The Gospel of St. Matthew:
A Bible Study

By
Michael D. Shepherd, B.S., M.R.E., D.Lit., D.Min.

Dedication

To my daughter, Elizabeth Diann Reece, who truly stretched my theology;

To my son, Newton Keith Shepherd, who as of this writing has not;

To my final editor and most constructive critic, my wife of fifty plus years, Betty who, as both the wife of a pastor and of a Shepherd (women married to guys named Shepherd have a special challenge), has had to put up with more than any wife should have to endure.

I must also include the two congregations who suffered through the first two drafts:

First Baptist Church, Lynwood, California and Maryvale Baptist Church, Phoenix, Arizona, finally

To Baptist Community Church, Arco, Idaho, where I began teaching it while their interim pastor and continued and concluded by the people in the church.

My thanks to those who have encouraged me to commit this to book-form and have offered suggestions to improve its final content.

And thanks to Koddie Snyder-Becker, then the graphic artist at Vineyard Church North Phoenix for the cover design.

Upon reflection, the genesis of this book was actually First Southern Baptist Church, Buckeye, Arizona where I served as associate minister and began to look more fully into the Gospel of Matthew.

Acknowledgments

And thanks to Koddie Snyder-Becker, then the graphic artist at Vineyard Church North Phoenix for the cover design.

Upon reflection, the genesis of this book was actually First Southern Baptist Church, Buckeye, Arizona where I served as associate minister and began to look more fully into the Gospel of Matthew.

Preface

This study is the result of a three-year Wednesday Bible study taught while I was pastor of First Baptist Church, Lynwood, California, and repeated at Maryvale Baptist Church, Phoenix, Arizona, and begun in my Interim Pastorate at Baptist Community Church, Arco, Idaho, and finally taught at our Vineyard Church North Phoenix small group Bible Study. Recently, while teaching from chapter 5 on being salt and light, I repeated the "I am not a role model" statement of (Sir) Charles Barkley then a few moments later referred to one of my favorite Bible commentators (William) Barkley without giving his first name and adding unintended humor (?) to the study…you may find more of that kind of thing within the written material. Normally I don't quote Sir Charles without referring to him by name.

This is NOT a "critical" commentary, as they are measured, but it might be considered a little more a devotional commentary or expanded Bible study. I began it at Lynwood with a few commentaries and over time have added more. They range from "liberal" to "conservative" and are all mostly "old." I pray the study will give you something to reflect upon and stretch you a little.

Having accepted Jesus as my personal Savior in 1948, at the age of eight, in First Southern Baptist Church, Yuma, Arizona; and being educated at Grand Canyon University (College back then); Phoenix, Arizona, and Golden Gate Baptist Theological Seminary, Mill Valley, California; and serving in Southern Baptist Churches until 1984; my theological "roots" are certainly very conservative and Southern Baptist to boot. My undergraduate work was in business administration (accounting) and I received a Master of Religious Education degree from Golden Gate, not a preacher's degree, so please don't blame the schools, they did the best they could with me.

In 1984, I became pastor of an American Baptist Church, Beatty Community Church in Beatty, Nevada, and remained in the ABC/USA and then Transformation Ministries while working in administrative positions in Evangelical Lutheran and United Methodist Churches until accepting a call to serve as Administrative Pastor of North Hills Church of God (Anderson, Indiana) in Phoenix, Arizona. Upon my retirement in April, 2009, my wife, Betty, and I joined Vineyard Church North Phoenix where our son served in worship arts and young adult ministries until becoming one of the pastors.

I concluded my formal educational journey at Southern California Theological Seminary, Stanton, California, where I was awarded an honorary Doctor of Literature degree while teaching Pastoral Theology there and completing requirements for a Doctor of Ministry in Pastoral Counseling. SCTS was affiliated with the Assemblies of God.

Because of my theological journey, I am confident that there is something in this study with which many of my friends will take exception…however, being somewhat controversial, and only slightly irreverent by most standards, this is my nature. I pray that I might stretch your theology a little also.

While at VCNP I lead the counseling and recovery ministries until re-retiring at the end of 2020. As of this revision, I am the Minister of Music at Emmanuel Baptist Church, Sun City, Arizona. What's next for me, only God knows and He hasn't let me in on it yet…

I pray you will enjoy my musings about this great gospel!

Primary Resources

All Scripture, unless otherwise noted, is taken from the World English Bible, identified as WEB, a Public Domain (no copyright) modern English translation of the Holy Bible based on the American Standard Version of the Holy Bible first published in 1901, the *Biblia Hebraica Stutgartensa* Old Testament, and the *Greek Majority Text New Testament*. It is in draft form, and currently being edited for accuracy and readability. I have, based on my, albeit limited understanding of the Greek, freely added my own additional meanings, set off in [brackets]. "NU" refers to *Nestle/Aland UBS* critical New Testament textual variants, and "TR" refers to *Textus Receptus* textual variants. Textual variants can occur when a copyist makes deliberate or inadvertent changes in the text being copied. Those alterations may, or may not have changed the meaning of the original text. Sometimes the changes were made to give a better understanding, sometimes they were to correct prior errors, sometimes they were made to support a particular doctrine or idea. The *Textus Receptus*, Latin meaning "received text," is the body of Greek manuscripts used to translate the original Greek New Testaments from the Reformation to the present. The WEB is a "work in progress."

AB   Albright, W.F. and Mann, C.S., *The Anchor Bible*, Vol. 26, (Garden City, NY: Doubleday & Company, Inc., 1971).

BBC   Stagg, Frank, *The Broadman Bible Commentary*, Vol. 8, (Nashville: Broadman Press, 1969)

CCE   Jamieson, R., Fausset, A. R., Fausset, A. R., Brown, D., & Brown, D. (1997). *A Commentary, Critical and Explanatory, on the Old and New Testaments*. Oak Harbor, WA: Logos Research Systems, Inc.

DSB   Barclay, William, *The Daily Study Bible Series, The Gospel of Matthew*, Volume 1, chapters 1-10, and Volume 2, chapters 11-28, (Philadelphia, The Westminster Press, 1975).

GN   Notes for the *Geneva Bible*, written by John Calvin, John Knox, Miles Coverdale, et al, from the 1599 edition, Geneva Notes, PC Study Bible formatted electronic database Copyright © 2003 Biblesoft, Inc. All rights reserved.

IB   Buttrick, George W., Ed. *The Interpreter's Bible*, Vol. 7, (New York: Abingdon Press, 1951).

IDB   Crim, Keith, Ed., *The Interpreter's Dictionary of the Bible*, (Nashville: Abingdon, 1962 & 1976).

KJV   The King James or Authorized Version, Public Domain.

LASB *Life Application Study Bible*, Tyndale House Publishers, Inc., (Wheaton, IL, 2004)

LXX   The Septuagint, the Greek translation of the Old Testament translated in Alexandria, Egypt and the version generally quoted in the New Testament.

MH   *Matthew Henry's Commentary on the Whole Bible*, PC Study Bible Formatted Electronic Database Copyright © 2006 by Biblesoft, Inc. All Rights reserved

NIV   *The Holy Bible, New International Version®*, NIV®. Copyright ©1973, 1978, 1984, 2011 by Biblica, Inc.™

NLTSB   *New Living Translation Study Bible*, Tyndale House Publishers, Inc., (Carol Stream, IL, 2008)

TNTC Tasker, R.V.G., *The Gospel According to St. Matthew*, (Grand Rapids: Wm. B. Eerdmans Publishing Company, 1961)

WP   Robertson, A. T., *Word Pictures in the New Testament*, Vol. 1, (Nashville: Broadman Press, 1930)

Table of Contents

Introduction to Matthew

Matthew "...forms the connecting link between the Old and New Testaments because of its emphasis on the fulfillment of prophecy (LASB, p. 1530)" and is one of four books in the New Testament called Gospels (meaning "good news"). The other three are Mark and Luke, which parallel Matthew and John. Each of these books record part of the life of Jesus the expected Jewish Messiah, or Christ in Greek, but they do not record all of the events or sayings that make up His life. John 21:25 says, "There are also many other things which Jesus did, which if they would all be written, I suppose that even the world itself wouldn't have room for the books that would be written."

Because they give an account of Jesus' life from the same perspective, Matthew, Mark and Luke are called Synoptic Gospels, from the Greek meaning "one eye" or "to see together." Each "book" contains something the other two books have and omits something included in the other two. The similarities are so numerous that most scholars agree that all three shared the same sources, and/or are used by one of the others as a basis/resource for their own study of Jesus' life.

Matthew is the first book of the New Testament because it was originally thought to have been written first, and there seems to be evidence that may be true, but scholars generally agree Mark is the earliest of the gospels. Their reasoning generally follows lines based on literary criticism (the critical study of sources and materials) of the available, early Greek texts.

Some things to note about the Synoptic Gospels include:
1. Mark can be divided into 105 sections, 93 are included in Matthew and 81 in Luke. Only four don't occur in either Matthew or Luke.
2. Mark has 661 verses. Matthew has 1,068 and includes 606 from Mark. Luke has 1,149 verses and includes 320 from Mark. Only 24 verses of Mark are not used by Matthew or Luke.
3. Both Matthew and Luke generally follow Mark's outline. Occasionally one deviates, but never do both change the order.
4. Both Matthew and Luke have more material than Mark and they share over 200 verses not found in Mark. This has led to the suggestion of another source. The theory is: Mark has what Jesus did; the other source, called *Q* (German for *Quelle* meaning "source"), contains what Jesus said.

Matthew was probably the tax collector Matthew, son of Alphaeus, whose Hebrew name was Levi. I say probably because the book itself makes no claim as to authorship and there is no definite proof as to who the writer actually was. The only evidence we have is that the early church called it "The Gospel According to Matthew."

Matthew shapes his Gospel according to two structural principals. First, following an introduction...Matthew alternates teaching material with narrative material. ... second, Matthew records Jesus' confrontation of Israel with God's message about the arrival of his kingdom in the last days...followed by the responses this message evoked from various people... Matthew then tells of Jesus Christ's death and resurrection...for the salvation of humankind. (NLTSB, p. 1573)

Some scholars don't believe Matthew wrote the book, but that he did supply Jesus' sayings; others suggest that he is possibly the author of *Q*, mentioned above. Their reasoning is that an eyewitness would not need to follow someone else's outline, but would know "first hand" what Jesus said and did so he would not need to rely on other sources. However, those familiar with the saying, "if it ain't broke, don't fix it," might disagree, (cliché alert) why "reinvent the wheel"?

As a tax collector, Matthew needed to be able to write and communicate well to enable him to "extract" the necessary taxes from people who undoubtedly hated him and even considered him a traitor for working with the Roman government collecting taxes from his own kinsmen. For that reason, he may have been one of the more "learned" of the Disciples.

It's relatively easy to identify Matthew's main themes. After introductory material, he lays out five major discourses: The Sermon on the Mount (chapters 5-7), apostleship, (chapter 10), parables about the kingdom (chapter 13), church discipline (chapter 18) and the end of the age (chapters 24-25). What is less obvious is the careful selection and organization in his material.

Matthew was probably written about AD 59 but some scholars date it as late as AD 80. It emphasizes the universality of Jesus and His kingship. He first sets out Jesus' lineage and then to show the fulfillment of Old Testament prophesies. About sixteen times we see something like "...this was to fulfill what the Lord had spoken by the prophets..." While addressing primarily Jews, Matthew also records the marching orders of the Church in Matthew 28:19 "Therefore go and make disciples of all nations..."

"Matthew argues the case that Jesus fulfills the ancient faith of Israel and the OT hope: In him the Messiah and the day of the Lord have come (NLTSB, p. 1574)."

Matthew's Gospel stresses Jesus' call to men and women to be baptized, to follow him as disciples, to obey his teachings (28:20), and to enjoy fellowship with him. Jesus summarizes the requirements of discipleship in his Sermon on the Mount (5:1–7:29), and this theme recurs throughout Matthew (e.g., 10:1-42; 16:24-26). Matthew shows the disciples overcoming their failures through Christ's help (NLTSB, p 1575; see 14:28-33; 16:5-12).

And so, we begin…

Taking Down the Barriers
Matthew 1:1-17

The book of the genealogy of Jesus Christ, [Messiah; Anointed One] the son of David, the son of Abraham. ² Abraham became the father of Isaac. Isaac became the father of Jacob. Jacob became the father of Judah and his brothers. ³ Judah became the father of Perez and Zerah by Tamar. Perez became the father of Hezron. Hezron became the father of Ram. ⁴ Ram became the father of Amminadab. Amminadab became the father of Nahshon. Nahshon became the father of Salmon. ⁵ Salmon became the father of Boaz by Rahab. Boaz became the father of Obed by Ruth. Obed became the father of Jesse. ⁶ Jesse became the father of King David. David became the father of Solomon by her who had been Uriah's wife. ⁷ Solomon became the father of Rehoboam. Rehoboam became the father of Abijah. Abijah became the father of Asa. ⁸ Asa became the father of Jehoshaphat. Jehoshaphat became the father of Joram. Joram became the father of Uzziah. ⁹ Uzziah became the father of Jotham. Jotham became the father of Ahaz. Ahaz became the father of Hezekiah. ¹⁰ Hezekiah became the father of Manasseh. Manasseh became the father of Amon. Amon became the father of Josiah. ¹¹ Josiah became the father of Jechoniah and his brothers, at the time of the exile to Babylon. ¹² After the exile to Babylon, Jechoniah became the father of Shealtiel. Shealtiel became the father of Zerubbabel. ¹³ Zerubbabel became the father of Abiud. Abiud became the father of Eliakim. Eliakim became the father of Azor. ¹⁴ Azor became the father of Zadok. Zadok became the father of Achim. Achim became the father of Eliud. ¹⁵ Eliud became the father of Eleazar. Eleazar became the father of Matthan. Matthan became the father of Jacob. ¹⁶ Jacob became the father of Joseph, the husband of Mary, from whom was born Jesus, who is called Christ. ¹⁷ So all the generations from Abraham to David are fourteen generations; from David to the exile to Babylon fourteen generations; and from the carrying away to Babylon to the Christ, fourteen generations.

Matthew opens his gospel with *biblos geneseōs*, we might translate it "genealogy," but it can carry other ideas as well. "But for the first readers of Matthew, it called attention to the birth (*genesis*) not only of Jesus, but of the whole new order to which that birth gave rise (AB, p.2)." This was a very good way to introduce a Jewish audience to Jesus because who your family was showed your proper place in the community. Jesus wasn't just a descendent of Abraham, he was also a descendent of the great king, David! The name Jesus, or Joshua in Hebrew, was a popular name Jewish parents gave their sons and means "the Lord saves" or "O save, Lord."

Because their status within the nation depended on it, the Jews were obsessed with genealogies and several such listings are included in the Bible, especially in the Old Testament in relation to kings and priests. A priest was required to trace his lineage back to Aaron and his wife had to be able to go back at least five generations. King Herod the Great was born about 74-73 BC, the son of an Idumean father and the daughter of an Arab sheik. When John Hyrcanus (164-104 BC) overran Idumea (Edom) he forced its inhabitants to convert to Judaism, so while technically a Jew, he certainly didn't practice it. He was also so depressed by his lack of family heritage that he had the official records destroyed so no one could prove ancestry better than he could. However, if you were a Levite or a descendant of King David, you can believe that your ancestry was drummed into you!

The way Joseph is introduced is different than the other fathers in Jesus' lineage. The words "the father of" occur until we reach Mary and Joseph when it changes to "of whom was born" and can be translated, "produce, originate and create." This may be a subtle way to make clear that Joseph was not the father of Jesus, except in an adoptive way.

In an attempt to reconcile the lineage listed in Luke 3:23-28, some have suggested that this is Joseph's family tree and Luke records Mary's lineage. Unfortunately, since Mary was related to Elizabeth, who was a descendant of Aaron, that can't be Jesus' "legal" lineage. The lineage through Joseph makes Him a descendant of Judah and therefore King David. On Mary's side, He is a descendant of Aaron. Jesus therefore combines the kingly and priestly offices.

Matthew used a memory device called a mnemonic to help people memorize this passage. He divided it into three sections of fourteen generations each; each division is one of the three great stages of Jewish history: from Abraham to David, from David to the Babylonian Captivity, and from the Babylonian Captivity to Jesus' birth. "We have no good reason to doubt that the genealogy was transmitted in good faith (AB p. 5)."

We should note that the last section contains only thirteen generations and, according to the genealogies in 2 Chronicles, three generations have been omitted, kings Ahaziah, Joash and Amaziah. Today we might want to omit the "black sheep" from our family tree, but we have a need for completeness that did not exist in ancient times; they did it without a pang of conscience. "[Verses] vss. 13-16 contain names not otherwise known to us in scripture, but they are names well enough known from Jewish sources of the Hellenistic period, including an increasing number of Aramaic documents (AB, p. 3)." Complete or incomplete, it doesn't change the heritage.

It was Abraham who founded the nation and for Jews the inhabitants of earth before Abraham held little significance. For Matthew, Abraham may have had greater significance because it was through him that all the people on earth would be blessed (Gen. 12:3).

The history of the Jews from Abraham to David was the time when they became a true nation. They were no longer just families of nomads wandering around in the land or in Egyptian bondage. The time from David to the Babylonian Captivity was a history of shame and tragedy which led to the destruction of Jerusalem. The third group tells of their rescue from slavery in Babylon and set the stage for Jesus to deliver them from the slavery of sin. The title "Christ" (Greek) and "Messiah" (Hebrew) both have the same meaning "the Anointed One."

The passage indicates two very important things about Jesus: first, He was the son of David, the great king, and second, He was the fulfillment of prophecy.

Two very interesting points in this passage are the women listed:

1. There are four women listed. Prior to Jesus' coming, women were not important. They were the property of their fathers until their marriage and afterward they were the property of their husbands.

2. The women listed are not the "right" kind of women. Tamar was an adulteress who, because Judah failed to give her his third son as her husband, prostituted herself with him (Gen. 38). Rahab wasn't an Israelite and while she protected the spies at Jericho, she was a prostitute and possible even a "madam" (Josh. 2:1-7). Ruth, the best of the lot, was still a foreigner, a Moabitess (Ruth 1:4). And, "An Ammonite

or a Moabite shall not enter into Yahweh's assembly; even to the tenth generation shall no one belonging to them enter into Yahweh's assembly forever… (Deut. 23:3)." This actually means that David, who wanted to build the temple and Solomon who built it were not "qualified" to enter it. Bathsheba, not even called by name, was seduced by David who had her husband Uriah killed so he could conceal, temporally, her unfaithfulness.

Matthew doesn't name the "good" women in Jesus' lineage and according to Barclay, "If Matthew had ransacked the pages of the Old Testament for improbable candidates, he could have not discovered four more incredible ancestors for Jesus Christ (DSB, p.17)."

The listing of these women indicates that three barriers truly have been torn down in the coming of the Messiah: The barrier between Jew and Gentile, male and female, "saint" and sinner. Paul states that fact in Galatians 3:28, "There is neither Jew nor Greek, there is neither slave nor free man, there is neither male nor female; for you are all one in Christ Jesus."

In the first 17 verses we meet 46 people whose lifetimes span 2,000 years. All were ancestors of Jesus, but they varied considerably in personality, spirituality, and experience. Some were heroes of the faith… Some had shady reputations… Many were very ordinary… And others were evil… God's work in history is not limited by human failures or sin, and he works through ordinary people. Just as God used all kinds of people to bring his Son into the world, he uses all kinds today to accomplish his will. And God wants to use you. (LASB, p. 1533).

The Birth of Jesus the Christ
Matthew 1:18-25

Now the birth of Jesus Christ was like this; for after his mother, Mary, was engaged to Joseph, before they came together, she was found pregnant by the Holy Spirit. [19] *Joseph, her husband, being a righteous man, and not willing to make her a public example, intended [resolved] to put her away secretly.* [20] *But when [while] he thought about these things, behold an angel of the Lord appeared to him in a dream, saying, "Joseph, son of David, don't be afraid to take to yourself Mary, your wife, for that which is conceived in her is of the Holy Spirit.* [21] *She shall give birth to a son. You shall call his name Jesus, for it is he who shall save his people from their sins."*

[22] *Now all this has happened, that it might be fulfilled which was spoken by the Lord through the prophet, saying,* [23] *"Behold, the virgin shall be with child, and shall give birth to a son. They shall call his name Immanuel"; which is, being interpreted, "God with us." (Isaiah 7:14)*

[24] *[So] Joseph arose from his sleep, and did as the angel of the Lord commanded him, and took his wife to himself;* [25] *and didn't know her sexually until she had given birth to her firstborn son. He named him Jesus.*

In Jewish practice there were three steps to marriage: engagement, betrothal and the marriage itself. Engagement took place when the girl was a child, possibly even at birth. Often the boy was very young also, but if there was a shortage of women or the boy died, the "fiancé" might be a man several years older than her.

Betrothal was an acceptance of the engagement and could happen any time after she had her first menstrual period. If she wanted to, the woman could break the agreement at that time; if she did not, it became binding and required a divorce to terminate. If she accepted, the young man would go and prepare a home for his bride and family, probably by adding a room on his father's house (see John 14:1 ff.). Things often were the same as marriage, except they were not to share a bed. At this point, unfaithfulness would be considered adultery which was punishable by the death of both parties involved, but the man was rarely punished (Lev. 20:10, Deut. 22:23 ff.).

Marriage usually took place about one year after the formalization of the betrothal and was an elaborate affair lasting for a week. For most, it was the one bright spot in an otherwise bleak life.

We all wish there were more information about Joseph, but there isn't and we must resist the temptation to create a background and life for him. Looking at Joseph, verse 19 says he was "a righteous man." This is the same word used of Zachariah and Elizabeth (Luke 1:6) and Simeon (Luke 2:25). Righteousness here carries the idea of right conduct or right living whether judged by God's standard or man's standard.

Righteousness requires doing what God wants us to do, even when it seems to be contrary to reason, tradition, or law. For Joseph not to divorce Mary was to admit that he was the adulterer because it would soon be evident to everyone that Mary was pregnant. Joseph and Mary's willingness to accept the stigma of being adulterers is evidence of God's wisdom in choosing this couple to be the parents for His Son, our Savior.

As was said, genealogies were very important to the Jews and one of the early battles Christians fought was over Jesus' "legitimacy." The Jews claimed that He was the product of a rape by an unnamed Roman soldier. Rape was definitely a tactic used to terrorize and intimidate the native population. If you were a descendent of King David, you can be sure that the family was extremely proud of that fact and you would be reminded and would remind your sons of it because the Messiah was expected to come from David's lineage.

A Jewish Christian such as Matthew could only deal faithfully with his traditions and set them down as he knew them. …at least [it] tells us something significant about the honesty of an evangelist dealing with what he knew would cause speculation and scandal (AB, p. 10).

The name assigned to the unborn child was actually "Joshua," meaning "Yahweh is salvation;" Jesus is the Greek form. "Jesus was not so much The Man born to be King as The Man born to be Saviour [sic] (DSB, p.19)." Jesus was to be the new Joshua, not to lead the people out of Caesar's oppression, but out of Satan's slavery and directly into God's presence.

According to Barclay, the Holy Spirit in Jewish thought did four things: one, He brought truth to men; two, He enabled men to recognize truth; three, He was connected with the work of creation; and four, He was involved in re-creation. The emphasis of the passage is not that Jesus was born of a virgin, but that He was born of the work of the Holy Spirit as an act of re-creation.

In these verses we have the beginning of what has become our doctrine of the Incarnation. "Incarnation is far more than the Indwelling of God by the Holy Spirit in the human heart. …he gave him a human mother, but not a human father so that Jesus Christ is both Son of God and Son of Man, the God Man (WP, p.7)."

We might note here that there is a Roman Catholic doctrine called the Immaculate Conception, which doesn't apply to Jesus' conception, but to Mary's conception and birth. It claims normal conception, but that God protected her from the stain of "original" sin. Briefly, it says that unless Mary had a miraculous birth, she could not be the "Mother of God." Protestants generally believe she is simply the mother of the incarnate Jesus, He was with God in His pre-incarnate state before coming to earth, and therefore she is not the mother of God, but the mother of the incarnate Jesus.

Mary could not produce a child on her own, but God could give her one. This parallels the fact that we cannot save ourselves on our own, but God can do it.

The virgin birth is not intended to explain Jesus' sinlessness... Sin belongs to personal, moral choice, not to biology. Neither sin nor salvation is biologically transmitted... That Jesus had no human father belongs to divine choice and not to Gnostic problems of sex (BBC, p. 84).

Verse 25 does not support the perpetual virginity of Mary, which is also a doctrine of the Roman Catholic Church that says that Mary remained a virgin after the birth of Jesus. Matthew 13:55-56 and Mark 6:3 indicate that Jesus had brothers and sisters and there is no evidence offered that these were Joseph's children by another wife and that he was a widower.

Had Joseph been a widower, based on how other difficult situations were handled in Scripture and by the Gospel writers, I'm sure we would have been told that fact.

Honor from Abroad; Hostility at Home
Matthew 2:1-12

Now when Jesus was born in Bethlehem of Judea in the days of King Herod, behold, wise men from the east came to Jerusalem, saying, ² "Where is he who is born King of the Jews? For we saw his star in the east, and have come to worship him." ³ When King Herod heard it, he was troubled, and all Jerusalem with him. ⁴ Gathering together all the chief priests and scribes of the people, he asked them where the Christ would be born. ⁵ They said to him, "In Bethlehem of Judea, for this is written through the prophet, ⁶ 'You Bethlehem, land of Judah, are in no way least among the princes of Judah: for out of you shall come a governor, who shall shepherd my people, Israel'" (Micah 5:2).

⁷ Then Herod secretly called the wise men, and learned from them exactly what time the star appeared. ⁸ He sent them to Bethlehem, and said, "Go and search diligently for the young child. When you have found him, bring me word, so that I also may come and worship him."

⁹ They, having heard the king, went their way; and behold, the star, which they saw in the east, went before them, until it came and stood over where the young child was. ¹⁰ When they saw the star, they rejoiced with exceedingly great joy. ¹¹ They came into the house and saw the young child with Mary, his mother, and they fell down and worshiped him. Opening their treasures, they offered to him gifts: gold, frankincense, and myrrh. ¹² Being warned in a dream that they shouldn't return to Herod, they went back to their own country another way.

This Bethlehem was not the only Bethlehem in Israel at that time, there was also one in Zebulon, by the Sea of Galilee. Our Bethlehem was situated in a saddle about 2,500 feet in elevation and looked out at

Jerusalem; Jacob buried Rachel there. It means "house of bread" and possibly gained that name because it was located in Israel's rich grain growing area. It was the home of Ruth and Boaz and their great-grandson David, the great king. It somehow seems appropriate for the "bread of life" to be born in the "house of bread."

Most religious leaders believed in a literal fulfillment of all Old Testament prophecy; therefore they believed the Messiah would be born in Bethlehem as foreseen by the prophet Micah seven century earlier (Micah 5:2). Ironically, when Jesus was born, these same religious leaders became his greatest enemies. (LASB, p. 1537).

Many homes in the area were built on the slope of the limestone cliff with a stall for cattle hollowed out underneath. Justin Martyr (ca. 150) established the tradition that the manger was actually in one of those caves and that cave is the site of the Church of the Nativity today.

It's unlikely that one day Joseph told Mary they needed to get down to Bethlehem because the Messiah had to be born there. It would be an arduous trek for a young, pregnant girl to make; it's more likely that they were caught unaware by Augustus' order and went reluctantly, however, it did fulfill prophesy (See Luke 2:1–6). It could also be argued that this was fulfillment of Genesis 49:10, "The scepter will not depart from Judah, Nor the ruler's staff from between his feet, Until he comes to whom it belongs."

"…in the days of King Herod" is the only way we have to estimate the year of Jesus' birth. Herod the Great, whom the Romans proclaimed king, became king in about 40 BC and died early in 4 BC; Jesus was born sometime during his reign, probably toward the end of it. Luke gave us a little more information, but it's still insufficient in light of recorded history of the time to set the time precisely.

The important thing is not when He was born, but that He was born. "But when the fullness of the time came, God sent out his Son, born to a woman, born under the law, (Gal. 4:4)" at the right time He was born into the world.

Since Herod killed all the boys age two and under (Matt. 2:16) and verse 11 says, "They came into the house and saw the young child with Mary, his mother, and they fell down and worshiped him." we assume they were no longer in the manger. Since He is called a "child" we further assume He wasn't an infant, but was about one year old. We know He was over eight days old because the offering at His circumcision would have been greater if they had already received the gifts from the Magi (see Lev. 12) before that time.

"When King Herod heard it, he was troubled, and all Jerusalem with him." Herod was not ignorant of the Jewish Messianic hope and the news of the Magi must have sent a shudder through him. When Herod was troubled, you knew "all" Jerusalem would be disturbed or frightened. Caesar Augustus' attitude toward Herod was that it was safer to be Herod's pig than his son. "Matthew is influenced by the knowledge that, when Jesus the Messiah was born at Bethlehem, the Judaean princes such as Herod regarded Him as a serious rival… (TCNT, p. 39)."

"Magi" is a transliteration of the Greek word from which we derive our word magician and is a better rendering than "kings" or even "wise men." Originally, they seem to have been a priestly tribe of Median similar to the Levites. They were philosophers, doctors, and scientists and often interpreted dreams and cast horoscopes. Part of their profession involved studying the stars. Later, the word was applied to Zoroastrian priests. In rabbinic usage, it was usually employed in an evil sense.

They were undoubtedly astrologers because, in those days, except for devout Jews, astrology was very much in vogue. By devout I don't mean the leadership because, like the church today, many Jews "dabbled" in astrology, and there are indications signs of the zodiac could be found in the synagogues and even the Temple.

The visit of the Magi has no parallel in early Christian writing. Two of the legends that have developed are: one, because there are three gifts, there were three "kings;" two, there was a young one, an old one and one was black, to represent all mankind. The truth is that we have no idea how many or what their ethnicity may have been; there is even the possibility that they were Jews (AB p.15).

The statement, "we saw his star in the east, and have come to worship him." is not only a miss location of words in English but a poor translation of the Greek. More accurately, it should read, "We saw his star at its rising, and are come to pay Him homage (TNTC, p.37)." Had they seen the star in the eastern sky, they would have traveled toward India not toward Canaan. The intention is to convey the idea that they saw the star when it first rose, at its genesis, above the horizon.

What about the star? Was it a miracle or just a natural occurrence? Does it need to be a miracle? No, it doesn't. Some of the natural occurrences that took place include:

1. Halley's Comet which was visible October 8, 12 BC, but a comet is unlikely because they were an omen of disaster to the ancients. This date also seems to be a little early and we don't have record of any other comets at that time to account for the other "star" events, which doesn't mean there were none.

2. The Chinese recorded a nova in 5 BC that was visible for seventy days. However, novae are not very impressive

3. In the 17th century Johannes Kepler suggested a conjunction of Jupiter, the planet associated with royalty, and Saturn, the planet associated with the Jews which came to be identified with the Messiah. Such a conjunction occurred three times in 7 BC, May 29, September 29, and December 4, in the Pisces constellation which was also associated with the Jews. This may have been how they knew it was "His" star and it fits the time requirements.

The Kepler star could have risen when He was born, and the Magi presumably saw it then. They traveled to Jerusalem, a journey of some three months after they got ready for the trip, and the star reappeared to lead them to Bethlehem. It may not be what happened, but it fits.

A fourth option is that the star was an out and out miracle, totally outside the natural realm. However, this would also require a supernatural revelation for the Magi to understand what was going on. Certainly, this isn't beyond God's power and should not be ruled out. Whatever it was, the timing was worked out by God and accomplished what God wanted. "He [Jesus] was revealed to the astrologers by a method suited to their habits and understanding; and their reason in coming to Jesus was not personal advantage, but solely to give Him homage (TNTC, p. 40)."

When the Magi left Herod, the star "went ahead of them" not to show them the town, they already knew it, but to show them the place. How it led them is also subject to speculation. My feeling is that it must have been like a flashlight would be used to light the path.

These men, like most of the people in the world "worshipped" many gods, so worship here probably means to worship as a god (small g) or to pay homage to. They were not necessarily recognizing Jesus as the one, true God. There are records of Magi, or Magus (singular), traveling to other lands to honor those they felt were noteworthy. "God safeguards our freedom; he gives the sign, but we may stay or journey (IB, p. 257)." Do you wonder, like me, why the Jewish leaders didn't go with them? Weren't they also looking for the Messiah to come?

Some interesting things about the Magi: They are assumed to be Gentiles, but there is nothing definitive that has been discovered to prove they were. They were busy about their jobs when they discovered the star, and they were quick to act to find the new king, they came to worship or honor him and they brought their best as gifts.

The significance of the gifts is often overstressed and many meanings have been assigned to them. However, these men brought a representation of their wealth; things that would be appropriate to give a king. We have assigned additional importance to both the men and their gifts: gold—value, worth, substance; frankincense—fragrance, inner treasure; myrrh—precious, sorrow and suffering. Gold or cash is truly the gift where one size fits all! Frankincense was use to prepare the oil used for anointing a king. Ink made using myrrh was used to write on charms and amulets. These were supplies and gifts that an astrologer would normally carry.

When confronted by the Christ, men react in one of three ways:

1. They react with hostility, like Herod, because they feel they will have to give up something; change their lives.

2. They react with indifference, like the Jewish leaders, because they were engrossed in their own selves and theology and there is no room for anyone or anything else.

3. They react with adoration, like these wise men, because they believe God's love is addressed to them personally.

The wise men were sensitive to God's leading, they found Jesus and offered their gifts, then, at God's direction, they went home a different way. "Finding Jesus may mean that your life must take a different direction, one that is responsive and obedient to God's Word (LASB, p. 1537)."

The Flight to Egypt
Matthew 2:13-15

Now when they had departed, behold, an angel of the Lord appeared to Joseph in a dream, saying, "Arise and take the young child and his mother, and flee into Egypt, and stay there until I tell you, for Herod will seek the young child to destroy him."

[14] He arose and took the young child and his mother by night, and departed into Egypt, [15] and was there until the death of Herod; that it might be fulfilled which was spoken by the Lord through the prophet, saying, "Out of Egypt I called my son" (Hosea 11:1).

Here we see yet another occasion when God speaks to Joseph in a dream, which isn't very unusual, because God often spoke to people in dreams in the Old Testament. The Holy Spirit doesn't come in power until Pentecost (Acts 2:1-4)

Will God's will always be done? Sadly, it will not, not even in our own lives. While people can thwart God's Will for a time, "...the devices of man can never thwart the ultimate purpose of God... (TNTC p. 42)."

At the time of Jesus' birth, Egypt was a Roman province, but was not under Herod. Most cities and many villages had Jewish residents. Barclay estimates Alexandria had "more than a million...and certain districts...were entirely handed over to them (DSB, p. 33)."

Egypt was considered the land of magic. According to the *Talmud*, a collection of Jewish oral tradition interpreting the *Torah*, the first five books of the Old Testament, "Ten measures of sorcery descended into the world; Egypt received nine, the rest of the world one." It's not strange that some have tried to make something out of this trip to Egypt and have attempted to discount his miracles by saying he learned magic there. The problem is he was a young child, not a young man (the same Greek word is used in 2:20 about the return from Egypt) and he was taken there under the guidance of the Holy Spirit for his protection.

Here is the first of Matthew's "prophetic" references. Matthew's purpose was to show the Jews that Jesus was the Messiah promised in the Old Testament. To do this he used passages that he believes could be connected to the events in Jesus' life. Today we would probably consider this "proof texting," but it was an accepted practice among ancient people.

Hosea 11:1 says, "When Israel was a child, then I loved him, and called my son out of Egypt." The original reference applied to God's redemption of His people when He led the Israelites out of slavery in Egypt. While Hosea didn't intend it to apply to the Messiah, Matthew sees a connection and reports it.

There is a parallel between Moses and Jesus. Moses fled Egypt to escape pharaoh and returned to bring the Israelites out of Egyptian bondage. Jesus fled Judea to escape Herod and returned to bring all humankind out of the bondage of sin. But Jesus is not a second Moses. While Moses gave the Law; Jesus came to bring the Law to completion, not to give a new Law.

The Slaughter of the Babies
Matthew 2:16-18

Then Herod, when he saw that he was mocked by the wise men, was exceedingly angry, and sent out, and killed all the male children who were in Bethlehem and in all the surrounding countryside, from two years old and under, according to the exact time which he had learned from the wise men. [17] *Then that which was spoken by Jeremiah the prophet was fulfilled, saying,* [18] *"A voice was heard in Ramah, lamentation, weeping and great mourning, Rachel weeping for her children; she wouldn't be comforted, because they are no more" (Jeremiah 31:15).*

Herod wanted to know the time the star appeared to the Magi; this would be important in setting the age of the child. In verses 16-18 Matthew shows how Herod used the information he obtained and it certainly fits his character. As soon as Herod became King, he began to murder anyone who threatened him and his reign. It's estimated that he caused the death of several hundred people, what were a few more?

History records the atrocities of Herod the Great. Among his victims were: his "favorite" wife, Mariamne; his brother-in-law, the high priest; several of his children; his mother-in-law; anyone who was a threat to his throne fell victim to his assassins. As death approached, Herod went to Jericho and had seventy important men from Jerusalem arrested with orders to kill them when he died. He wanted people to mourn his death and otherwise they would have celebrated.

"Herod's order...implies that Jesus...was beyond his first year or that the heartless king made his net wider than necessary...as long as he reached his intended victim (BBC, p.89)." Herod left no stone unturned.

We often see a picture of hundreds of babies being killed; this isn't accurate. While one is too many, based on the population at the time, about 300 people, Robertson estimates fifteen to twenty were killed (WP, p. 20), but others would have a lower number. We can see in Herod the extent to which some people will go to get rid of Jesus. The problem is that you cannot get rid of Him and you often hurt innocent people in trying.

In Jeremiah 31:15, "Yahweh says: 'A voice is heard in Ramah, lamentation and bitter weeping, Rachel weeping for her children. She refuses to be comforted for her children, because they are no more." here we have another of Matthew's appropriated prophecies. The passage originally was applied to the deportation of Jews from Jerusalem by the Babylonians in the 6th century BC. The picture is that it was so sad an occasion that when they passed Rachel's tomb in Ramah, Rachel began to cry. It would be similar to our "turning over in his grave" idiom. There is no mistaking, or minimizing, the ignominy and sadness of this situation.

The Return to Nazareth
Matthew 2:19-23

But when Herod was dead, behold, an angel of the Lord appeared in a dream to Joseph in Egypt, saying, [20] "Arise and take the young child and his mother, and go into the land of Israel, for those who sought the young child's life are dead."

[21] He arose and took the young child and his mother, and came into the land of Israel. [22] But when he heard that Archelaus was reigning over Judea in the place of his father, Herod, he was afraid to go there. Being warned in a dream, he withdrew into the region of Galilee, [23] and came and lived in a city called Nazareth; that it might be fulfilled which was spoken through the prophets: "He will be called a Nazarene."

Herod changed his will, again, and split the kingdom up. Archelaus, the worst of his remaining sons succeeded him in Judea, but was given the title ethnarch not king; he reigned from 4 BC until he was banished in AD 6. From that time on Palestine was an imperial province ruled by a procurator, except for the period from 41-44 when it was under Herod Agrippa I. Herod Antipas, often called just Antipas received Galilee and Herod Phillip, a rather weak son, received the northeast and beyond the Jordan River. Like his father, Archelaus was a brutal, immoral tyrant which might give anyone concerns about living in such close proximity.

This paragraph indicates that Jesus was a Nazarene. We don't know of a direct reference Matthew would be referring to, it could even be just a term of contempt. "Nathanael said to him, 'Can any good thing come out of Nazareth?' Philip said to him, 'Come and see' (John 1:46)."

Why Galilee and Nazareth? That is where Mary and Joseph lived before moving to Bethlehem. Luke 1:26-27 tells us, "Now in the sixth month, the angel Gabriel was sent from God to a city of Galilee, named Nazareth, to a virgin pledged to be married to a man whose name was Joseph, of David's house. The virgin's name was Mary." But why return to a town where their reputations were marred by their "hasty marriage"? The answer is found in Scripture, "Being warned in a dream, he withdrew into the region of Galilee, and came and lived in a city called Nazareth…" We can certainly see how Joseph and Mary relied on the leadership of the Spirit in many situations.

There is a passage Matthew may have in mind from Isaiah 11:1 "A shoot will come out of the stock of Jesse, and a branch out of his roots will bear fruit." which could be the reference, but we can't be certain. If so, it's a play on words; branch is *nezer*. If this is the situation, Matthew is making a case for Jesus being a new shoot on the tree of Israel and Paul does talk of the Christians as being grafted into the stump after the Jews rejected Christ (Rom. 11:11-24).

We often think of Nazareth as a sleepy little town of no importance, but that was not true. It was located in a hollow in the hills of southern Galilee at the crossroads of the world. By climbing the hills, you could see the Mediterranean Sea with its trading ships sailing into nearby ports. It was on the caravan route called the Way of the South, or the Road to the Sea, which ran from Damascus to Egypt, and was used for centuries by traders. Another road, through Nazareth was the Road to the East; it left the sea coast at Ptolemais and was used by Roman legions going out to the frontier and traders bringing silk and spices from the east.

So, it would appear that Jesus grew up in the heart of a cosmopolitan area and had opportunity to see all kinds of people with many problems and concerns. Nazareth was truly a crossroads of the world!

John the Baptizer
Matthew 3:1-12

In those days, John the Baptizer came, preaching in the wilderness of Judea, saying, ² "Repent, for the Kingdom of Heaven is at hand [ᵃis fast approaching]!" ³ For this is he who was spoken of by Isaiah the prophet, saying, "The voice of one crying in the wilderness, make ready the way of the Lord. Make his paths straight" (Isaiah 40:3).

⁴ Now John himself wore clothing made of camel's hair, with a leather belt around his waist. His food was locusts and wild honey. ⁵ Then people from Jerusalem, all of Judea, and all the region [neighborhood] around the Jordan went out to him. ⁶ They were baptized by him in the Jordan, confessing their sins. ⁷ But when he saw many of the Pharisees and Sadducees coming for his baptism, he said to them, "You offspring of vipers, who warned you to flee from the wrath to come? ⁸ Therefore produce fruit worthy of repentance! ⁹ Don't think to yourselves, 'We have Abraham for our father,' for I tell you that God is able to raise up children to Abraham from these stones.

¹⁰ "Even now the ax lies at the root of the trees. Therefore every tree that doesn't produce good fruit is cut down, and cast into the fire. ¹¹ I indeed baptize you in water for repentance, but he who comes after me is mightier than I, whose shoes I am not worthy to carry. He will baptize you in the Holy Spirit (some translations add "with fire"). ¹² His winnowing fork is in his hand, and he will thoroughly cleanse his threshing floor. He will gather his wheat into the barn, but the chaff he will burn up with unquenchable fire."

Five main subjects are covered in chapters 3 and 4. First is the preaching of John the Baptizer (3:1-12), and the baptism of Jesus (3:13-17) in chapter three. Chapter four covers the formal temptation of Jesus (4:1-11), the move to Capernaum (4:12-17), and the call of the disciples (4:18-25).

Since Malachi there had been no prophetic voice in Israel; without much introduction, John the Baptizer just seems to burst on the scene in the wilderness of Judea preaching a call to repentance. (Matthew and Luke tell us only about His birth and nothing more.) John the Baptizer is better than John the Baptist because he was doing something new and unexpected, calling Jews to repent and to be baptized...he wasn't a "Baptist." The "Chosen" calls him "Crazy John," and seems to belittle him behind his back, and even has Jesus smiling about it. That is not correct, he was saner and more "on target" than any of the others!

As introduction to John's life, Luke 1 tells us the following: His father, Zechariah, was a priest in the division of Abijah. His mother, Elizabeth, was a relative of Mary the mother of Jesus. John was born in Judea and is mentioned by Josephus, the gospel writers, and the writings of his disciples.

John's preaching marked the end of the prophetic era and Jesus' coming opened the kingdom era. Like other prophets, his influence did not die when he was killed. He was identified by Jesus as the anticipated return of Elijah and his clothing even resembled that of Elijah (2 Kings 1:8). I wonder if that was lost on the Pharisees? He grew up in close proximity to the wilderness and his food and dress were made up of things found in the desert that would be ceremonially "clean." His manner was not so much ascetic as it was legally pure. John's dress was reminiscent of the prophet Elijah and may unknowingly be a statement that he was the one Malachi predicted would precede the coming of the Messiah (Mal. 4:5).

According to the Synoptic Gospels, his preaching called for repentance, a change of heart and mind, because God's judgment was about to be poured out on the earth. He also emphasized ethical living, sharing an extra coat, not over charging and being content with wages. Most of the people John baptized were ordinary people who returned to their jobs and families to await the one who was to come.

Let's take a look at this somewhat controversial word "baptism." The Greek noun *baptisma* and the verb *baptismos* were used to refer to immersing or dipping something into a liquid medium, in this case, water. It was the process used to dye cloth or garments. Unfortunately, by the time the Bible was translated into English the belief that baptism was a part of salvation and the practice of infant baptism was fully established. Further, sprinkling" and/or "pouring" had replaced immersion as the accepted mode of baptism except by those who practiced "believer's baptism." It's my belief that the translators took the easy way and simply transliterated, rather than translated, the Greek. To have done otherwise would have flown in the face of established practice.

It would be natural that the Gentiles needed to repent and be baptized, but never had Jews been willing to admit their need to repent or to be baptized; after all, they thought they had Abraham as their father (John 8:39). (Baptism was used by the Jews in the process of proselyte conversion, not as a symbol of repentance but as an acceptance of Judaism.) The unusual thing about John's baptism is that he put Jews on the same level as Gentiles; both were required to repent prior to baptism. "There is nothing that shuts up the way of mercy and salvation from us so much as the opinion of our own righteousness does. True repentance is an inward thing which has its seat in the mind and heart (GN)."

Matthew uses the phrase "the Kingdom of Heaven is near" some thirty times to emphasize the fact that the expected Messianic Age was rapidly dawning. At that time there was a great national movement; people were returning to God, but never had a prophet asked Jews repent and be baptized. Note [a] in the text is from *The Anchor Bible* translation to catch that urgency they felt (p. 25). "This prophecy quoted is Isaiah 40:3. Isaiah was one of the greatest prophets of the Old Testament and one of the most quoted in the New (LASB, p. 1538)."

Although there is no "real" evidence, many scholars believe that John, and possibly Jesus himself, was a part of the Essenes and the Qumran community. Baptism was a rite of admission into the sect and, since they were largely Jews already, it too was a baptism of repentance. The method John used for baptism, undoubtedly, was immersion and isn't debated by anyone (other forms began emerging in the third century as baptism came to be seen as sacramental and therefore necessary to salvation).

Since baptism doesn't save us or remove our sins, the method shouldn't become a "test of faith" or fellowship. The important thing is obedience on the part of a new Christian who may be ignorant about the meaning and form of the rite. It's interesting that the Pharisees and Sadducees apparently came seeking baptism, which seems to be doing the right thing. However, John called for evidence of their repentance before baptizing them.

> That John did not view his baptism as having saving value follows from the fact that he denied it to Pharisees and Sadducees who failed to produce "fruit" of "repentance." Had John seen saving power in baptism itself, he would have been without excuse for denying it to those who by his own pronouncement were in the path of coming judgment (BBC, p. 92).

Like John, Jesus referred to the Pharisees and Sadducees, who "...[are] rather consistently representative of disbelief and opposition to Jesus as "vipers" in Matthew 12:34 and 23:33 and it may have been a rather common expression for despicable people because it is found in that manner in other material (AB, p. 26)."

The "wrath" of God sadly has fallen into the arena of political incorrectness. Part of that is because we have 'preached' it incorrectly. Here it's presented in a way that suggests God has gotten mad at human beings and in vengeance is raining down lightning bolts, or the like. In reality God's wrath is the result of God dispensing justice on those who disobey His laws.

The Jewish leaders were proud that they were descended from Abraham and felt an entitlement to whatever rewards there would be, but John, using a play on the Hebrew words for "children," *banim*, and bread *abanim*, insisted that God had a voice in the matter. As Americans, do we ever feel the same way? Aren't we special and blessed by God and therefore "entitled" to preferential treatment. Throw in the fact that we may also be Christians and we believe we "trump" everyone else's rights.

"Baptism, as administered by John, is here contrasted with the forthcoming baptism by the Messiah (AB, p. 26)". Speaking about the work of the Messiah John said, "He will baptize you in the Holy Spirit (some translations add "with fire")." Since all who accept Jesus as Savior are baptized with the Holy Spirit, like it or not, there are no non-charismatic Christians (Eph. 4:5).

The Baptism of Jesus
Matthew 3:13-17

Then Jesus came from Galilee to the Jordan to John, to be baptized by him. [14] But John would have hindered him, saying, "I need to be baptized by you, and you come to me?"

[15] But Jesus, answering, said to him, "Allow it now, for this is the fitting way for us to fulfill all righteousness." Then he allowed him. [16] Jesus, when he was baptized, went up directly from the water: and behold, the heavens were opened to him. He saw the Spirit of God descending as a dove, and coming on him. [17] Behold, a voice out of the heavens said, "This is my beloved Son, with whom I am well pleased."

The second theme addressed is the baptism of Jesus (3:13-17). John's fame had reached Nazareth and according to Matthew, the reason Jesus left Galilee was to be baptized by John. The fact that Jesus was baptized by John was not a problem for Jesus, but it became a problem for the early Church fathers.

How old was Jesus? Luke says, "Jesus himself, when he began to teach, was about thirty years old, being the son (as was supposed) of Joseph, the son of Heli, (Luke 3:23)." Why wait so long? The time wasn't right yet. When John began to preach, Jesus saw it was time to start his own ministry.

It's interesting to me that John's baptism was a baptism of repentance, yet Jesus came and asked to be baptized. Although John didn't yet recognize Jesus as the Messiah (John 1:31), he apparently knew Jesus' behavior as not requiring repentance and didn't want to baptize him. Actually, John wanted Jesus to baptize him (verse 14).

There is nothing in any biblical or extra-biblical material to indicate that Jesus thought He needed to repent. So, why would Jesus want to be baptized? It identified Him with the people He came to save (DSB, p. 60), and it linked the ministries of John and Jesus (WP, p. 29).

In verse 11 "…this is the fitting way for us to fulfill all righteousness" does not suggest that His baptism in some way turned Him into the Messiah, as the Gnostics thought, He was already that. It suggests an appropriateness in launching His formal mission and it was a means of identifying with His future followers who were called on to be baptized.

In Jesus' baptism we have representation of all three persons in the God-head. There is the voice of the Father, the baptism of the Son, and the Holy Spirit "descending like a dove." A dove, swift yet gentle settling down, like a Spirit, hovering over the water (Gen. 1:2). The dove, a symbol of Israel (Hos. 7:11, 11:11 and in the Song of Solomon) was to birds what a lamb was to animals and came to represent the Holy Spirit in the early church.

Each of the Synoptic Gospels describes the event a little differently:

In those days, Jesus came from Nazareth of Galilee, and was baptized by John in the Jordan. Immediately coming up from the water, he saw the heavens parting, and the Spirit descending on him like a dove. A voice came out of the sky, "You are my beloved Son, in whom I am well pleased" (Mark 1:9-11).

Now when all the people were baptized, Jesus also had been baptized, and was praying. The sky was opened, and the Holy Spirit descended in a bodily form like a dove on him; and a voice came out of the sky, saying "You are my beloved Son. In you I am well pleased." (Luke 3:21-22)

There is no indication that the bystanders saw or heard anything, but Matthew does seem to have the voice address the crowd.

"This is my beloved Son;" quotes Psalms 2:7. And "with him I am well pleased" comes from Isaiah 42:1 and is not simply "happy." "The Greek word [translated *well pleased*] signifies a thing of great worth and such as highly pleases a man (GN)."

Interestingly, there are no recorded miracles prior to Jesus' baptism and the Spirit's descent upon Him.

The Formal Temptation of Jesus
Matthew 4:1-11

Then Jesus was led up by the Spirit into the wilderness to be tempted by the devil. ² When he had fasted forty days and forty nights, he was hungry afterward. ³ The tempter came and said to him, "If you are the Son of God, command that these stones become bread."

⁴ But he answered, "It is written, 'Man shall not live by bread alone, but by every word that proceeds out of the mouth of God'" (Deut. 8:3).

⁵ Then the devil took him into the holy city. He set him on the pinnacle of the temple, ⁶ and said to him, "If you are the Son of God, throw yourself down, for it is written, 'He will put his angels in charge of you.' And, 'On their hands they will bear you up, so that you don't dash your foot against a stone'" (Psalm 91:11-12).

⁷ Jesus said to him, "Again, it is written, 'You shall not test the Lord, your God'" (Deut. 6:16).

⁸ Again, the devil took him to an exceedingly high mountain, and showed him all the kingdoms of the world, and their glory. ⁹ He said to him, "I will give you all of these things, if you will fall down and worship me."

¹⁰ Then Jesus said to him, "Get behind me (some translations read "Go away"), Satan! For it is written, 'You shall worship the Lord your God, and you shall serve him only.'" (Deut. 6:13).

¹¹ Then the devil left him, and behold, angels came and served him.

So often we think serving God should, or will, exempt us from difficulty, sort of a vaccination against problems. And, this expected, even demanded, special care dominates Christian attitudes in the United States. However, "…Jesus was led" is better translated "…Jesus was driven" because the Greek word used here, *ekballo* is the same word used for driving out demons, so Jesus was driven, by the Spirit to be tempted. As Matthew Henry so aptly stated,

Concerning Christ's temptation, observe, that directly after he was declared to be the Son of God, and the Saviour [sic] of the world, he was tempted; great privileges, and special tokens of Divine favour [sic], will not secure any from being tempted (MH).

In English, to tempt is to entice or encourage to behave badly. The word used here more correctly means "test." This testing is similar to the testing of Abraham in Genesis 22. God does not tempt men to do evil, but He does test them. "Let no man say when he is tempted, "I am tempted by God," for God can't be tempted by evil, and he himself tempts no one. (James 1:13)." And we also need to consider: "No temptation has taken you except what is common to man. God is faithful, who will not allow you to be tempted above what you are able, but will with the temptation also make the way of escape, that you may be able to endure it. (1 Cor. 10:13)."

This time of testing showed that Jesus was the Son of God, able to overcome the devil and his temptation. A person has not shown true obedience if he or she has never had an opportunity to disobey. … When temptations seem especially strong, or when you think you can rationalize giving in, consider whether Satan may be trying to block God's purposes for your life or for someone else's life. … Jesus wasn't tempted inside the Temple or at his baptism but in the wilderness, where he was tired, alone, and hungry, and most vulnerable. … Jesus was able to resist all of the devil's temptations because he not only knew Scripture, but he also obeyed it. (see Ephesians 6:17) Note that Satan had memorized Scripture, but he failed to obey it. (LASB, p. 1542).

Testing is an opportunity to succeed or fail, "...men and steel are alike [they are] uncertain until they are tested (IB, p. 269)." Temptation of this type is intended to help us exercise our spiritual muscles and develop and improve them. "...the test...comes to a man whom God wishes to use (DSB, p. 63)."

Power to overcome temptation is obtained not in the time of crisis, but before the testing occurs. D. L. Moody was criticized when "...he failed to attend a prayer meeting in the midst of threatened shipwreck, he replied: 'I'm prayed up' (IB, p. 269)."

Is Satan so well versed in Scripture as to be able to quote it readily? Matthew Henry says he is. Further, "It is possible for a man to have his head full of Scripture notions, and his mouth full of Scripture expressions, while his heart is full of bitter enmity to God and to all goodness (MH)." However, Satan will take it out of context and twist it to his own devises. Was Satan the original "spin-doctor"? I think so, how about the Garden of Eden?

The wilderness would not be unlike much of the desert which surrounds us in Arizona. It was hot and dry; there wasn't much shade. God sent Jesus on a mission and it was time to withdraw and prepare. The wilderness was a place to be alone; alone with God. Sometimes we also need to stop and be alone with God so we can recharge our spiritual batteries and be sure we are heading in the right direction.

The Synoptics all place the "formal" temptation of Jesus right after His baptism. Barclay warns us that often when we are high because of what God is doing, we are in danger of attack from the devil. Some do not believe in a personal devil, but cannot otherwise account for the presence of evil in the world.

These temptations were designed to attack Jesus as Messiah; to show Him an "easy way" to get the job done. "Eternal vigilance is the price of freedom" applies as much to the Christian as it does to the nation. However, this was not the only time Jesus was tempted, it's just the most prominent time.

These temptations were designed especially for Jesus and His power. He had the power Satan asked Him to use and He knew how to use it. When Satan comes to us, he approaches us on our level. He knows what we can do and seeks to get us to do it for his glory rather than for God's glory.

Verse 40 says, "After fasting forty days and forty nights, he was hungry." This is interesting, why wasn't he hungry before that? This was apparently true for Moses (Ex 34:28) and Elijah (1 Kings 19:8) also. "A supernatural power of endurance was of course imparted to the body, but this probably operated through a natural law – the absorption of the Redeemer's Spirit in the dread conflict with the tempter (CCE)."

Since Jesus was alone, He had to be the source for this Scripture and this may account for the close similarity in the Synoptic gospels. Look at the small differences:

1. Matthew 4:1, "Then Jesus was led up by the Spirit into the wilderness to be tempted by the devil.
2. Mark 1:12, "Immediately the Spirit drove him out into the wilderness."
3. Luke 4:1, "Jesus, full of the Holy Spirit, returned from the Jordan, and was led by the Spirit into the wilderness."

While Matthew and Luke use "led by the Spirit," Mark uses "the Spirit drove…" Both Mark and Luke infer the temptations occurred during the forty days, while Matthew places them at the end.

The WEB says, "The tempter came." A better translation of Greek is "on coming to him" and is a word Matthew uses some fifty-two times in his Gospel.

Mark doesn't cover specific temptations as do Matthew and Luke. Luke reverses temptation numbers two and three, but the temptation and response are the same.

In Luke 4:6 Satan says about the kingdoms of the world (Matthew's third temptation) "I will give you all this authority, and their glory, for it has been delivered to me; and I give it to whomever I want."

These temptations were not just games without any real threat or consequence. They were very real and designed by Satan to overthrow the Christ. Hebrews 4:15 says, "For we don't have a high priest who can't be touched with the feeling of our infirmities, but one who has been in all points tempted like we are, yet without sin."

There are three tests that come to Jesus to use miracles: first, to meet immediate needs, second, to give a sign, and third, to gain political power.

The First Temptation – To Feed Himself

The tempter came to him and said, "If you are the Son of God, command that these stones become bread." Notice the subtlety, "If you are..." Questioning? Why not test out your power Jesus? If you are, then you'll know for sure!

There is no article before "Son" in the Greek. The devil refers to the words of the Father at Jesus baptism, "This is my Son." So, he challenges Him to prove it by using His power (WP, p. 31).

The small round stones lying all around Him could easily remind Jesus of the loaves of bread baked every day. We are told the people believed that God continued to make manna in heaven and the Messiah would feed the people with it when He came. The same image of stones and bread is used in Matthew 7:9 "Or who is there among you, who, if his son asks him for bread, will give him a stone?"

The First Response

But he answered, "It is written, 'Man shall not live by bread alone, but by every word that proceeds out of the mouth of God' (Deut. 8:3)."

We will see that each temptation is rebuffed by a quotation from Deuteronomy. "It is written" means more than just written down. It means "it is written and is still in force." That is, it hasn't been replaced by a new law of God.

Does man live by bread? Yes! But, not by bread alone! The philosopher Thomas Carlyle (1795-1881) suggested that...not all the finance ministers and upholsterers and confectioners of modern Europe...in joint stock company could make one shoeblack happy...above an hour or two. I believe he was correct. It's good to have things, but they will never keep us happy very long.

The Second Temptation – Put on a Big Show

Then the devil took him into the holy city. He set him on the pinnacle of the Temple, and said to him, "If you are the Son of God, throw yourself down, for it is written, 'He will put his angels in charge of you.' and, 'On their hands they will bear you up, so that you don't dash your foot against a stone'" (Psalm 91:11-12).

Again, notice the subtlety, "If you are...jump off..." Show your faith in God to protect you and show the people your power at the same time. Jesus reminded the rich man "He said to him, 'If they [his brothers] don't listen to Moses and the prophets, neither will they be persuaded if one rises from the dead.'" (Luke 16:31) "...this second one might well be the most subtle and dangerous to one who is spiritually sensitive" (IB, p. 272).

Satan used, and still uses, Scripture to defend his proposals, his temptations. All he did then, and continues to do now, was misinterpret it, misapply it, and omit part of it. Scripture used improperly can become a poison to those who unwittingly and unknowingly receive it.

As an example, consider the follow portions of verses which have been taken out of context to "prove" you should commit suicide right now. From Matthew 27:5, "He [Judas] threw down the pieces of silver in the sanctuary, and departed. He went away and hanged himself." Next, Luke 10:37b, "Go and do likewise." Finally, John 13:27b, "What you do, do quickly." You can "prove" just about anything you want with Scripture taken out of context and/or by using portions of verses. "Only if you really understand what the *whole* Bible says will you be able to recognize errors of interpretation when people take verses out of context and twist them to say what they want them to say (LASB, p 1542)."

The Second Response

Then Jesus said to him, "Again, it is written, 'You shall not test the Lord, your God'" (Deut. 6:16). Presumption on God is not a good idea. God is not bound to us, we are bound to Him; that is, He doesn't need us, we need Him. Conviction doesn't come from what we see, but from what we believe. "God is not our magician in the sky ready to perform on request...God wants us to live by faith, not magic. Don't try to manipulate God by asking for signs. (LASB. P. 1524)."

The Third Temptation – Take the Easy Way

Again, the devil took him to an exceedingly high mountain, and showed him all the kingdoms of the world, and their glory. He said to him, "I will give you all of these things, if you will fall down and worship me." The devil drops the "prove your sonship" and throws his highest card on the table. Satan claims ownership of the world and offers it to Jesus if he will worship him. Satan will happily give what he doesn't own to anyone, if we will worship him. It costs him nothing, he doesn't own it, and it costs us everything.

For the "flat earth" Hebrews, there might be a mountain high enough to explain the ability to see all the nations. We recognize that would not be possible, but we could "parade" them on a wide screen television "in an instant," I imagine that Satan could do the same kind of thing.

The Third Response

Then Jesus said to him, "Get behind me, Satan! For it is written, 'You shall worship the Lord your God, and you shall serve him only.'" (Deut. 6:13). Jesus didn't argue about the ownership of the world. He simply ordered him away and once more quotes Scripture. How is Satan defeated? The word of God! The picture of the "Son of Man" in Revelation 1:16 shows him with a two-edged sword coming out of his mouth indicating to me that the word of his mouth is truly mightier than any sword. When He says, "Bang! You're dead!" like we did as kids, it really happens! You're dead!

Matthew says, "Then the devil left him, and behold, angels came and served him." Luke 4:13 points out that "When the devil had completed every temptation, he departed from him until another time." For Jesus, it was not over until the resurrection.

The Conclusion

Now that Jesus had finished this particular temptation, the angels came and did as the devil had said they would do when he quoted Psalms 91 to him; they came and ministered to him. But they came because he was faithful to God's word, not frivolous.

The Move to Capernaum
Matthew 4:12-17

Now when Jesus heard that John [the Baptizer] was delivered up [put into prison], he withdrew into Galilee. [13] Leaving Nazareth, he came and lived in Capernaum, which is by the sea, in the region of Zebulun and Naphtali, [14] that it might be fulfilled which was spoken through Isaiah the prophet, saying, [15] "The land of Zebulun and the land of Naphtali, toward the sea, beyond the Jordan, Galilee of the Gentiles, [16] the people who sat in darkness saw a great light, to those who sat in the region and shadow of death, to them light has dawned" (Isa. 9:1-2).

[17] From that time, Jesus began to preach, and to say, "Repent! For the Kingdom of Heaven is at hand."

John's arrest came as the result of his condemnation of Herod and Herodias, Herod's brother's wife living together and his evil reign (see Luke 3:19). Herodias wanted John killed immediately, but Herod feared the people and refused.

The arrest of John the Baptist was the sign for Jesus to lift the banner of the kingdom. When one ministry ended, another and better ministry began: the promise of dawn gave place to the daybreak (IB, p. 273).

This second event in chapter four is Jesus' relocation from Nazareth to Capernaum. Luke 4:14-30 says that Jesus returned to Nazareth where He was raised but was not welcomed there so He moved on to Capernaum. Capernaum was a fishing village located on the northwest shore of the Sea of Galilee not far from the Jordan River. It was the home of Peter and Andrew and comes as close as any to being Jesus' "home."

The Sea of Galilee is about fifty miles north to south and twenty-five miles from east to west at the widest part and is located in the most fertile part of Palestine. When Josephus was governor, ca 66-70 AD he says there were 204 villages with at least 15,000 people, but that may be exaggerated.

The Jews were not ready to accept Jesus and His message and more threats came from them. Since He found a better reception among the Gentiles, He spent a great deal of time with them. Capernaum was a commercial fishing village which was more tolerant than Judea. It was occupied by a mixed-race people who were involved with traders traveling the caravan route from Damascus to Egypt. The population was probably about 1,000 with a large Jewish population. Excavation of the synagogue, built a few hundred years later, indicates it was sixty-five feet long and two stories high. There was also a large, octagonal church from the same era built on the traditional site of Peter's house.

In verses 15 and 16, Matthew appropriates another "prophecy." It originally addressed the idea that the Messiah would bless the entire world, including the Gentile areas listed.

The evangelist is interested in the fact that the Messiah resided at Capernaum not merely because he himself lived in it, but also because he finds in this a fulfillment of Isaiah's prophecy that a great light would one day dawn upon the downtrodden region ravaged by the Assyrian invader [in the 7th century BC] (see Isa. 9:1-7) (TNTC, p. 56)

"The early Galilean ministry of Jesus had two complementary features. It consisted of both preaching and healing (TNTC, p. 56)" and it paralleled John the Baptizer's call for repentance... "in view of the coming kingdom of God (TNTC, p. 56)." However, that is where the similarity ended because Jesus "brought" the promised kingdom with Him.

The word translated "repent" means to "change one's mind." The Jewish idea followed in the LXX, the Greek translation of the Old Testament, and translated "repent" meant to "grieve for one's sins." "It involved profound sorrow for sin, restitution so far as possible, and a steadfast resolution not to commit that particular sin again (IB, p. 274)." There was strong argument that you could only know you had truly repented when you refused to yield to the same temptation the next time it occurred.

"Death," in verse 16, is personified, like our "grim reaper."

Jesus had been teaching before, but now His ministry goes into high gear. It is interesting that He is usually called "teacher," but now He is a "preacher." "Properly, the verb [preach], is used to mean the proclamation of important news by means of a herald, whose office and person in classical times were inviolate (AB, p. 39)."

The terms "Kingdom of Heaven" and "Kingdom of God" are used interchangeably in the Synoptics. Hebrew writers preferred using Heaven to avoid using God's name and inadvertently violating the third commandment.

Barclay lists three things about Jesus' preaching that all preaching should contain:

1. A note of certainty: a man cannot make others sure of that about which he himself is in doubt.
2. A note of authority: the application of prophetic authority to the present situation.
3. The message comes from a source beyond himself, it must be the voice of God speaking to men.

The Call of the Disciples
Matthew 4:18-25

Walking by the Sea of Galilee, he (some translations read "Jesus") saw two brothers: Simon, who is called Peter, and Andrew, his brother, casting a net into the sea; for they were fishermen. ¹⁹ He said to them, "Come after me, and I will make you fishers for men."

²⁰ They immediately left their nets and followed him. ²¹ Going on from there, he saw two other brothers, James the son of Zebedee, and John his brother, in the boat with Zebedee their father, mending their nets. He called them. ²² They immediately left the boat and their father, and followed him.

²³ Jesus went about in all Galilee, teaching in their synagogues, preaching the Good News of the Kingdom, and healing every disease and every sickness among the people. ²⁴ The report about him went out into all Syria. They brought to him all who were sick, afflicted with various diseases and torments, possessed with demons, epileptics, and paralytics; and he healed them. ²⁵ Great multitudes from Galilee, Decapolis, Jerusalem, Judea and from beyond the Jordan followed him.

The final section in chapter 4 covers the call of the disciples in verses 18-25. "Next to Jesus, interest in the Gospel of Matthew is focused upon his disciples (BBC, p. 100)." Jesus first called two pair of brothers. One of them, Andrew was a disciple of John the Baptizer and influenced Peter to follow Jesus (John 1:35-42). James may have been aggressive, because he was the first martyr (Acts 12:2), and his brother John.

Jesus could have selected anyone to be His disciples (pupils) and then to be the leaders of the church that would have emerged. Who did He choose? He didn't choose the educated, the established religious leaders. He chose ordinary men, "For you see your calling, brothers, that not many are wise according to the flesh, not many mighty, and not many noble; (1 Cor. 1:26)." While this passage doesn't refer specifically to the disciples, it is appropriate.

Some characteristics of a fisherman listed by Barclay are:
1. They are patient and have learned to wait for the fish to take the bait.
2. They have perseverance and do not discourage easily.
3. They have courage because there was often danger on the sea.
4. They are alert and they watch for the right time and place to fish.
5. They know their prey. They use the right bait or lure for their game.

In the same way, a fisher of men must be like a fisher of fish.

What kind of men were these men? They were ordinary, average men; they were individual men, not carbon copies of each other or of Jesus. There was headstrong Peter; quiet, loyal Andrew; and the "sons of thunder." They were also reverent men; not in the sense the Jews understood reverence, but in the true sense of the word.

Augustine says, "...Peter did not lay aside his nets but changed them (IB, p. 276)." To catch men was used negatively in both rabbinic and Greek tradition (see Jer. 16:16), but as so often happened, Jesus reinterpreted the adage.

That these men left so readily to follow Jesus indicates that they may have been acquainted with Him already. Now it was time to begin in earnest. Teaching in rabbinic and Greek cultures involved intimate daily contact it was by example as well as precept (IB, p. 276).

Verse 23 indicates that Jesus was involved in a threefold ministry: teaching in the synagogues, preaching the good news, and healing.

"This is the first of three tours of Galilee Jesus made... The second time he took the twelve. On the third he sent the twelve on ahead by twos and followed after them (WP, p. 36)."

Wherever there were ten adult males, there was a synagogue which was used primarily for worship and teaching the Law, but it also may have served as a sort of community center for secular Jewish activities, much like the churches in some the small towns I grew up in where the church was the center of activities, the synagogues were the center of life for the Jews. They were under control of laymen, not the priests. (I have used laymen here because there was a very real distinction between the "clergy" and the "laity" in Judaism. Such a distinction should not exist in the Church!) The fact that Jesus taught in the synagogues indicates that He didn't wish to break with historic Judaism.

His healing ministry shows that He cared and cares about the whole person, not just the soul. "Three diseases are named; the palsy [paralysis], which is the greatest weakness of the body; lunacy [epilepsy], which is the greatest malady of the mind; and possession of the devil, which is the greatest misery and calamity of both; yet Christ healed all... (MH)." Many times we see that Jesus' healing was motivated by His compassion for the physical plight of the people.

Verse 24 demonstrates the extent of the news of Jesus' activity. The statement "all who were ill with various diseases," could also be rendered 'Those who had it bad,' [the] cases that the doctors could not cure (WP, p. 36)." These were the ones who sought Him out.

Verse 25 says there were crowds, not just a crowd; many people in great groups came from everywhere for healing.

The Decapolis was a league of ten Greek speaking city-states on the northwest side of the Sea of Galilee.

Why a Mountain?
Matthew 5:1-2

Seeing the multitudes, he went up onto the mountain. When he had sat down, his disciples came to him.
² He opened his mouth and taught them, saying,

"The Sermon on the Mount challenged the proud and legalistic religious leaders of the day. It called them back to the messages of the Old Testament prophets, who, like Jesus, taught that the heartfelt obedience is more important than legalistic observance (LASB, p. 1545)."

Notice "...the multitudes... He opened his mouth and taught them, saying," Some raise the question, did Jesus teach the crowds or was He speaking to the disciples and the others "eavesdropped"? I'm in favor of His teaching the people because according to Matthew only four disciples have been called at this point, Matthew himself isn't called until Matthew 9:9. Matthew 7:28-29 indicates the reaction of the crowds to

Jesus' teaching. "When Jesus had finished saying these things, the multitudes were astonished at His teaching, for He taught them with authority, and not like the scribes."

You might ask, "Why a mountain?" Jesus was transfigured on a mountain (17:1), gave His last command from a mountain before He ascended to Heaven (28:16), and Moses received the Ten Commandments on a mountain (Exodus 19). The setting "seems to suggest that the evangelist is deliberately portraying Jesus as the second Moses, who…gives to the new Israel a new 'law'… (TNTC, p. 59)." However, this law isn't a list of "dos" and "don'ts" that we can "check off." As Jeremiah said, "'But this is the covenant that I will make with the house of Israel after those days,' says Yahweh: I will put my law in their inward parts, and I will write it in their heart. I will be their God, and they shall be my people. (Jer. 31:33)."

And, there are many other occasions that have events set on a mountain. "Mountain top experiences" have always had great significance for people; so much so that, we use it as an expression for something especially moving.

When we address the beatitudes, one thing is certain; they are a clear statement of a new standard for living. I hope that it will also become clear to us that God's standard is set in absolutes, not in "shoulds" and "oughts," but in "demands" upon our lives.

Sitting down to teach was the norm. When a Rabbi taught, he always sat down. When the Pope speaks *ex cathedra*, it is from his Chair and we have professorial "chairs" in our universities and seminaries. Some examples applied to Jesus include: Mark 4:1 "Again he began to teach by the seaside. A great multitude was gathered to him, so that he entered into a boat in the sea, and sat down. All the multitude were on the land by the sea." Luke 4:20a, "He closed the book, gave it back to the attendant, and sat down." John 8:2, "Now very early in the morning, he came again into the temple, and all the people came to him. He sat down, and taught them."

The best teaching doesn't just come off the "top of the head" or from your study notes; it is sharing a part of yourself; it is from the heart. The best teaching still comes from diligent study followed by personal sharing and is best done on the same level as the student, not stand over them, but parallel to them.

I prefer the WEB translation of the Greek in verse 2, "and opening his mouth" Because this phrase has special significance in Greek and has two usages. One is for solemn, grave and dignified utterances and the other is used of teaching that comes from the teacher's heart (DSB, p. 86).

"…teach them, saying:" is in the imperfect past tense indicating that it was a continuing action. An example might be this; "It was his habit to always shut the gate when he came in…" versus, "He shut the gate when he came in."

Introduction to the Beattitudes

One of the oldest and possibly the least important questions about the beatitudes is, "How many beatitudes are there?" There are nine verses that begin "Blessed…" so it would seem to give us nine beatitudes. But some find two in verses 11-12 and others contend that these verses are a "gloss," something added by a copyist at a later time.

25

The gloss theory says that the first eight verses are written in the third person and the ninth is in the second person. The first eight also have a rhythm and parallelism that is not found in the ninth.

However, the ninth is similar to Luke's fourth beatitude, all of which are written in the second person. Numerology was important to ancient people, but we must not assume that it was so all consuming that everything had to be forced into some numerological pattern.

"The beatitudes stress the striking contrast between outward appearance and inner reality (BBC, p.104)." "The beatitudes are all promises of the kingdom of God, for to be in the kingdom is to 'be comforted,' to 'inherit the earth,' or the promised land, to 'be satisfied,' to 'obtain 'mercy,' to 'see God,' and to be called his 'sons' (IB, p. 280)."

"Blessed are..." is an inadequate way to begin each beatitude. They begin with the Greek word *makorioi* which can be translated "to be blessed," which is more a declaration of a state of blessedness, like the blessing given to the children by the father before his death. In Greek *makorioi* was applied to the gods, it was a godlike joy or happiness. Barclay says it describes "joy which has its secret within itself (DSB, p. 89)."

"Of the two words which our translators render 'blessed' the one here used points more to what is *inward,* and so might be rendered 'happy,' in a lofty sense; while the other denotes rather what comes to us *from without* (as Matt. 25:34) (CCE)."

According to Fisher, the first four beatitudes speak of our relationship to God, the next four with our submission to Him (Fisher, p. 34-35). These beatitudes follow the outline of Psalm 85:10, a description of God, "Mercy and truth meet together. Righteousness and peace have kissed each other." "Mercy is required where men wrong other men; purity of heart is required where mixed motives abound; peacemakers are needed in a world where men are estranged; righteousness is persecuted in an unrighteous world (Fisher, p. 36)."

If we look carefully, I believe we will see that each Beatitude, like the "fruits of the Spirit," builds on the preceding one until we are able to be what is required of the Christian and the final Beatitude acts as the crown for all the others. "The Beatitudes are not simple statements; they are exclamations...not pious hopes of what shall be...they are congratulations on what is (DSB, p. 88)."

The Beatitudes - Part 1 – Poor in Spirit
Matthew 5:3

"Blessed are the poor in spirit,
for theirs is the Kingdom of Heaven (Isa. 57:15; 66:2)."

"Jesus began his sermon with words that seem to contradict each other. But God's way of living usually contradicts the world's [way] (LASB, p. 15415)." The Jews held two opposite positions about being poor. One position said poor people were cursed by God, the other held that God blessed the poor. Matthew points out that material possession doesn't indicate a person's spiritual condition. Jesus said in John 16:22, "Therefore you now have sorrow, but I will see you again, and your heart will rejoice, and no one will take your joy away from you." The poverty expressed here is absolute destitution; no relief is available. The

Hebrew concept is that of the destitute person who can only rely upon God. When a person's situation is totally hopeless, they have only one place to turn and that is to God.

"Poverty of spirit runs counter to the pride of men's heart… (CCE)." The Psalmist had much to say about the poor and their relationship to God. Some examples include: "For the needy shall not always be forgotten, nor the hope of the poor perish forever. (Ps. 9:18)." "This poor man cried, and Yahweh heard him, and saved him out of all his troubles (Ps. 34:6)." "All my bones shall say, 'Yahweh, who is like you, who delivers the poor from him who is too strong for him; yes, the poor and the needy from him who robs him?' (Ps. 35:10)." "He will judge the poor of the people. He will save the children of the needy, and will break the oppressor in pieces (Ps. 72:4)."

Do we need wealth, that is to say, things? When we acquire them, we don't really own them, they own us. Do you ever have to work on the house, the car, the dog? Do they ever keep you from doing what you really want to do?

We place great store in material wealth and its effect on people, some use it for God's glory, and some waste it on worldly things. But wealth is neutral; we shouldn't make the mistake of assuming that material poverty is beneficial in God's sight. The same is true of spiritual poverty it can cause us to turn to God or cause us to turn away.

The poverty spoken of here isn't the lack of material wealth; it is a spiritual poverty. It is such great poverty that it is like a beggar crying out for God's Spirit, not money. Those who think they are spiritually wealthy, that is the proud, have no need to turn to God. This is what Jesus meant in Matthew 9:12b, "Those who are healthy have no need for a physician, but those who are sick do."

If there is a greatest sin, it may be the sin of pride, which is the root or beginning of all sin. It is pride that prevents us from doing those things we need to do. It is pride that causes us to behave in "bull-headed" ways that end up embarrassing the Savior and us. It is pride that prevents us from asking for forgiveness from God and our fellow man.

The word translated "theirs" is emphatic in the Greek; the Kingdom belongs to these people alone. "The poor in spirit not only shall have – they already have – the kingdom (CCE)." No one will be able to take it from them!

We also have a problem with the word "Kingdom." For us it is a geographical area, a nation, but for the Greeks and Hebrews it meant the "reign of a king." Therefore, since Jesus is reigning, the Kingdom is here, and the Kingdom belongs to all who are subjects of the King!

The two passages from Isaiah that are referenced in the "notes" on the verse say:

For thus says the high and lofty One who inhabits eternity, whose name is Holy: "I dwell in the high and holy place, with him also who is of a contrite and humble spirit, to revive the spirit of the humble, and to revive the heart of the contrite. (Isa. 57:15).

"For my hand has made all these things, and so all these things came to be," says Yahweh: "but to this man will I look, even to he who is poor and of a contrite spirit, and who trembles at my word." (Isa. 66:2)

They speak of God's compassion for the "poor," contrite, humble in spirit further emphasizing that this poverty can only be resolved by God's love and forgiveness!

The Beatitudes - Part 2 – Mourners
Matthew 5:4

"Blessed are those who mourn,
for they shall be comforted (Isa. 61:2; 66:10, 13)."

"Luke substituted 'weep' for 'mourn' and 'laugh' for 'comforted' (Luke 6:21). He also included a corresponding woe on those who 'laugh now' saying that they shall 'mourn and weep' (Luke 6:25) (Fisher pp. 28-29)." "Christianity is caring (DSB, p. 94)." Have you shared the pain of a friend? Do you hurt with them or just feel sorry for them? Does your sin cause you agony? What about the sin of a loved one or a neighbor?

In Exodus 32:31-32 we have these words related to our responsibility to our friends and their sin:

Moses returned to Yahweh, and said, "Oh, this people have sinned a great sin, and have made themselves gods of gold. Yet now, if you will, forgive their sin—and if not, please blot me out of your book which you have written."

"Not all mourning is blessed and much sorrow finds no comfort (BBC, p. 105)." It is the grief that follows the realization of our utter spiritual poverty (verse 3) that is of benefit. The word used here is one used for mourning at death, "the passionate lament for one who was loved (DSB, p. 93)." It is the same word used in the LXX of Jacob's grief at the loss of Joseph, when his sons tricked him. "Those who mourn..." it is spiritual poverty that leads to genuine sorrow; sorrow for our spiritual condition. Our comfort comes only from God and His forgiveness.

This "mourning" must not be taken loosely for that feeling which is wrung from men under pressure of the ills of life, nor yet strictly for sorrow on account of committed sins. Evidently it is that entire feeling which the sense of our spiritual poverty begets; and so the second beatitude is but the complement of the first. The one is the intellectual, the other the emotional aspect of the same thing. (CCE)

It's great to live in the sunshine, but the Arabs have a proverb: "All sunshine makes a desert." Sorrow can bring about two things: it can show us the love of our friends and the love of our God. Just as the rain makes the desert bloom, so sorrow can produce strength and beauty in us. Think about the beauty of the night. The stars are there all the time, but the sun is so bright it hides them from our view. Only in the darkness can we look up and see the flickering specks of light that dot the sky all the time.

Sadly, grief can also make us bitter and drive us away from God and friends. This happens any time we lose focus and decide God has it "in" for us. Everyone suffers loss; it began with the death of Abel and continues to this day. Internalized grief is a tool of the devil to distract us from God's love through the Holy Spirit and our Christian family.

"The world says, 'Enjoy!' Christ says, 'Grieve!' (IB, p. 281)." Another paradox of Christianity is that joy has its roots in sorrow. Jesus knew, and we know, that all sorrow doesn't bring joy.

The prayer of Psalms 51:1-3 is certainly appropriate.

Have mercy on me, God, according to your loving kindness. According to the multitude of your tender mercies, blot out my transgressions. Wash me thoroughly from my iniquity. Cleanse me from my sin. For I know my transgressions. My sin is constantly before me.

The first word in the message of both John the Baptizer and Jesus is "Repent!" But you cannot repent until you are first sorry for your sins. "And when a man sees sin in all its horror, he cannot do anything else but experience sorrow for his sin (DSB, p. 95)."

The example Jesus gives in Luke 18:10-14 is self-explanatory: Jesus said:

"Two men went up into the temple to pray; one was a Pharisee, and the other was a tax collector. The Pharisee stood and <u>prayed to himself</u> [my underline for emphasis] like this: 'God, I thank you, that I am not like the rest of men, extortionists, unrighteous, adulterers, or even like this tax collector. I fast twice a week. I give tithes of all that I get.' But the tax collector, standing far away, wouldn't even lift up his eyes to heaven, but beat his breast, saying, 'God, be merciful to me, a sinner!' I tell you, this man went down to his house justified rather than the other; for everyone who exalts himself will be humbled, but he who humbles himself will be exalted."

We also fail to understand the word "comforted." For us it is probably sitting in an easy chair as we relax and enjoy our favorite TV show. The message the Greek carries is different. It is that of a person laboring to carry a load up a hill and having someone come along to assist them in their struggle (Fisher p. 30).

Be careful how you live your life, but beware when you think nothing in your life would displease God. Poverty of spirit should naturally lead us to mourning for our situation.

The Beatitudes - Part 3 – Meekness
Matthew 5:5

"Blessed are the gentle,
for they shall inherit the earth (or land; Ps. 37:11)."

Since Luke doesn't record this Beatitude, some have suggested that it was a later insertion. It reflects, if not quotes, Psalm 37:11, "But the humble shall inherit the land, and shall delight themselves in the abundance of peace." According to Barclay, Aristotle would define a virtue as the "happy medium" between two extremes. Thus, meekness [gentleness] became the medium between too much anger and too little anger (DSB, p. 96).

Moses is described as "humble," in many translations which is a poor translation, because it is the same Greek word translated "meek" in the LXX. "Now the man Moses was very humble, above all the men who were on the surface of the earth" (Num. 12:3). Yet, I don't think we can say Moses just stood by and allowed Pharaoh to ignore God's demands. The meek are not the weak and cowardly, but those who accept God's will for their lives over their own desires. "...one lives by dying, receives by giving, and is first precisely when willing to be last (BBC, p.105)." A domesticated animal was said to be meek. That is, they were trained to obey commands, respond to the reins and accept control of the master. For the Christian the key then is not in being self-controlled, but in being God controlled.

In English, "meek" and "submissive" have often been connected but they shouldn't be because they are not necessarily related. There are three words we need a spiritual understanding of: meek, aggressive and assertive. Meek, means God directed; its opposite, aggressive, which I will define as self-directed; and assertive, which I call God's limit for how far He is willing for us to be pushed, but we need to be careful that our assertiveness doesn't become aggression.

In an effort to color the meaning correctly, the French translated it "debonair." "This hints a man who is so gladdened and overcome by God's greatness that he counts his own life as nothing, but gaily gives it for love's sake (IB, p. 282)."

Gentleness develops after we mourn for our sins and submit to God's will and direction. If "poor in spirit" is the opposite of proud in spirit, then "meek" is the opposite of aggressive. "Others claim their rights, but the meek are concerned about their duties (IB, p. 282)." Peter, talking about Jesus said, "Who, when he was cursed, didn't curse back. When he suffered, didn't threaten, but committed himself to him who judges righteously;" (1 Pet. 2:23). The meek do not trust in themselves, but in God.

"The Jews asserted their pride of race, the Romans their pride of power, the Greeks their pride of knowledge...modern nations insist on their 'place in the sun;' but the meek are content to walk in the shadow where God keeps watch over his own (IB, p. 282)."

The word "inherit" indicates a bequest, a gift. The meek Christian would never seize it, but it will come to them as a gift from God.

The Beatitudes - Part 4 – Hunger and Thirst
Matthew 5:6

"Blessed are those who hunger and thirst after righteousness,
for they shall be filled."

"Hunger and thirst..." know anyone who is spiritually overweight? Gentleness leads to a desire to know better the One who has done so much for us. "Words do not exist in isolation; they exist against a background of experience and of thought; and the meaning of any word is conditioned by the background of the person who speaks it (DSB, p. 99)." Most of us don't know what it means to be hungry and thirsty. We're like a child who is "starving" within an hour of a great meal.

The Greek words used here are strong words. These are people who knew what it was to go without food and water; they had experienced great hunger and thirst. It would be unusual for a working man to have meat more than once a week. Theirs was a subsistence economy, but the words are used metaphorically here. Our hunger for righteousness should be so great that a "snack" won't do anything but make us hungrier. How much do you want righteousness? As much as a man crawling across the desert wants a drink?

Fisher suggests three possible applications for this verse: personal uprightness, personal salvation, and the victory of God's cause in the world, (Fisher, p. 33). Barclay says, "The true wonder of man is not that he is a sinner, but that even in his sin he is haunted by goodness (DSB, p. 100)." King David wanted desperately to build a temple for His God. That desire was not fulfilled, but the Scripture says, "Now it was in the heart of David my father to build a house for the name of Yahweh, the God of Israel. But Yahweh said to David my father, Whereas it was in your heart to build a house for my name, you did well that it was in your heart:" (1 Kings 8:17-18).

According to Barclay, Greek grammar calls for the verbs "hunger" and "thirst" to be followed by modifiers that indicate a desire for a part of something, (genitive case). "I hunger for a piece of bread and a glass of water," not the whole loaf or the whole bucket. But here it is a direct accusative, "hunger and thirst" for all there is. Only total and complete righteousness will satisfy my soul, I cannot be content with only a part.

Notice the requirement is to hunger and thirst for righteousness, not to be righteous. It is a journey for the Christian, ever traveling toward righteousness. The more we are "filled" the more we can hold. It may be impossible for us to be perfect, in our usage of the word, but we should be getting better.

The word "filled" is a word used for "stuffed," as after finishing a Thanksgiving feast. You have eaten until there isn't even room for Jell-O. "There are bread and water for the hunger of the mouth, and there is light for the hunger of the eyes. Why should it be hard for us to believe that there is fulfillment for the thirst of the soul? (IB, p. 283)."

The Beatitudes - Part 5 - Merciful
Matthew 5:7

"Blessed are the merciful,
for they shall obtain mercy."

"Merciful..." is the natural outgrowth of having a loving relationship with God and our family. By family, I mean more than just related to us by blood or law; I mean the family of God. As we understand how merciful God has been to us, we share that love and mercy with others which helps them understand God's love for them. "In mercy and forgiveness, receiving is bound up with giving. ...in the nature of mercy and forgiveness there cannot be receiving without giving (BBC, p. 105)."

One of the great fallacies today is that people grant mercy and forgiveness for someone else. However, we cannot extend mercy and forgiveness to someone unless we have the right and the power to execute judgment on the person who has wronged us. It is the one whose property was stolen that can extend mercy and forgive the thief. "The New Testament is insistent that to be forgiven we must be forgiving (DSB, p. 102)." We have incorrectly made mercy a noun; it is a verb and requires action. (See Matthew 6:12 and 18:21-35.)

This beatitude was given to people who believed in an "eye for an eye." Justice or vengeance, not mercy, was the cry of the day and "the commonly accepted explanation of suffering saw in it only the deserved punishment for sin (IB, p. 284)."

While the New Testament was written in Greek, they were using the language of the day to record thoughts that were rooted in their Hebrew language. The Hebrew word for mercy is *chesedh* and is untranslatable into English because it requires the ability to get into the other person's skin, to see with his eyes, to think with his mind, to feel his feelings, (DSB, p. 102). It is the Native American idea of walking a mile in the other guy's moccasins. In the strictest sense of the word, sympathy comes close. The meaning, in Greek is to suffer with, to literally go through what the other person is going through.

If we made this kind of deliberate effort, it would make a big difference. Barclay points out three things: it would save us from being kind in the wrong way; it would make forgiveness and tolerance easier; and it is how God in Jesus relates to us (DSB, p. 103-104).

There is a reason for everything we do. To understand what the other person is feeling would make forgiveness and tolerance easier. If we understood what is going on in the mind of the other person, we could minister more readily and effectively and be ready to forgive oversights and acts that "hurt" us. Didn't Jesus and Stephen forgive their murderers? A French proverb states, "To know all is to forgive all."

It is how God in Jesus relates to us. God got inside man's skin. In becoming a man, He saw with a man's eyes; He felt with a man's feelings; He thought with a man's mind. God knows what life is like, because He became a man. The best example of *chesedh* is God coming in Jesus.

Wherever there is injury, mercy is required!

The Beatitudes - Part 6 – Pure in Heart
Matthew 5:8

"Blessed are the pure in heart,
for they shall see God."

"This saying is peculiar to Christianity; and it is more largely insisted upon than any of the rest (MH)." "Here is the beatitude which demands that every man who reads it should stop, and think, and examine himself (DSB, p. 105)." Fisher says that "to attain purity of heart is like a child reaching for the moon (Fisher, p. 38)."

In the Bible, "heart" has a broader meaning than it does for us today. We consider it the seat of human emotions, but for the Hebrews, it was that and more, it represented the inner man. It included his will, thoughts, purpose in life. Purity was also primarily a religious word for them. The psalmist asks, "Who may ascend to Yahweh's hill? Who may stand in his holy place? He who has clean hands and a pure heart; Who has not lifted up his soul to falsehood, and has not sworn deceitfully. He shall receive a blessing from Yahweh, Righteousness from the God of his salvation" (Psalm 24:3-5).

"Pure in heart..." clean, single-minded, sincere. Not just a ceremonial washing prior to worship or eating, but a good, deep cleaning to remove everything improper. The NLT has "...those whose hearts are pure," they are "contrasted with those who thought that they had satisfied God's will through ceremonial conformity to tradition (NLTSB, p. 1584)." Remember that the heart was a symbol of the whole person, the outward life reflecting the inner life. "...for most people this sixth beatitude is the 'bright particular star' in the constellation. It seems almost inaccessible (IB, p. 285)."

Pure is the translation of *katharos* which has three basic meanings.

1. It means clean and can be applied to washing dirty clothes.
2. It was used of grain which had been winnowed to remove chaff and when addressed to the army it meant to remove the discontented, cowardly, unwilling and inefficient soldiers leaving only the first-class fighting men.
3. It was used to apply to milk, wine and metal that were pure or unadulterated (DSB, p. 106).

In our culture it is the grieving process that removes the pain of death or disappointment.

Purity of heart is perhaps the hardest to attain. Most of us love because of what we get in return. Purity of heart is that of a small child who loves because it is so much fun to love. Often our service to people is not based solely on a desire to help, but on the fact that we will also receive some recognition. The great preacher John Bunyan was known to respond to a compliment on his sermon with "The devil already told me that as I was coming down the pulpit steps (DSB, p. 106)." Rebuffing compliments isn't necessarily good, and I don't think accepting compliments is bad because God uses people to accomplish His Will. Is our work done out of a heart of love, or because we will be "paid" in some way?

Do we read the Bible and pray because we sincerely desire fellowship with God, or is it just something we have become accustomed to doing or is it so we can say "I prayed for the church like the pastor asked us to do and I'm all current in my effort to read the Bible through this year."?

"Purity of heart and wholeness go together, the outward life reflecting the inner beauty (BBC, p. 106)." Luke 6:43-45 tells us:

> For there is no good tree that brings forth rotten fruit; nor again a rotten tree that brings forth good fruit. For each tree is known by its own fruit. For people don't gather figs from thorns, nor do they gather grapes from a bramble bush. The good man out of the good treasure of his heart brings out that which is good, and the evil man out of the evil treasure of his heart brings out that which is evil, for out of the abundance of the heart, his mouth speaks.

"So, says Jesus, it is only the pure in heart who shall see God (DSB, p. 108)." Remember we keep our hearts clean by God's grace and soil our hearts by our own desires. We generally think of purity of heart as an ethical ideal, but try considering it as a relational ideal instead. It is not so much how we live, but how our manner of life discloses our relationship with God. John put it this way, "If we say that we have fellowship with him and walk in the darkness, we lie, and don't tell the truth" (1 John 1:6). And "…he who says he remains in him ought himself also to walk just like he walked" (1 John 2:6).

What does it mean to "see God"? Paul says that we shall see Him in heaven, "For now we see in a mirror, dimly, but then face to face. Now I know in part, but then I will know fully, even as I was also fully known" (1 Cor. 13:12). But there is more to it than that. Moses dared to stand against Pharaoh because he had seen God. "By faith, he left Egypt, not fearing the wrath of the king; for he endured, as seeing him who is invisible" (Heb. 11:27). He had learned to see God around him. We also need to learn to recognize God in the people we meet. We need to see Him in the beauty of life that surrounds us.

The Beatitudes - Part 7 – Peacemakers
Matthew 5:9

"Blessed are the peacemakers,
for they shall be called children of God."

Shalom "peace" is the traditional Hebrew greeting and means more than the absence of strife; it goes to the social and personal wellbeing of the person greeted. "In the Bible peace means not only freedom from all trouble; it means enjoyment of all good (DSB, p. 108)."

Some have suggested this beatitude was a gloss, an addition based on Psalms 34:14, "Depart from evil, and do good." This is the only place peacemaker is used as an adjective in the New Testament; generally, it is the verb form, "to make peace." But this "sounds" like Jesus, as we will see. Could it be targeting the Zealots who sought to bring about the Kingdom through bloodshed?

Who are peacemakers? They are those who show love and compassion toward people who have indicated that they are enemies of the peacemaker. We are not simply to be bridge-builders who bring alienated parties together; we are to be precipitators of peace.

Paul said:

Therefore if anyone is in Christ, he is a new creation. The old things have passed away. Behold, all things have become new. But all things are of God, who reconciled us to himself through Jesus Christ, and gave to us the ministry of reconciliation; namely, that God was in Christ reconciling the world to himself, not reckoning to them their trespasses, and having committed to us the word of reconciliation. We are therefore ambassadors on behalf of Christ, as though God were entreating by us: we beg you on behalf of Christ, be reconciled to God. (2 Cor. 5:17-20).

"Peacemakers..." positive action is required not just sitting and allowing the problem to go away or resolve itself. It is appropriate that the followers of the "Prince of Peace" would be peacemakers. The central thrust is generally assumed to mean peace between man and God, but that may not be the only meaning here. Jesus demanded that we be "peacemakers," not just peace "lovers" (Fisher, p. 41). We are also to make peace between man and man. The Rabbis taught that the highest work a man could do was to help reconcile man to man.

If we love peace in the wrong way, we make trouble. How do we do that? We do that by simply allowing the wrong to succeed. Tolstoy thought that we should enact the Sermon on the Mount into law and do away with police and armies. But laws are usually made because wrongs have been committed, not to prevent them, so it isn't a peace at all costs mentality.

"Peacemaking is positive and active, not passive (BBC, p. 106)." Biblical peace "springs from trust, love, and obedience toward God (IB, p. 287)." Also examine Ephesians 2:13-17:

But now in Christ Jesus you who once were far off are made near in the blood of Christ. For he is our peace, who made both one, and broke down the middle wall of partition, having abolished in the flesh the hostility, the law of commandments contained in ordinances, that he might create in himself one new man of the two, making peace; and might reconcile them both in one body to God through the cross, having killed the hostility thereby. He came and preached peace to you who were far off and to those who were near.

Terry Waite, an official of the Church of England and a peace envoy successfully negotiated the release of British hostages in Iran in 1981 and Libya in 1985. He was warned not to return for further talks or he would be placing his own life at risk. His efforts in 1987 to free United States hostages in Beirut resulted in his kidnapping by Shiite Muslims during talks. He was finally released in November 1991. That's what peacemakers do; they put themselves at risk for the sake of others.

Fisher suggests a peacemaker is the opposite of a troublemaker; "He is the kind of man who creates peace in any group where he is—the church, the lodge, the labor union or the bridge club (Fisher, p. 42)."

There are always people who try to stir up trouble among other people. They are in every part of society and in every church I've ever been a member of. "The man who divides men is doing the devil's work; the man who unites men is doing God's work (DSB 110)."

Why are they "called the sons of God"? Because they look like God, who is their Father. In the human family, there is often a familial resemblance and there is a family resemblance in the heavenly family. But it isn't physical, it is deeper. We should remind people about God by our attitudes, by our speech, and by our actions. Peacemakers are those who are doing the work of God.

To be "called" in this sense is to become. On the morning of February 6, 1952, Princess Elizabeth knelt before the Archbishop of Canterbury, but she rose Queen Elizabeth II of England. She was not the same person who entered Westminster Abbey, she had become someone else. That's how it should be with us. When we kneel before God, we should rise changed people. Lincoln is reported to have said, "Die when I may, I would like it to be said of me, that I always pulled up a weed and planted a flower where I thought a flower would grow (DSB, p. 109)."

Possibly the best commentary on this verse is found in Matthew 5:38-45, Jesus said:

"You have heard that it was said, 'An eye for an eye, and a tooth for a tooth.' But I tell you, don't resist him who is evil; but whoever strikes you on your right cheek, turn to him the other also. If anyone sues you to take away your coat, let him have your cloak also. Whoever compels you to go one mile, go with him two. Give to him who asks you, and don't turn away him who desires to borrow from you. You have heard that it was said, 'You shall love your neighbor, and hate your enemy.' But I tell you, love your enemies, bless those who curse you, do good to those who hate you, and pray for those who mistreat you and persecute you, that you may be children of your Father who is in heaven. For he makes his sun to rise on the evil and the good, and sends rain on the just and the unjust."

The Beatitudes - Part 8 - the Persecuted
Matthew 5:10-12

"Blessed are those who have been persecuted
for righteousness' sake,
for theirs is the Kingdom of Heaven.
[11] "Blessed are you when people reproach
you, persecute you, and say all kinds of
evil against you falsely, for my sake. [12] Rejoice, and be exceedingly glad, for great is your reward in
heaven. For that is how they persecuted the prophets who were before you."

Some find two beatitudes here, verse 10 is one and 11 is the other. Part of the rational is the phrase "for theirs is the Kingdom of Heaven" which is an echo of verse 3. Another point is the style change from poetic to prose in verse 11. There is also a shift of voice to second person plural (you); Matthew had been using "the" and "those." I will treat it as one like most of my commentators.

Is it better to be persecuted than to live in peace? Some have taken this literally and put themselves in a position to be persecuted to gain a greater reward in heaven. Is this valid? Not if the rest of the Bible is true. The emphasis is on peacemaking, on restoring and forgiving one another.

Everyone knew where Jesus stood; He was, above all, honest with people. His followers knew what was ahead for them if they chose to follow Him and He expected them to be persecuted. Why? Not because they behaved in an obnoxious manner, but because they followed Him. Wasn't He persecuted? Weren't the prophets persecuted? Are we any better than they? If we are persecuted, "…persecution should never be allowed to become a martyr complex or a morbid self-pity (IB, p. 287)."

This blessing is only applicable when we suffer in Christ's service and the charge of evil doing is false. As we have seen in the other beatitudes, there is no special virtue or added grace for being on the short end. But when, or if it comes, be ready for it and God will take care of your reward.

Barclay sights three areas a person's Christianity should affect his life.

1. Their ability to make a living. What if you were a brick layer and your boss got a job building a pagan temple, should you quit your job?

2. Their social life. Most "parties" were in connection with a pagan temple and even an ordinary meal began with an offering to the gods, much like we say grace.

3. Their family life was often disrupted. A wife or child was usually thrown out of the family if they became Christians, so they were forced to choose between Christ and those dearest to them (DSB, pp. 111-112).

"Reproach" can also be translated "ridicule" or even "hassle." The idea is that of verbal abuse. Our defamation of character might fit this. "Persecute" is probably better understood as "scorn." First century hatred should be thought of in terms of behavior like many religious zealots; anyone whose views were different than their interpretation of their "holy writ" was treated as a heretic and could be subject to death.

Who persecuted the Christians? Primarily two groups were involved, slanderers and religious/political fanatics. The slanderers accused them of four atrocities:

1. Cannibalism, they twisted the symbolic meaning of body and blood of the Lord's Supper into a feast where a small child was sacrificed and eaten.

Jesus therefore said to them, "Most certainly I tell you, unless you eat the flesh of the Son of Man and drink his blood, you don't have life in yourselves. He who eats my flesh and drinks my blood has eternal life, and I will raise him up at the last day. For my flesh is food indeed, and my blood is drink indeed. He who eats my flesh and drinks my blood lives in me, and I in him. As the living Father sent me, and I live because of the Father; so he who feeds on me, he will also live because of me. (John 6:53-57)."

2. The Agape Feast they perverted into an orgy. After all the Christians kissed each other in public what kind of things would they do at a "Love Feast" behind closed doors?

3. The Christians spoke of the coming end of the world; therefore, they were plotting the overthrow of Rome.

4. They were accused of splitting up the family and thereby destroying the state.

On the religious/political line, the Roman Empire was huge. It stretched from Britain to the Euphrates and from Germany to North Africa. Its people were ethnically and culturally diverse. They spoke many different languages and worshiped many different gods. The only thing they had in common was worship of the goddess *Roma* who was the personification of the spirit of Rome. This gradually deteriorated into the worship of dead emperors and finally to living emperors. At its height, every man was required to make an offering of a pinch of incense and say "Caesar is Lord" each year. Then they could worship any god they wanted. Failing to make the offering automatically made you an outlaw.

When we follow the commandments of Jesus, scorn and persecution may follow close at hand. "The Bible everywhere assumes that God's servants must remain true even at the risk of their lives. The rabbis later ruled that a man might, if his life were in danger, break any commandment except those against idolatry (IB, p. 287)." This was not to be the way of the Christ followers!

The early church looked forward to persecution as an opportunity to show their loyalty. Polycarp, Bishop of Smyrna, prior to his martyrdom reportedly said, "Eighty and six years have I served Christ and he has done me no wrong. How can I blaspheme my King who saved me?" It also allowed them to follow the same path as the prophets of the Old Testament, the saints of the New Testament, and the martyrs of all ages. Nothing makes you a part of an institution like sharing in their treatment. It is wonderful to be a player on the championship team, but just to be there when it happens is something we can never forget. Because we share in the victory, our actions make things easier for those who are following. To know what someone has already been able to accomplish gives us confidence for our part of the journey.

Finally, they were able to undergo persecution because they believed they would not suffer alone. In the fiery furnace in Daniel 3:16-18:

Shadrach, Meshach, and Abednego answered the king, Nebuchadnezzar, we have no need to answer you in this matter. If it be so, our God whom we serve is able to deliver us from the burning fiery furnace; and he will deliver us out of your hand, O king. But if not, be it known to you, O king, that we will not serve your gods, nor worship the golden image which you have set up.

Jesus said we are to celebrate by jumping for joy in the midst of our persecution. How can this be? Because God will reward us! But what are the rewards? They are: not measurable and not in proportion to service rendered but they are a gift of grace. The ultimate reward is becoming a part of the "Kingdom of Heaven." Please remember, we don't "earn" our heavenly reward by suffering persecution, but God has promised He will reward and He does.

Thus the 'golden chain' of the beatitudes is completed. The same man stands before us always. He is described in various ways—poor in spirit, mourning, meek, hungering and thirsting after righteousness, merciful, pure in heart, peace maker, and persecuted for righteousness' sake. But is always the same man, looked at now from his relationship to God and now from his relationship to other men (Fisher, pp. 44-45).

The Salt of Discipleship
Matthew 5:13

"You are the salt of the earth, but if the salt has lost its flavor, with what will it be salted? It is then good for nothing, but to be cast out and trodden under the feet of men."

Verse 13 isn't something new and, "…as it stands in our English versions makes virtually no sense at all… Sodium chloride does not lose its taste or savor except by dilution? (AB, p. 54)." But,

If a seasoning has no flavor, it has no value. If Christians make no effort to affect the world around them, they are of little value to God. …we should affect others positively, just as seasoning brings out the best flavor in food (LASB, p. 1546).

If you have made the beatitudes genuine in your life, this verse is the natural outcome. There is a parallel found in Mark 9:50, Jesus said, "Salt is good, but if the salt has lost its saltiness, with what will you season it? Have salt in yourselves, and be at peace with one another." And in Luke 14:34-35 "Salt is good, but if the salt becomes flat and tasteless, with what do you season it? It is fit neither for the soil nor for the manure pile. It is thrown out. He who has ears to hear, let him hear."

Salt…to preserve it from corruption, to season its insipidity, to freshen and sweeten it. The value of salt for these purposes is abundantly referred to by classical writers as well as in Scripture; and hence its symbolical significance in the religious offerings as well of those without as of those within the pale of revealed religion. (CCE)

"That guy is the salt of the earth." Can any higher compliment be paid anyone than this expression? It says we hold this person in the very highest regard. Salt was so highly valued that the Greeks called it divine and Roman soldiers were often paid in salt because it would be as acceptable as "money." Salary comes from the Latin *Salarium* or salt money. In some societies a man's life was worth a bag of salt, making a salt thief akin to a rustler in the Old West.

Calling the disciples "salt" had the effect of elevating them. "But how…are Christians to do this office for their fellow men, if their righteousness only exasperates them…? The answer is…a small but noble band would receive and hold it fast… (CCE)."

Salt was primarily a preserving agent and while pure salt cannot lose its saltiness, much of their salt came from the Dead Sea and was a mixture containing more than just sodium chloride.

There are some important questions to answer before we can interpret this verse: What use of salt in the ancient world became the example the people would understand and transfer to this verse? What does "earth" mean; is it a metaphor for people as "world" is in v. 14? Does Jesus mean that salt actually loses its chemical properties and thus "loses its saltiness"? And if so, does that mean a Christian can lose his salvation?

It was long recognized that salt is essential to life. There were many common uses of salt in Old Testament times among the Jews: the most obvious is to season food (Job 6:6), it was also added to some sacrifices (Lev. 2:13; Ezekiel 43:24) and burning of incense (Eze. 16:4). It was used to purify the spring at Jericho (2 Kings 2:19-22) and Abimelech plowed salt into the land around Shechem to destroy its growing potential for crops (Jud. 9:45). It was also a symbol of friendship (Num. 18:19).

There were two other major uses of salt: first, to preserve food from spoiling, a practice that is still used in many parts of the world today, and second in the form of sodium nitrate, as fertilizer.

Three positions have arisen from these comparisons. The most popular idea uses salt as essential, making Christians an essential ingredient to the world. They flavor without overpowering. This forces the "earth" to equal people which would be unnatural to a New Testament person because it isn't used anywhere else in that way. This also hints that there can be too much "Christianity" and spoil the result.

Actually, there can't be too much Christianity, but there can be too much religion. I recall Dr. Jess Moody saying in a sermon, "Beware of pious people; they pious all over you!" You know them; you go to church with them. However, they don't know who they are and they think they are the real followers of Christ.

Barclay finds that often Christians have the opposite effect on the world. Julian wanted to restore the old gods and wrote to Ibsen:

Have you looked at these Christians closely? Hollow-eyed, pale-cheeked, flat-breasted all; they brood their lives away, unspurred by ambition: the sun shines for them, but they do not see it: the earth offers them its fullness, but they desire it not; all they desire is to renounce and to suffer that they may come to die.

The second most popular idea has salt as a preservative. This view puts the Church in a negative position, fighting against corruption rather than for righteousness. Again, the first century Christian would have trouble finding that meaning.

A third position draws on the fertilizer picture. "It is the earth itself which is in need of attention. But if the salt is of poor quality, of low grade, then the earth will suffer loss (AB, p. 55)." As fertilizer prepares and improves growing conditions for the earth, so the Church works in the world to improve its conditions and allow God's love to grow. This allows "earth" to equal earth and puts our task in a positive context. It also answers our third question, about losing saltiness.

The fertilizer could lose its power as the rain washed away its essential chemicals making it useless, no longer a good fertilizer. But how does it apply to Christians? Can they lose their salvation? I don't think that's what Jesus meant, but they can lose their effectiveness as the problems of life are allowed to rob them of their essential "fertilizing" ingredients. Speaking about the moral laxity of the clergy in his time, Chaucer said, "If golde ruste, what shuld iren doo? (IB, p.289)."

There seems to be a strange tradition in the synagogue and early church. Anyone expelled for apostasy and seeking re-admittance was required to lie in the doorway and invite the members to trample on them because they had become useless.

Another suggestion is that salt stands for wisdom. This is suggested because the literal translation is: "If salt should become foolish." This form is also a valid interpretation. Matthew 7:26 "Everyone who hears these words of mine, and doesn't do them will be like a foolish man, who built his house on the sand."

Finally, Paul encourages the Christians at Colossae, "Let your speech always be with grace, seasoned with salt, that you may know how you ought to answer each one" (Col 4:6).

...the disciples of Christ must not, through fear of being an unworthy influence, remain silent about their religion. They can, and they must, bear witness to the faith that is in them through personal example (TNTC, p. 64).

Disciples of Light
Matthew 5:14-16

"You are the light of the world. A city located on a hill can't be hidden. [15] Neither do you light a lamp, and put it under a measuring basket, but on a stand; and it shines to all who are in the house. [16] Even so, let your light shine before men; that they may see your good works, and glorify your Father who is in heaven."

In the 1920s, Harry Dixon Loes wrote a song that is appropriate to this passage: "This little light of mine, I'm gonna' let it shine. This little light of mine, I'm gonna' let it shine. This little light of mine, I'm gonna' let it shine. Let it shine, let it shine, let it shine."

"Ministry belongs not optionally but essentially to Christ's people (BBC, p. 106)." I believe it can best be said like this: "To him therefore who knows to do good, and doesn't do it, to him it is sin (Jam. 4:17)." Every member of the Kingdom has been both "called" and "SHAPEd," to use Rick Warren's acronym, for ministry within the congregation. According to Paul:

Now there are various kinds of gifts, but the same Spirit. There are various kinds of service, and the same Lord. There are various kinds of workings, but the same God, who works all things in all. But to each one is given the manifestation of the Spirit for the profit of all. For to one is given through the Spirit the word of wisdom, and to another the word of knowledge, according to the same Spirit; to another faith, by the same Spirit; and to another gifts of healings, by the same Spirit; and to another workings of miracles; and to another prophecy; and to another discerning of spirits; to another different kinds of languages; and to another the interpretation of languages. But the one and the same Spirit produces all of these, distributing to each one separately as he desires. (1 Cor. 12:4-11)

So, get in the "game," find your place and be a blessing, even as you are being blessed!

Following the parable of salt, Jesus gives two more comparisons. Emphatically Jesus says, "You are" [my underline] not "you ought to be" or even "you should be," but *You are*. Neither salt nor light are effective unless they give of themselves.

The Essene community at Qumran called themselves "the children of light." If that was their desire, why did they move away from the people and keep to themselves. How could they light anything? We become "the children of light" when we become a Christian. Then we have the responsibility to shine the light with others and cannot withdraw into a Christian ghetto.

Light was meaningful in Jewish thought and was used metaphorically of God's good gifts: "Every good gift and every perfect gift is from above, coming down from the Father of lights, with whom can be no variation, nor turning shadow (Jam. 1:17)."

It delights, Ecc. 11:7. It means life, Job 3:16. It is equated with salvation, Job 3:20, Psalm 49:18-19. Those who receive light give out light: Ecc. 8:1, Pro. 4:18-19, Dan. 5:11, Isa. 49:5-6, 60:1-5, 62:1. God is light, 1 John 1:5. Jesus is light, John 8:12. We have received light, Heb. 6:4 and are children of light, Luke 16:8, John 12:35-36, Eph. 5:8-10.

Barclay points out three purposes of light: it is meant to be seen, it is a guide, and it can be a warning of danger (DSB p. 123-124).

This being the distinctive title which our Lord appropriates to Himself (John 8:12; 9:5; and see John 1:4, 9; 3:19)—a title expressly said to be unsuitable even to the highest of all the prophets (John 1:8)—it must be applied here by our Lord to His disciples only as they shine with His light upon the world… (CCE)

We are not the light; Jesus is the light. But we are the lamps that allow the light to shine in the present age. How does the light shine through us? It shines through our ministry in the world. It should shine in an ever-widening circle until it reaches the entire world. Care must be taken that our light shines to glorify God, because "it is not an advertising light: it is an altar flame. (IB p. 291)"

The emphasis is on living, not simply telling the "good news." The reason is, most people are drawn to the Savior by our actions before they believe our words (1 Peter 2:12). Consider your life like a check, or debit card, when you use them to make a purchase, there must be funds in the bank or you cannot complete your transaction. We are not credit cards that can draw on future promises to pay. We must back up our deeds with God's love! In fact, our actions should cause them to ask why we are ministering to them. There is no room for secret discipleship. We are required to do good works, not to impress others, but to glorify God (Matt. 6:3-6, 16-18).

There is a tension in regard to ministry. Sometimes, we do not want to draw attention to ourselves so we do nothing. However, then we do not draw attention to God either. Some refuse to accept recognition for a job, or a performance that is well done with a "just give glory to God." But doesn't that call more attention to ourselves than a simple "Thanks, God is good to me."?

There are two Greek words we translate good, *agathos* meaning "good quality" and *kalos* which also means "good quality" and adds to it "beautiful." Our works are to be the *kalos* kind. They are to be beautiful as well as the very best they can be (DSB p. 125). In Jesus' day, and in our own time, God's true self was obscured by formalized, dead religion and rampant paganism (Fisher p. 54). The Religious leaders sought praise for themselves rather than glory for God.

The Law of Righteousness
Matthew 5:17-20

"Don't think that I came to destroy the law or the prophets. I didn't come to destroy, but to fulfill. [18] *For most certainly, I tell you, until heaven and earth pass away, not even one smallest letter (literally, iota) or one tiny pen stroke (or, serif) shall in any way pass away from the law, until all things are accomplished.* [19] *Whoever, therefore, shall break one of these least commandments, and teach others to do so, shall be called least in the Kingdom of Heaven; but whoever shall do and teach them shall be called great in the Kingdom of Heaven.* [20] *For I tell you that unless your righteousness exceeds that of the scribes and Pharisees, there is no way you will enter into the Kingdom of Heaven."*

At this point in Jesus' ministry, I might even say His early ministry, Jesus has not addressed Gentiles. Gentiles may have sought Him out, but He has not yet sought them out. And,

There is no shred of evidence that Jesus at any [future] point repudiated his obligation to the Law to which both his birth and circumcision committed him, Moreover, we know from Acts 21:20 that many Jews who embraced the teaching of Jesus nevertheless maintained their adherence to the Law (AB, p.57).

There are interesting contrasts in Jesus' teachings. At some points He stresses the total acceptance of the old religion; at others, He contrasts them rather violently. Some passages to consider are: Matthew 11:12-13, Luke 16:16-17, Mark 7:14-15, Luke 13:10-17, Mark 3:1-6. As with all Scripture, the best commentary on any one verse is the totality of the Word. "If Jesus did not come to abolish the law, does that mean all the Old Testament laws still apply to us today? (LASB, p. 1546)."

In this section Jesus insists that in His teaching He is in no way contradicting the Mosaic law, though He is opposed to the legalistic type of religion that the scribes had built upon it... At the same time, it is also clear that He regards His own teaching as equally binding... (TNTC, p. 64).

Barclay feels this may seem to be one of the most astonishing statements Jesus made in the Sermon on the Mount. Over and over, He broke what the Jews called the Law. He didn't observe hand-washings, He healed on the Sabbath, and He was crucified as a law breaker. Tasker points out that Jesus emphasized the fact "that God's demands in these matters are far more comprehensive and exacting than current interpretations...might suggest (TNTC, p. 65)." The scribes had made the Law a burden rather than a blessing.

So-called scholarly debate has sometimes clouded and diluted the strength of these verses. They feel this is such a strange saying for Jesus. Some feel Matthew, the writer of the most Jewish gospel, put these words into Jesus' mouth. There is no question, these are strange words for Jesus to say, but before deciding, let's consider the Jewish understanding of Law.

"Law" is used in four ways. First, it is the Ten Commandments. Second, it is the Pentateuch, the first five books of the Old Testament. Third, it is "The Law and the Prophets" identifying the entire Old Testament. Finally, it is the oral or scribal law.

It was this last usage, the scribal law, which both Jesus and Paul condemned so radically. There are few actual rules for living in the Old Testament. Since there are not many explicit rules and since the Law was given for our guidance, they reasoned that the rest of the rules must be implicit. To solve this problem a caste of scribes developed; men who devoted their lives to studying, interpreting and arguing the Law.

An example of that development is given by Barclay. Consider Exodus 20:8-9, "Remember the Sabbath day, to keep it holy. You shall labor six days, and do all your work..." Okay then, what is work? Classifications of work began to develop.

Carrying a burden is work. What is a burden? Enough ink to write two letters of the alphabet. Then to write two letters is breaking the Law if it is done with ink, paint, chalk or any permanent material. If you write with juice or any non-permanent material it is not work. However, there are exceptions, you cannot write on more than one piece of paper that can be read together, as in a ledger.

Healing on the Sabbath was acceptable if the person's life was in danger, but the emphasis was on stabilizing the patient, not improving their condition. A bandage could be applied to a wound to stop the bleeding, but it must be without medication.

The compilation of these laws in the second century became the *Mishnah*; it began as an Oral Tradition during the Babylonian Captivity and is made up of sixty-three treatises or tracts that touch all the Jewish religious-legal system. In English they are about eight hundred pages. Sometime later, scholars began making commentaries on the *Mishnah* called the *Talmud*. There are two editions, Jerusalem and Babylonian. The former has twelve printed volumes and the latter has sixty. And, thus the Scribal Law expanded.

"Pharisees" means "separated ones." They were men who separated themselves and dedicated their lives to living those rules set forth by the scribes. The scribes and Pharisees were right to attempt to obey the implicit "law" of God, but they went about it incorrectly. Their attempt brought self-righteousness not God-righteousness.

Often Jesus was misunderstood. We must recognize that Jesus accepted the principle of the Law and considered it binding; His problems were with making ritual superior to obedience and the development of purity laws (small "l"). He didn't propose any changes in the Ten Commandments. He wasn't a revolutionary, He was a pioneer. He would take us where we had not been able to go alone. As a pioneer, He recognized there would be hazards ahead. He knew that new wine could not be put in old wineskins. He reinterpreted the negative "thou shalt not" into the blessed are they that... (IB, p. 292).

"Don't think" could mean "How dare you!" It was inconceivable for them to believe Jesus wanted to change the Law. "Destroy" here may mean to relax or weaken. This would destroy very subtly. Some find in verse 17 Jesus' purpose in coming to earth. This raises the question: does this purpose statement eliminate the other uses of the "I am come" sayings of Jesus. Does it push us into another form of attempting to live righteously? Similar "I am come" passages are: Matthew 10:34, Mark 1:38, Luke 12:49, and 19:10.

"Fulfill" carries the idea of completion; to bring to its maximum potential; "to unfold them, to embody them in living form, and to enshrine them in the reverence, affection, and character of men, am I come (CCE)." He wanted to remove the stress from the legalistic interpretation and place it on the spiritual side, not to ignore actions, but to develop spiritual character. It echoes Matthew 5:48 "Therefore you shall be perfect, just as your Father in heaven is perfect."

Verse 18 begins with the Hebrew word *Amen* which has no Greek or English equivalent. "Truly," "verily" or "I tell you the truth," come close. It is used in solemn statements, as in prayers; Jesus uses it to prepare for a divine statement of fact.

As noted in the text, the phrase "not even one smallest letter" is "iota" the smallest Greek letter, "i" in English, yodh, like an apostrophe, in Hebrew. The "one tiny pen stroke" is not a dot, but probably like crossing a "T" or the placement of the tail on an "a" or an "o" which could confuse or change the meaning of a word (the Hebrew alphabet had no vowels). In other words, nothing is going to change!

Fisher suggests there were three types of laws and not all of them were intended to remain in force forever. The food laws were meant to separate Israel from the pagan nations and Jesus announced their death in Mark 7:19, "because it [food] doesn't go into his heart, but into his stomach, then into the latrine, thus making all foods clean…" Later, God validated it for Peter in Acts 10.

The ritual or cultic laws were intended to point people to Jesus; when He came, they were no longer needed. "…which are a shadow of the things to come; but the body is Christ's" (Col. 2:17). "For by one offering he has perfected forever those who are being sanctified" (Heb. 10:14)

The final section was the moral law based on the Ten Commandments and other specific passages. These are the laws Jesus meant will not pass away or be changed and are still in effect today.

"…break" in verse 19 is the same word translated "loosed" in Matthew 18:18 "Most assuredly I tell you, whatever things you will bind on earth will be have been bound in heaven, and whatever things you will release on earth will have been released in heaven." The idea is a relaxing of the rules: by allowing your friends to join the clubs with one set of requirements, but making them more difficult for someone you want to keep out. I have long contended that legalistic people can justify any action they want (I know I did, and probably still do) and that is the idea here.

The scribes had identified 613 commandments in the Scriptures. These were divided in two groups, "heavy" and "light," we might compare them to venial and mortal sins. In their minds it was better to break or relax a "light" law than a "heavy" law. To Jesus, sin was sin!

The antinomian Christians, those who were anti-Law or claimed there was no law Christians must obey, thought they could live any way they wanted because they were free of all Law. It could well be that Jesus is warning them not to be in a hurry to throw out the Ten Commandments (BBC, p. 108).

Even worse is the person who "shall break one of these least commandments, and teach others to do so, shall be called least in the Kingdom of Heaven." (See James 2:8-13). Breaking the law is bad and Paul cautions us against subjecting ourselves to the Law, because it opens a new set of requirements. To "be called least in the Kingdom of Heaven" doesn't necessarily mean to be excluded "Most assuredly I tell you, among those who are born of women there has not arisen anyone greater than John the Baptizer; yet he who is least in the Kingdom of Heaven is greater than he" (Matt. 11:11).

What about greatness? How is it acquired? It is acquired by serving! The problem here is: you cannot make yourself humble to gain a greater reward; your motivation is wrong. Your humility must come from inside, then allow the reward to be whatever God wishes.

What can Jesus mean, "…that unless your righteousness exceeds that of the scribes and Pharisees…"? The NLT has "better," which might be easier to understand. These people had very high standards of righteousness. They emphasized not only personal holiness, but social responsibility. What did they do wrong? They made allowances for their own weaknesses. The *Mishnah* teaches that a man will be judged on the basis of the majority of his deeds (Aboth 3:16). If there is more "good" than "bad" you're okay. Jesus required His followers to live "as though they were already living in the age to come (IB, p. 294)."

Our righteousness must be a "better" righteousness. As Butterick says it must be long enough to reach to the outcast, the "unclean." It must be broad enough to reach into all of our life, not just the obvious faults. It must be deep enough to share with everyone. It must be high enough to exceed the limits of anything that seeks to contain it. This wasn't the case with the Jews; they killed Jesus and thought they did God a service (IB, p. 293).

Jesus said this about them: "…those who devour widows' houses, and for a pretense make long prayers. These will receive greater condemnation." (Mark 12:40). Jesus warns:

Woe to you, scribes and Pharisees, hypocrites! For you tithe mint, dill, and cumin, and have left undone the weightier matters of the law: justice, mercy, and faith. But you ought to have done these, and not to have left the other undone (Matt. 23:23).

Their righteousness was all on the outside, not on the inside where it belongs, "Woe to you, scribes and Pharisees, hypocrites! For you are like whitened tombs, which outwardly appear beautiful, but inwardly are full of dead men's bones, and of all uncleanness" (Matt. 23:27).

Matthew follows this introduction with six examples of how Jesus fulfilled the Law and how our righteousness can exceed that of the scribes and Pharisees. The crown of this section is the conclusion: Matthew 5:48, "Therefore you shall be perfect, just as your Father in heaven is perfect." "Augustine summed up how a Christian should live in the statement, 'Love God, and do what you like' (DSB, p. 133)."

The Importance of Forgiveness
Matthew 5:21-26

"You have heard that it was said to the ancient ones, 'You shall not murder;' (Ex. 20:13) and 'Whoever murders will be in danger of the judgment.' 22 But I tell you, that everyone who is angry with his brother without a cause (NU omits "without a cause") will be in danger of the judgment; and whoever says to his brother, 'Raca!' ("Raca" is an Aramaic insult, related to the word for "empty" and conveying the idea of empty-headedness) will be in danger of the council; and whoever says, 'You fool!' will be in danger of the fire of Gehenna (or, Hell).

23 "If therefore you are offering your gift at the altar, and there remember that your brother has anything against you, 24 leave your gift there before the altar, and go your way. First be reconciled to your brother, and then come and offer your gift. 25 Agree with your adversary quickly, while you are with him on the way; lest perhaps the prosecutor deliver you to the judge, and the judge deliver you to the officer, and you be cast into prison. 26 Most certainly I tell you, you shall by no means get out of there, until you have paid the last penny (literally, kodrantes, a small copper coin worth about 2 lepta (widow's mites)).

"To us it seems as plain as possible that our Lord's one object is to contrast the traditional perversions of the law with the true sense of it as expounded by Himself (CCE)." One of the things we will see Jesus do is to contrast true righteousness with the traditions the scribes and Pharisees foisted on the people. This may be the reason several translations have not followed the KJV translation "Ye have heard that it was said by them of old time…"

There are two approaches to righteousness, legalism and love. Legalism is easier because it only requires that we learn the rules and live by them. As long as we correctly interpret and follow the rules, we don't need to be concerned about the results. However, we must not miss any of them; that was the Pharisees' problem and their need for such meticulous rules.

All the Jews held the Law in the highest regard. They began their service by parading the Torah around, like a saint's statue in a festival, so everyone could show their love for it. It was this very veneration which caused the development of their system of Oral Tradition we discussed in the prior section.

Love is much more difficult than legalism because everything we do requires us to give ourselves totally in ministry. It isn't enough to "do," we must also "be." I believe Joseph Fletcher and his treatment of situation ethics may have had something; in dealing with another human being, all ethics are ultimately situation ethics. In relation to God, there are "absolutes," but in relation to another person, things are always best understood and responded to in the "situation."

Jesus launches into a discussion to illustrate the intention of the Law. He is not expanding, as we will see, but is fulfilling it (bringing it to maturity), as He said. He is showing us how our righteousness can surpass that of the Pharisees.

He set forth the ideals of Christian behavior; ideals that cannot be relaxed because we don't like them or feel they are too stringent. Many would like the Bible rewritten every few years to take into consideration changes in social morals. That is not possible! This section is one of the most important sections in the whole New Testament, possibly even the entire Bible.

He uses what will become a familiar introduction, "You have heard that it was said to the ancient ones…" Most people couldn't read, but they heard the Law read, heard the teachers teach and listened to the Rabbis debate it. The prophets always said, "Thus says the Lord." The rabbis cited the Law or restatement and commentary on the Law. Jesus says, "But I tell you…" How could He get away with it? "…he taught them with authority, and not like the scribes" (Matt. 7:29). Listen to your teachers; you can tell if they know the subject and have the right and authority to speak about it.

He begins with what many of us would consider the most serious crime possible, murder. (Murder is the better word here, not "kill" as some translations have.) In Judaism, only a few offenses were considered capital crimes: adultery, idolatry, murder. Notice how Jesus' interpretation shifts the emphasis from objective (following the rules) to subjective (what is happening here).

It's important for us to recognize that for a Christian, attitude is as important as action. Most of us are able to resist physically assaulting one another, but we have difficulty with how we feel about someone. We must learn that the root of sin is in the anger and contempt in our hearts; the act is only the blossom of the plant. "Killing is a terrible sin, but anger is a great sin, too, because it also violates God's command to love. … Anger keeps us from developing a spirit pleasing to God. (LASB, p. 1547)."

Two Greek words are translated anger. *Thumos* is anger which erupts quickly and is quickly gone; it is the passion of the moment. The word used here is *orgizesthai*, the slow burning, long lasting, brooding anger which is nursed by its owner. It is selfish in its orientation and it is the anger Jesus forbids.

Life was cheap in New Testament times. Poor people were often treated with contempt, almost like non-people. If we depersonalize people of other races and nationalities, it is easier to justify their abuse. In World War II, we didn't take away the rights of all people; we only took away the rights of the "Japs." The Japanese were depicted as subhuman and many popular Japanese icons of the day either changed nationality or dropped out of sight. The Green Hornet's sidekick, Kato, who was Japanese, became Filipino.

46

"Without a cause" is not found in the older manuscripts and is not commented on by the early Church fathers, so we believe it was probably added by a copyist who felt it was unreasonable to expect us never to get mad at one another. Everyone gets angry; it's what we do about it that makes the difference. "Be angry, and don't sin" (Eph. 4:26a) has a derivative of *orgizesthai* used for anger.

"Brother" in verse 22 could mean another Jew but it could also reflect Jesus' attitude expressed in the story about neighbors of the Good Samaritan.

Raca has been translated in many ways, but it is also more a sound than a word; it is a sneer with a sound attached and was addressed to someone considered detestable. Some cultures spit at the person. It is ultimate arrogance and self-centeredness. (Also see the note within the text.)

"You fool!" translates the Greek word *moros* from which we get our word moron. What you may not know about moron is that it is a moral judgment, not just an intellectual judgment. This is not a stupid person, but a base person. At best it is derogatory and at its worst it is slanderous.

There are two words translated "hell" in the New Testament and they are sometimes confused. *Hades* is not hell at all; it is the same as the Old Testament place called *sheol* the place of the dead and was thought to be a gray world where all the dead before Christ's sacrifice and the lost dead awaited judgment.

The other word is *gehenna* meaning "Valley of Hinnom," located southwest of Jerusalem; it was a place used for human sacrifices by Ahaz (2 Chr. 28). Josiah turned it into the city dump and it became a place where fire was always burning and the bodies of the poor and criminals were often left for disposal. It was a heinous place used by the Jews to describe the place of torment where sinners would be punished.

When we injure a person's name, Jesus says we are in the same grave danger of judgment that accrues to a murderer; not from the courts of the land, but from God.

Jesus set a new standard for behavior. It is no longer enough simply not to murder someone; it is only enough not even to want to murder. When transferred to the rest of life: it isn't enough not to do wrong; it is only enough not to even think about doing wrong. This position makes clear our inability to meet God's standard and our need for Jesus.

He [Jesus] speaks of the judgment of God, and of the difference of sins, and therefore applies his words to the form of civil judgments which were then used. … by three men, who had the hearing and deciding of money matters, and such other small causes. … [The council] which stood of 23 judges, who had the hearing and deciding of weighty affairs, as the matter of a whole tribe or of a high priest, or of a false prophet.

The covetous Pharisees taught that God was appeased by the sacrifices appointed in the law, which they themselves devoured. But Christ on the contrary side denies that God accepts any man's offering, unless he makes satisfaction to his brother whom he has offended: and says moreover, that these stubborn and stiff-necked despisers of their brethren will never escape the wrath and curse of God before they have made full satisfaction to their brethren (GN).

Sacrifices were not offered directly, but were brought to the Temple by the sinner for sacrifice by the priest. They came into the Temple, walked through several gateways to the entry of the Court of the Priests and placed their hands on the offering, recited the sins it covered and gave it to the priest. It is important to understand that the sacrifice only covered those sins recited!

One other thing required for the sacrifice to be effective was penitence and this included reconciliation and restoration to the fullest extent possible. The sacrifice was just a symbol of what had already taken place in the heart. If you feel you are not getting through to God, maybe you're not. How often we come into worship with anger working away at our insides. Jesus says here that that kind of worship isn't going to be counted. He said, "Get up! Go find the one you have trouble with; resolve your difficulty and return."

Jewish justice was swift, like "wild west justice." Claims were heard by three to twenty-three elders, based on city size and the number available. Their decision was rendered swiftly and was carried out just as swiftly. There was no opportunity to haggle or appeal to a higher court.

Removing the Lust
Matthew 5:27-30

"You have heard that it was said, (TR adds "to the ancients") 'You shall not commit adultery;' (Exodus 20:14) [28] *but I tell you that everyone who gazes at a woman to lust after her has committed adultery with her already in his heart.* [29] *If your right eye causes you to stumble, pluck it out and throw it away from you. For it is more profitable for you that one of your members should perish, than for your whole body to be cast into Gehenna (or, Hell)* [30] *If your right hand causes you to stumble, cut it off, and throw it away from you. For it is more profitable for you that one of your members should perish, than for your whole body to be cast into Gehenna (or, Hell).*

What is adultery? The Jews considered it a violation of a husband's property rights. The rules were drawn from the tenth commandment, regarding coveting. Exodus 20:17, "You shall not covet your neighbor's house. You shall not covet your neighbor's wife, nor his male servant, nor his female servant, nor his ox, nor his donkey, nor anything that is your neighbor's." While there doesn't seem to be a problem in New Testament times, polygamy and concubines were common in Old Testament times. In practice, a man could not commit adultery against his wife and the seduction of a single, unengaged, or non-Jewish woman was not considered adultery.

The penalty for adultery was set in Leviticus 20:10. "The man who commits adultery with another man's wife, even he who commits adultery with his neighbor's wife, the adulterer and the adulteress shall surely be put to death." However, it wasn't generally enforced against the men.

Adultery is so serious because it glorifies sex. It expresses lust, not love. It is the desire of one person to control another. This wasn't God's intent. Sadly, for our society, love should generally be spelled "L U S T." Fisher says, "There is no greater travesty in the English language than our modern use of 'making love' for the physical act of sexual intercourse (Fisher, p. 74)." We see the results of sexual license every day and it causes more problems than simply unplanned pregnancies.

The Rabbis taught that good intentions were added to our "account" as good, but evil intentions were not counted unless actually carried out. Once again, Jesus draws the line beyond the normal behavior patterns of the Scribal law. To not commit adultery was not enough.

"Jesus is not condemning natural interest in the opposite sex or even healthy sexual desire but the deliberate and repeated filling of one's mind with fantasies that would be evil if acted out (LASB, p. 1546)."

Temptation is not sin, but neither is not "doing" the act not sin. Sin is done as soon as we give consent to do it, even if prevented from completing the act. We must look to the heart because the best way to prevent any sin is to straighten out the heart.

The word "looks" is better translated, "keeps on looking." God intended men to be attracted to women and women to men. There isn't anything wrong with looking; the problem begins when we start to "pant," when we keep on looking. I'm not sure who said "Looking at a beautiful woman isn't sin." And the follow up usually is, "How long can I look before it is?"

The word translated "causes you to stumble" is *skandalon* and is the bait stick in an animal trap. It applies to anything that causes us to sin. In our text, "stumbling block" is a good rendering of it. We must remove the "stumbling block" at all cost.

If we keep eye-balling things that cause us to sin, does God expect us to "gouge it out and throw it away"? If we do things with our right hand which cause us to sin, are we to "cut it off and throw it away"? If it would make us quit sinning, yes, but we may become a bunch of one-eyed, one-armed sinners. Sin begins in the heart not in the eye or hand. We must correct the heart problem. Removal of the eye or the hand cannot remove the desire; in fact, it may even serve to increase the desire. "The *eye* is here regarded as the medium through which temptation comes, and the *hand* as the instrument by which sin is committed (TNTC, p. 69)." Job said, "I made a covenant with my eyes, how then should I look lustfully at a young woman? (31:1).

This passage is similar to Matthew 18:8-9:

If your hand or your foot causes you to stumble, cut it off, and cast it from you. It is better for you to enter into life maimed or crippled, rather than having two hands or two feet to be cast into the eternal fire. If your eye causes you to stumble, pluck it out, and cast it from you. It is better for you to enter into life with one eye, rather than having two eyes to be cast into the Gehenna of fire.

How can we remove the problems that pull us into sin? Our experience has shown us that we can't begin by not thinking about the sins we enjoy; Satan brings it into our mind anyway. We cannot drive it from our mind by not thinking about it, but there are two things we can do.

1. We can fill our lives with the things of the Lord. The more we are involved with the work of the Lord, the less opportunity there will be for Satan to slip in.

2. We can fill our minds with study and meditation on God's word. We must push evil out with good. "By their fruits you will know them. Do you gather grapes from thorns, or figs from thistles? Even so, every good tree produces good fruit; but the corrupt tree produces evil fruit. A good tree can't produce evil fruit, neither can a corrupt tree produce good fruit" (Matt. 7:16-18).

The key is purity and recalls Matthew 5:8, "Blessed are the pure in heart..." The Christian should be the bright white that shows the contrast of the evil in the world.

New Rules for Divorce
Matthew 5:31-32

"It was also said, 'Whoever shall put away his wife, let him give her a writing of divorce' (Deut. 24:1). [32] *but I tell you that whoever puts away his wife, except for the cause of sexual immorality, makes her an adulteress; and whoever marries her when she is put away commits adultery.*

Here Jesus is concerned about divorce, not remarriage; however, we will look at that problem also. He is not interested is setting up "grounds" but in setting forth a principle, an ideal, for Christian marriage, "'For I hate divorce,' says Yahweh, the God of Israel," (Mal. 2:16).

Among the Greeks, the marriage relationship was not taken seriously, the husband's infidelity was not only condoned; it was expected. Demosthenes said, "We have courtesans for the sake of pleasure; we have concubines for the sake of daily cohabitation; we have wives for the purpose of having children legitimately, and of having a faithful guardian for all our household affairs (DSB, p. 153)." The mistresses of famous men were often better known than their wives. Divorce was accomplished by returning the dowry intact and dismissing the wife in the presence of two witnesses (DSB, p. 155).

In Rome the home was the most important institution and was to be preserved at all cost. A son never came of age as long as his father lived; the wife was held in high regard. There wasn't one recorded divorce in the first five hundred years of the empire. Then Rome conquered Greece and Hellenism began to take over the empire. Divorce became so common that Seneca talked about women who were married to be divorced and divorced to be married. Marriage became an unfortunate necessity, because there were special taxes on the unmarried and the childless (DSB, p. 156-157).

Slaves were not generally married; they were property and as such were bred like other livestock. Their offspring became property of their master and, if they were lucky, might be raised by their parents, but there was no promise or guarantee that would happen. They had no rights and were traded on the open market.

This is the situation into which this saying was thrust. Male chastity and women's rights, while better in Judaism, were not very high on anyone's to-do list. It was Christ and the Church that would begin to restore a proper attitude toward women and marriage.

Today, some denominations consider marriage a sacramental agreement between a man and a woman. It's hard to find fault with this attitude. The ideal is permanence and mutual benefit in the marriage relationship. "Even so ought husbands also to love their own wives as their own bodies. He who loves his own wife loves himself" (Eph. 5:28). "Nevertheless each of you must also love his own wife even as himself; and let the wife see that she respects her husband" (Eph. 5:33).

A similar saying is found in Luke 16:18. "Everyone who divorces his wife, and marries another, commits adultery. He who marries one who is divorced from a husband commits adultery." Jesus also addresses the problem of divorce in Matthew 19:3-9 which is like Mark 10:2-12 and 1 Corinthians 7:10-11.

Among the Jews, every man was expected to marry and raise a family. The only reason not to do so was to dedicate your life to the study of the Law. The Jews opposed divorce in theory, but not in practice.

The passage is directed primarily to the husband, since it he could divorce easier, if at all, and is intended to protect an innocent wife. A woman could not divorce her husband, but under certain circumstances could force him to divorce her. Those included his getting certain diseases, engaging in certain obnoxious trades, or making vows or forcing her to make vows to her detriment.

A certificate of divorce was required by Deuteronomy 24:1 to protect the woman's rights, i.e., that she was in fact divorced and free to remarry:

When a man takes a wife, and marries her, then it shall be, if she find no favor in his eyes, because he has found some unseemly thing in her, that he shall write her a bill of divorce, and give it in her hand, and send her out of his house.

This indecency could be anything the husband disliked in the opinion of the rabbinic school of Hillel but was limited to infidelity in the school of Shammai.

Today most scholars feel the "exception clause," "…except for marital unfaithfulness," is not from the lips of Jesus, but was added, possibly by Matthew. However, there are no ancient texts that do not contain the clause, so if it was added by anyone, it had to be very early.

Why do some think Jesus didn't say it? Two reasons could be listed:

1. It would have made Him appear to take sides in a current rabbinic debate on the subject.
2. He didn't make exceptions for other things and this exception would weaken His teaching on marriage.

Why would Matthew have added the clause? Possibly because of conditions that existed in the Church at the time. The feeling is that there must be some way to sever a marriage that is not satisfactory. The "unfaithfulness" could be pre-marital or extra-marital and this clause would place a "guilty" wife's fate in her own hands.

If Jesus said this, what does He mean? Is He setting up a legalistic system, establishing rules for divorce and remarriage? If so, then any remarriage, except of the innocent party, is adulterous and the people are living in adultery. This would of necessity disqualify all those people from any religious leadership, especially those requiring ordination.

According to Fisher, there are four things wrong with this idea. First, Jesus did not make rules, He set forth ideals. Second, there rarely is, as opposed to never, an "innocent" party. Third, this position ignores the equally important teaching about forgiveness and restoration by God. Fourth, it makes remarriage of "guilty" parties an unforgivable sin.

Possibly the biggest problem with the clause is that it has the "tail wagging the dog." It has taken our attention from the emphasis of Jesus' ministry to look for loop holes. Remember, "God hates divorce."

If you are considering divorce, no one can tell you that you should do it, however, divorce should be only as a last resort. If you are divorced and remarried, no one can tell you that you did the right thing. Dr. Laura Schlessinger, a popular conservative radio, an orthodox Jew, and family advocate, says that when there are children in the home, there are only three reasons for divorce: addiction, abuse and/or adultery. I add a fourth, abandonment. When we bring children into the world, our first responsibility is in raising them and statistics provide ample evidence that children raised in a two-parent home, even a bad one, do far better than those raised by a single parent.

Is Your Word Your Bond?
Matthew 5:33-37

"Again you have heard that it was said to them of old time, 'You shall not make false vows, but shall perform to the Lord your vows,' ³⁴ but I tell you, don't swear at all: neither by heaven, for it is the throne of God; ³⁵ nor by the earth, for it is the footstool of his feet; nor by Jerusalem, for it is the city of the great King. ³⁶ Neither shall you swear by your head, for you can't make one hair white or black. ³⁷ But let your 'Yes' be 'Yes' and your 'No' be 'No.' Whatever is more than these is of the evil one."

Fisher reminds us, "Every command finds its root in the character of God (Fisher, p.82)." What he is saying is everything reflects God and therefore our behavior reflects on God. This is true because many people only know God as they know us. They think God is like we are because we claim to be His children.

Verse 33 reminds us of the third commandment, "You shall not take the name of Yahweh your God in vain, for Yahweh will not hold him guiltless who takes his name in vain." (Ex. 20:7). It also reflects the restatement found in Leviticus 19:12 and Numbers 30:1-15.

Isn't it strange how often Jesus told the Jews what they already knew? The Old Testament makes little distinction between vows, but insists that all vows be honored. The Jewish teachers agreed; there were many proverbs about the importance of truthfulness. Barclay tells us the school of Shammai even forbade the common, polite courtesies of society lest they inadvertently make an oath (DSB, p. 158).

These same people developed a system of prioritizing vows and allowing loop-holes (sound familiar?). They could pretend to keep a vow while finding a way around keeping it. Jesus severely criticized them for that attitude in Matthew 23:16-22, holding that all vows are sacred.

In New Testament times there were two problems associated with oaths:

1. Frivolous swearing. Oaths were given where they weren't appropriate and were unnecessary.

2. Evasive swearing. Oaths were divided into two groups, binding and non-binding. Any oath containing God's name must be kept, but the others could be broken. The use of God's name made Him a partner (DSB, p. 159). However, not everyone knew about these rules.

In verse 34, Jesus discourages us, from taking vows, but Paul uses them in his writing. He also asked the Thessalonians to take a vow in 1 Thessalonians. 5:27 "I solemnly charge you by the Lord that this letter be read to all the holy brothers." The writer of Hebrews says God took a vow, "For when God made a promise to Abraham, since he could swear by none greater, he swore by himself..." (Heb. 6:13).

Jesus even allowed Himself to be put on oath without objecting at His trial When He was questioned by the High Priest: "But Jesus held his peace. The high priest answered him, 'I adjure you by the living God, that you tell us whether you are the Christ, the Son of God.' Jesus said to him, 'You have said it. Nevertheless, I tell you, henceforth you will see the Son of Man sitting at the right hand of Power, and coming on the clouds of the sky'" (Matt. 26:63-64).

There is no reason to consider that solemn oaths in a court of justice, or on other proper occasions, are wrong, provided they are taken with due reverence. But all oaths taken without necessity, or in common conversation, must be sinful… The worse men are, the less they are bound by oaths; the better they are, the less there is need for them (MH).

We put people under oath so we can prosecute them for perjury if we later learn they have lied thus inferring that lying is acceptable, unless we are "under oath." When honesty is the rule, everything we say becomes an oath so we don't need to make oaths to emphasize our sincerity.

Then why is Jesus opposed to our taking oaths? Because the necessity of the oath implies that we cannot be trusted. Oaths are usually carefully worded and are like a tent; they cover everything, but touch nothing. Our word or statement should be sufficient. The Essenes refused to take oaths at all as did the Quakers and Anabaptists, even to swearing a political oath of office.

Fisher lists three reasons for not taking oaths:

1.   Reverence for God. Some oaths were binding and some weren't, verses 34 and 35.
2.   Man cannot control the natural color of his own hair, verse 36.
3.   Oaths come from the fact that we cannot trust each other, verse 37 (Fisher p. 83-84). (See also John 8:44).

The doubling of the "yes" and "no" in verse 37 is for emphasis and is echoed by James 5:12.

You Cannot Be Too Good!
Matthew 5:38-42

"You have heard that it was said, 'An eye for an eye, and a tooth for a tooth.' [39] *But I tell you, don't resist him who is evil; but whoever strikes you on your right cheek, turn to him the other also.* [40] *If anyone sues you to take away your coat, let him have your cloak also.* [41] *Whoever compels you to go one mile, go with him two.* [42] *Give to him who asks you, and don't turn away him who desires to borrow from you."*

This "…an eye for eye, and a tooth for a tooth" expression is called *Lex Talionis*, roughly meaning "equivalent retaliation" and was a law limiting vengeance. It echoes Exodus 21:23-25, Leviticus 24:19-22, and Deuteronomy 19:21 and was part of the Code of Hammurabi and Roman law. Retaliation was more balanced and justice replaced vendettas and feuds.

This law did not require retaliation, it simply limited it. The practical effect was the development of a system of payment for "damages," similar to that in effect today, instead of a literal "tit for tat," or more, response.

Lex Talionis was not the only rule in effect in the Old Testament. "Don't say, 'I will do to him as he has done to me; I will render to the man according to his work'" (Pro. 24:29) and "You shall not take vengeance, nor bear any grudge against the children of your people; but you shall love your neighbor as yourself. I am Yahweh." (Lev. 19:18). Paul also quotes other verses we will see later.

Jesus went further than this however, He said, don't retaliate at all. There is a potential problem in nonresistance, it may not work, but we must try. He said: "don't resist him [my underline] who is evil." "Do not resist evil," as some translations have is an incorrect translation because Jesus resisted evil and we are ordered to resist evil. But we, like Jesus, are not to resist or fight an evil person. Paul tells us, "Don't be overcome by evil, but overcome evil with good." (Rom. 12:21). This is the basis of the modern nonviolence movement to overcome the British Raj rule in India initiated by Gandhi and picked up by Dr. Martin Luther King, Jr. in the civil rights movement in America.

In Romans 12:19, Paul says, "Don't seek revenge yourselves, beloved, but give place to God's wrath. For it is written, 'Vengeance belongs to me; I will repay, says the Lord'" and is a quotation of Deuteronomy 32:35. This doesn't mean our sense of justice is to be dulled, but we must emphasize the need to be active in loving people into a right relationship with God. It also doesn't mean we should hurt people with kindness, but that we should leave the entire thing to God.

What about the problem of being struck "on the right cheek?" Does Jesus literally expect us to "turn...the other also"? First, recognize that a right-handed person would normally hit you on the left cheek, so this blow came from the back of the hand; a blow of contempt, an insult. Jewish law set a fine of "thirty-four dollars" for such a blow. What does Jesus expect? Don't retaliate when insulted?

Turning the other cheek is a statement of how nonresistant we are to be. Isaiah, talking about the Messiah, said, "I gave my back to the strikers, and my cheeks to those who plucked off the hair; I didn't hide my face from shame and spitting" (Isa. 50:6). And the writer of Lamentations offers this advice, "Let him give his cheek to him who strikes him; let him be filled full with reproach" (Lam. 3:30).

To many Jews of Jesus' day, these statements were offensive. Any Messiah who would turn the other cheek was not the military leader they wanted to lead a revolt against Rome. They wanted retaliation against their enemies, whom they hated (LASB, p. 1549).

Looking at the law suit, a Jewish man had two primary garments, a "coat" and a cloak or tunic. The cloak was ankle-length for women and knee length for men and was a long-sleeved garment, worn next to the skin. The coat, worn over the cloak, served double duty, a coat during the day and blanket at night. Even a poor man would have a change of cloaks, but most people had only one coat. In Jewish law a person could sue you for your coat, but not your cloak. If the coat was security for a loan, it had to be returned before sundown (Exodus 22:25-27). Jesus requires us to go beyond the legal requirements, not just in regard to clothing, but in setting forth a principle. We must always go beyond the minimum.

We live in an atmosphere of law suits for any reason. Swift justice is our demand. Most law suits don't come from pure motives. There is often a desire to "get even" to "get what's coming to us." But, "revenge is not sweet, despite the proverb: it is poison, strife breeding strife in endless circle (IB, p. 301)." If Jesus had demanded justice, He wouldn't have died. Our motivation must be the same: a desire to reclaim and restore, not to revenge and destroy. We must not lower ourselves to the standard of our detractors. A Christian should not stand on his legal rights. "The Christian thinks not of his rights, but of his duties; not of his privileges, but of his responsibilities (DSB, p. 167)."

In verse 41, "compels" is a Greek word which came from Persia. The royal courier could commandeer whatever supplies and help he needed to speed the mail on its way. It came into the English legal system and was outlawed, without "due process," by the United States Constitution. It was this law that allowed the Roman soldiers to force Simon the Cyrene to carry Jesus' cross (Matthew 27:32). The Jews considered this an especially odious law. Again, we must go beyond the minimum. Give until it hurts? No! Give until it helps!

Jesus now turns His discussion to lending and helping others which was based on Deuteronomy 15:7-11. It required the Jews to help any Jew who asked, even if they didn't have the ability to repay or return the favor. We aren't sure why Matthew included this verse here, but he did, so we will look at it. Often, we get hung up with the question, "Do they deserve our help?" We should be more concerned about how we can help. They may not deserve our help, but we don't deserve to be able to help either. "...Christian response is to be controlled by the need of others, not his merit or one's own 'rights' (BBC, p. 111)."

According to Barclay, the rabbis had five rules for giving:

1. Giving must not be refused. To refuse to help a fellow Jew put you in the same group as an idolater. The reason was partly practical, someday you may be the one needing help.

2. Giving must benefit the needy person. It must be what he needs and enough to allow him to retain the standard of comfort he had known. It should relieve his poverty and the humility associated with it.

3. Giving must be done privately and secretly. The best giving is done in such a way that the person helped doesn't know who helped him and the person helping doesn't know who is being helped.

4. The manner of giving must fit the character and temperament of the recipient. If a person was too proud to ask for help, a loan should be offered, but no request for repayment should ever be made. It was, in fact a gift not a loan.

5. Giving was both a privilege and an obligation because all giving is giving to God (DSB, pp. 170-1).
It is a good rule to remember: it is better to help many who don't need it than to fail to help one who does.

Whom Should We Love?
Matthew 5:43-48

"You have heard that it was said, 'You shall love your neighbor and hate your enemy.' [44] But I tell you, love your enemies, bless those who curse you, do good to those who hate you, and pray for those who mistreat you and persecute you, [45] that you may be children of your Father who is in heaven. For he makes his sun to rise on the evil and the good, and sends rain on the just and the unjust. [46] For if you love those who love you, what reward do you have? Don't even the tax collectors do the same? [47] If you only greet your friends, what more do you do than others? Don't even the tax collectors (NU reads "Gentiles" instead of "tax collectors") do the same? [48] Therefore you shall be perfect, just as your Father in heaven is perfect.

We don't find a command to hate our enemies in the Old Testament, but there are passages the Jews felt urged them to treat enemies with hostility. The Qumran communities *Manual of Discipline* calls for the Essenes to love the people of God and hate all others.

In this passage, Jesus gives us "A double reason: the one is taken of the relatives, the children must be like their father: the other is taken of comparisons, the children of God must be better than the children of this world (GN)."

Leviticus 19:18 commands, "You shall not take vengeance, nor bear any grudge against the children of your people; but you shall love your neighbor as yourself. I am Yahweh." The Jews interpreted neighbor to mean a fellow Jew, but not a foreigner, so they interpreted this to mean they should hate non-Jews. Jesus sited this passage as the second greatest commandment and gave a new definition to the word neighbor.

In spite of the absence of a command to love your enemy in the Old Testament, there are many examples of that happening. David spared Saul in 1 Samuel 24:7. Elisha intervened for the blinded Syrian army in 2 Kings 6:22-23. Proverbs 25:21 calls for us to feed our enemies.

Do we have enemies? Yes, but they are not just those people who don't like us; they are those people who don't love God. They are "those who persecute you." They are enemies of God, therefore, they "hate you...curse you...mistreat you." (Luke 6:27-28).

There are four Greek words we translate with one word "love," they are: *eros, storge, philia,* and *agape.* *Eros* is sexual love; the physical love of a man for a woman, and vice versa, and is not used in the New Testament; while it isn't "lust," it certainly can lead to lust. *Storge* is the word used for family affection; the love between husband and wife, parent and child. *Philia* is love for our fellow man; it is the word used for a warm relationship within the brotherhood.

The word used here is *agape* which originally carried the meaning of showing hospitality and is used that way in the LXX. It is a love that implies a relationship even if it is a unilateral relationship; it is not about simply liking someone, it involves compassion. It continues even if there is no positive response. It is not a feeling, nor is it based on feelings.

Barclay states that six things occur when we *agape* someone:
1. The love we express to our enemy is different from the love we express to a friend.
2. The love we express to our enemy is not from the heart, but from the will.
3. We allow our enemy to do exactly what they want without retaliation, even if it injures us.
4. It is the basis for our personal relationships.
5. It can only be expressed by Christians through the grace of Jesus.
6. It requires us to pray for them regardless of their attitude toward us (DSB, pp. 174-175).

I would like to add a seventh, it is the kind of love God had for us before we became believers and it's the kind of love He continues to have for us, even when we fail to do His will.

"What is meant by 'love' is not to be derived from a Greek word but from what we see of God revealed in Jesus Christ (BBC, p. 112)." It is the picture Jesus painted for us in the story of the Good Samaritan, Luke 10:25-37. It is the example He gave us in His life.

Love is a verb and requires action on our part. We have robbed it of its strength and purity by turning it into a "four letter word." To love, in this way, is to do something to help someone, not for what they can do for us, but in spite of their inability to do something for us. Love doesn't expect or require repayment. If love involves any emotion, it is compassion. When we give in order to get benefit, we are not practicing love of any kind, except possibly self-love. While some have considered the "hate your enemy" phrase to be a gloss, the attitude of the Jews toward all Gentiles was one of utter hatred. So much so that the "Romans charged the Jews with hatred of the human race (CCE)."

The translation "children of your Father who is in heaven" is an unfortunate rendering because it follows the Hebrew syntax where possessive pronouns are made by the use of a construct. Thus "Father's sons" becomes "sons of the father." It also fails to indicate the quality of sonship implied in the word used. We are to be "true children," children who have His character, godlike children. Then our love is spontaneous, springing from our changed character. Children are constantly trying to imitate their parents; are we imitating our Heavenly Father?

As verse 45 says, God does not discriminate between the good and bad on earth. If He did, good things wouldn't happen to bad people and bad things would not happen to good people.

Verses 46 and 47 show the deep contrast between the love of a "true child" and the love of others; our love must go beyond the love of all others, because we are now different. "Therefore, if anyone is in Christ, he is a new creation; the old has gone, the new has come!" (2 Cor. 5:17).

Why single out tax collectors? Many taxes were collected directly by Roman representatives. Export and import taxes were contracted out to these men. They contracted for a certain sum and they retained everything else they collected. The system encouraged dishonesty. To say they were often less than equitable would be a gross understatement.

Verse 48 should begin with "You." Not only that, but in the Greek it is emphatic. Everything we have seen in the Sermon on the Mount has been stated in absolute terms, a description of our growth needed toward this perfection, maturity. There is no way to dodge the command in the following verse. Yet, often we try to escape or explain it away.

In our understanding of the word, and in the whole of Scripture, we find only one person who is perfect, and that is Jesus. In Luke 17: 10, Jesus says, "…when you have done all the things that are commanded you, [you can but] say, 'We are unworthy servants. We have done our duty.'" So, how does this stack up with the command, not suggestion, to "be perfect"?

We're afraid of the word perfect, and rightly so, but this is a different word. The word used is *teleios* meaning mature or correct for the intended task. It is not an abstract or philosophical perfection. It is a man or woman who has reached their physical maturity. It is a student who has learned the lessons and is ready to graduate. It is an animal without blemish suitable for sacrifice. So, Jesus was perfect in both our understanding of the word and in the sense intended by the Greek. While we cannot be flawless, we can have that perfection that means "correct for the task" God has called us to do.

Many people in the LXX are called *teleios*. David is in 1 Kings 11:4-6. Certainly, David wasn't perfect, but he was in tune with God's task for him. Before him *teleios* is used of both, Noah, Genesis. 6:9, and Job, Job 1:1. It is also the word used in Ephesians 4:11-14 to speak of the "maturing" of the saints.

God demands perfection, completeness, maturity, and does not release us from the demand, He accepts us in mercy. That acceptance includes His assurance that He will be with us; ideally, that is in the presence of the Holy Spirit and our Christian brothers and sisters. We are not expected nor required to live this life alone.

Doing Good the Wrong Way
Matthew 6:1-4

"Be careful that you don't do your charitable giving before men, to be seen by them, or else you have no reward from your Father who is in heaven. ² Therefore when you do merciful deeds, don't sound a trumpet before yourself, as the hypocrites do in the synagogues and in the streets, that they may get glory

from men. Most certainly I tell you, they have received their reward. ³ But when you do merciful deeds, don't let your left hand know what your right hand does, ⁴ so that your merciful deeds may be in secret, then your Father who sees in secret will reward you openly."

Fisher feels the key to the first eighteen verses of this chapter is sincerity. Jesus assumed His followers would respond to the needs of people. His concern was that they might lack sincerity, hence the warning to be "careful" (p. 98). He begins the passage with a command issued in the present tense meaning "to be on guard." We need to be "careful," on guard, that we do not do things to impress the people who might be watching us.

He wants us to do the right thing, but not for the wrong reason. "What we do, must be done from an inward principle, that we may be approved of God, not that we may be praised of men (MH)." This attitude is borne out in the "sheep and goats judgment" of Matthew 25:31-46.

The KJV, "do your alms" is not a good a rendering of the Greek, which is actually "do your acts of righteousness," the WEB rendering is also good. The merciful deeds expected of a Jew certainly included charitable giving, that is alms, which they considered more important even than making sacrifices, but since almsgiving is not required by the law, the Jews considered it to have extra merit, like doing extra credit work in school. "Ambition makes alms vain (GN)." Other "acts of righteousness" they might do included praying and fasting.

Yes, Jesus did things in public and it is true that His actions were done in the streets, in full view of the people, but they were not done to be seen. They were done "before men," but not to "be seen by men." Some have become so obsessed with secrecy that they do nothing to help others, lest someone see it.

Is there a conflict between Matthew 5:16 "...let your light shine before men," and the apparent desire for secrecy Jesus expressed here? *The Interpreter's Bible* recommends a rule for "show and tell." "Show when tempted to "hide," hide when tempted to "show" (IB, p. 306).

Barclay listed three motives a Jew had for giving:

1. A sense of duty: he gave not because he wanted to give, but because he could not escape the requirement. The poor might even have been placed in the world to allow him to help them. He gave his money, but not himself.

2. To gain prestige: not to glorify God, but to glorify himself. He built a memorial to himself.

3. Because of love: he was so filled with compassion for his fellows, he could not keep from giving (DSB, pp. 189-190).

The phrase "to be seen" comes from the Greek theater and describes a performance. It was not something to benefit a person as much as it was to impress an audience. What happens if you "perform"? People applaud. "...you will have no reward from your Father in heaven." This can suggest that there is only one reward for each deed of righteousness. If men see and applaud your action, then God does not. If men do not see it, or see but misunderstand it, God applauds it. This interpretation would be consistent with Jewish theology at that time.

What about rewards? Three times in this chapter (vs. 4, 6, 18) and in Matthew 5:12, 10:42, 25:14-46, Jesus talks about rewards. What rewards will God give us? This is a tough question, but we should never give in order to get a reward. If we do, we are going to be greatly disappointed. We must allow God to decide the reward.

Fisher suggests three things about rewards:

1. The Bible does not suggest there is a system where we can add to our account. The Christian is a slave and slaves do not get paid.

2. Material reward is not promised. Rewards are spiritual.

3. Rewards are not "payment in kind" (Fisher, p. 100).

Barclay would add, "…the highest reward never comes to him who is seeking it (DSB, p. 182)."

As to the "trumpets," we do not have examples of Pharisees actually blowing, or having a trumpet blown to attract attention, so we are not sure what is meant here. It could also be similar to our expression about "tooting your own horn." It could also refer to the practice of using a horn to call the people to prayer during times of drought. At that time, a collection to aid the poor was taken. It is also possible that a trumpet was blown to recognize major gifts.

The word "hypocrite" is an interesting word. It is used about seventeen times in the New Testament and thirteen are in Matthew. When Matthew uses it, it is usually on the lips of Jesus and in connection with the Pharisees. But what does it mean? Albert Mann translates it "overscrupulous." "In the face of the evidence nothing can justify the continued use if the word 'hypocrite' in our English versions (AB, p. 73)." Fisher prefers to translate it "misguided."

The word came from the Greek theater and meant "to speak from behind the mask." Greek actors often played more than one role in a production. To change roles, they went off stage, picked up the appropriate mask, returned to the stage and held it in front of their face while speaking their lines.

The term *hypocrites*, as used here, describes people who do good acts for appearance only—not out of compassion or other good motives. Their actions may be good, but their motives are hollow. These empty acts are their only reward, but God will reward those who are sincere in their faith (LASB, p. 1550).

Fisher suggests three requirements for determining what Jesus meant when he used it:

1. It must have negative connotation because Jesus did not approve of the "hypocrite."

2. It must be a sincere word because the Pharisees thought their actions were pleasing to God.

3. It must give indication of the practices of the Pharisees which, because of their legalism, were a danger to Jesus' followers. (p. 103)

The phrase "they have received their reward" comes from the business community and applies to a bill that is "paid in full." As has been suggested, there is only one recognition of our actions either man pays us or God does.

Verse 3 shows that Jesus expected us to give alms, but it was to be a private matter. How can we not let our left hand know what your right hand does? He may mean reach into your wallet and pull out some money and give it, but don't look at the amount. That could be dangerous! You could get a $20 bill instead of a $1 or a $5. He may mean do not let your best friend, your "right hand," know what you have done.

"Openly" is not in the oldest and best texts. It was probably a gloss, added by a copyist. Allow God to reward you in His own way. You cannot make a deal with God, "I'll help these people if you'll help me." You must give only from an intense, sincere desire to help.

Preparation for Prayer
Matthew 6:5-8

"When you pray, you shall not be as the hypocrites, for they love to stand and pray in the synagogues and in the corners of the streets, that they may be seen by men. Most certainly, I tell you, they have received their reward. [6] But you, when you pray, enter into your inner room, and having shut your door, pray to your Father who is in secret, and your Father who sees in secret will reward you openly. [7] In praying, don't use vain repetitions, as the Gentiles do; for they think that they will be heard for their much speaking. [8] Therefore don't be like them, for your Father knows what things you need, before you ask him."

"When you pray..." assumes that all Christians will pray and we have already seen that prayer was one of the three "acts of righteousness" required of the Pharisees. It was also important to pagan people, but for a different reason. The Pharisees, prayed to impress God and the people listening; the pagans prayed to coerce their gods into doing their will. Christians are in danger of doing the things that both the Pharisees and the pagans did.

Prayer was such a serious matter for the Jews that it became formalized and was subject to abuse. The proper posture for prayer among the Pharisees was to stand with their hands lifted toward heaven and head bowed. But what was the proper "attitude" of prayer, and by attitude, I mean physical as well as mental? That may be the impetus for Jesus' teaching on prayer. Jesus didn't lay down any physical requirements. Some bow their heads and close their eyes; some keep their eyes open; some kneel or prostrate themselves. There is no right or wrong physical position for prayer.

Barclay tells us there were two prayers the Jews were required to repeat. The *Shema*, "Hear, Israel: Yahweh is our God. Yahweh is one. You shall love Yahweh your God with all your heart, with all your soul, and with all your might. (Deut. 6:4-5)." which was to be repeated in the morning and the evening and the *Eighteen*, or *Amidah*, which was repeated three times a day. There were also special prayers for almost every occasion, meals, new moon, seeing a river, etc.

The appointed times of prayer were the third (9 am), sixth (noon), and ninth (3 pm) hour. Wherever you were, you were required to stop, turn toward the Temple and pray, much like Muslims turn toward Mecca today. The Pharisees felt that the best place to pray was in the Temple, next best was in the synagogue, but you were to pray wherever you were. Those who wanted to make an impression on others arranged their schedules so they could be in a prominent place at the appointed time of prayer. We should note that "this is no condemnation of praying in a synagogue or public place *as such* (AB, p. 74)."

I'd like to share just a few personal words about public prayer before we move on. I don't want to offend anyone, but sadly much public prayer in our churches is still more exhibition than prayer. I sometimes wonder if our brains are "turned on" before we start "speaking." Speaking about prayer in his introduction in the *Message* to the book of Psalms Eugene Peterson says:

Untutored we tend to think that prayer is what good people do when they are doing their best. It is not. Inexperienced, we suppose that there must be an "insider" language that must be acquired before God takes us seriously in our prayer. There is not. Prayer is elemental, not advanced, language. It is the means by which our language becomes honest, true, and personal in response to God. It is the means by which we get everything in our lives out in the open before God.

I am often disappointed by people I'll call eloquent prayers who change the tone of their voice and their language to "churchy" language full of "Thee's" and "Thou's" and often try to cover the entire world while asking God to bless the offering that is about to be received. It is also onerous to use prayer as a platform for making announcements or soliciting volunteers to work in a ministry, praying for those things should be relegated to the prayer closet.

Jesus tells us, "[to] enter into your inner room, and having shut the door, pray..." so I assume that this model is not necessarily for public prayer, but for private prayer. Will this make us sincere? No! While it may solve the problem of wanting "to be seen by men," we may still use it to try to manipulate God. Is public prayer wrong? No, Jesus and the disciples prayed in public. However, <u>everything</u> the Pharisees did was done "to be seen by men." "...and your Father who sees in secret will reward..." What kind of reward? The same kind we discussed in verse 1-4. Whether we will be "openly" rewarded as some translations have it, or not, God will do it.

Pagan prayer usually involved then, as it does today, the repetition of a "mantra," a special phrase repeated over and over that was intended to get a god's attention and align the person's spirit with their god. This may be what Jesus meant when he said, "don't use vain repetitions, as the Gentiles do; for they think that they will be heard for their much speaking." If you were speaking to a friend, and God, while our Heavenly Father, is our friend, would you keep repeating your friend's name with every phrase/sentence you spoke? I doubt it! Yet we do it in prayer. We should not simply "plug" in Father, Lord, God, etc. when we are praying. Think, "If I were talking to Mike, would I repeat his name this many times in one conversation?"

Elijah ran into this problem with the prophets of Baal, "They took the bull which was given them, and they dressed it, and called on the name of Baal from morning even until noon, saying, 'Baal, hear us!' But there was no voice, and nobody answered. They leaped about the altar which was made." (1 Kings 18:26). Luke tells of one such experience: "But when they perceived that he [Paul] was a Jew, all with one voice for a time of about two hours cried out, 'Great is Artemis of the Ephesians!'" (Acts 19:34)

The Jews believed that if fifteen minutes of praying was good, then thirty minutes was twice as good. The rabbis taught that to properly pray aloud one should spend one hour in preparation before and one hour in meditation afterwards (DSB, p. 197). That isn't a bad suggestion because too often we rush into prayer and then rush to something else immediately after saying, "Amen."

Does Jesus mean that we are not to pray for something more than once? No. He prayed three times for His "cup" to be removed (26:36, 42, and 44). He also told of a woman who would not give up seeking relief from a judge in Luke 18:1-9, because her continued request wore the judge down and brought her justice. However, we don't have to wear down God, He wants to grant our requests.

Christians should have a different attitude toward prayer. We do not need to be God's window on the world, "for your Father knows what you need before you ask him." If God already knows what you need, why do you prayer at all? Prayer is not for God; it is for us. It encourages us to trust Him more. What we need is childlike simplicity and trust. And, "If you then, being evil, know how to give good gifts to your children, how much more will your Father who is in heaven give good things to those who ask him! (Matt. 7:11)."

Prayer Related to God's Rule in the World
Matthew 6:9-10

"Pray like this: 'Our Father in heaven, may your name be kept holy. ¹⁰ Let your Kingdom come. Let your will be done, as in heaven, so on earth.'"

The prayer consists of six parts which can be divided into two groups of three. The first group focuses on God and His rule of the world; the second group on the individual's needs.

Quite probably the most quoted and misquoted passage in the Bible is this passage we call "The Lord's Prayer." It is used in more worship services than any other Bible passage and serves two functions. First, it is used as a prayer, second it is used as a "school of prayer." "...but unlike other schools, it is both a kindergarten and a university (Fisher, p. 110)."

The prayer is not intended to be a substitute for what might be called "a prayer from the heart" and isn't meant to be said by rote, rather than prayed, without connecting the heart and/or brain. Remember that this prayer was taught to the disciples by Jesus himself. Therefore, unless it is used by a disciple, it is meaningless. Barclay says it "is not a child's prayer... [it is] not meaningful for a child (DSB, p. 199)."

Luke's treatment is shorter and has a different setting than Matthew's. Luke 11:1-4 says:

When he finished praying in a certain place, one of his disciples said to him, "Lord, teach us to pray, just as John also taught his disciples."

He said to them, "When you pray, say,

'Our Father in heaven,

May your name be kept holy.

May your Kingdom come.

May your will be done on Earth, as it is in heaven.

Give us day by day our daily bread.

Forgive us our sins,

For we ourselves also forgive everyone who is indebted to us.

Bring us not into temptation,

But deliver us from the evil one.'"

It is suggested that because Luke's version is shorter, it is older. Fisher gives three possible reasons for Matthew's additions: they are explanations; they may come from different translation of the language used or they may be the result of addressing a different [larger] audience.

"Our Father" or "The Father" was a more formal address of God that the Jews used. Many nations addressed God as father, but not in the same sense the Jews did. The Jews knew Him as Father in His selection of Israel for His special blessing and in their deliverance from enemies, but Jesus took it further calling him "*abba,*" which I prefer to translate as "daddy," in Mark 14:36 and echoed by Paul in Romans 8:15 and Galatians 4:6.

When we truly call God Father, Barclay believes we can correctly settle all our relationships:

1.   Our relationship to the unseen world: men were haunted by the gods they thought lived in everything around them waiting to hurt or play tricks on them; we can trust our heavenly Father.

2.   Our relationship to the seen world: their world was a dark, hostile world in which they suffered greatly; the loving God will use even the bad things to help us.

3.   Our relationship to our fellow-men: if God is our Father, then he is Father of all; there is no I, me, or mine in the Prayer, only "our," and "us." True brotherhood is based on true fatherhood.

4.   Our relationship to ourselves: everyone dislikes himself sometimes, but if we matter to God, we can matter to ourselves.

5.   Our relationship to God: it does not remove the might, majesty and power of God, but makes that might, majesty and power approachable for us.

"...in heaven" states not only the residence of God, but expresses one of the great paradoxes of the biblical revelation; while God is right here with us, He is also transcendent, that is He is in Heaven.

To deism, God is distant and out of reach [transcendent]; to pantheism, God is everything and everything is God; to the sentimentalist, God may be "the man upstairs." To Jesus, God is none of this. He is Father and he is God, near and ever to be held in reverence (BBC, p. 115).

"...may your name be kept holy" may be the most difficult phrase for us to understand. In Greek the word *hagios* translated "holy" has to do with the way a person or thing is treated. The root meaning is "different" or "separate." A Temple was *hagios* because, not only was it dedicated to God, but it was different from other buildings.

A better word in English might be "revered." If we are going to revere God's name, we must first believe there is a God. This is a peculiar statement for a Christian to make, but there are many who do not believe there is a God, and it is strange that the Bible does not offer any proof of God. For the Jews, the fact of God was self-evident and did not require confirmation because they saw His hand in everything. So, they felt they did not need to prove that which everyone knew and accepted to be true.

To reverence God, we must know what kind of God He is. Is He capricious like the Greek and Roman gods who were feared, but were not revered? To reverence God, we must be aware of His presence with us at all times and in all places, we must submit to His reign over us.

In Hebrew to know the name of a person meant more than just simply to know the name they were called. It meant the person was a friend you could call upon. Consider, "Those who know your name will put their trust in you, for you, Yahweh, have not forsaken those who seek you" (Ps. 9:10). We know that just knowing God's name is not enough; we must have a personal relationship with and trust in Him. "Some trust in chariots, and some in horses, but we trust the name of Yahweh our God" (Ps. 20:7). That doesn't infer that God's name will defeat the foe but that God will fight for His people.

"...your Kingdom come," speaks both of the desire to reach people now, and looks forward to the *parousia,* the end of the age, when His Kingdom comes on earth. The kingdom is both here now and will be here at the end of the ages. The Greek and Hebrew idioms carry a different meaning than the English. It is not a nation or a place, but a people who recognize the King as their ruler wherever they may live or be.

The message Jesus brought to the people was about the Kingdom (Mark 1:14, 38, Luke 4:43, 8:1). He spoke of the Kingdom and related it to the past. "I tell you that many will come from the east and the west, and will sit down with Abraham, Isaac, and Jacob in the Kingdom of Heaven," (Matt. 8:11). And to the present, "...neither will they say, 'Look, here!' or, 'Look, there!' for behold, the Kingdom of God is within you" (Luke 17:21). In the Prayer, He speaks of the Kingdom that is yet to come.

"Let your will be done, as in heaven, so on earth" echoes and amplifies the coming of the Kingdom; it was a common practice for Jews and Greeks to repeat or reword a phrase for emphasis.

In Greek "will" is a noun that stresses more a desire than an action, but what is God's desire? It is one thing to pray this word, but another thing how we pray it. Do we pray in a tone of perfect love and trust because we can depend on a God who loves us? Or do we pray in a tone of resignation because God wants it? Or is it a tone of resentment because God has beaten us into submission?

Remember what Paul said, "He who didn't spare his own Son, but delivered him up for us all, how would he not also with him freely give us all things? (Rom. 8:32)."

Prayer Related to Personal Needs
Matthew 6:11-15

Give us today our daily bread. [12] Forgive us our debts, as we also forgive our debtors. [13] Bring us not into temptation, but deliver us from the evil one. For yours is the Kingdom, the power, and the glory forever. Amen.'(NU omits "For yours is the Kingdom, the power, and the glory forever. Amen.")

[14] *"For if you forgive men their trespasses, your heavenly Father will also forgive you. [15] But if you don't forgive men their trespasses, neither will your Father forgive your trespasses.*

This prayer teaches us to seek first the kingdom of God and his righteousness, and that all other things shall be added. After the things of God's glory, kingdom, and will, we pray for the needful supports and comforts of this present life. Every word here has a lesson in it (MH).

The human needs it deals with are the three essential needs of people. The three arenas of life are bread for today, forgiveness for the sins of the past and relief from temptation in the future. (DSB, p. 199).

Luke's version says, "Give us each day our daily bread. Forgive us our sins, for we also forgive everyone who sins against us. And lead us not into temptation." (Luke 11:3-4)

"...daily" translates the Greek word *epiousion* which occurs in the New Testament only in this Prayer and has been only found once in other existing Greek records. Ironically, that was a woman's shopping list for the food she needed that day. It may be related to the "manna" experience in Exodus 16 when God fed the Israelites with bread that was sufficient for the day. It was an urgent situation, as was the feeding of the five thousand in Matthew 14:13-21.

Several interesting positions have been taken about what "bread" means. Barclay lists four suggestions:

1. It was identified with the Lord's Supper. Early in Church history the prayer was used in conjunction with the Supper.
2. It has been identified as the Spiritual food which comes from the Word of God.
3. It is said that Jesus is the "bread" [of life] (John 6:33-35).
4. In the Jewish sense, it is the "bread of heaven" reserved for the Messianic feast (DSB, p. 215-216).

While these are interesting ideas, that is probably all they are because we must not overlook the obvious. There is no need to spiritualize what is so plainly stated. It is a petition to satisfy the need of the day. The Bible teaches that God cares about us and our needs on a daily basis.

"Give" does not infer that we have no responsibility in the process. Many passages clearly teach our responsibility in that matter however, we must recognize that it is God who gives us the ability to "get."

"Debts" is a Jewish expression for "sins," as Luke has stated, so it had great meaning for Matthew's Jewish audience. I prefer the "trespasses" or "sins" as the translation because it states more clearly that we have stepped over God's line into sin. The condition for receiving forgiveness is that to be forgiven we must first forgive. It is a two-way street.

Here is a promise, if you forgive, your heavenly Father will also forgive. We must forgive, as we hope to be forgiven. Those who desire to find mercy with God must show mercy to their brethren. Christ came into the world as the great Peace-maker, not only to reconcile us to God but one to another (MH). When we pray this prayer without forgiving others, we are actually asking God not to forgive us.

Before we can pray this part of the prayer, we must be aware of sin in our lives. "Forgiving others is a reflection of a repentant, regenerate heart which makes our own forgiveness possible. Those who have experienced forgiveness will forgive (NLTBS, p. 1588)." While we all recognize we are sinners, it is more a superficial recognition than an examination and desire to be wholly what God wants us to be?

The Greek words the New Testament uses to describe sin are interesting, they are subtle, almost innocent, in their meaning, yet there is a "hook" in them.
1. *Hamartia*, to miss the mark, to be less than you are capable of being.
2. *Parabasis*, to step across the line.
3. *Paraptoma*, to slip across, not as deliberate as *parabasis*.
4. *Anonia*, lawlessness, to know what is right and choose to do wrong.
5. *Opheilema*, failure to pay what is due. This is the word used in the Prayer.

Everyone was expected to forgive, but surely there must be a limit to how much (see Matthew 18:21-35). Barclay thinks we must learn to do three things before we can truly forgive:
1. To understand. There is always a reason for why people do what they do and their reason does not have to make sense to us.
2. To forget. There is no forgiveness as long as we continue to brood over a thing. Certainly, we can't actually forget, but we can refuse to allow it to remain on our minds for long.
3. To love; *agape* (see Matthew 5:43-48).

Whenever we ask God to forgive us for sin, we should ask, "Have I forgiven the people who have wronged me?"

Basically, there are only two classes of sin: sins of commission and sins of omission, and no, sins of omission are not sins that we should have committed and didn't. Growing up Southern Baptist, I was convinced that I was constantly sinning; after all, that is the nature of the human condition. It was mostly those sins of omission, things that I know I should have done but didn't do.

Today, I am convinced that we don't, I would even say can't, sin accidentally, because sin must be an act of the will. We make a decision to do something we know we shouldn't do or we make a decision to refuse to do something we know we should do. There is a deliberateness required to sin. James warns: "To him therefore who knows to do good, and doesn't do it, to him it is sin (Jam. 4:17)."

As John reminds us: "If we confess our sins, he is faithful and righteous to forgive us the sins, and to cleanse us from all unrighteousness. (1 John 1:9)." God is always ready to forgive us. We must be just as ready to forgive others. Sometimes this takes a little while for us, but we must keep working at it.

When we consider "bring us not into temptation," the word translated "temptation" can also be translated "test" and is possibly what Matthew and Luke had in mind. Here it is testing, not luring into evil, as with Jesus in Matthew 4:1; "Then Jesus was led by the Spirit into the desert to be tempted by the devil." Testing is done to determine the quality of a product.

In James 1:13-16, James tells us that God does not tempt us, but He does test us. If this is the case, we should not be asking to be excused from the testing, because it is for our good. Another possibility is that the second half holds the key to the first half, "but deliver us from the evil one," which is not in the oldest texts available. The evil one is Satan, the accuser, also called the devil, the slanderer. He often appears in the guise of a friend, even a loved one, luring us away from the task before us.

Paul has assured us that God is with us and will help us, if we allow him:

No temptation has taken you except what is common to man. God is faithful, who will not allow you to be tempted above what you are able, but will with the temptation also make the way of escape, that you may be able to endure it (1 Cor. 10:13).

The final phrase of the prayer, "for yours is the kingdom and the power and the glory forever. Amen." is not in the older MSS and several translations omit it. It is considered to be a gloss added sometime later "to round the prayer out liturgically (IB, p. 315)." Some denominations omit it when they use the prayer in their services.

The pattern of the prayer is: brief, simple, universal, childlike. It is a prayer of commitment and the prayer of a humble man (Fisher, p. 119).

How Not to Fast
Matthew 6:16-18

"Moreover when you fast, don't be like the hypocrites, with sad faces. For they disfigure their faces, that they may be seen by men to be fasting. Most certainly I tell you, they have received their reward. [17] But you, when you fast, anoint your head, and wash your face; [18] so that you are not seen by men to be fasting, but by your Father who is in secret, and your Father, who sees in secret, will reward you.

Having concluded His supplementary directions on the subject of prayer with this Divine Pattern, our Lord now returns to the subject of *Unostentatiousness* in our deeds of righteousness, in order to give one more illustration of it, in the matter of fasting (CCE).

This saying, as many of Jesus' sayings, was in direct conflict with the accepted practices in His day. Anointing the head was forbidden by custom, but not by commandment, on any fast day. It is as though you are not supposed to look happy when you are dedicated to God. But, "Fasting should be occasional, secret, and joyous—as with gifts of charity (IB, p. 317)."

Fasting was important to the Jews and early Christians and it is still an important part of many eastern religions but sadly few in the Christian church today continue the practice. Fasting only lasted from dawn, as soon as you could tell a white thread from a black one, until sunset. You were not allowed to eat, drink, bathe, smoke, smell perfume, etc. Tradition says Reuben fasted seven years for his part in selling Joseph and Simeon fasted two years to repent for his hatred of Joseph. The only required Jewish fast was on *Yom Kippur*, the Day of Atonement.

Mourners were required to fast from the time of death until burial, which often took place within hours. Fasting was closely connected to repentance. The nation was called to repent and fast in Judges 20:26, 1 Samuel 7:6 and Nehemiah 9:1. Fasting was also called for to prepare for God's revelation: Daniel 9:3 and Matthew 4:2.

The Pharisees fasted twice a week as a display of piety, on Monday and Thursday. According to tradition those were the days Moses ascended and descended Mt. Sinai. It also happened to be the main market days and there were more people to see their piety. To be sure that it was not overlooked, they did not groom themselves and often would put ashes or flour on their faces to emphasize their fast.

Barclay lists three ideas behind the Jewish fasting:

1. It was a deliberate attempt to get God's attention, as though God would pay more attention to a person fasting.
2. It would show that their repentance was real, however it became a substitute for repentance.
3. It was vicarious, designed to cause God to feel sorry for them (DSB, pp. 234, 235).

When the Pharisees challenged Jesus' disciples about fasting, He asked them:

Can you make the friends of the bridegroom fast, while the bridegroom is with them? But the days will come when the bridegroom will be taken away from them. Then they will fast in those days (Luke 5:34-35).

The statement, "when you fast," suggests that He expected His followers would fast and Christians fasted Wednesday and Friday, but it was never as important to them as it was to the Pharisees. In verses 17 and 18, Jesus addresses how not to fast. As we saw in 4:2 and will see in 9:14-17, Jesus fasted.

Generally, the Pharisees wanted people to know when they were doing one of the required "acts of righteousness," but Jesus warned, "...do not look somber as the hypocrites do." "It was not the *deed*, but *reputation* for the deed which they sought; and with this view those hypocrites multiplied their fasts (CCE)." As in everything a Christian does, attitude is the key. Things done for men to see are rewarded by being seen.

With all the problems, and potential problems, associated with fasting, should we do it? Barclay comes to our aid and lists five benefits for us:

1. It is good for your health. Most of us eat too much.
2. It is good for self-discipline to deny ourselves occasionally. We have become totally self-indulgent.
3. It helps us avoid becoming slaves of habit; often we eat because it is time to eat, not because we are hungry.
4. It helps us learn to do without things. Few things are essential, but we have come to regard many luxuries as necessities.
5. It helps us appreciate things more. There is very little "thrill" to life for most of us (DSB, pp. 237-238).

I would add a sixth, digestion requires a great deal of energy, when we fast that energy used for digestion is available to use in focusing on God.

Jesus is suggesting that when you fast, behave in the same way you do every other day so that it will not be obvious to others that you are fasting, but only to God who will see what you are doing and will reward you appropriately.

Your Best Investments
Matthew 6:19-21

"Don't lay up treasures for yourselves on the earth, where moth and rust consume, and where thieves break through and steal; [20] *but lay up for yourselves treasures in heaven, where neither moth nor rust consume, and where thieves don't break through and steal;* [21] *for where your treasure is, there your heart will be also.*

To say that we live in a world where money is important would be a gross understatement. Not only is it important, but it is a necessity for a variety of things: food, clothing, shelter, medical care, school, and many other good things.

Most of us do not realize it, but we are more controlled by the things we own than controllers of them. Do you own a car? How much time do you spend taking care of your car? It needs maintenance, washing, etc. How many things have you added to it to enhance its beauty or functionality since you bought it? Now, do you own the car, or does it own you? The accumulation of money has become the most important factor in life for many people. Here, and in the rest of chapter six, Jesus addresses how to free ourselves from the control of money.

The interpretation of this passage is very important to a Christian understanding of wealth. "Lay up for yourself treasures in heaven" "…was a common image for Jews of Jesus' day; doing God's commands became virtually equivalent to accumulating treasures with God. (NLTSB, p. 1588)." The issue is not that we should not have money or use money to buy things that are expensive or might not last very long, but to have a proper view of possessions. Paul indicated that when we use money properly, it becomes a treasure for many:

Not that I am looking for a gift, but I am looking for what may be credited to your account. I have received full payment and even more; I am amply supplied, now that I have received from Epaphroditus the gifts you sent. They are a fragrant offering, an acceptable sacrifice, pleasing to God (Philippians 4:17-18).

Jesus condemned the attitude of the rich fool (Luke 12:13-21) who is told: "Sell your possessions and give to the poor." His problem, and that of the rich young ruler of Mark 10:17-22, was that his money was keeping him from the Kingdom. Paul reminds us, "For the love of money is a root of all kinds of evil (1 Tim. 6:10)". Not money, "the love of money" is the problem!

However, Lazarus apparently was a wealthy man and we have no record of Jesus telling him to give it away. Likewise, Zacchaeus, in Luke 19, wasn't ordered to give his money away but did it because he wanted to do it; money was no longer his god.

The primary forms of wealth in New Testament days were fine garments and rugs, storable food, and jewels and precious metals. The best clothes and rugs were woven of wool, which was often attacked by moths (2 Kings 5:22, Josh. 7:21). Food stuff, in the form of grain, was stored in barns and was vulnerable to mice and fungus. Valuables, gold, silver, and jewels were usually buried in a field or stored in the house and thieves would watch and try to steal them.

Jesus addressed the three great destroyers of that kind of wealth: the moth, who laid her eggs in the wool and the larva fed on it; the vermin who lived in the barns and ate the grain and the thief, who dug through the dirt wall of the house to steal the valuables. The word "destroy" is the Greek word *brosis* which means "eating away" and was used to describe mice nibbling away at something and is a better translation than the KJV "corrupt."

The two problems addressed here are: earthly treasures are perishable and investments in them usually follow our heart's desire. The advantage of the proper use of wealth is that it cannot be destroyed. Someone wisely said, "You only keep what you give away." Money we have given to help others continues to work even after we and they are gone.

"On earth and in heaven are qualitative adjectives telling the nature of the treasure. It is not a question of location, but nature (Fisher, p. 121)." Unfortunately, we want to amass a treasure here rather than sending it ahead of us, so is it possible that many who are rich on earth are going to be broke in heaven?

The Generous Eye
Matthew 6:22-23

"The lamp of the body is the eye. If therefore your eye is sound, your whole body will be full of light. [23] *But if your eye is evil, your whole body will be full of darkness. If therefore the light that is in you is darkness, how great is the darkness!*

Luke gives a little different slant on the passage.

Your eye is the lamp of your body. When your eyes are good, your whole body also is full of light. But when they are bad, your body also is full of darkness. See to it, then, that the light within you is not darkness. Therefore, if your whole body is full of light, and no part of it dark, it will be completely lighted, as when the light of a lamp shines on you (Luke 11:34-36)

There is more to this than simply to say that a clean, clear window allows good light into a room and a dirty, obscure or distorted window does not do the same thing in; we must also consider the quality of the light. The contrast here is between the good "eye" that works properly to bring things into focus and the bad "eye" that can't properly focus (cataracts, tunnel vision, etc.), but that still misses the point. "Men maliciously and wickedly put out even the little light of nature that is in them (GN)."

The problem is with how we "see" things. Do we look at a scene and see the litter or do we see the possibilities. There are many things that can distort our vision: prejudice, jealousy, and conceit to name only a few. Jesus is saying, "It is impossible to properly focus on both God and the world." If the wording is confusing, the meaning is clear. "A man needs spiritual insight to discern where the true values of life lie (Fisher, p. 123)."

Much of the difficulty is because the Greek adjectives used do not seem to fit the nouns they modify; "sound," translates *haplous* which the KJV renders "single," and "evil," translates the word *poneros*.

Haplous means "simple, with no ulterior motive." When used in an ethical sense it means "pure" and is translated "generously" in James 1:5, "If any of you lacks wisdom, he should ask God, who gives "generously" to all without finding fault, and it will be given to him" and has the same meaning in Romans 12:6-9, 2 Corinthians 8:2 and 9:11-13.

Poneros means "bad or useless" and usually has to do with poverty of some type. We sometimes speak of a "jaundiced eye." In the LXX, it is used to describe wicked people in Deuteronomy 15:9-10 and Proverbs 23:6-8. It is the word used to describe the disgruntled laborers, in the parable of the landlord, Matthew 20:1-16.

It appears that the choice was intended to tell us the importance of viewing the world properly. If we do, we will see people and things as God does, with a "sound" eye. If we have a "bad" eye, we are not going to do the "God" thing, but the opposite." "The judgment of the mind: that as the body is with the eyes, so our whole life may be ruled with right reason, that is to say, with the Spirit of God who gives light to us (GN)."

Barclay lists "three great evils" of those with bad vision:

1. It is impossible to live with ourselves. Bitterness and resentment rob us of our happiness.

2. It is impossible to live with others. Love might cover a multitude of sins, but stinginess covers a multitude of virtues.

3. It is impossible to live with God. No one is as generous as God and there can be no fellowship with two of such opposite attitudes (DSB, p. 247).

Whose Servant Are You?
Matthew 6:24

"No one can serve two masters, for either he will hate the one and love the other; or else he will be devoted to one and despise the other. You can't serve both God and Mammon."

This is not a threat or confrontation for the Christian; it is a simple statement of fact. Everyone has a "master," a spouse, a child, a job, a sports team, anything which has become the all-consuming director of their life. If you are going to be a good mechanic, golfer or musician, you must dedicate a large part of your life to that, but does it become your "master"? It doesn't have to.

"Masters" is a good translation, but "owners" would be better, because the idea is of the slave/owner relationship. A slave was the property of the "master," a living tool, and had no rights of his own. He could be sold, beaten or killed at the whim of the "master." For two owners to hold joint title to one slave would surely result in the slave being killed by one of them, because a slave's time was not his own. He was forever on call to wait on his master, but which one? In the same way, a Christian has no rights of his own. He is to be at the disposal of his "Master," the Lord Jesus Christ.

In the New Testament, "love" and "hate" are not expressions of emotion, but of relationships and attitudes. Here "love" is a derivative of *agape*. The way "hate" is used, it is the opposite of "love," which is not always the case in the New Testament.

While "Money" is not used in the Greek text, it might be easier for us to understand than "Mammon," "wealth" or "net worth" would be good words to use also. "Mammon," was not a god in any pantheon, but comes from Hebrew and means personal wealth or treasure; especially wealth used in opposition to God and it is a transliteration and personification of the Syrian word *mammon*, meaning "wealth, riches, earthly goods."

Jesus' days were much like our own, money was everything to many people, so everyone would understand its personification by Jesus. We need to put possessions in their proper place. Barclay suggests three things that will help: first, all things belong to God; second, people are always more important than things; and third, wealth is always a subordinate "good." He also says there are two questions we should ask about wealth. How was it obtained and how is it used? (DSB, pp. 250-252.)

"It is significant that Jesus makes money, not Satan, the rival to God's claim upon us (BBC, p. 118)." Paul says:

> But if we have food and clothing, we will be content with that. People who want to get rich fall into temptation and a trap and into many foolish and harmful desires that plunge men into ruin and destruction. For the love of money is a root of all kinds of evil. Some people, eager for money, have wandered from the faith and pierced themselves with many griefs. But you, man of God, flee from all this, and pursue righteousness, godliness, faith, love, endurance and gentleness (1 Tim. 6:8-11).

"God calls for self-dedication and sacrifice; mammon calls for self-assertion and self-seeking. There is a radical incompatibility between the two (Fisher, p. 125)." The interesting thing about this verse is that Jesus has narrowed the choices to only two, which is typical of Him.

We live in a world of a thousand shades of gray. However, ultimately there are not thousands of choices, only two: good or bad, right or wrong, "God" or "Money." In his farewell address, Joshua challenged the people,

> If it seems evil to you to serve Yahweh, choose today whom you will serve; whether the gods which your fathers served that were beyond the River, or the gods of the Amorites, in whose land you dwell; but as for me and my house, we will serve Yahweh (Joshua 24:15).

We cannot escape choosing. "A choice allowed to go by default is still a choice (IB, p. 320)." "The only escape from the rule of things is submission to the rule of God (BBC, p. 11)."

The Illusion of Worry
Matthew 6:25-34

"Therefore I tell you, don't be anxious for your life: what you will eat, or what you will drink; nor yet for your body, what you will wear. Isn't life more than food, and the body more than clothing? [26] See the birds of the sky, that they don't sow, neither do they reap, nor gather into barns. Your heavenly Father feeds them. Aren't you of much more value than they?

[27] *"Which of you, by being anxious, can add one moment (literally "cubit") to his lifespan? [28] Why are you anxious about clothing? Consider the lilies of the field, how they grow. They don't toil, neither do they spin, [29] yet I tell you that even Solomon in all his glory was not dressed like one of these. [30] But if God so clothes the grass of the field, which today exists, and tomorrow is thrown into the oven, won't he much more clothe you, you of little faith?*

[31] *"Therefore don't be anxious, saying, 'What will we eat?' 'What will we drink?' or, 'With what will we be clothed?' [32] For the Gentiles seek after all these things; for your heavenly Father knows that you need all these things. [33] But seek first God's Kingdom, and his righteousness; and all these things will be given to you as well. [34] Therefore don't be anxious for tomorrow, for tomorrow will be anxious for itself. Each day's own evil is sufficient."*

In something of a continuation of the prior verses, and an argument for lesser to greater, birds to people, we are warned not to be preoccupied with extraneous matters. Mark warned, "but the worries of this life, the deceitfulness of wealth and the desires for other things come in and choke the word, making it unfruitful" (Mark 4:18). Fisher calls this section "How to be serene" and reminds us that "in spite of the storm, stress, and trial, he [Jesus] knew peace. In the face of the cross, he said, 'Peace I leave with you; my peace I give to you' (John 14:27) (Fisher, p. 127)."

However, Jesus is not encouraging idleness. "Idleness is for neither the Christian nor the birds. Birds exemplify not idleness but freedom from anxiety (BBC, p. 118)." "God's providence is not in baskets lowered from the sky, but through the hands and hearts of those who love him (IB, p. 322)." Man can cooperate with God by planting and harvesting, the birds can't. If God provides for them, why won't He also provide for us? "A man must think about food and clothing, but he should not think about them first (IB, p. 323)."

We have known for many years that worry causes some illnesses, and we are continuing to learn that it can be a major contributor, worsening almost any disease. Rather than adding to our life, it may subtract from it. Five times Jesus tells us not to worry. "Trusting God is Christian; worry about things is pagan (Fisher, p. 130)."

Jesus' statement "you of little faith" suggests worry is evil, because we don't trust God to take care of us, but worry about them instead. "Little faith results from the failure to understand one's value to God and the extent of God's providential protection (NLTSB, p. 1589)." Paul exemplifies the Christian's attitude in his message to the Philippian church:

I am not saying this because I am in need, for I have learned to be content whatever the circumstances. I know what it is to be in need, and I know what it is to have plenty. I have learned the secret of being content in any and every situation, whether well fed or hungry, whether living in plenty or in want. I can do everything through him who gives me strength (Phil. 4:11-13).

When Jesus said "all these things will be given to you as well," it was not an absolute, it was conditional. If we put God first, He will take care of us. This is the same promise God made over and over to Israel. When we are totally committed to God, the "worry" is His, not ours…

Since Luke doesn't report this verse, many feel that Matthew added it on his own. They feel Jesus would not say something like that. Fisher doesn't agree; he says, "…worry about tomorrow hinders God's care for his children (Fisher, p. 131)."

We need to be careful about confusing planning and "worry." Planning is, simply stated, preparing for the future and is not being discouraged here; it's a good thing to do. "Worry" concerns either past actions or future events we can't control, and must be avoided. Go ahead and make your plans, work on them, but leave the results in God's hands. "Planning for tomorrow is time well spent; worrying about tomorrow is time wasted. Sometimes it's difficult to tell the difference (LASB, p. 1552)"

Barclay finds seven arguments against "worry" in these ten verses:

1. God gives us life and can be trusted to take care of it.
2. Birds do not pile up a store house of food; they go out every day and pick it up. They work, but they do not worry.
3. Worry is useless because it cannot increase our height or life span.
4. God clothes the flowers of the field in great beauty, in spite of their brief life.
5. Worry is characteristic of heathens, people who do not trust God, because He is not their Father.
6. When we seek God's kingdom first, He will provide everything else we may need.
7. When we live one day at a time, we are not concerned about what may happen tomorrow.

Medical science has shown us the effects of worry: it damages our health, our productivity, and how we treat others. All of these arguments are intended to show us how much God would like to take care of us, if we would only let Him (DSB, pp. 257-8).

These things are concerned with the future: what about worrying about the past? Most often our worry is about things we did or didn't do somewhere in our past. There are two things we can do in this regard.

First, be reconciled, as much as possible with our past. The Jews used to say there are two things God cannot do, recall a word that has been spoken or undo a deed that has been done. Therefore, we must apologize; make restitution, or whatever we can to restore a "proper" relationship with people we may have injured. Paul commanded, "If it is possible, as far as it depends on you, live at peace with everyone (Rom. 12:18)."

Second, we need to learn from our mistakes. If we have made a mistake, and tried to repair the damage, then learn from our mistake and move on, possibly "building" on the error. We can also use it to help others avoid the same problem(s) we had. Paul encourages us:

Brothers, I do not consider myself yet to have taken hold of it. But one thing I do: Forgetting what is behind and straining toward what is ahead, I press on toward the goal to win the prize for which God has called me heavenward in Christ Jesus (Phil. 3:13-14).

Paul didn't allow the damage he had done to the Church prior to his conversion to prevent him from doing what God was calling him to do.

"Take no thought for your life. Not about the length of it; but refer it to God to lengthen or shorten it as he pleases; our times are in his hand, and they are in a good hand (MH)." The way to know where we are in this is to complete Paul's statement in Philippians 1:21 "For to me, to live is..."

The Foolishness of Judging
Matthew 7:1-5

"Don't judge, so that you won't be judged. [2] For with whatever judgment you judge, you will be judged; and with whatever measure you measure, it will be measured to you. [3] Why do you see the speck that is in your brother's eye, but don't consider the beam that is in your own eye? [4] Or how will you tell your brother, 'Let me remove the speck from your eye;' and behold, the beam is in your own eye? [5] You hypocrite! First remove the beam out of your own eye, and then you can see clearly to remove the speck out of your brother's eye."

Luke records this section in chapter 6:37-38, and 41-42. These words wouldn't be strange to the Jews. The *Mishnah* says: "Do not judge your fellow until you are in his position." and "When you judge any man weight the scales in his favor." Here again is the idea of walking a mile in the other guy's moccasins.

"The secret to a creative life is to be like Jesus (Fisher, p. 133)." Creativity involves not only ourselves, but the people we have opportunity to help and influence. Everything Jesus did was to build people up. He didn't even try to injure His enemies and detractors. Remember the woman caught in adultery in John 8? What did He do? He recognized the frailty of humanity and helped her. The Law required the death penalty. Jesus showed her compassion and mercy and urged her to become what God wanted her to be by saying, "Neither do I condemn you. Go your way. From now on, sin no more. (John 8:11b)." He didn't just give her a "get out of jail free" card, as some would like. He also told her to change her lifestyle!

"Do not judge" is in the Greek present tense and means to stop doing what you are continually doing. As has already been cited, Nathanael repeated a common idea of the day when told about Jesus. "'Nazareth! Can anything good come from there?' Nathanael asked. 'Come and see,' said Philip (John 1:46)." Likewise, the Pharisees based their judgment on the people Jesus associated with, "But the Pharisees and the teachers of the law who belonged to their sect complained to his disciples, 'Why do you eat and drink with tax collectors and "sinners"'?" (Luke 5:30). "Mercy is a dominant theme in Jesus' teaching and practice, but not at the expense of clear opposition to sin...God measures us by our treatment of others (NLTSB, p. 1589)"

Jesus tells us to examine our own motives and conduct instead of judging others... [His] statement, "Do not judge others," is against the kind of hypocritical, judgmental attitude that tears others down in order to build oneself up. It is not a blanket statement to overlook wrong behavior of others but a call to be *discerning* rather than negative (LASB, p. 1552).

All of us make judgments, but we don't have to express them. When we do, we bring judgment on ourselves. If we refuse mercy to others, mercy is often refused to us. "He [Jesus] draws a line between ethical appraisal and sharp-tongued criticism, and bids us keep on the right side of the line (IB, p. 325)."

There is real humor in verses 3-5. Jesus uses hyperbole to show how foolish we often are. The "beam" is a large building beam that would be used to hold up the roof of a house. The "speck" is just that, a small, dry piece of wood, a piece of saw dust. Here I am with a board in my eye that is so big I can't carry it by myself and I notice you have a speck of something in your eye. I have to look very closely to see something like that.

"Jesus is not telling us to ignore 'the speck' in our brother's eye. ... But one is in position for this ministry [speck removal] only after 'the log' is out of his own eye (BBC, p. 119)." Fisher says of us, "You misguided nitpicker[s]," when we ignore our own sin to point out the "sin" of others (Fisher, p. 137).

In chapter five, we have been commissioned to be "salt of the earth" and "light of the world," But we have become so involved in "fruit inspection" that we have no time to fertilize or enlighten.

Barclay lists three reasons why we should not judge one another:

1. We never know the whole facts or the whole person. We cannot know the strengths or weakness of another person. What we might do may be different in different circumstances.

2. It is almost impossible for any man to be strictly impartial in his judgment. We can be swayed by many things: looks, nationality, race, etc.

3. No man is good enough to judge any other man. Only the faultless has a right to look for the faults in others (DSB, pp. 263-265).

Judgment should be left to God for he alone is able to judge rightly. Paul reminds us:

Therefore judge nothing before the appointed time; wait till the Lord comes. He will bring to light what is hidden in darkness and will expose the motives of men's hearts. At that time each will receive his praise from God" (1 Cor. 4:5).

Be Discerning

Matthew 7:6

"Don't give that which is holy to the dogs, neither throw your pearls before the pigs, lest perhaps they trample them under their feet, and turn and tear you to pieces."

This is one of the most difficult sayings of Jesus, because it seems to contradict the command to reach the entire world with the gospel. Many explanations are offered, but no one knows exactly what it means. The LASB offers a good suggestion:

Pigs were unclean animals… Jesus says that we should not entrust holy teaching to unholy or unclean people. It is futile to try to teach holy concepts to people who don't want to listen and will only tear apart what we say. We should not stop giving God's Word to unbelievers, but we should be wise and discerning in our witnessing, so that we will not be wasting our time (p. 1552).

We speak of "pearls of wisdom," and rabbis considered important ideas and Scripture to be pearls. The early Church used it in two ways.

1. Both dogs and pigs were despised by the Jews because they were both considered unclean and were often equated with Gentiles so some of the Jewish Christians used this statement to "prove" Gentiles should become Jews before they could become Christians.

2. The Church faced two dangers. Dangers that came from both outsiders and insiders who introduced heresy and compromise into the message and we still face these dangers today. There was danger from outside where pagan people tried to dilute the power of the gospel. There was danger from inside where factions attempted to interpret the message in their own way.

The early Church also identified this passage with the Lord's Supper, so they were very careful who was allowed to participate or even attend the observance of the Supper. This is possibly where the practice of "closed," "close," and "open" communion in churches today came from. This didn't mean the early Church wasn't missionary minded, but they were trying to maintain the "purity" of the Church.

Closed communion is the practice of excluding all who are not members of that congregation. They may be members of the same denomination, but that doesn't matter. Close communion allows all who are members of the denomination but members of other churches to participate. Open communion allows any Christian to participate; some might phrase it to include any baptized Christian while others don't make any distinction.

In regard to interpreting the passage, Fisher offers these suggestions.

1. It prohibits using your talents for unworthy purposes and it could imply refusing to associate with "sinners."

2. It prohibits sharing spiritual experiences with unholy people and since they cannot understand, they ridicule and scorn the experience.

3. It prohibits "beating our head against a wall." It is foolish to witness to people set against the gospel (pp. 138-9).

Barclay suggests that this passage has been altered in its transmission to us. He sees it as a good example of Hebrew parallelism. "Give" is parallel to "throw;" "dogs" to "pigs" but "sacred" isn't related to "pearls." In Hebrew, where there were no written vowels, the consonants in "sacred" and "earring" are the same, K D SH. In the *Talmud*, "an ear ring in a swine's snout" is a proverb for something that is totally out of place; he suggests the original text would then be "Give not an earring to the dogs; neither cast ye your pearls before swine." If this is the true meaning, Barclay says, it would mean that certain people are not fit, not able to receive the message we offer (pp. 267-8).

Jesus isn't telling us not to tell the good news to everyone, but he is warning us of some dangers that exist when we try. Stagg lists three hazards to sharing with those who are not discerning:

1. He may further damage the one he tries to help.

2. He may force himself or his values on another.

3. He may unnecessarily imperil himself or others.

Plato said, "To find the maker and founder of this universe is a difficult task; and when you have found him, you cannot speak of him before all people."

Keep on Asking, Seeking and Knocking
Matthew 7:7-11

"Ask, and it will be given you. Seek, and you will find. Knock, and it will be opened for you. ⁸ For everyone who asks receives. He who seeks finds. To him who knocks it will be opened. ⁹ Or who is there among you, who, if his son asks him for bread, will give him a stone? ¹⁰ Or if he asks for a fish, who will give him a serpent? ¹¹ If you then, being evil, know how to give good gifts to your children, how much more will your Father who is in heaven give good things to those who ask him!

Luke's parallel, reads a little differently and follows his presentation of the Lord's Prayer.

So I say to you: Ask and it will be given to you; seek and you will find; knock and the door will be opened to you. For everyone who asks receives; he who seeks finds; and to him who knocks, the door will be opened. Which of you fathers, if your son asks for a fish, will give him a snake instead? Or if he asks for an egg, will give him a scorpion? If you then, though you are evil, know how to give good gifts to your children, how much more will your Father in heaven give the Holy Spirit to those who ask him! (Luke 11:9-13).

While focusing on persistence in our prayers, Jesus isn't promising that, because of our persistence, God will grant any request we make.

Do you notice the progression in intensity? "Ask, seek, knock," each is more emphatic than the last. Each is also in the Greek present imperative tense which indicates we are to make a habit of doing these things, "keep on…" but if they were in the aorist imperative, it would mean do it one time. In Christianity, the emphasis is on constantly praying. "With this in mind, we constantly pray for you…" (2 Thess. 1:11a). But while we are to "keep on…" we "must never imagine that persistency in prayer is necessary in order to overcome some unwillingness on the Father's part to respond to His children's requests (TNTC, p. 80)."

"We *ask* for what we *wish;* we *seek* for what we *miss;* we *knock* for that from which we feel ourselves *shut out* (CCE)."

One may not receive what he requests, he may not find what he seeks, and the door upon which he knocks may not be the one opened; but the assurance is that where there is asking there will be receiving, where there is seeking there will be finding, and where there is knocking God will open a door (BBC, p. 121)."

The Jews were a nation that loved to pray and the Rabbis said much about prayer. One of their expressions says, "God is as near to his creatures as the ear to the mouth (DSB, p. 270)" and may be the origin of our expression "from your mouth to God's ear." On the other hand, the Greeks prayed, but because the Greek gods were precocious, they were almost afraid of the answer they might receive.

Jesus chooses His examples carefully. As we saw in Matthew 4:3, there were small limestone rocks that could look like a small loaf of bread. No father would be so mean as to give his son a rock to eat. The word "snake" would be better translated "eel." Thus, it was a fish, but it was "unclean" because it didn't have fins and scales, so it would satisfy the request for a fish, but it would not be ethical for a Jew to eat it. "Anything living in the water that does not have fins and scales is to be detestable to you" (Lev. 11:12).

Luke adds the "egg...scorpion" section. A pale scorpion when curled up could look very much like an egg, but it would be an awful trick to play on anyone.

Jesus also makes it clear that if men, who are "evil," give good gifts to people, God can certainly be trusted to give "good" gifts to people also. While Matthew doesn't tell us what God wants to give us, Luke makes it very clear the gift God most wants to give us is the Holy Spirit.

The children in Jesus' example asked their father for bread and fish—good and necessary items. If the children had asked for a poisonous snake, would the wise father have granted their request? Sometimes God knows we are praying for "snakes" and does not give us what we ask for, even though we persist in our prayers. ... Christ is showing us the heart of God the Father. God is not selfish, begrudging, or stingy, and we don't have to beg or grovel as we come with our requests (LASB, p. 1553).

Not only are we to pray constantly, that is habitually, but we are to pray about everything. Jesus doesn't put any limitations on how we are to pray or what we can pray for. He only assures us that our prayers will be answered. There are those who say God answers all their prayers; some time he says "yes," sometimes "no" and sometimes "not right now." I think that last one is a "cop out." And, while we may not say it in a sing-song way, this is how most of us "hear" it. It excuses the fact that we didn't get a direct answer to that specific prayer.

"Prayer is the appointed means for obtaining what we need. Pray; pray often; make a business of prayer, and be serious and earnest in it. Ask, as a beggar asks alms (MH)." What should we pray for? Barclay says there are two tests, "Do we really want a thing?" and "Can we pray about it? (DSB, p. 272)." If it meets these requirements then keep on asking, keep on seeking, and keep on knocking.

Be Careful What You Do
Matthew 7:12

"Therefore whatever you desire for men to do to you, you shall also do to them; for this is the law and the prophets."

Every society has rules, both written and unwritten, for how people are to live with their neighbors. This statement, which is Jesus' summary of those rules, isn't particularly new. Similar, but not the same, statements have also come from Confucius, Plato, Loa-Tzu, and several Old Testament prophets. The problem with them is that they are usually stated negatively.

How can you sum up the whole of Christian ethics in a verse? How about the "Golden Rule"? The "Golden Rule" isn't meant to apply to everyone; "The Golden Rule presupposes discipleship that is submission to the rule of God (BBC, p.121)." Barclay calls this "the Everest of all ethical teaching (DSB, p. 273)."

The "Silver Rule" states, "Do not do unto others what you would not have them do to you" and was championed by Hillel, Gandhi and others. The good thing is that it doesn't require us to do anything; that is also the bad, may I say, the worse thing about it also.

When a rule is stated negatively, it is easier to follow. I can say, "If you want to be good, don't hit other people." If you follow that rule, you feel you can be a good person simply by not hitting others.

Unfortunately, you don't help people just by not doing something to or for them. "Do not" is a legal principle. "Do" is a Christian principle. It requires us to "do to others." "Do not" can be kept by a person with no love at all for his fellow man. The Golden Rule requires action.

If we follow Jesus' admonition, we must again seek to understand people from their viewpoint. The question is not, "What would I want to happen to me?" But, "If I were in his position, what would I want to happen to me?" That is what Jesus did for us. He asked, "If I needed a Savior, what would I want someone to do for me?" The answer cost Him His life.

James Cash Penny opened his first store in 1902 and called his store the "Golden Rule Store." Often it is suggested that following the Golden Rule would be good for your business, as it was for his, and for our social relationships. That may be true, but it shouldn't be our motivation. We behave like we do because it is a reflection of our heavenly Father's love. Everything we do should reflect that attitude. Paul indicated that in his admonition to Timothy. "The goal of this command is love, which comes from a pure heart and a good conscience and a sincere faith" (1 Tim. 1:5).

For many years there has been great debate about which is more important, preaching the gospel or meeting the physical needs of people who are lost? One of my favorite passages is the "sheep and goats" judgment scene found in Matthew 25:31-46. It has to be a thorny passage for many, because Jesus doesn't ask how many sermons we preached. He doesn't even ask how many accepted Him as Savior. The measure He uses is how we served. The entire book of James focuses on "doing."

The classic example of a neighbor is the "good Samaritan" found in Luke 10:25-37. Again, the yardstick used is ministry. These are examples of *agape* in practice. They are expressions of selflessness. But we will have to learn how to do it; we cannot just jump in and do it. The "heart' of the Law and the prophets is love! Because "Whoever does not love does not know God, because God is love." (1 John 4:8 NIV)

It's interesting to me that Luke places this section just before the command to love our enemies (Luke 6:31-36). Is there a connection?

Making Choices
Matthew 7:13-14

"Enter in by the narrow gate; for wide is the gate and broad is the way that leads to destruction, and many are those who enter in by it. [14] How (TR reads "Because") narrow is the gate, and restricted is the way that leads to life! Few are those who find it."

Matthew now gives us four warnings; the broad road (v. 13-14), the false prophets (v. 15-23), the false profession, (v. 21-23) and the foolish builder (v. 24-27). Stagg suggests that Matthew might have the *antinomian* threat (Christians who believed they didn't need to follow any laws or rules because they were now under grace) in mind (BBC, p. 121).

How easy is it to go to Heaven? It's as easy as making the right choice (singular, choice, not plural, choices). How hard is it to go to Heaven? It's as hard as not making the right choice. Again, our choices come down to two. Two choices that are as different as day and night, but that are often disguised to look the same. Two gates, two destinations. As Jeremiah said, "Furthermore, tell the people, 'This is what the

Lord says: See, I am setting before you the way of life and the way of death'" (Jer. 21:8). The same theme is followed in Deuteronomy 30:15-20 and Joshua 24:15.

You need to know where you want to go before you can select the way to get there. Therefore, the destination we desire must be determined <u>before</u> we select the gate. Fisher says, "...only determined self-discipline can lead to life (p. 146)." Do you seek life? Then select the gate that leads to life because all roads in the ancient world may "lead to Rome," but they don't all lead to Heaven.

Many people and religious doctrines suggest that all of us are trying to get to the same place: Heaven. We may all be "trying," but no matter how hard we try, if we aren't on the same, right road, we're going to end up in a different place. "Jesus answered, 'I am the way and the truth and the life. No one comes to the Father except though me'" (John 14:6). I'm sorry, He didn't say "a way," but "<u>the</u> way." Proverbs 14:12 warns, "There is a way that seems right to a man, but in the end it leads to death."

The gate that leads to eternal life (John 10:7-9) is called "narrow." This does not mean that it is difficult to become a Christian but that there is only *one* way to eternal life with God and that only a few decide to walk that road. Believing in Jesus is the only way to heaven, because he alone died for, our sins and made us right before God... (LASB, p. 1553).

We must be careful. "This plain declaration of Christ has been disregarded by many who have taken pains to explain it away... (MH)." "Religion easily becomes a rigid, legalistic system, stressing attainable goals or rules, whether ritual, doctrinal, ascetic or whatever (BBC, p.121)."

Barclay offers four differences in the two ways before us:

1. The difference between the "hard" and "easy" way. Greatness is the product of hard work. The "overnight success" often spends many years preparing. It isn't uncommon for a professional golfer to spend all day hitting balls to perfect his swing. A basketball player may shoot over 200 baskets before a game.

2. The difference between the "long" and the "short" way. We know that Plato wrote at least thirteen versions of the opening sentence to the *Republic*, because we have found them, and Thomas Gray spent eight years writing "Elegy written in a Country Churchyard".

3. The difference between the "disciplined" and "undisciplined" way. How many of us would like to be something great? What's the problem? We lack the discipline, the ability to stick-to-it.

4. The difference between the thoughtful and thoughtless way. This is the ability to look not just at this moment in time, but the future. What will be the effect on those to come? (DSB, pp.278-280).

Salvation requires "decision, commitment, and obedience to God (BBC, p. 121)."

On Fruit Inspection
Matthew 7:15-20

"Beware of false prophets, who come to you in sheep's clothing, but inwardly are ravening wolves. [16] *By their fruits you will know them. Do you gather grapes from thorns, or figs from thistles?* [17] *Even so, every good tree produces good fruit; but the corrupt tree produces evil fruit.* [18] *A good tree can't produce*

evil fruit, neither can a corrupt tree produce good fruit. [19] *Every tree that doesn't grow good fruit is cut down, and thrown into the fire.* [20] *Therefore by their fruits you will know them."*

Notice two things in this passage. First, He isn't talking about the scribes and Pharisees who never claimed to be prophets. Second, by prophet, He doesn't necessarily mean foretellers of the future; these are people posing as prophets who work from the inside, not the outside. The Jews knew about "false prophets," that they called "wolves." Jeremiah and others warned about them. Jesus warned the apostles, "For false Christs and false prophets will appear and perform signs and miracles to deceive the elect – if that were possible. So be on your guard; I have told you everything ahead of time" (Mark 13:22-23).

> False prophets were common in Old Testament times… False teachers are just as common today. Jesus says to beware of those whose words sound religious but who are motivated by money, fame, or power. You can tell who they are because in their teaching they minimize Christ and glorify themselves. (LASB, p. 1553).

Few people could read and the New Testament hadn't been written yet so preaching and teaching were very important in the early years of the church. When Paul listed the leadership in Ephesians 4:11-13, they were all communicators whose task was to "build up" the Church. In that passage the order is interesting "apostles," "prophets," "evangelists," and "pastors and teachers." After the ascension of the Lord, these people became the new, living word of God. Because of the importance of prophesy, "false prophets" began to arise. Peter and John expressed concern about the problem, 2 Peter 2:1 and 1 John 4:1-3. Paul listed discernment as the gift to help us identify false prophets in 1 Corinthians 12:8-10.

How do we identify "…false prophets"? Many occupations have distinctive costuming. Anyone dressing and acting like a doctor is assumed to be a doctor. Anyone dressing and acting like a prophet was assumed to be a prophet because they looked and acted like the real thing. Many were also sincere about what they taught and believed, but they were on the wrong road, some of them may even have been misled or poorly instructed Christians. The problem was that the source of their inspiration was not God, but Satan. Jesus said "…by their fruits you will know them."

In the New Testament, "fruit" isn't necessarily used as a metaphor for works and the fruit isn't identified by Jesus. Paul says, "...the fruit of the Spirit is love, joy, peace, patience, kindness, goodness, faithfulness, gentleness and self-control" (Gal. 5:22-23a). That may be the best place to start. See also Matthew 3:8 and John 15:1-10.

A "bad tree" isn't just a sick tree, but can mean the wrong kind of tree, "unclean," like the fish Matthew described, "When it was full, the fishermen pulled it up on the shore. Then they sat down and collected the good fish in baskets, but threw the bad away" (Matt. 13:48).

Life-style or character won't always identify them because a "true prophet" makes mistakes and a "false prophet" may appear to be righteous. The real test, according to Fisher, is the doctrine he teaches. He suggests three things that will characterize the teaching of a true prophet: it will be in harmony with the Scriptures; Christ will be central; it will lead people to know, love, and honor God in Christ (Fisher, p. 148).

As He usually did, Jesus drew His application from the things people were familiar with. The buckthorn had small berries that resembled grapes. There was also a thistle which had flowers that looked like figs. At a distance either of them could be easily confused, especially if you were hungry.

Jesus concludes with a warning: "Every tree that does not bear good fruit is cut down and thrown into the fire." This is the same warning John the Baptizer gave: "The ax is already at the root of the trees, and every tree that does not produce good fruit will be cut down and thrown into the fire" (Matt. 3:10).

Barclay gives five potential problems of false teachers. They teach:

1. A religion which consists solely or mainly in the observance of externals. The scribes and Pharisees did this. Obey the Law! Make the sacrifices! Pay the tithe!

2. A religion which consists of prohibitions. Based on "thou shalt nots." Don't dance! Don't go to movies! [But] the essence of Christianity is doing.

3. An easy religion. It removes the Cross, minimizes the voice of Christ, it pushes judgment into the background and makes men think lightly of sin.

4. A religion that divorces religion and life. This is what the monks did; a soldier of the Cross belongs in the battle.

5. A religion which is arrogant and separatist. Our task is tearing down walls, not building them up. Bringing men together, not driving them apart.

Put Your Money Where Your Mouth Is
Matthew 7:21-23

"Not everyone who says to me, 'Lord, Lord,' will enter into the Kingdom of Heaven; but he who does the will of my Father who is in heaven. 22 Many will tell me in that day, 'Lord, Lord, didn't we prophesy in your name, in your name cast out demons, and in your name do many mighty works?' 23 Then I will tell them, 'I never knew you. Depart from me, you who work iniquity.'"

This is an interesting passage because it appears that some of those who were rejected by Jesus in the judgment were people who both spoke and did good things Jesus condemned them for not "doing." The problem is that they were saying and doing their "thing," they weren't saying and doing "the will of my Father." We'll meet these people again in Matthew 25:31-46.

The proclamation "Lord, Lord..." was the basic confession of New Testament Christians:

…that if you confess with your mouth that Jesus is Lord, and believe in your heart that God raised him from the dead, you will be saved. For with your heart, one believes unto righteousness; and with the mouth confession is made unto salvation (Rom. 10:9-10).

Paul also tells us that that confession cannot be made without aid of the Holy Spirit, "Therefore I make known to you that no man speaking by God's Spirit says, 'Jesus is accursed.' No one can say, 'Jesus is Lord,' but by the Holy Spirit" (1 Cor. 12:3). However, that doesn't mean that a person cannot say the words. Proper confession comes from the heart, not the mouth, "The Lord said, 'Because this people draws near with their mouth and honors me with their lips, but they have removed their heart far from me, and their fear of me is a commandment of men which has been taught...'" (Isa. 29:13). Confession involves a changed life.

Jesus warned about "false prophets," now He looks at false miracle workers. Why were they a problem? Most people believed illnesses were caused by demons, therefore, healing came about by exorcism and these healers could make a good living traveling around "healing" people.

How could they do it? Today we recognize that many illnesses are psychosomatically caused. If someone can convince you they can help you, that they can heal you with a word, then they often can. Actually, they haven't done it, you have. Since Jesus was a popular healing figure, anyone using His name would be assumed to be just as effective.

"That day," is the Day of Judgment; the day all masks and disguises will be removed. Apparently, some used the name Jesus as a part of a magical formula, their "abracadabra," "But some of the itinerant Jews, exorcists, took on themselves to invoke over those who had the evil spirits the name of the Lord Jesus, saying, 'We adjure you by Jesus whom Paul preaches.'" (Acts 19:13). In that day, the use of a name implied they had the authority of the person whose name was used.

The question "didn't we?" is a request for acknowledgment that they were, in fact, ministering on Jesus' behalf. In 1 Corinthians 13:1-4, Paul warned us that it is possible to do miracles without the love of God in our lives. As always, the critical issue is attitude. Once again, more is required than just doing something. Jesus brushed aside any claim the usurpers put forth. In His banishment, he invoked Psalm 6:8 "Away from me, all you who do evil, for the Lord has heard my weeping." Jesus didn't want anything to do with those who didn't recognize Him as Lord.

Preparing for a Rainy Day
Matthew 7:24-29

"Everyone therefore who hears these words of mine, and does them, I will liken him to a wise man, who built his house on a rock. [25] The rain came down, the floods came, and the winds blew, and beat on that house; and it didn't fall, for it was founded on the rock. [26] Everyone who hears these words of mine, and doesn't do them will be like a foolish man, who built his house on the sand. [27] The rain came down, the floods came, and the winds blew, and beat on that house; and it fell - and great was its fall."

[28] When Jesus had finished saying these things, the multitudes were astonished at his teaching, [29]for he taught them with authority, and not like the scribes.

In this section, Jesus' topic is assurance. The answers to all the prior questions are brought together in this section. How can you be sure you're walking in the right way? Following the right prophets? Living the right kind of life? Doing the right acts of righteousness? "Practicing obedience becomes the solid foundation to weather the storms of life (LASB, p. 1554)."

In the prior section Jesus talked about saying and doing, now He discusses hearing and doing. Obedience is indispensable for discipleship. The differences between Matthew and Luke are relatively minor. Luke emphasizes the man "dug and went deep." (Also see Luke 6:47-49.)

The passage is another example of Jesus' familiarity with the Scriptures. "When the storm has swept by, the wicked are gone, but the righteous stand firm forever" (Pro. 10:25). It also shows that the lessons in carpentry He received from Joseph were well learned. There is also a study in the practical. Undoubtedly, He had seen buildings fall when shortsighted men had not properly prepared before beginning.

An interesting aspect of this particular discussion is that there doesn't seem to be any difference in the houses; the difference is the foundation. The "wise man" is the prudent, sensible, practical man who does the work properly. On the other hand, the "foolish man" is the stupid, sluggish man who throws up a building in a hurry. It's as much a character judgment as an intellectual valuation.

The problems that come into each of our lives are similar. Dealing with the in-laws. Making a living. Raising children. Handling medical problems. There is no exemption or special consideration for Christians. If anything, there are additional pressures on the Christian. To tithe or not to tithe. To lead a small group or not.

The results should be different. Why? Because the foundation is different. Fisher makes two applications: the claim of Jesus that people ignore His teaching to their own peril and Jesus' words must be obeyed; not debated (Fisher, p. 153).

Jeremiah recorded these words of God:

This is what the Lord says: "Cursed is the one who trusts in man, who depends on flesh for his strength and whose heart turns away from the Lord. He will be like a bush in the wastelands; he will not see prosperity when it comes. He will dwell in the parched places of the desert, in a salt land where no one lives. But blessed is the man who trusts in the Lord, whose confidence is in him. He will be like a tree planted by the water that sends out its roots by the stream. It does not fear when heat comes; its leaves are always green. It has no worries in a year of drought and never fails to bear fruit" (Jer. 17:5-8).

As he concludes the Sermon on the Mount, Matthew says: "the multitudes were astonished at his teaching, for He taught them with authority, and not like the scribes" Do we come away with the same amazement or have we heard the "stories" so many times our senses are dulled? If we have a problem in our generation, it is that of hearing. I don't mean listening, I mean hearing. There are so many competing voices: radio, TV, politicians, theologians, the internet, do we tend to close our ears so tightly that we can't even hear the voice of Jesus?

Touching a Life!
Matthew 8:1-4

When he came down from the mountain, great multitudes followed him. ² Behold, a leper came to him and worshiped him, saying, "Lord, if you want to, you can make me clean."

³ Jesus stretched out his hand, and touched him, saying, "I want to. Be made clean." Immediately his leprosy was cleansed. ⁴ Jesus said to him, "See that you tell nobody, but go, show yourself to the priest, and offer the gift that Moses commanded, as a testimony to them."

Having finished the first of five discourses, Matthew inserts a narrative consisting of ten miracles in chapter 8 and four events in chapter 9. Jesus' teaching in the Sermon on the Mount was "with authority." In this section He continues to show that authority, this time by His actions.

Most of Jesus' miracles showed His compassion for those who were hurting. Faith was usually a prerequisite of healing, but not for those which exercised control over nature or demons. There is no doubt Jesus healed people, both His friends and His enemies agreed. The only question was about the source of His power.

It's interesting that Matthew chose to report on the healing of a leper as the first person Jesus healed. "Leprosy…was a terrifying disease because there was no known cure (LABS, p. 1554)." In spite of the fact that lepers were barred from all social life (Lev. 13:45-46) and only touching a dead body was more defiling than touching a leper, Jesus still reached out to touch this man. "Sin is also an incurable disease - and we all have it. Only Christ's healing touch can miraculously take away our sins and restore us to real living (LASB, p. 1554)."

Every skin problem from simple dermatitis, like ringworm and psoriasis, to the disease we know as leprosy were all classed together and included in the same group with leprosy. True leprosy lasts from nine to thirty years, with parts for the body dying and dropping off; it ends in mental decay, coma and death. It is a death by inches.

There are two surprising elements in this event. First, the leper approached Jesus, how close he came we do not know but it was close enough for Jesus to hear him; second, Jesus reached out and touched him, which was forbidden by the Law, common sense, and practice. Barclay notes three things about the leper's approach:

1. He came with confidence. He would not have approached a scribe or Rabbi because he would have been stoned.

2. He came with humility. He didn't demand, but recognized Jesus' power over disease.

3. He came with reverence. He "knelt [KJV]" before him. The word used, *prokunein*, is only used in Greek in relation to worship of the gods (DSB, p. 298).

The Greek word *kurios* is a common form of address for Jesus in the gospels and is appropriately translated "lord," but should probably be translated "sir" most of the time.

How did Jesus respond? The way He always did, with compassion, "Being moved with compassion, he stretched out his hand, and touched him, and said to him, 'I want to. Be made clean'" (Mark 1:41). To prevent the spread of leprosy, the Law forbade physical contact with lepers but the law of love often requires us to go against our natural inclination. Jesus didn't do this to attract attention, quite the opposite; he did it because the man needed healing.

In this case, as in many others, He asked for no publicity but in Mark 1:45, he, the leper, "…went out, and began to proclaim it much …" Often Jesus told the people He healed not to tell what had happened, but they did anyway. Why keep quiet? Jesus didn't heal for show or fame, but because people needed healing. Some have suggested that if He became too well known, it could have brought His ministry to a conclusion before its time, I am not one of those people. Jesus handled other attempts to kill Him without any problem and I believe He could have handled this also.

Some even suggest that Jesus was using reverse psychology, wanting those He healed to tell others. That kind of manipulation would not only be repulsive, it would be sinful!

Jesus could have spoken the cure, but He reached out and touched him. In spite of the statement "immediately," some feel the healing wasn't instantaneous, but took place as he was on his way to Jerusalem as was the case with Naaman, 2 Kings 5:1-14 and the ten lepers, Luke 17:12-14. Why do they think that? I honestly don't know! When the Bible says it, I have a tendency to accept it. Why Jerusalem? Jerusalem was the only place the proper offering, described in Leviticus 14, could be made.

What does Jesus mean "as a testimony to them"? To whom? The people? The Jewish establishment? Whomever, it does indicate that Jesus is <u>not</u> attempting to overturn the Law.

Faith of a Foreigner
Matthew 8:5-13

When he came into Capernaum, a centurion came to him, asking him, ⁶ and saying, "Lord, my servant lies in the house paralyzed, grievously tormented."

⁷ Jesus said to him, "I will come and heal him."

⁸ The centurion answered, "Lord, I'm not worthy for you to come under my roof. Just say the word, and my servant will be healed. ⁹ For I am also a man under authority, having under myself soldiers. I tell this one, 'Go,' and he goes; and tell another, 'Come,' and he comes; and tell my servant, 'Do this,' and he does it."

¹⁰ When Jesus heard it, he marveled, and said to those who followed, "Most certainly I tell you, I haven't found so great a faith, not even in Israel. ¹¹ I tell you that many will come from the east and the west, and will sit down with Abraham, Isaac, and Jacob in the Kingdom of Heaven, ¹² but the children of the Kingdom will be thrown out into the outer darkness. There will be weeping and gnashing of teeth." ¹³ Jesus said to the centurion, "Go your way. Let it be done for you as you have believed." His servant was healed in that hour.

While Matthew and Luke change the circumstances of this event, the dialogue and emphasis are almost identical. The main point here isn't the healing but the faith of a Gentile, who was a Roman centurion. A centurion was career military officer, and… "of all people, were hated by the Jews for their oppression, control and ridicule (LASB, p. 1555)."

He was the commander of about a hundred men; a Roman legion was made up of 6,000 men divided into sixty centuries of one hundred men (plus or minus) each. The centurion was a professional soldier responsible for making the army what it was. That they were among the very best men in the army is witnessed by the fact that each one mentioned in the New Testament is spoken of with honor.

This man was special. How do we know? By the centurion's attitude toward his ill servant, who was probably a slave! His point of view is opposite that of most slave owners, whose concern would be more for the loss of a "tool" than with the suffering of a human being. "Jesus told the crowd that many religious Jews, who should be in the Kingdom, would be excluded because of their lack of faith (LASB, p. 1555)" and inferred that this Roman soldier, and other Gentiles, would not be excluded. Matthew emphasizes the universality of Christianity, something Isaiah and Malachi prophesied but the New Testament Jewish leaders ignored. Everyone must decide for themselves, God has no grandchildren…

In Luke's presentation, we discover the Jews respected him so much they made the request for the centurion, who had built a synagogue and respected their nationality. This also would be somewhat in opposition to the attitude toward many foreign rulers and of the Jews themselves toward outsiders. These may be some of the reasons Jesus was willing to go to his home, even though he was not a Jew. Jesus made it clear; it is not the label; it is the content that matters. "...the man who cares for men is always near to Jesus Christ (DSB, p. 302)."

Another unusual thing about this man is his faith; these actions are evidence of that faith. It would be natural that he would know about the Jewish religious laws and customs. But those laws, actually rabbinic custom, wouldn't, and never did, stop Jesus, however the centurion didn't know that. He only knew that his servant was sick and Jesus could heal him.

We live in an "age of reason," we have been taught to believe anything that can be proven. There isn't anything wrong with that attitude but, do you realize that faith is the driving force behind reason? It was faith in the idea that polio could be prevented that drove researchers to find a vaccine. When we lose faith that is when we give up.

To "sit down with Abraham, Isaac, and Jacob in the Kingdom of Heaven" refers to the banquet the Jews expected to take place when the Messiah came at the end of the age. They looked forward to it with great anticipation, but never thought a gentile could be included, because they believed the gentiles would have been destroyed by then. "For that nation and kingdom that will not serve you shall perish; yes, those nations shall be utterly wasted." (Isa. 60:12).

While "children of the Kingdom" is a good translation of the literal "sons," it doesn't carry the play on words the Greek does. The Jews thought they would be alright because of their family connection. The implication of Jesus' words is "they will be disinherited" and their "estate" will go to someone else...the sinners and gentiles...

Jesus spoke the word and the man was healed. Isn't it interesting; He could have spoken the cure for the leper, but He reached out and touched him? He could have gone to the home of the centurion, but He healed him with a word. Jesus always seems to do what people needed, not what they expected.

Healing Peter's Mother-in-Law
Matthew 8:14-17

When Jesus came into Peter's house, he saw his wife's mother lying sick with a fever. [15] He touched her hand, and the fever left her. She got up and served him. (TR reads "them" instead of "him") [16] When evening came, they brought to him many possessed with demons. He cast out the spirits with a word, and healed all who were sick; [17] that it might be fulfilled which was spoken through Isaiah the prophet, saying, "He took our infirmities, and bore our diseases" (Isa. 53:4).

Capernaum, and Peter's home, seem to be Jesus' unofficial headquarters for His ministry in the area. According to Mark this incident occurred on the Sabbath after Jesus had delivered a demon possessed man. Mark 1:29-34 and Luke 4:38-41 relate the same incident.

Was Peter married? What happened to his wife? The only other reference we have about her is "Have we no right to take along a wife who is a believer, even as the rest of the apostles, and the brothers of the Lord, and Cephas?" (1 Cor. 9:5) That, coupled with this passage about his mother-in-law, indicates that he certainly was married. What happened to her we don't know for sure, but Clement of Alexandra said they were martyred together.

Malaria and typhoid were serious problems in that area of the world, so one of those could have been the problem. The fact that Jesus saw Peter's mother-in-law when He entered the house probably indicated that it was a typical one room house. This also means that everyone there would have been able to see the miracle. Mark, who probably got his information from Peter, says Jesus "…took her by the hand and raised her up."

This passage again indicates that Jesus wasn't just concerned with redemption of the soul, but redemption from disease also. There was no period of recuperation; the cure was instantaneous and complete and she was able to immediately begin serving. Everyone has something to do; how do you use the gifts God has given you?

When word got out that Jesus had healed Peter's mother-in-law, the people came with their sick friends and family members. It had already been a long day, but it didn't seem to matter to Jesus. As long as there were people who needed His help, He never seemed to be too tired to give it. We too must serve as long as there are people who need ministry.

Who Should Bury the Dead?
Matthew 8:18-22

Now when Jesus saw great multitudes around him, he gave the order to depart to the other side.

19 A scribe came, and said to him, "Teacher, I will follow you wherever you go."

20 Jesus said to him, "The foxes have holes, and the birds of the sky have nests, but the Son of Man has nowhere to lay his head."

21 Another of his disciples said to him, "Lord, allow me first to go and bury my father."

22 But Jesus said to him, "Follow me, and leave the dead to bury their own dead."

There are always people who are attracted to spectacular events. From this and other passages we see that Jesus was often mobbed by the local people and He often withdrew from the crowds who had come to see the "show" or to just have their own needs met.

One of the strange things about Jesus was His toughness toward those who wanted to become His disciple; it's almost as if He didn't want people to follow Him. "The *teachers of religious law* [the scribe] had a prestigious vocation of preserving, learning, and interpreting the Scriptures for the good of society. The way to God was thought to be through them (NLTSB, p. 1592)." However, the statement in verse 21, "Another of his disciples…" as well as the use of "Lord" to address Jesus suggests that the scribe was already a disciple.

Often, we are guilty of convincing people to join a cause when they didn't really want to belong. We're excited about the group and its goals, so we bring everyone we can in. Unfortunately, they often don't share our zeal.

Jesus wanted followers, but not at any cost. To follow Jesus meant to give up self. For a scribe to call someone "teacher" was the supreme complement. Jesus was being honest in His enlistment of His followers, but here is a scribe, a teacher of the law, who wants to become a follower. This was a great opportunity for Jesus to pick up an educated man, trained in the law; who better to make some exceptions for than this man?

It has been suggested that the homelessness Jesus spoke about applied to more than just a home to sleep in. He may be speaking of another home; the home of their traditions. Jesus was in the process of forcing the Jews to make an examination of their traditions and this scribe would no longer have the safety of his traditions to retreat into (IB, p. 344).

"Son of Man" appears about 80 times in the Gospels and 31 are in Matthew. It is used in Ezekiel, often in reference to the coming Messiah, more than 90 times and Isaiah uses it also. In the New Testament, it appears to be Jesus' favorite title for Himself because we only find it in words attributed to Him. While it often has Messianic implications, it can also be applied to any man. "Jesus did not use "Son of Man" to distinguish his humanity from his deity ("Son of God"); by using this title, Jesus could define himself as Messiah on his own terms." (NLTSB, p. 1593).

On the surface, "Lord, allow me first to go and bury my father" seems to be a reasonable request.

If *another of his disciples* in verse 21 is interpreted strictly it would be necessary to suppose that the *certain scribe* of verse 19 was either already a disciple when he made his rash assertion, or became one later. …The second man…appears to be anxious to postpone committing himself to the full implications of his vocation till after the funeral of his father, who may be dead already or expected to die soon (TNTC, p. 90, 91).

In Judaism there was no greater obligation on a son than the proper burial of his parents. It was so sacred that a man was even excused from saying the Shema and priests were allowed to desecrate themselves for this purpose.

Because burial took place on the day of death, the problem here is that the father probably isn't dead yet; if the father were already dead, he would have been buried before the man came to hear Jesus. This then becomes a request for deferred discipleship; some day in the future, after my father dies, I want to become a follower.

Another interesting aspect is that in many religions, including Judaism, when a family member deserts the family religion, there is often a funeral and the individual is declared dead and loses his inheritance. Jesus' demand is to place God above family. "He who loves father or mother more than me is not worthy of me; and he who loves son or daughter more than me isn't worthy of me. He who doesn't take his cross and follow after me, isn't worthy of me" (Matt. 10:37-38).

When Jesus said, "leave the dead to bury their own dead," He certainly didn't mean we have no obligation to our families. He was probably reminding us to "…seek first God's Kingdom, and his righteousness; and all these things will be given to you as well." (Matt. 6:33).

Power over Nature
Matthew 8:23-27

When he got into a boat, his disciples followed him.[24] *Behold, a violent storm came up on the sea, so much that the boat was covered with the waves, but he was asleep.* [25] *They came to him, and woke him up, saying, "Save us, Lord! We are dying!"*

[26] *He said to them, "Why are you fearful, O you of little faith?" Then he got up, rebuked the wind and the sea, and there was a great calm.*

[27] *The men marveled, saying, "What kind of man is this, that even the wind and the sea obey him?"*

Both Matthew and Luke shorten Mark's version of this story of Jesus' power over nature. Healing was one thing, they had seen many healers, but commanding nature was something else, no one had been able to control nature.

The fact that Jesus was asleep should not surprise us. Most people don't realize how much physical and emotional energy is involved in ministry. I can assure you that if it is done right, ministry can be exhausting. He had been working very hard; as He always did, teaching and healing. People followed Him everywhere, or arrived as soon as word got out that He was there. He didn't get much time off.

Storms of this type were normal on the Sea of Galilee which is 680 feet below sea level and surrounded by mountains that funnel the wind down onto the small lake. The words translated "violent storm" is *seismos* which can mean earthquake. In Luke's presentation, "squall" can be translated whirlwind, which better represents the nature of this kind of storm; we might call it a microburst or a tornado. Several have said that the wind on the lake seems to come from everywhere.

This particular passage was probably allegorized by the early Christians to show that Jesus could protect His followers in any kind of storm; natural, political, or whatever. While we must be careful in allegorizing Scripture, Jesus is truly with us, no matter what storm rages in our lives.

The question, "What kind of man is this?" can also mean "where did this man come from?" Could a mere human have this kind of power? Remember that Jesus said? "For most certainly I tell you, if you have faith as a grain of mustard seed, you will tell this mountain, 'Move from here to there,' and it will move; and nothing will be impossible for you" (Matt. 17:20b).

We might think the disciples, who were fishermen, would take this more in stride; surely they had been in these storms while fishing, but apparently they were like most of the Jews, who had no navy or merchant marine, and were afraid of sailing so they relied on others for their shipping needs. For them heaven was described as a place with "no more sea" (IB, p. 345).

We cannot overemphasize the need for faith. Faith doesn't necessarily change the outcome, but it sure can change the effect on the one undergoing the trial. The storm may continue to rage around us, but we can have peace within.

Casting out Demons
Matthew 8:28-34

When he came to the other side, into the country of the Gergesenes, (NU reads "Gadarenes") two people possessed by demons met him there, coming out of the tombs, exceedingly fierce, so that nobody could pass that way. [29] Behold, they cried out, saying, "What do we have to do with you, Jesus, Son of God? Have you come here to torment us before the time?" [30] Now there was a herd of many pigs feeding far away from them. [31] The demons begged him, saying, "If you cast us out, permit us to go away into the herd of pigs."

[32] He said to them, "Go!"

They came out, and went into the herd of pigs: and behold, the whole herd of pigs rushed down the cliff into the sea, and died in the water. [33] Those who fed them fled, and went away into the city, and told everything, including what happened to those who were possessed with demons. [34] Behold, all the city came out to meet Jesus. When they saw him, they begged that he would depart from their borders.

Again, we see that Matthew and Luke have shortened Mark's account. One of Mark's favorite subjects involves demons recognizing Jesus as the Son of God when humans don't. It's strange that Matthew omits what we might consider the most important element of the Mark account, the man "…sitting, clothed, and in his right mind… (Mark 5:15b).

One historical problem is where this miracle actually took place. Mark and Luke set it in the region of the Gerasenes while Matthew has Gadarenes and he has two men. The best guess seems to be that the city Matthew knew best was Gadara, so he used that city. Mark and Luke are probably more accurate; however, there were several cities in the area on the eastern side of the lake that could meet the requirements.

When Jesus crossed the lake; He also crossed national and racial lines to heal a Gentile and this isn't just any Gentile, he's an insane man who was feared by most people and pitied by few. LASB points out that the men were unclean in three ways: they were Gentiles, they were demon possessed, and they lived in a cemetery (p. 1556).

As we have discussed, ancient people lived in fear of demons overtaking them at any time. They believed that millions of them lived in the air; there were so many of them that it was thought to be impossible to stick a needle into the air without hitting one. For them demons caused almost every medical problem known (DSB, p. 320).

Today Christians are divided: some believe in demons and some don't, others opt strictly for psychology. They might say the man was manic and suicidal, and certainly he may have been, but Jesus didn't deny the reality of demons and neither should we. And "…when Jesus comes, demons must go (BBC, p. 127)."

The question, "What do you want with us?" is really more a question of "What do we have to do with each other?" Whatever is meant, Jesus freed us from the fear of all kinds of demons (BBC, p. 127).

Jews didn't keep swine and this was Gentile territory, so there's no reason to think that these people were Jews, but much stress has been placed on the destruction of private property, the pigs. We should leave the question to God's judgment but He probably places the value of a person above that of any animal.

However, it is clear that Jesus cared more about one man than a whole herd of pigs...have we gotten it backwards today...

It is a good bet that the townspeople did not want Jesus to leave because of their economic loss. More likely in their world, a man who could command demons might send those demons to attack them. This could be the reason Jesus left the demoniac there, so he could be a missionary to his own people.

The Faith of Friends
Matthew 9:1-8

He entered into a boat, and crossed over, and came into his own city. [2] Behold, they brought to him a man who was paralyzed, lying on a bed. Jesus, seeing their faith, said to the paralytic, "Son, cheer up! Your sins are forgiven you."

[3] Behold, some of the scribes said to themselves, "This man blasphemes."

[4] Jesus, knowing their thoughts, said, "Why do you think evil in your hearts? [5] For which is easier, to say, 'Your sins are forgiven;' or to say, 'Get up, and walk?' [6] But that you may know that the Son of Man has authority on earth to forgive sins..." (then he said to the paralytic), "Get up, and take up your mat, and go to your house."

[7] He arose and departed to his house. [8] But when the multitudes saw it, they marveled and glorified God, who had given such authority to men.

It is suggested that this is the same healing reported in Mark 2:1-12 and Luke 5:17-26. If it isn't, there are certainly enough similarities, especially in Mark, that most commentators treat them all as the same event.

His "own city" was Capernaum, a wealthy city involved in fishing and trading on the Sea of Galilee. It had a large population and a Roman garrison to keep the peace. "The city was a cultural melting pot, greatly influenced by Greek and Roman manners, dress, architecture, and politics (LASB, p. 1557)."

Everything Matthew reports is designed for a specific purpose. Barclay lists four charges leveled at Jesus in chapter nine: blasphemy—curing by forgiving sins; immorality—hanging out with the wrong group; impiety—did not go through the orthodox motions related to the scribal law; and in league with the devil—working miracles with the power of the devil not God (DSB, pp. 324-5).

Among the first words Jesus said to the paralyzed were "Your sins are forgiven." ...Both the man's body and his spirit were paralyzed—he could not walk, and he did not know Jesus. But the man's spiritual state was Jesus' first concern (LASB, p. 1557).

Blasphemy is "to speak wickedly: and among the more eloquent Greeks, to slander (GN)." You may recall that in Judaism, it was a capital offence. The Pharisees would not even use God's name lest they inadvertently used it improperly. The Jewish leaders recognized that Jesus was claiming to be God, and, to them, that was blasphemous; for Him, it was truth. And, Jesus backed up His claim by healing the invalid.

While we can't make decisions for others, we can do everything possible to help them. This seems to be the situation with the "friends;" they couldn't heal the man, but they could bring him to Jesus.

Why did Jesus begin with the man's sin? Possibly because people then, as now, believed that sickness was often caused by sin. They also felt that the greater the sickness, the greater the sin. We cannot doubt that sin causes sickness, but there isn't necessarily a direct cause and effect relationship between them either.

Another reason for beginning with the sin could have been to prepare for the forgiveness. If the man believed his sins were forgiven, it could break the sin cycle holding him in the prison of his infirmity and that would require faith. The friends had faith, was it sufficient for him also?

In Jesus' day, it was considered to be easier to forgive sin than to heal disease. After all, how would we know if they were actually forgiven? But there was a problem, only God could forgive sins and "…breaking the power and dominion of sin and of the dominion of evil is one of the signs of the dawning of the Kingdom (AB, p. 102)." None of the Rabbis would consider giving this kind of absolution. Jesus assumed that authority and confirmed His divinity. If the man actually got up that would be ample evidence that his sins had been forgiven and that Jesus had the authority to forgive those sins.

Because of our great advances in health care, and our lack of desire to forgive others, the opposite may be true today. Remember, we need to forgive others. In the Catholic tradition, forgiveness follows confession, but there is no indication of any confession on the part of this man. Scripture to support their position include: "If you forgive anyone's sins, they have been forgiven them. If you retain anyone's sins, they have been retained" (John 20:23). And

> Now I also forgive whomever you forgive anything. For if indeed I have forgiven anything, I have forgiven that one for your sakes in the presence of Christ, that no advantage may be gained over us by Satan; for we are not ignorant of his schemes. (2 Cor. 2:10-11).

Response to the Challenge
Matthew 9:9-13

As Jesus passed by from there, he saw a man called Matthew sitting at the tax collection office. He said to him, "Follow me." He got up and followed him. [10] As he sat in the house, behold, many tax collectors and sinners came and sat down with Jesus and his disciples. [11] When the Pharisees saw it, they said to his disciples, "Why does your teacher eat with tax collectors and sinners?"

[12] When Jesus heard it, he said to them, "Those who are healthy have no need for a physician, but those who are sick do. [13] But you go and learn what this means: 'I desire mercy, and not sacrifice,' (Hosea 6:6) for I came not to call the righteous, but sinners to repentance" (NU omits "to repentance").

Have you noticed the many boundaries Jesus has already crossed? He is not through yet! In extending His hand to Matthew (Levi) He again went against tradition and common sense. For the Pharasees, there couldn't have been a less likely prospect for discipleship than a tax collector. Because they collected public funds, tax collectors were called "publican" from Latin *publicani*. The right to collect taxes in an area was auctioned off. Anything over the auction amount was the collector's pay. The system was rife with abuse because the rates weren't known and the amount collected was based more on what the collector could get from the individual than what was fair or required.

Three set taxes were commonly collected. One, a land tax of 10% of the grain or 20% of the fruit, paid in cash or produce. Two, an income tax of 1% of income. Three, a poll tax on males from 14 to 65 and women from 12 to 65.

In addition, there were taxes for: imports and exports from 2½% to 12½%; toll road fees (yes, they existed way back then!) and bridge fees; fees for entering market places and harbors; pack animals and wheels and axles on carts were taxed; sales taxes on goods bought and sold; and government-controlled items. Sound familiar? It's no wonder these men were hated by everyone.

A creative tax collector could do much with these and other "taxes" at his "disposal." When I was Tail Twister of Prescott Sunrise Lions Club, I usually came up with a fine for everyone in attendance, it was my job, and I did it with great relish, however, I didn't get to keep the money myself. In Jewish law they were considered unclean and barred from the synagogues and Temple and, since they were presumed to be dishonest, they weren't allowed to testify in court.

One thing Jesus may have seen that everyone overlooked was Matthew's ability with the pen and his years of conniving that would have honed his thinking skill and were translated into this book we are studying. Because of his dealing with peoples, he possible spoke several languages. In my opinion, Matthew was probably the best trained and educated of the original twelve apostles. "…when Christ called him. He left it [tax collecting], and though we find the disciples, who were fishers, occasionally fishing again afterwards, we never more find Matthew at his sinful gain (MH)."

The word "sinners" was also used to describe a special group of people, the "people of the land" we have discussed before. These were

…those who either could not because of ignorance, or would not because of the intolerable burden involved, observe the intricacies of the Jewish law as elaborated by the tradition of the scribes. (TNTC, p. 97).

Many of the things Jesus did were shocking to the orthodox who tried so hard to keep the law that they destroyed the message it contained. You already know they separated people into two groups, Jews and Gentiles. They also divided Jews into two groups, those who tried to keep the minutia of the scribal law and "people of the land." If you wanted to maintain your status, you weren't allowed to travel with or do business with or entertain or allow the people of the land to entertain you. Barclay lists three problems with their view:

1. Like a doctor who won't take care of the sick lest he becomes sick; they were more concerned with maintaining their own holiness than with helping a sinner come to God.

2. Like a doctor who looks at a serious injury and turns away in repulsion instead of helping the injured person; they were more concerned with criticism than encouragement.

3. Like a doctor more concerned with diagnosis than healing; they pointed out the sins of others instead of helping them overcome them; condemnation rather than forgiveness (DSB, p. 334-5).

Jesus categorically rejected this attitude in the statement, "Those who are healthy have no need for a physician, but those who are sick do." For Him, there was no difference between the sacred and the secular; all was sacred and all was secular. Jesus didn't wait for men to come to Him, He went to them. "He not only received sinners; he sought them out! (BBC, p. 129)."

In stating, "I came not to call the righteous, but sinners to repentance," Jesus implies that all are sinners. His quotation is found in Hosea 6:6 "For I desire mercy, and not sacrifice; and the knowledge of God more than burnt offerings." Not only does it point out the need for an attitude adjustment but it is a favorite of His because it points out the importance of attitude over actions.

When to Leave the Past
Matthew 9:14-17

Then John's disciples came to him, saying, "Why do we and the Pharisees fast often, but your disciples don't fast?"

[15] Jesus said to them, "Can the friends of the bridegroom mourn, as long as the bridegroom is with them? But the days will come when the bridegroom will be taken away from them, and then they will fast. [16] No one puts a piece of unshrunk cloth on an old garment; for the patch would tear away from the garment, and a worse hole is made. [17] Neither do people put new wine into old wine skins, or else the skins would burst, and the wine be spilled, and the skins ruined. No, they put new wine into fresh wine skins, and both are preserved."

Weekly fasting was expected of "good" Jews, but the only required fasts were *Yom Kippur* and days proclaimed fast days because of some disaster (like famine). As we have seen, the Pharisees fasted twice each week and on other occasions when they felt it would show their "righteousness." We have already seen in Matthew 6:16-18 that Jesus wasn't opposed to fasting, but He wanted fasting to be motivated by need; not the calendar or a desire to "prove" something.

The analogy of the wedding is a good one. The couple didn't go away on a honeymoon like we do, but stayed home seven days and held "open house." They were treated like royalty! They, and their "attendants," were exempt from many religious obligations, including fasting, for the seven days that made up the wedding celebration.

It would be somewhat natural for us to consider Jesus to be the bridegroom, because He is the cause for rejoicing to all who know Him as Savior. This is also the first indication in the Gospels that Jesus knew that sooner or later, He would be put to death and His disciples would be left to mourn.

At first glance there doesn't seem to be a connection between verses 15, 16 and 17 and we might wonder why Matthew put them together. After the grapes were crushed, the juice was put into specially prepared, new wine skins to ferment, which would stretch the skins. It was common practice to keep good, used wine skins to transfer wine from broken or cracked skins. The skins are only a vessel, they aren't the end and they could be changed as necessary. Jesus knew His message would be difficult to accept because, like us, the Jews liked things just the way they were. They saw changes not as just mistakes, but as sin. They did everything they could to protect the Law which is why the Scribal laws developed. But a new order was dawning and it was going to be impossible to continue to "do church" the way they were doing it.

Jesus used this description to explain that he had not come to patch up the old religious system of Judaism with its rules and traditions. His purpose was to bring in something new… This new message, the Good News, said that Jesus Christ, God's Son, came to earth to offer all people forgiveness of sins and reconciliation with God. The Good News did not fit into the old rigid legalistic system of religion (LASB, p. 1559).

The Church often continues in that attitude today. The seven last words of orthodoxy, then and now are: "We never did it that way before." Most people made the adjustment from kerosene lamps to electric lights, but don't want anyone to mess with the Sunday school or worship service.

Think about it, in the last two hundred years, we've changed the way we do everything in our lives, but we still worship almost the same way we believe our congregations did back then. Is the form of worship a wine skin that can and should be changed from time to time? Congregations that have changed the form of their worship and outreach, not the message, have continued to reach people and grow, but those that have not made the change, have not.

Barclay sheds some light on that, "We read God's word to 20th century men and women in Elizabethan English, and seek to present the needs of the 20th century man and woman to God in prayer language which is four hundred years old." "...the Church dare not be the only institution which lives in the past (DSB, pp. 339-40)." ...and it's been another 70 years since he wrote that...

The Importance of Faith
Matthew 9:18-26

While he told these things to them, behold, a ruler came and worshiped him, saying, "My daughter has just died, but come and lay your hand on her, and she will live."

[19] *Jesus got up and followed him, as did his disciples.* [20] *Behold, a woman who had an issue of blood for twelve years came behind him, and touched the fringe (or, tassel) of his garment;* [21] *for she said within herself, "If I just touch his garment, I will be made well."*

[22] *But Jesus, turning around and seeing her, said, "Daughter, cheer up! Your faith has made you well." And the woman was made well from that hour.*

[23] *When Jesus came into the ruler's house, and saw the flute players, and the crowd in noisy disorder,* [24] *he said to them, "Make room, because the girl isn't dead, but sleeping."*

They were ridiculing him. [25] *But when the crowd was put out, he entered in, took her by the hand, and the girl arose.* [26] *The report of this went out into all that land.*

In this story within a story, it is hard to decide which is more important. Possibly the main message is the need for faith in Jesus, not necessarily as Savior, but as healer. Mark and Luke give a little more coverage.

This woman "who had an issue of blood for twelve years" had a very humiliating and serious health problem. And, because of her condition, she was considered unclean and excluded from all religious activity. This is possibly why she "came up behind him." Her touch would have made Him "unclean."

There can be little doubt that Jesus was being touched, there was a crowd moving along, following Him. But one of them had a driving need, the need to be healed. It was she and she alone who thought, "If I just touch his garment, I will be made well." In doing so, she is probably proclaiming more a superstitious faith than a faith in God.

When she wanted to "touch his garment" she was reaching for the tassels, made up of four knotted threads, which hung at the four corners of a Jew's cloak. The tassels were meant to remind them of their special relationship with God. Barclay reports that in times of persecution, the tassels were worn on undergarments and later only on prayer shawls.

The phrase "Your faith has made you well" is the same Greek word translated "saved." In the Jewish mind, salvation relates to the whole person, including the physical body, and Jesus' ministry was always to the whole person: body, mind, and spirit.

The resurrection of this girl isn't the only resurrection event recorded in the Bible. Elijah (1 Kings 17:17-24), Elisha (2 Kings 4:17-37), and Peter (Acts 9:36-42) also raised people from the dead and Jesus raised Lazarus (John 11:11-15) and the son of the widow of Nain (Luke 7:14). In each of those incidents, except the raising of Lazarus, the crowd was made to leave.

In picking up the details from Mark and Luke we learn the man was probably the ruler, the *archisynagogos*, who wasn't a priest or a rabbi but a "layman" chosen as the leader of the synagogue and was named Jairus. He would be in charge of the synagogue service and of the business of the synagogue and was elected by the elders. He would need to be very careful what he did because people would be watching him and he would probably go to Jesus only as a last resort. He must have had great faith in Jesus' ability to work miracles, because we have no record of any similar event prior to this. As with everyone, Jesus treated him with respect and didn't "lord it over" him. "Christ can [still] make a difference when it seems too late for anyone else to help (LASB, p. 1559)."

Everyone wonders if the little girl was really dead? As far as they could determine, she was. There is ample evidence that people in comas were buried, but they didn't have the sophisticated equipment we have to make the judgment. Whether she was actually dead or not, Jesus saved her from death, because she would be buried shortly. There were no known signs of life, so they assumed she was dead and brought in the mourners and flutes. Mourning was very serious in Judaism. Three customs were expected to be followed.

1. Tearing the clothes. The tear was over the heart and big enough to put the fist into. It was left open seven days, then loosely stitched for thirty days, then repaired. Women reversed the inner garment to avoid exposing their breasts.

2. Wailing, not just weeping. There were then, and there are now, professional mourners in the Near East. When you came into the home, they would immediately begin wailing and, if possible, calling the names of your departed relatives to bring you into distress also.

3. Flute players. The flute was associated with death throughout the Mediterranean. The *Talmud* required at least two flute players and one mourner for a dead wife. Roman law limited flutes to ten for anyone who died.

In Greek and English, the word sleep is used to describe death and cemetery comes from *kiometerion* meaning a place where people sleep.

Faith and Follow Through
Matthew 9:27-31

As Jesus passed by from there, two blind men followed him, calling out and saying, "Have mercy on us, son of David!"

28 When he had come into the house, the blind men came to him. Jesus said to them, "Do you believe that I am able to do this?"

They told him, "Yes, Lord."

29 Then he touched their eyes, saying, "According to your faith be it done to you." 30 Their eyes were opened. Jesus strictly commanded them, saying, "See that no one knows about this." 31 But they went out and spread abroad his fame in all that land.

There is no direct Scripture parallel, but there are similar passages in Matthew 20:29-34, Mark 10:46-52, and Luke 18:35-43. We'll look at them when we get to Matthew 20.

It is remarkable that in the only other recorded case in which the blind applied to Jesus for their sight, and obtained it, they addressed Him, over and over again, by this one Messianic title, so well known—'Son of David' (Matt. 20:30). Can there be a doubt that their faith fastened on such great Messianic promises as this, 'Then the eyes of the blind shall be opened,' (Isa. 35:5). (CCE)

The title "Son of David" in the New Testament was used by people who only knew Jesus from afar, from the crowd, and it is used in a messianic sense, that is, someone of David's line would restore their freedom and lead them in reestablishing the glory of their Kingdom.

Should we ask, in prayer, for something more than once? The text seems to say these men continued to call out. When you want something very badly, how many times should you ask it? Ask a child how many times! People who want a thing badly do everything they can to get it.

Blindness was, and is, one of the most severe handicaps. There's an interesting parallel in the physical blindness and the spiritual blindness of men. As bad as physical blindness is, spiritual blindness is even worse. It not only keeps us from seeing our need for God, but it also keeps us from seeing what God wants us to do for others. Physical blindness was common in Jesus' day, as it was in most countries until recently. In those days, a blind man was reduced to begging; today there are more medical and employment options available to them.

The emphasis here is on the question, "Do you believe...?" and the effect "According to your faith." Jesus didn't always require faith before healing, He often just acts, but here He not only asks for it, He almost demands it. We know the importance of faith in the healing process today. It is vital to any healing and is true of both medical and faith healing. We must have faith in the doctor or we won't go see him. We must have faith in the medicine or we won't buy it and take it. We must have faith in the one who prays and the One to whom he prays.

Again, Jesus doesn't want to call attention to himself. LASB suggests,

Jesus told people to keep quiet about his healings because he did not want to be known only as a miracle worker. He healed because he had compassion on people, but he also wanted to bring *spiritual* healing to a sin-sick world (p.1559).

It shouldn't surprise us that He never attracted attention to Himself, but reflected it to the Father or the disciples.

Where Does the Power come from?
Matthew 9:32-34

As they went out, behold, a mute man who was demon possessed was brought to him. [33] *When the demon was cast out, the mute man spoke. The multitudes marveled, saying, "Nothing like this has ever been seen in Israel!"*

[34] *But the Pharisees said, "By the prince of the demons, he casts out demons."*

There is a parallel in Matthew 12 that we will look at when we get there.

According to Isaiah 35:5-6, this event is also a sign that the Kingdom of God is breaking through.

If this healing follows close on the healing for the blind men as Matthew indicates, then "the first person the blind men [saw] was a fellow-sufferer…destined to experience the same divine power as themselves (TNTC, p. 101)."

Do you ever get tired, as I do, of trying to help people who seem to be helpless and hopeless and won't do anything to help themselves? I wonder if Jesus did. If He did, He helped anyway! The easy cases were treated at home with the remedies they knew about. Those more difficult cases went to the doctor for his remedy, if you had the money to pay him. Jesus got the impossible cases. When no one else could heal them, like us, they turned to the Great Physician.

Here we have a mute man; the Greek word also means deaf and probably implies a person who was both deaf and mute and the inability to speak had been attributed to demon possession. Superstitious nonsense? Maybe. Maybe not. Trauma caused by "bad" things in our lives can be used by Satan to afflict us and keep us in bondage. It is possible that his problem was simply he couldn't speak because he couldn't hear, they often go together. It's also possible the trouble is just as the Bible said it was.

The real story is not in the man or even in the healing, it is in the reaction of the multitudes and the Pharisees; there is an interesting contrast between their attitudes. The crowd was amazed, but the Pharisees were cynical. This contrast shows the impossibility of neutrality toward Jesus. Barclay finds three things in the attitude displayed by the Pharisees:

1. They are too set in their ways to change. All the great things belong to the past; to change what we are doing today would be deadly sin. New is wrong!

2. They are too proud in their self-satisfaction to accept the fact that Jesus is the only way. Recognizing the need to change would require admitting they are wrong.

3. They are too prejudiced to see; they are so blinded by their own ideas that they cannot see the truth. DSB pp. 351-2.

While the learned, sophisticated people may become jaded, the simple people will always be amazed by the wonder of the risen Lord. Our congregational leaders need to be careful that they are following the Holy Spirit rather than the spirit of tradition. "Why did the Pharisees do this? (1) Jesus bypassed their religious authority. (2) He weakened their control over the people. (3) He challenged their cherished beliefs (4) He exposed their insincere motives (LASB, p. 1560)."

"Nothing can convince those who are under the power of pride. They will believe anything, however false or absurd, rather than the Holy Scriptures; thus they show the enmity of their hearts against a holy God (MH)."

The Critical Commentary points out that this is the first time the Pharisees attributed Jesus' power to Satan, a ploy they would continue to use.

Harvest What You Got
Matthew 9:35-38

Jesus went about all the cities and the villages, teaching in their synagogues, and preaching the Good News of the Kingdom, and healing every disease and every sickness among the people. [36] But when he saw the multitudes, he was moved with compassion for them, because they were harassed (TR reads "weary" instead of "harassed") and scattered, like sheep without a shepherd. [37] Then he said to his disciples, "The harvest indeed is plentiful, but the laborers are few. [38] Pray therefore that the Lord of the harvest will send out laborers into his harvest."

Teaching, preaching and healing were Jesus' three-pronged approach to ministry, they were the emphasis of the early Church and they are our approach to mission work. Shouldn't they be the emphasis of the church's ministry in our communities?

We place heavy emphasis on the need for preaching, or proclaiming the gospel, and our primary weekly service is built around singing, giving, and preaching, but many in our communities lack direction. New direction for living comes from changed hearts and lives and that comes from proclaiming the Good News of Jesus.

But it is not enough to simply preach; we must also teach the significance of the Good News to believers; discipleship is a good word to use here. New believers must be discipled so they can disciple others. Please don't forget, every Christian is a teacher and the best teaching is by example, living before the pupil, not the eloquent stringing together of words and ideas.

The final element, healing, is preaching and teaching put in action and covers not only medical needs, but also other physical, emotional and spiritual needs. Jesus spent much more time ministering to the needs of people than he did to preaching and teaching. Can we do less?

If you will, the work of the shepherd is a healing ministry; it is caring for the flock: feeding and watering them, seeking out those that wander away, taking care of their wounds, protects them from danger. The work of the reaper is that of evangelism; gathering the crop and adding it to what has already gathered. Both are essential.

"But when he saw the multitudes, he was moved with compassion for them." The word used for "compassion" is the strongest Greek word available; it is a feeling that cuts as deeply into the soul as is possible. In the New Testament, except for some parables, it is only used in connection with Jesus. When was the last time you were so moved by the needs of people that you had that kind of feeling for them?

The Greek elite separated themselves from the common man and the Jewish religious leaders saw them as unclean and unworthy. For both, they were a source of embarrassment and chaff for the fires of hell. Jesus' love for the common man was so great that He felt their pain; He never saw them as "cases" or "disadvantaged;" He saw them as people whom He loved and could help. Is our attitude toward the poor, the homeless any better than that of the Greek and Jew?

Jesus uses the picture of a flock of sheep, a familiar picture of God's people in the Bible. In 1 Kings 22:17a, the prophet Micaiah quoted Yahweh as saying about the northern kingdom of Israel, "I saw all Israel scattered on the mountains, as sheep that have no shepherd…" Why sheep? Because there is probably no more helpless animal in creation, except a human infant.

These sheep "were harassed [or weary]." In Greek "harassed" carries the picture of "skinned." It is all right to shear sheep; actually, it is good for them because they can grow more wool. But when you skin them, they die.

The common people, then and now, desperately want to have a relationship with God, but religious people can't find a place for them. Instead of helping men and women stand before God do we set up rules and walls that keep them out? Do we give them a religion that cripples instead of strengthens them? Zechariah warned "Woe to the worthless shepherd who leaves the flock! The sword will be on his arm, and on his right eye. His arm will be completely withered, and his right eye will be totally blinded!" (11:17).

We are asked to pray for "laborers" not because God doesn't want to send them out, but because we "laborers" don't want to go; we often substitute prayer for labor. Prayer is important, but it is not a substitute for doing. They are different sides of the same coin. The picture here is of workers who are praying while they are reaping.

At the time Jesus said this, there were already plenty of religious leaders working in Israel but they were "skinning" the flock, not shepherding them. Jesus' request is for quality leadership; people who will do the work of ministering to the needs of the hurting flock.

"Send out" is *ekballo* and carries the idea of violently throwing something out; remember, it is the word used to describe "casting out a demon." I believe the prayer is for God to wake us up and force us out into the fields to do the work before us. There are always more fields to harvest than there are harvesters to do the work. Why is that?

The Call and Commission of the Twelve
Matthew 10:1-4

He called to himself his twelve disciples, and gave them authority over unclean spirits, to cast them out, and to heal every disease and every sickness. ² Now the names of the twelve apostles are these. The first, Simon, who is called Peter; Andrew, his brother; James the son of Zebedee; John, his brother; ³ Philip; Bartholomew; Thomas; Matthew the tax collector; James the son of Alphaeus; Lebbaeus, who was also called (NU omits "Lebbaeus, who was also called") Thaddaeus; ⁴ Simon the Canaanite; and Judas Iscariot, who also betrayed him.

While this is the first mention of twelve disciples in the New Testament, Paul is the first, chronologically, to refer to them in that way, "…and that he appeared to Cephas [Peter], then to the twelve" (1 Cor. 15:5). This is the only time Matthew uses the word "apostle," "meaning one sent," in his gospel, "but the concept of 'sending on a mission'…is common in his gospel" (AB, p. 117).

"Jesus *called* his 12 disciples. He didn't draft them, force them, or ask them to volunteer; he chose them to serve him in a special way (LASB, p. 1560)." Twelve is an important number to Jews and Christians alike; remember Jesus and the early Church saw their group not as a new movement, but as an extension of what began with Abraham. Like Martin Luther, the goal was reform and renewal; no break was ever intended.

Mark indicates that Jesus paired the disciples up and sent them out. This may be because the Old Testament required two witnesses to establish facts: "One witness shall not rise up against a man for any iniquity, or for any sin, in any sin that he sins: at the mouth of two witnesses, or at the mouth of three witnesses, shall a matter be established" (Deut. 19:15).

It seems clear from the many references that there were certainly twelve disciples/apostles, but it is unfortunate we don't know very much about most of them. It's also interesting that in the four lists, there are three groups of four; Peter is always the first in the first group and Judas Iscariot is always the last name in the last group.

Matthew says, "…first, Simon (who is called Peter)." Since Peter is always listed first, "first" may carry more impact than just as a location on a list. After Jesus' ascension, Peter appears to be the titular head of the Church until James, the half-brother of Jesus, comes on the scene. "But he, beckoning to them with his hand to be silent, declared to them how the Lord had brought him out of the prison. He said, 'Tell these things to James, and to the brothers.' Then he departed, and went to another place" (Acts 12:17). From this point on, Peter seems to be involved in some kind of missionary work.

The choice of these particular men to be leaders is a statement of the confidence God has in ordinary people; they were uneducated, working men. There wasn't one professional in the bunch; they came from varied backgrounds and interests, and I might add they had different, very different personalities; and Jesus placed the eternal success of the Church in them. "When you feel small and useless, remember that God uses ordinary people to do his extraordinary work (LASB, p. 1560)."

It is clear that Jesus is giving authority here. Power without the accompanying authority is useless. Luke says "…and gave them power and authority over all demons, and to cure diseases" (Luke 9:1b) "in other words, He both *qualified* and *authorized* them (CCE)."

Go and Tell
Matthew 10:5-15

Jesus sent these twelve out, and commanded them, saying, "Don't go among the Gentiles, and don't enter into any city of the Samaritans. ⁶ Rather, go to the lost sheep of the house of Israel. ⁷ As you go, preach, saying, 'The Kingdom of Heaven is at hand!' ⁸ Heal the sick, cleanse the lepers, (TR adds "raise the dead,") and cast out demons. Freely you received, so freely give. ⁹ Don't take any gold, silver, or brass in your money belts. [10] Take no bag for your journey, neither two coats, nor shoes, nor staff: for the laborer is worthy of his food. [11] Into whatever city or village you enter, find out who in it is worthy; and stay there until you go on. [12] As you enter into the household, greet it. [13] If the household is worthy, let your peace come on it, but if it isn't worthy, let your peace return to you. [14] Whoever doesn't receive you, nor hear your words, as you go out of that house or that city, shake off the dust from your feet. [15] Most certainly I tell you, it will be more tolerable for the land of Sodom and Gomorrah in the day of judgment than for that city.

The word "commanded" is the Greek word *paragellein* and carries four implications: it was a military command used by officers to send men into a campaign; it was a call to friends for help; it described a teacher giving rules and instruction; and it was an imperial command (DSB, p. 362).

"Don't go among the Gentiles" could be translated "do not take any road which will lead you into Gentile territory (TNTC, p. 107)." When we look at this passage, it seems strange to us. Why did Jesus restrict His disciples "to the lost sheep of Israel"? One theologian suggested it was because Matthew was concerned with Christological not missional interests; Jesus was the "son of David," sent to be Israel's Messiah. It was after the Jews rejected Him that He sent the disciples to the Gentiles. Paul put it this way, "For I am not ashamed of the Good News of Christ, for it is the power of God for salvation for everyone who believes; for the Jew first, and also for the Greek" (Rom. 1:16). We should note that "Being lost is the result of neglect by their shepherds (NLTSB, p.1597)."

Jesus did go first to Israel, but undoubtedly, it was not a permanent command as evident from His total ministry. He didn't ignore the Gentiles He came in contact with. A few examples include, His journey to Samaria to minister in John 4, He healed the Syro-Phoenician child in Matt 15:28, and Matthew concludes His gospel with the "Great Commission" and instruction to "go, and make disciples of all nations…" (28:19). It was never God's plan to leave out non-Jews, see Genesis 12:2-3 and, Isaiah 49:6. But because of the prejudice of the Jews, if He had gone to the Gentiles first, they probably would have totally rejected Him and His ministry. Another suggestion is that these men are just beginning their "seminary" training and were not yet ready to face the entire world with their polytheistic beliefs.

The ministry Jesus sent the disciples to accomplish was the same one we have seen Him carrying out: preaching and healing. The instruction, "Heal the sick, cleanse the lepers, [raise the dead,] and cast out demons" has often been considered to have both physical and spiritual implications. These activities were "signs" the "The Kingdom of Heaven is at hand." What kind of preaching would these men be able to do? At this stage, it was probably the same message any Christian can give, a personal testimony of what Jesus had done for them.

Further, since the disciples had received their authority at no cost, there was to be no charge for their ministry. They were to "travel light" without a knapsack to carry provision, which would accomplish several things. It would speed them on their way, it would keep them unencumbered from the world, and it would force them to depend on God for their needs.

However, this shouldn't be considered an injunction against a paid ministry, quite the contrary, "Jesus said that those who minister are to be cared for. The disciples could expect food and shelter in return for the spiritual service they provided (LASB, p. 1561)." Paul refused pay, but defended his right to receive it (1 Cor. 9:4-18). Unfortunately, pay is a two-edged sword. The advantage is that it frees the minister from

103

concerns of "making a living" and allows for better preparation for ministry; the danger is that the minister may fear dismissal more than God and may address or fail to address problems in relation to the desires of the congregation rather than the direction of the Holy Spirit.

The admonition of verses 11-15 are sound advice for us today. It is important to provide a worthy house for ministers to stay in because it can affect their ministry and their families. They are ordered to stay there until they are finished, not to move around "upgrading(?)".

In the east, words are believed to have a life of their own and it is true that things said to us continue to affect us long after they are heard. Curses can become self-fulfilling for those who believe them. So, a blessing rejected and recalled could have serious effect on the people of that house. The Hebrew greeting "shalom" meant "peace," but it was more than just the absence of strife, it meant peace in everything they did.

To "shake the dust off your feet" was a common practice among devout Jews and was done whenever they returned to Judea after traveling in Gentile country. It was also done as a sign of contempt for some action or person. When you "shake the dust off your feet" be careful; your attitude cannot be that of the Pharisees.

Christians Held on Phony Charges
Matthew 10:16-25

"Behold, I send you out as sheep among wolves. Therefore be wise as serpents, and harmless as doves. [17] *But beware of men: for they will deliver you up to councils, and in their synagogues they will scourge you.* [18] *Yes, and you will be brought before governors and kings for my sake, for a testimony to them and to the nations.* [19] *But when they deliver you up, don't be anxious how or what you will say, for it will be given you in that hour what you will say.* [20] *For it is not you who speak, but the Spirit of your Father who speaks in you.*

[21] *"Brother will deliver up brother to death, and the father his child. Children will rise up against parents, and cause them to be put to death.* [22] *You will be hated by all men for my name's sake, but he who endures to the end will be saved.* [23] *But when they persecute you in this city, flee into the next, for most certainly I tell you, you will not have gone through the cities of Israel, until the Son of Man has come.*

[24] *"A disciple is not above his teacher, nor a servant above his lord.* [25] *It is enough for the disciple that he be like his teacher, and the servant like his lord. If they have called the master of the house Beelzebul, (Literally, Lord of the Flies,) or the devil how much more those of his household!*

We know from our study of the Sermon on the Mount that Matthew presents an orderly, thorough discussion of the subject he is handling. We have just seen Jesus send out the disciples to the Jews, but the warning that follows includes trials before Gentiles. This is a continuation of the prior section and continues through the end of chapter 10.

"We are not to be gullible pawns, but neither are we to be deceitful connivers (LASB, p. 1562)." As we have seen, sheep are often used as an image for people, so we will not deal with it again. The wolves are interesting though, here they are "religious" people and religious councils as well as civil authorities;

remember, in Judaism, there was no difference between religious and civil authority and the trial and punishment could both take place in the synagogue.

The word "wise" means prudent and "harmless" and refers to sincerity. They seem to be strange words to put together, but they are not. We need complete knowledge of God's word and pure motives when we use that knowledge.

The statement, "do not worry about what to say or how to say it. At that time you will be given what to say," is used by some as evidence that we don't need to prepare sermons or Bible studies, because the Holy Spirit will tell us what to say. That is only true if we omit the first phrase, "But when they deliver you up [arrested you] …" So, if your class or congregation meets the condition: "On my account you will be brought before governors and kings as witnesses to them and to the Gentiles," you are right, the Holy Spirit will take care of it, otherwise you had better prepare.

The Jews divided time into two ages, the present age and the age to come, separated by the "Day of the Lord." For them the present age was an evil time when sin was rampant. The age to come would be the "golden age" of God. The Day of the Lord was a time of judgment when friend would turn against friend and family would turn against family. What Jesus is saying to them is, "Today is the Day of the Lord!"

"Enduring to the end is not a way to be saved but the evidence that a person is really committed to Jesus. Persistence is not a means to earn salvation, it is a by-product of a truly devoted life (LASB, p. 1562)." There is one big thing this passage shows, Jesus never underestimated the path He asked His followers to take. The world promises honor and glory to those that take its way, but the reward is destruction and despair. Jesus promises difficulty, but gives Heaven as a reward.

Jesus warns that we cannot, and should not, expect special treatment because we are Christians; actually, we should expect worse treatment. In some places Christians are persecuted, and even killed for their faith, but not in most of Europe and the United States. What went wrong with us? Where is the persecution Jesus promised? Is it yet to come? Maybe we have blended in to society too well…

When people are challenged to accept big risks, they are more willing to accept the task. "It may be that the Church must learn again that we will never attract men to an easy way; it is the call of the heroic which ultimately speaks to men's hearts (DSB, p. 375)." The call to salvation is a call to service. There is no requirement to serve so that we might be saved, but having received salvation, we cannot help but serve. "It is the consistency which reflects one's salvation, not the holding out which earns salvation (BBC, p. 137)."

Fear the Right Things
Matthew 10:26-33

Therefore don't be afraid of them, for there is nothing covered that will not be revealed; and hidden that will not be known. [27] What I tell you in the darkness, speak in the light; and what you hear whispered in the ear, proclaim on the housetops. [28] Don't be afraid of those who kill the body, but are not able to kill the soul. Rather, fear him who is able to destroy both soul and body in Gehenna (Hell).

29 "Aren't two sparrows sold for an assarion coin? (An assarion is a small coin worth one tenth of a drachma or a sixteenth of a denarius. An assarion is approximately the wages of one half hour of agricultural labor.) Not one of them falls on the ground apart from your Father's will, 30 but the very hairs of your head are all numbered. 31 Therefore don't be afraid. You are of more value than many sparrows. 32 Everyone therefore who confesses me before men, him I will also confess before my Father who is in heaven. 33 But whoever denies me before men, him I will also deny before my Father who is in heaven.

In the prior passage believers were told to flee persecution, now it seems there is a time, not to fight, but to stand your ground to testify. In these few verses, three times we are told not to be afraid in verses 26, 28, and 31. Who or what is it that we are not to fear? Those who accuse us and Satan and his minions!

Are you afraid of Satan? I hope not! Is it Scriptural to fear him? No! We are to resist Satan not be afraid of him, "Resist the devil, and he will flee from you (Jam. 4:7b)." The "them" here are the accusers, people who are agents of the devil. Paul admonishes us to "Put on the whole armor of God, that you may be able to stand against the wiles of the devil" (Eph. 6:11).

Why can we have courage? Because the truth will be revealed and we should not fear it. Who is going to tell the truth? The proclaimer! What does the proclaimer proclaim? In verse 27, Jesus tells us, "What I tell you in the dark, speak in the light; and what you hear whispered in your ear, proclaim on the housetops." But who is the proclaimer? I am! You are!

Before we can speak, we must first listen, "in the dark," possibly in your prayer closet, then we will have something to "proclaim from the roofs." We must speak the message we have heard, even if it is not popular and causes us to take our lives into our hands. It was common practice for a teacher to whisper secret teachings and/or interpretations to his disciples, but Jesus did not have any secret teachings like many of the teachers of His day.

Still, we are only to "be afraid of the One who can destroy both soul and body in hell." Who can destroy body and soul? Satan? No! Only God has that power. While I don't think it is Jesus' intent, some use this to suggest that Hell is not eternal and the unbelieving will simply be obliterated in the end. However, that is not taught in the balance of Scripture.

How can we love someone whom we fear, and how can we fear someone we love? It can only happen with God. Our fear is not that we dread His punishment, but we are to reverence and be in awe of Him. Paul tells us, "For you didn't receive the spirit of bondage again to fear, but you received the Spirit of adoption, by whom we cry, 'Abba! Father!' (Rom. 8:15)."

In relation to the sparrow, the expression "fall to the ground" may mean die, but it may also simply mean land on the ground. Can it be that God knows each time a sparrow lands? Why not? And if He cares this much about a sparrow, how much more does He care for us.

How is it possible for believers to "deny" Christ? Barclay suggests three ways:

1. By our words, by using the wrong words we blend into society so well that people cannot tell that we are followers of Christ.

2. By our silence and by failing to proclaim the good news.

3. By our actions, if our life and attitudes deny our faith, our words will not be effective.

"*Objection:* But this may cost us our life? *Answer:* It may, but there their power ends… (CCE)." What are you willing to die for? However, dying only happens once…what are you willing to live for? By that, I mean change your lifestyle and expectations to align with God's Will.

I often see verses 32 and 33 posted in memes on social media suggesting that if you don't "like,' "repost," or do something positive to proclaim your faith on their meme, you are denying God. Not only is that incorrect, it is manipulative and therefore sinful!

Contrast this passage with the situation of Peter's denial and restoration. "But go, tell his disciples and Peter, 'He goes before you into Galilee. There you will see him, as he said to you'" (Mark 16:7). God is always ready to offer forgiveness and restore us, all we need to do is ask: "If we confess our sins, he is faithful and righteous to forgive us the sins, and to cleanse us from all unrighteousness" (1 John 1:9).

The Problem of Relationships
Matthew 10:34-39

"Don't think that I came to send peace on the earth. I didn't come to send peace, but a sword. ³⁵ For I came to set a man at odds against his father, and a daughter against her mother, and a daughter-in-law against her mother-in-law. ³⁶ A man's foes will be those of his own household (Micah 7:6) ³⁷ He who loves father or mother more than me is not worthy of me; and he who loves son or daughter more than me isn't worthy of me. ³⁸ He who doesn't take his cross and follow after me, isn't worthy of me. ³⁹ He who seeks his life will lose it; and he who loses his life for my sake will find it.

This is a strange saying and is a quotation of Micah 7:6 and echoes Psalm 41:9. Didn't Jesus come to reconcile man to man as well as man to God? Yes, He did! There is a clue in verse 39; another of those strange opposites that exist in Christianity: we find by losing and lose by trying to keep. I'm not sure why many scholars think these words are hyperbole, that is to say, deliberate exaggeration to make a point. There is great, simple truth in these words.

We have already noted Jesus' honesty about the ministry He called His followers into; that honesty is continued here. When Jesus talks about discipleship, He is emphatic

…a saying which our Lord once and again emphatically reiterates (Matt. 16:24; Luke 9:23; 14:27). We have become so accustomed to this expression—taking up one's cross'—in the sense of 'being prepared for trials in general for Christ's sake,' that we are apt to lose sight of its primary and proper sense here—'a preparedness to go forth even to crucifixion,' as when our Lord had to bear His own cross on His way to Calvary—a saying the more remarkable as our Lord had not as yet given a hint that He would die this death, nor was crucifixion a Jewish mode of capital punishment (CCE).

Barclay says Jesus offers four areas of conflict:

1. Warfare between members of their own family; the Jews expected this to happen during the Day of the Lord. Great causes have always divided people and families. This was echoed in the history of the United States during the Civil War when brother fought brother.

2. Choices must be made as loyalties are tested; loyalty to God must surpass loyalty to family. Neutrality is not possible.

107

3. A cross is offered to followers, a cross is a means of sacrifice. A sacrifice may include personal ambition, convenience and comfort.

4. Adventure is offered; again, and again the disciples were thrust into unexpected adventure. We can also testify to the excitement that may come into the life of a believer. (DSB 395-6).

Jesus is insistent that His reign is not like that of earthly kings who impose an uneasy peace on their subjects by force-of-arms. "On the contrary, his coming will involve painful decisions. He will not interfere with man's freedom (AB, p.130)."

Why does Jesus say, "a daughter-in-law against her mother-in-law"? What about son-in-law against father-in-law? As a marriage counselor, I can testify that there are far more mother-in-law—daughter-in-law conflicts than there are father-in-law—son-in-law conflicts.

The *Mishnah* required a man to honor God and the Law more than his teacher and his teacher more than his father. True family relationships are found not in a physical blood line, but in a spiritual blood line. If we seek to achieve personal goals, we may reach them, but we may not be happy with them. The call to salvation is the call to total commitment and to service.

How to Get Rewards
Matthew 10:40-42

He who receives you receives me, and he who receives me receives him who sent me. [41] He who receives a prophet in the name of a prophet will receive a prophet's reward. He who receives a righteous man in the name of a righteous man will receive a righteous man's reward. [42] Whoever gives one of these little ones just a cup of cold water to drink in the name of a disciple, most certainly I tell you he will in no way lose his reward."

I'm not a "prosperity gospel" teacher, but there is a proper way to obtain rewards, and it isn't by seeking them, it's by serving others! Jesus sets out four groups: "me," "prophet," "righteous man" and "little ones." What He is saying here is our relationship to Him is the same as our relationship to other people. Receiving the "disciples," is the same as receiving Him. A "prophet" was similar to an apostle and is mentioned several times in the New Testament. A "righteous man" is one who lives as God intends, not just righteous in the eyes of the Law. The "little ones" here are not just children, but "little" people; ordinary, unimportant people, and those with diminished abilities, those who are often overlooked by everyone. There are no unimportant people to Jesus!

Could He have been referring to someone specific in this use of "prophet" and "righteous man"? Some have suggested that He and His disciples are inferred. However, He also had special regard for those who were ignored by the religious community, "the people of the land," we have seen before. Since many of Jesus' followers were the poor, they may well be the "little ones" referred to here.

Not all of us can be "prophets." The Jews knew that and recognized that those who enabled the prophet to do his work had a share in his reward. Without the people "behind the scenes" the work could not be done and there would be no "scene" to see. On any given Sunday, there are only a few people "featured," but there are many people working to make it happen.

Examine your gifts and talents. What are they? Can you sing? Then sing and you'll receive a "singer's reward." Can't sing? Then help a singer sing and you'll receive a "singer's reward." That's what Jesus is saying. Those who have a talent or a "calling," pursue it, those who do not, use what they have to help the others.

Jesus knew there would be difficulties for His followers and He knew it would not be easy for people to help the persecuted followers. Anyone who did would receive the same reward as those persecuted. This is more than charity; it is motivated by a sincere desire to accomplish God's will for the Church.

A "cup of cold water" would have greater significance for Jesus' listeners than most of us because their water was drawn from cisterns and the water would be warm and somewhat stale. To get "cold water" would require a trip to a well to draw it. "How much we love God can be measured by how well we treat others (LASB, p. 1563)."

The final test is a test of discipleship requiring us to put forth effort that goes beyond normal, convenient exertion.

John's Question
Matthew 11:1-6

When Jesus had finished directing his twelve disciples, he departed from there to teach and preach in their cities. 2 Now when John heard in the prison the works of Christ, he sent two of his disciples 3 and said to him, "Are you he who comes, or should we look for another?"

4 Jesus answered them, "Go and tell John the things which you hear and see: 5 the blind receive their sight, the lame walk, the lepers are cleansed, the deaf hear (Isa. 35:5) the dead are raised up, and the poor have good news preached to them (Isa. 61:1-4) 6 Blessed is he who finds no occasion for stumbling in me."

About verse 1, Staggs says, "Stephan Langston in 1228, in making our modern chapter divisions, could well have included this verse in chapter 10, for it belongs to the section of Matthew's five formulas indicating a major division of his work (cf. 7:35; 13:53; 19:1; 26:1)." p. 139.

John, though a unique figure in biblical history, was no superman. He was subject…to depression and disappointment. …he was becoming impatient and beginning to wonder why Jesus was not asserting His messianic claims more forcibly and more openly. (TNTC, pp. 113-114)

John the Baptizer was the end of the old order, the Law and the Prophets; Jesus was the beginning of the new order. There is evidence that John's disciples continued his ministry for a time after the death of their leader and that may account for the Gospel of John's emphasis on the "fore runner" mission of John the Baptizer. John was a fearless preacher and, as we saw earlier, that landed him in jail because he spoke out against Herod's abhorrent behavior.

Everyone wonders why John was asking if Jesus was truly the Messiah. Was he confused because Jesus wasn't acting like the Messiah was expected to act? That confused everyone else, why not John? Barclay sees three possibilities in John's question:

1. It was not for his sake, but for the sake of his disciples. It is as if John was saying, "If you have any doubts, go and see what Jesus is doing and your doubts will be at an end."

2. It could be a question of impatience, when was Jesus going to get started and the Day of Destruction begin.

3. It could be that he was asking for confirmation of the hope of the new age the Messiah would bring (DSB, pp. 2-3)

Some leaders do not like to be challenged with questions, but Jesus didn't mind John's questioning and God does not mind our questioning either, "'Come now, and let us reason together,' says Yahweh: 'Though your sins be as scarlet, they shall be as white as snow. Though they be red like crimson, they shall be as wool.'" (Isa. 1:18.)

If you sometimes doubt your salvation, the forgiveness of your sins, or God's work in your life, look at the evidence in Scripture and the changes in your life. When you doubt, don't turn away from Christ; turn to him (LASB, p. 1563).

Verse 6 takes the same form as the Beatitudes, that is, "Blessed are…" Could it be an additional declaration? The phrase "finds no occasion for stumbling," ("take offense" in the KJV) is a fair translation of the Greek *skandalon*, which we have seen before and means the "bait stick" (in a trap). Jesus might be saying, "Blessed is the person who is not lured away because I do not do what they expect."

Paul also addressed the problem like this:

For Jews ask for signs, Greeks seek after wisdom, but we preach Christ crucified; a stumbling block to Jews, and foolishness to Greeks, but to those who are called, both Jews and Greeks, Christ is the power of God and the wisdom of God. Because the foolishness of God is wiser than men, and the weakness of God is stronger than men. (1 Cor. 1:22-25).

Jesus' answer to John's disciples was simply "Tell John what you see me doing, 'The blind receive their sight, the lame walk, the lepers are cleansed, the deaf hear, the dead are raised up, and the poor have the good news is preached to them.'" "Jesus was the only person who could ever demand without qualification to be judged, not by what he said, but by what he did (DSB, p. 3)." He can still stand the test!

The falling away is because of the ministry Jesus performed, it was simply not what everyone expected. Men are often offended by Jesus when His teaching cuts across their behavior patterns, expectations, and the religion they have developed.

The Greatest People May Not Look Like It
Matthew 11:7-15

As these went their way, Jesus began to say to the multitudes concerning John, "What did you go out into the wilderness to see? A reed shaken by the wind? [8] But what did you go out to see? A man in soft clothing? Behold, those who wear soft clothing are in kings' houses. [9] But why did you go out? To see a prophet? Yes, I tell you, and much more than a prophet. [10] For this is he, of whom it is written, 'Behold, I send my messenger before your face, who will prepare your way before you' (Mal. 3:1) [11] Most certainly I tell you, among those who are born of women there has not arisen anyone greater than John the Baptizer; yet he who is least in the Kingdom of Heaven is greater than he. [12] From the days of John the Baptizer until now, the Kingdom of Heaven suffers violence, and the violent take it by force (or, plunder it). [13] For all the prophets and the law prophesied until John. [14] If you are willing to receive it, this is Elijah, who is to come. [15] He who has ears to hear, let him hear.

"What Christ said concerning John, was not only for his praise, but for the people's profit (MH)." They, the people, flocked to "see," and hear, John. In fact, the Greek word is the word from which we get our word "theater" and can mean to go to see a show or demonstration.

Since there was no punctuation in the original manuscripts, it is left to the translators to determine where and what punctuation is required. The question we have seems appropriate, but some suggest that the phrasing could also have been "Why did you go out into the desert to see a reed swayed by the wind?" But that does not make good sense (see below).

"A reed shaken by the wind?" Reeds blowing in the breeze were a common sight, so this could mean one of two things. It is either a person easily swayed by the gentlest argument or something so common that it was not worth watching.

"A man in soft clothing?" Courtiers wore fine clothes and learned to flatter the king. Do you get tired of seeing preachers wearing fancy clothes and driving fancy cars? Do you get tired of seeing preachers who look like their wardrobe came from the Salvation Army thrift store and driving clunkers? Do you want a preacher that fits nicely in between the two, not too flashy or too ragged? What is the answer?

"To see a prophet?" A prophet had to possess two characteristics, first a message from God and second the courage to deliver it.

The phrase "born of women" probably only means a human being. Where does John fit? John, like each of us is called to be himself, not someone else. John was who God called him to be. As ministers, each of us, for we are all ministers, should be who God calls us to be. John was a prophet and more. We shouldn't be surprised at Jesus' statement "yet he who is least in the Kingdom of Heaven is greater than he," but it doesn't diminish John's importance. John, and all the prophets, were extremely important and will be appropriately rewarded by God in the Judgment. Here Jesus is comparing the pre-Kingdom work of the prophets with the work the disciples and those who will follow them are to do.

John stood on the dividing line of time. I don't mean between BC and AD; I mean the line between the promise of the Messiah and the fulfillment of that promise. Was John a "Christian"? Maybe not in the classical sense, but in the broader sense, he was no less a Christian than any Old Testament prophet. The sadness is that he was not in a position to "see" the fulfillment of God's promise. "John was not a resurrected Elijah, but he took on Elijah's prophetic role—boldly confronting sin and pointing people to God (LASB, p. 1564)."

"Violent" as used here is in the middle voice to indicate that there is a shaking of the old order. If it were passive, as some take it to be, it would indicate that the kingdom is totally in the future.

As we have already seen, the Kingdom of God is a kingdom of people, not territory; it knows no boundaries of geography or time. Therefore, it cannot be taken by force, as the Jews wanted; it is a Kingdom of love.

Are You Behaving Like Children?
Matthew 11:16-19

"But to what shall I compare this generation? It is like children sitting in the marketplaces, who call to their companions [17] and say, 'We played the flute for you, and you didn't dance. We mourned for you, and you didn't lament.' [18] For John came neither eating nor drinking, and they say, 'He has a demon.' [19] The Son of Man came eating and drinking, and they say, 'Behold, a gluttonous man and a drunkard, a friend of tax collectors and sinners!' But wisdom is justified by her children" (NU reads "actions" instead of "children").

"Christ reflects on the scribes and Pharisees, who had a proud conceit of themselves (MH)." He compared them to a group of children trying to decide what game to play and not being able to agree. They didn't want to play wedding or funeral; they were what some might call "contrary."

They criticized John because He "came neither eating nor drinking," He was too strict. They criticized Jesus because He "came eating and drinking," He was a "party animal." These people would not be happy if they were "hung with a new rope," but they probably would have been "good Baptists." "…the methods of both John and Jesus have place in God's providence, for all their seeming disparity and seeming failure (AB, p. 139)."

Jesus condemned the attitude of His generation because "No matter what he said or did, they took the opposite view. They were cynical and skeptical because he challenged their comfortable, secure, and self-centered lives (LASB, p. 1564)."

Stagg says, "Jesus did plunge deeply into life, often offending religious leaders by the freedom and joy with which he moved among people of all kinds and by his refusal to let superficial rules or customs take priority over people (BBC, p. 143)."

Jesus could not have feasted very often, no one did, but He found true enjoyment in everyday life. He went where He was invited and/or needed and ministered to all He found there regardless of their social or religious status.

Willful Rejection
Matthew 11:20-24

Then he began to denounce the cities in which most of his mighty works had been done, because they didn't repent. [21] "Woe to you, Chorazin! Woe to you, Bethsaida! For if the mighty works had been done in Tyre and Sidon which were done in you, they would have repented long ago in sackcloth and ashes. [22] But I tell you, it will be more tolerable for Tyre and Sidon on the day of judgment than for you. [23] You, Capernaum, who are exalted to heaven, you will go down to Hades (or, Hell). For if the mighty works had been done in Sodom which were done in you, it would have remained until today. [24] But I tell you that it will be more tolerable for the land of Sodom, on the day of judgment, than for you."

Korazin, the nearest town, was about an hour north of Capernaum. Bethsaida, meaning "fishing house," was a fishing village on the west bank of the Jordan River where the river entered the north end of the Sea of Galilee. Tyre and Sidon were prosperous Phoenician cities often reviled in the Old Testament for their sinfulness.

We don't know what great miracles were done in Korazin, but Mark says that Bethsaida was where the blind man was healed, Mark 8:22-26. (The things we don't know about Jesus far outnumber the things we do know.)

What sins could these two villages be accused of that would be worse than the sins of Tyre, Sidon and Sodom? Whatever it was, it must have been very serious to elicit such a statement. I know I'm speculating, but could it have been their indifference?

Not unlike today, they didn't drive Jesus away or seek to harm Him; they just ignored Him. The Church is accepted and its ministry rewarded with titles, but it has become impotent, because of indifference to the message. "It does not burn a religion to death; it freezes it to death (DSB, p. 13)."

We are only responsible for those people and things the Lord has placed in our path or placed on our hearts. Greater privilege carries greater responsibility. "Let not many of you be teachers, my brothers, knowing that we will receive heavier judgment" (James 3:1).

Capernaum, you will remember, was the home of Peter, James and John and the "headquarters" for Jesus' ministry in the area. However, they didn't seem to respond to His message either.

The Custom-Made Yoke
Matthew 11:25-30

At that time, Jesus answered, "I thank you, Father, Lord of heaven and earth, that you hid these things from the wise and understanding, and revealed them to infants. [26] Yes, Father, for so it was well-pleasing in your sight. [27] All things have been delivered to me by my Father. No one knows the Son, except the Father; neither does anyone know the Father, except the Son, and he to whom the Son desires to reveal him.

[28] "Come to me, all you who labor and are heavily burdened, and I will give you rest. [29] Take my yoke upon you, and learn from me, for I am gentle and humble in heart; and you will find rest for your souls. [30] For my yoke is easy, and my burden is light."

Because they are similar in style and thought to John's Gospel, verses 25-27 are called the Johannine portion of Matthew; there isn't anything like them in the rest of the Synoptics.

The "wise and understanding" could well be the religious leaders and/or those who believe they can "figure" out God without God's revelation. The "infants" mentioned could be those, regardless of age, whose minds, and hearts, are open to what God may be doing. The former of these terms points to the men who pride themselves upon their speculative or philosophical attainments; the latter to the men of worldly shrewdness—the clever, the sharp-witted, the men of affairs (CCE.)

But Jesus is not condemning education or knowledge, He is condemning "intellectual pride," which is often a problem today, as it was in ancient Judaism (DSB, p. 14). The knowledge of God was "hidden...from the wise and learned, and revealed...to little children." "Man does not discover God, but God reveals himself to those who trust him (BBC, p. 144)."

113

To whom is this revealed? It goes "…to babe-like [little children] men; men of unassuming docility, men who, conscious that they know nothing, and have no right to sit in judgment on the things that belong to their peace, determine simply to 'hear what God the Lord will speak' (CCE)."

The statement, "All things have been delivered to me by my Father" is the clearest claim Jesus has made to the fact that He, and no one else, is the center of the faith we claim. "Other men may be sons of God; he is 'The Son' (DSB, p. 15)."

To "know," as used here, means more than just to have knowledge of; it means to know someone well enough to trust them. Jesus says to know the Father, the Son must "reveal him." God the Father, through God the Son, still takes the initiative in salvation.

The Jews used the yoke as a symbol for submission to something. The study of the Law was considered a "yoke," and a "burden," we'll see some examples of how true this was in Chapter 12. The invitation of the Pharisees had been a great burden to the people so instead of the study of God's word being a joy, it became a burden.

Jesus' invitation to "all you who labor and are heavily burdened," is an invitation to "rest," but "rest" might better be translated "relief." "Jesus does not promise…a life of inactivity or repose, nor freedom from struggle, but He does assure them that…they will find relief from such crushing burdens… (TNTC, p. 122)" "…easy" means kind and good and can mean well fitted; a poorly fit yoke would chafe the neck and injure the animal. If this is the idea, then Jesus is claiming to be the master yoke maker.

"Jesus…also calls His disciples to accept a yoke' but how different is His yoke! …it is not really obedience to any external law at all, for it is first and foremost loyalty to a Person (TNTC, p. 122)." It should also be noted that a yoke is designed for two animals working together. Often that was an experienced, trained animal pulling with an untrained animal. The one pulling with us is the Holy Spirit. "[My yoke] may easily be carried. For his commandments are not grievous, for all who are born of God overcome the world… (GN)." "For whatever is born of God overcomes the world. This is the victory that has overcome the world: your faith." (1 John 5:4).

I have labeled this "The Custom-Made Yoke" because God's expectation of us is unique to each of us; it is not a "cookie cutter," "one size fits all" approach. God does not expect us to do things that He has not gifted and equipped us to do, but He does often expect us to stretch to do it. And God has often confounded the religious professionals and experts by revealing His plans to the seemingly unimportant and unimpressive in the Kingdom.

What about "Blue Laws"?
Matthew 12:1-8

At that time, Jesus went on the Sabbath day through the grain fields. His disciples were hungry and began to pluck heads of grain and to eat. ² But the Pharisees, when they saw it, said to him, "Behold, your disciples do what is not lawful to do on the Sabbath."

³ But he said to them, "Haven't you read what David did, when he was hungry, and those who were with him; ⁴ how he entered into God's house, and ate the show bread, which was not lawful for him to eat, neither for those who were with him, but only for the priests (1 Sam. 21:3-6)? [5] *Or have you not read in the law, that on the Sabbath day, the priests in the temple profane the Sabbath, and are guiltless?* [6] *But I tell you that one greater than the temple is here.* [7] *But if you had known what this means, 'I desire mercy, and not sacrifice' (Hos. 6:6) you would not have condemned the guiltless.* [8] *For the Son of Man is Lord of the Sabbath."*

In Chapter 12 we see a series of developments in the Pharisees' opposition to Jesus' ministry. These are decisive events in Jesus' life that show the movement of the religious leaders to a decision that Jesus must be eliminated. Barclay says that four things are taking place:

1. Verses 1-8 show a growing "suspicion" of a teacher that disregarded the minutiae of the Sabbath law.

2. Verses 9-14 show a hostile "investigation" with a "malignant eye" seeking charges that may be brought against him.

3. Verse 14 shows evil "determination" as they seek a way to put an end to their enemy.

4. Verses 22-32 show a deliberate, prejudiced "blindness;" Jesus could not do anything right in their eyes (DSB, p. 19).

Barclay also finds five ways Jesus met their opposition:

1. Verses 9-14 show courageous "defiance," His actions were not done in secret, but in public.

2. Verses 22-32 issues a "warning," do not shut out the grace of God.

3. Verses 6, 41 and 42 are "claims: of who He is."

4. Verses 43-45 state that His teaching is "essential," the law leaves a man empty, the Gospel fills him up.

5. Verses 46-50 issues an "invitation" to become a part of the family of God (DSB, pp. 19-21).

Based on their interpretation of the Law, the Pharisees had 39 categories of things that were forbidden on the Sabbath. Harvesting grain by cutting or plucking it from the stalks was one of those categories. Then the disciples "doubled-down" but rubbing it in their hands and "thrashing" it so they could eat it. There was no room for compassion toward their fellow-man in their system but the point of the Law was to bring people to God, not drive them away.

For Jesus, nothing was more important than a person's relationship to God. The Sabbath, or day of rest, was unique to Israel and the rules the Pharisees developed over time were strictly enforced. The thing that enraged them was this: Jesus made himself "Lord of the Sabbath" and placed Himself and mankind above the Sabbath. This view was the opposite of that held by the Pharisees. In fact, they would even rather be killed than defend themselves on the Sabbath (1 Maccabees 2:31-38).

When the Pharisees said: "Behold, your disciples do what is not lawful to do on the Sabbath," they were not accusing them of stealing. "When you come into your neighbor's standing grain, then you may pluck the ears with your hand; but you shall not move a sickle to your neighbor's standing grain" (Deut. 23:25). The fields were laid out in long strips with a path between them. People traveling down the path were then, and still are, allowed to take an ear and eat it.

The Fourth Commandment, "Remember the Sabbath day, to keep it holy" (Ex 20:8) is at the heart of the problem here. And in spite of the commandment, the Sabbath was observed in varying degrees even among the Pharisees and they were often more apt to "enforce" it among others than themselves.

When Matthew says, "His disciples were hungry" he tells us that this wasn't just a casual event; they were hungry! The problem was that "work" on the Sabbath was forbidden and what they were doing was considered "work." Jesus' defense of his disciples takes four fronts:

1. There is an appeal to David's actions in 1 Samuel 21:1-6. There was no condemnation of David's actions reported in Scripture. The implication is that man and his wellbeing are more important than the Sabbath laws.

2. There is a statement of the Sabbath laws as it related to the priests. Jesus pointed out that the priests have required duties on the Sabbath and they required "work." "On the Sabbath day two male lambs a year old without blemish, and two tenth parts of an ephah of fine flour for a meal offering, mixed with oil, and the drink offering of it: this is the burnt offering of every Sabbath, besides the continual burnt offering, and the drink offering of it" (Numbers 28:9-10).

3. There is a reminder of God's statement "For I desire mercy, and not sacrifice; And the knowledge of God more than burnt offerings" (Hosea 6:6) "...we have no evidence that Jesus ever conducted a church service in all his life on earth, but we have abundant evidence that he fed the hungry and comforted the sad and cared for the sick. Christian service is not the service of any liturgy or ritual; it is the service of human need (DSB, p. 25)."

4. There is a statement concerning the priority of the Sabbath. Jesus said, "For the Son of Man is Lord of the Sabbath." There are two possible interpretations of the phrase "Son of Man." First, Jesus is the "Son of Man" and as such, He is superior to the Law, even as the temple regulations are superior to the Law." Second, the statement "Son of Man" in English simply means "a man," actually any man.

We cannot be certain what is meant, because the early manuscripts do not have an indication, the letters are all capitalized, not just Son. Mark says, "He said to them, 'The Sabbath was made for man, not man for the Sabbath. Therefore, the Son of Man is lord even of the Sabbath'" (Mark 2:27-28). This does not clarify the problem, but may mean that actually both interpretations are correct.

Jesus doesn't infer that we do not need rules or that we should throw out our tradition, but we must set proper priorities. The "Blue Laws" of the past forbidding doing business on Sunday never brought people to Jesus, but they were used by Satan to drive a wedge between believers and nonbelievers. When rules and traditions hurt people, we need to examine them carefully.

Choose Your Battleground Carefully
Matthew 12:9-14

He departed there, and went into their synagogue. [10] And behold there was a man with a withered hand. They asked him, "Is it lawful to heal on the Sabbath day?" that they might accuse him.

[11] He said to them, "What man is there among you, who has one sheep, and if this one falls into a pit on the Sabbath day, won't he grab on to it, and lift it out? [12] Of how much more value then is a man than a

sheep! Therefore it is lawful to do good on the Sabbath day." ¹³ Then he told the man, "Stretch out your hand." He stretched it out; and it was restored whole, just like the other. ¹⁴ But the Pharisees went out, and conspired against him, how they might destroy him.

Is this the hill you want to die on? As Jesus' "radical" behavior continued, the Pharisees saw a continued threat to a tradition lost in antiquity and to their authority to set the religious rules. The unnamed man is identified in the *Gospel According to the Hebrews*, which is not an accepted part of our Bible, as a stone mason. Clearly the man's life was not in danger and one more day wouldn't matter to him. Or would it?

What's really happening here? Verse 10b says, "They asked him, 'Is it lawful to heal on the Sabbath day?' that they might accuse him." They knew full well that it was "lawful" to heal on the Sabbath, but in their interpretation, only if the person were in immediate danger of death. They also knew Jesus well enough to that know He would accept their "challenge." Unfortunately for them, again they weren't prepared for His response.

Jesus turned the encounter into a reevaluation of the worth of people. He asked, "What man is there among you, who has one sheep, and if this one falls into a pit on the Sabbath day, won't he grab on to it, and lift it out?" The answer was obvious, sheep had value. They needed them for food, wool, wealth, etc. naturally they would rescue it.

His response to their silence was, "Of how much more value then is a man than a sheep!" Are we also guilty of valuing things above some people? We are when we ignore the hurt around us while we enjoy what "we're entitled to."

Jesus' statement, "Therefore it is lawful to do good on the Sabbath day" clearly states a new principle; failure to do good is evil. In healing the man, Jesus did more than just restore his health; he gave him back his ability to earn a living and thereby restored his dignity.

From Mark 3:5 we learn that Jesus, "When he had looked around at them with anger, being grieved at the hardening of their hearts, he said to the man, 'Stretch out your hand.' He stretched it out, and his hand was restored as healthy as the other" "This is one of the very few passages in the Gospel history which reveal our Lord's *feelings*. How holy this anger was appears from the 'grief' which mingled with it at 'the hardness of their hearts' (CCE)."

The failure of the argument is expressed in the Pharisee's response, "But the Pharisees went out, and conspired against him, how they might destroy him." According to their rules, planning what you are going to do was considered work, so they broke their interpretation of the Law. If you're going to argue with someone, be sure you can win.

Do the Right Thing because It's the Right Thing to Do.
Matthew 12:15-21

Jesus, perceiving that, withdrew from there. Great multitudes followed him; and he healed them all, ¹⁶ and commanded them that they should not make him known: ¹⁷ that it might be fulfilled which was spoken through Isaiah the prophet, saying,

[18] *"Behold, my servant whom I have chosen; my beloved in whom my soul is well pleased: I will put my Spirit on him. He will proclaim justice to the nations. [19] He will not strive, nor shout; neither will anyone hear his voice in the streets. [20] He won't break a bruised reed. He won't quench a smoking flax, until he leads justice to victory. [21] In his name, the nations will hope"* (Isa. 42:1-4).

Jesus was receiving increased opposition from the Pharisees for the miracles He was performing and increasing pressure from the crowds to do even more. It is possibly because of this that he took one of His rare respites as "the perversity of man temporarily limits divine grace (IB, p. 395)."

Why would He command those healed not to "make him known"? Could it be because He didn't want people coming to Him for the wrong reasons? Could it be because it would take time away from His teaching time? Both of these are good options, but there are probably other good reasons also.

The Jews expected the Messiah to be a king, but He wasn't the kind of king they were expecting. "Like the crowd in Jesus' day, we may want Christ to rule as a king and bring great and visible victories in our life. But often Christ's work is quiet, and it happens according to *his* perfect timing, not ours (LASB, p. 1566)."

With, "that it might be fulfilled which was spoken through Isaiah the prophet," Matthew appropriates another fulfillment of prophesy. The passage originally referred to Cyrus, the Persian king who was seen as an instrument of God to bring judgment on the Jews. The interesting thing about this quotation is that it is not a direct quote from either the Greek or the Hebrew version of Isaiah 42:1-4:

Behold, my servant, whom I uphold; my chosen, in whom my soul delights—I have put my Spirit on him. He will bring justice to the nations. He will not shout, nor raise his voice, nor cause it to be heard in the street. He won't break a bruised reed. He won't quench a dimly burning wick. He will faithfully bring justice. He will not fail nor be discouraged, until he has set justice in the earth, and the islands will wait for his law.

This is one of the "Suffering Servant" portions originally applied to the nation of Israel and then to the coming Messiah. Like many of us, Matthew, either paraphrased or misquoted it.

The statement, "He will not strive, nor shout;" could be used to refer to a brawler, a barking dog, a cawing raven or the uproar of a discontented audience in a theater. Jesus' conquest would be a quiet conquest of love, not a violent overthrow of the existing government.

Some of us have a harsh view of justice; we see it as being meted out by a dispassionate judge but the picture here is of a gentle judge. Isaiah says, "He won't break a bruised reed. He won't quench a smoking flax, until he leads justice to victory." "Instead of crushing people, he seeks to heal the mortally wounded and to fan each spark of faith into a flame (BBC, p. 148)."

The reed could be worthless, used for fuel for the fire, or it could be turned into a musical instrument. It would depend on who plucked it and how it was used. A smoldering wick would be of little use, but if it were trimmed and taken care of, it could again be used to bring light to the house.

Jesus will lead the faithful to victory and "will pronounce sentence and judgment, in spite of the world and Satan, and show himself conqueror over all his enemies (GN)."

What Is Unforgivable?
Matthew 12:22-32

Then one possessed by a demon, blind and mute, was brought to him and he healed him, so that the blind and mute man both spoke and saw. [23] *All the multitudes were amazed, and said, "Can this be the son of David?"* [24] *But when the Pharisees heard it, they said, "This man does not cast out demons, except by Beelzebul, the prince of the demons."*

[25] *Knowing their thoughts, Jesus said to them, "Every kingdom divided against itself is brought to desolation, and every city or house divided against itself will not stand.* [26] *If Satan casts out Satan, he is divided against himself. How then will his kingdom stand?* [27] *If I by Beelzebul cast out demons, by whom do your children cast them out? Therefore they will be your judges.* [28] *But if I by the Spirit of God cast out demons, then God's Kingdom has come upon you.* [29] *Or how can one enter into the house of the strong man, and plunder his goods, unless he first bind the strong man? Then he will plunder his house.*

[30] *"He who is not with me is against me, and he who doesn't gather with me, scatters.* [31] *Therefore I tell you, every sin and blasphemy will be forgiven men, but the blasphemy against the Spirit will not be forgiven men.* [32] *Whoever speaks a word against the Son of Man, it will be forgiven him; but whoever speaks against the Holy Spirit, it will not be forgiven him, neither in this age, nor in that which is to come.*

Does this passage remind you of Lincoln's "House Divided" speech? It should because he doubtlessly borrowed it from Jesus. What Lincoln said was true of our nation is also true of spiritual kingdoms.

We have seen before that it is dangerous to debate with Jesus; that truth has not changed here. In response to their accusation, Jesus offered three irrefutable answers:

1. To use the power of demons to cast out demons would divide the kingdom to which they both belonged. If that were the case, the kingdom would collapse.

2. Some of the Jews, presumably Pharisees, practiced exorcism; was their power from "Beelzebub" also? (However, they didn't do it the way Jesus did, by speaking a word, but with a liturgy dating back to Solomon.)

3. Since Jesus' healing was for the good of the individual, the demon in charge, "the strongman," had to be neutralized, bound, first. If this was the case, when was he bound?

In driving out the demons, the power of the Kingdom of God was demonstrated as being stronger than the power of the kingdom of Satan. Something more important than that has also occurred; "But if I by the Spirit of God cast out demons, then God's Kingdom has come upon you." This is the only time Matthew refers to God's Kingdom, a term he reserves to refer to the Kingdom after Christ's return, as having come. In the Greek, the wording is very strong. "The very proclamation of the Kingdom was a victory over demonic forces (AB. p. 156)."

Barclay points out "the sign of the coming of the Kingdom was not full churches and great revival meetings, but 'the defeat of pain' (DSB, p. 39)" the pain of guilt has been banished forever. "The kingdom of Christ and the kingdom of the devil cannot abide together (GN)."

There were apparently Jewish exorcists going about in the land driving out demons. What power were they using "...if they said that Jesus cast out devils by the prince of the devils, they could not prove that their children cast them out by any other power (MH)."

In verse 30, we have two problems, Jesus says: "He who is not with me is against me, and he who doesn't gather with me scatters." The first problem is the possible contradiction with Mark 9:40 "For whoever is not against us is on our side." and Luke 9:50 "Jesus said to him, 'Don't forbid him, for he who is not against us is for us.'" Looking at the context we find the event takes place when the disciples rebuked someone who was not from their group, but was casting out demons in Jesus' name. In other words, they were part of the wrong "denomination." The Arabs have an interesting saying, "The enemy of my enemy is my friend."

Barclay suggests we should apply the "Matthew" test to ourselves: "Am I truly on the Lord's side...?" And apply the Mark/Luke test to others: "Am I limiting the Kingdom of God to those who think as I do? (DSB, pp. 40-41)."

The second problem is that there is no possibility for neutrality. As He usually does, Jesus poses the argument so that there are only two sides. You either fight with Him or against Him; refusal to join Him gives aid to the enemy. And, like the fellow in the Civil War who wore a grey coat and blue pants, you are shot at by both sides. "...the campaign between God and Satan has begun in earnest, and in that campaign neutrality is impossible (TNCT, p. 128)." Not to choose God is to choose Satan, however, not to choose Satan doesn't mean that you choose God.

What about the unforgivable sin? What is unforgivable? Divorce? Remarriage? No, they aren't IT! Women pastors? Maybe, he said tongue firmly implanted in cheek. No, not even that. Sorry, but Jesus said only one thing is unforgivable and that is "blasphemy against the Holy Spirit."

Isaiah warned, "Woe to those who call evil good, and good evil; who put darkness for light, and light for darkness; who put bitter for sweet, and sweet for bitter!" (Isa. 5:20). However, that is exactly what the Pharisees were doing.

Stagg says, "As Jesus ministered in their midst, a blind man saw and religious leaders went 'blind' (BBC, p. 148)." Why? Probably because the father of all sin is pride and they were proud: proud of their parentage, proud of their righteousness, proud of their religious position, proud of their understanding of the Law. They were so proud; they could not accept anyone who disagreed with or diminished their status. A very sad fact of life is that many of us "conservatives" may fall into that same trap.

What about God, isn't He forever forgiving? "Jesus is not saying that God is ever unwilling to forgive but that man can render himself unforgivable (BBC, p. 149)." The principle is this: closing your eyes does not put out the light; it just blinds you to the light. I think this is the best way to understand "the unforgivable sin."

"Two things are here implied—first, that the bitterest enemies of our Lord were unable to deny the reality of His miracles; and next, that they believed in an *organized internal kingdom of evil,* under one chief (CCE)." The argument presented is impossible to argue:

No organized society can stand—whether kingdom, city, or household—when turned against itself; such intestine war is suicidal: But the works I do are destructive of Satan's kingdom: That I should be in league with Satan, therefore, is incredible and absurd. … If this expulsion of Satan is, and can be, by no other than the Spirit of God, then is his Destroyer already in the midst of you, and that kingdom which is destined to supplant his is already rising on its ruins (CCE).

In verses 31 and 32, it is clear that Jesus is saying the Pharisees, by attributing His power to Beelzebub rather than the Holy Spirit, are committing the very sin they are accusing Jusus of committing, blasphemy! Are you worried that you may have committed the "unforgivable sin"? Then relax! "But humble and conscientious believers, at times are tempted to think they have committed the unpardonable sin, while those who have come the nearest to it, seldom have any fear about it (MH)." Buttrick feels, and most agree, that the process along the road to committing this sin involves three preparatory steps: grieving the Holy Spirit (Eph. 4:30); resisting the Holy Spirit (Act 6:9-10); and quenching the Holy Spirit (1 Thess. 5:19). Buttrick says, "At long last there is no pardon, because there is no desire for pardon - or even recognition of [a need for] it (IB, p. 400)." Uneducated people can be taught, weak people can be strengthened, but people whose minds are made up cannot be helped until they are ready.

Using Good Judgment
Matthew 12:33-37

"Either make the tree good, and its fruit good, or make the tree corrupt, and its fruit corrupt; for the tree is known by its fruit. [34] You offspring of vipers, how can you, being evil, speak good things? For out of the abundance of the heart, the mouth speaks. [35] The good man out of his good treasure brings out good things, and the evil man out of his evil treasure (TR adds "of the heart") brings out evil things. [36] I tell you that every idle word that men speak, they will give account of it in the day of judgment. [37] For by your words you will be justified, and by your words you will be condemned."

Matthew places this saying right after the passage where the Pharisees attributed Jesus' power to Satan. Satan is bad and his fruit is bad. God is good and His fruit is good. Where is the center of evil? Don't look around, look inside. Luke's coverage is very similar (Luke 6:43-45).

The trouble with the scribes and Pharisees was like the problem of the root that feeds a tree. If a tree gets proper nutrients, it will produce good fruit. But if the tree is fed poisons, not only will the fruit be bad, but it will eventually kill the tree.

There are two special problems addressed, "out of the overflow of the heart the mouth speaks" and men will "give account...for every careless word they have spoken."

The first difficulty is stated in the saying of Menander the Greek dramatist, "A man's character can be known from his conversations." After talking casually and candidly to a person for a little while, you can usually find out what kind of person they are.

The second hurdle is more difficult. The word "careless" is *aergos*. Remember, "a" on the front of a Greek word means no or not, *ergos* means deed, so we have something that is not meant to produce deeds of any kind. It is applied to a barren tree, uncultivated land, and a lazy person.

Normally, we are careful what we say. We select our words carefully to be sure not to offend or not to say too much about something. But, the "idle" word is that which is not thought out, like a "Freudian slip," it jumps out in an unguarded moment, as when angry or upset.

Verse 36 presents a real problem for people like me who are quick with a quip or a remark that may not be understood by everyone. I have no idea how many times I've had to go and apologize to someone, and those are the ones I know about. Even worse, what about those who were hurt and I didn't learn about them.

There is also a problem with those who want to play the "devil's advocate." There is no place in the church for a Christian to offer his or her services to take Satan's position. There is room for debate and questioning, but trust me, Satan will supply his own advocate. We are to be united in Christ! You do no service to the Lord when you act for Satan. "Let us keep constant watch over ourselves, that we may speak words agreeable to the Christian character (MH)."

Judgment
Matthew 12:38-42

Then certain of the scribes and Pharisees answered, "Teacher, we want to see a sign from you."

39 But he answered them, "An evil and adulterous generation seeks after a sign, but no sign will be given to it but the sign of Jonah the prophet. 40 For as Jonah was three days and three nights in the belly of the whale, so will the Son of Man be three days and three nights in the heart of the earth. 41 The men of Nineveh will stand up in the judgment with this generation, and will condemn it, for they repented at the preaching of Jonah; and behold, someone greater than Jonah is here. 42 The queen of the south will rise up in the judgment with this generation, and will condemn it, for she came from the ends of the earth to hear the wisdom of Solomon; and behold, someone greater than Solomon is here.

Some have suggested, and there seems to be some evidence, that this was a different group of sincere, but confused Pharisees with a genuine desire to understand who and what Jesus was. They sought "something of an immediate and decisive nature, to show, not that His miracles were *real*–that they seemed willing to concede—but that they were from above, not from beneath (CCE).

However, the Pharisees, in general, had witnessed several miracles and now they requested a "sign." What had they been seeing? Often a Rabbi, or teacher, for that was their primary function, was requested to perform some wonder to validate his teaching. "To demand the kind of sign that the Pharisees were demanding was evidence of a lack of trust that God could and would reveal Himself and His purposes when He willed, and in the way He willed (TNTC, pp. 132-133)." It's like a boy asking a girl to "prove her love." Neither the Pharisees nor the boy are open to the evidence that is already there.

"Signs were granted to those who desired them to confirm their faith, as Abraham and Gideon; but denied to those who demanded them to excuse their unbelief (MH)." These wanted to see God in the supernatural, not in the ordinary, everyday events. What they needed was a willingness to believe, not more proof. The proof of Jesus' truth would be obvious to anyone whose mind wasn't already closed and made up.

To call them "evil and adulterous" is to echo the prophets cry against the unfaithfulness of their ancestors, another good word might be "apostate." They had already attributed the work of God to the devil, whatever Jesus did would also be explained away. Remember that Jesus said to the rich man who wanted someone from the dead to go talk to his brothers, "If they don't listen to Moses and the prophets, neither will they be persuaded if one rises from the dead." (Luke 16:31).

The only "sign" Jesus offered was that "of the prophet Jonah," but there must be more to it than the "three days and three nights in the belly of the whale" because Luke does not mention the whale at all. Jonah was a reluctant prophet preaching to people with no religious background, yet the Ninevites repented, and Jesus is certainly much more than Jonah was. Jonah himself was God's "sign" to the Ninevites and Jesus was God's "sign" to Israel.

It is very sad when people would rather stumble in the darkness than use the light they have available to them from the flashlight they are carrying in their hand. "Christ teaches, by the sorrowful example of the Jews, that there are none more miserable than they who put out the light of the gospel which was kindled in them (GN)."

Jesus' first prediction of His death, burial and resurrection came in John 2:19 when He "cleansed" the Temple. "Jesus answered them, 'Destroy this temple, and in three days I will raise it up.'"

Some will suggest that the statement "three days and three nights in the heart of the earth" is not to be taken literally; they will explain that any portion of a day would qualify as a day for them and that may be true, but they are trying to force the crucifixion to (Good) Friday to meet the established Christian calendar. Had Jesus only said, "three days," I would have less of a problem with the Friday crucifixion, but when He added the "nights" it moved into a new realm. I believe Jesus said what He meant and meant what He said in other places, why would I make an exception here? But does it really matter when He died? No! Certainly, it is not enough to create a new field of battle between Christians, we have more than enough already!

The Danger of Inactivity
Matthew 12:43-45

When an unclean spirit has gone out of a man, he passes through waterless places, seeking rest, and doesn't find it. ⁴⁴ Then he says, 'I will return into my house from which I came out,' and when he has come back, he finds it empty, swept, and put in order. ⁴⁵ Then he goes, and takes with himself seven other spirits more evil than he is, and they enter in and dwell there. The last state of that man becomes worse than the first. Even so will it be also to this evil generation."

This parable represents the case of the Jewish church and nation. It is also applicable to all those who hear the word of God, and are in part reformed, but not truly converted. The unclean spirit leaves for a time, but when he returns, he finds Christ is not there to shut him out; the heart is swept by outward reformation, but garnished by preparation to comply with evil suggestions, and the man becomes a more decided enemy of the truth. Every heart is the residence of unclean spirits, except those which are temples of the Holy Ghost, by faith in Christ (MH).

More than giving up bad habits is required of a Christian; first, follow Jesus and second, we must learn good ones. Several times in Israel's history idolatry was banned and the idols destroyed, but the hearts of the people were not changed and the idols returned.

By the time Jesus arrived on the scene, there was no longer any visible sign of idolatry, but it had been replaced by a new idolatry. An idolatry of pride, laws about the Sabbath, work, fasting, etc. These idols were actually worse than Baal and the other gods.

According to Jewish folklore, demons needed water to find rest and that may be why this one wandered and returned. Nature abhors a vacuum, having no faith is as bad as what we might call having "bad faith." Faith must be positive. The Pharisees had removed the "big" sins from their lives, but they were left empty and the "unclean spirit" returned with his friends and established himself. There was nothing left but loyalty to Judaism and the Law and now the entire nation was in danger of collapse. Barclay finds three things to notice:

1. The evil spirit is banished, not destroyed. Evil can be conquered, but it is always looking for an opportunity to counter-attack.

2. Negative religion is never enough. It may clean up a person, but it cannot keep him clean.

3. The only permanent cure for evil action is Christian action. The one fatal disease is idleness (DSB, p. 51).

Who Is Your Family?
Matthew 12:46-50

While he was yet speaking to the multitudes, behold, his mother and his brothers stood outside, seeking to speak to him. [47] One said to him, "Behold, your mother and your brothers stand outside, seeking to speak to you."

[48] But he answered him who spoke to him, "Who is my mother? Who are my brothers?" [49] He stretched out his hand towards his disciples, and said, "Behold, my mother and my brothers! [50] For whoever does the will of my Father who is in heaven, he is my brother, and sister, and mother."

This statement about family makes one thing perfectly clear: Kinship does not come from blood, unless it is the blood of Jesus! However, there is no hint that family is not important; He made provision for His mother during His crucifixion and He used the word "Father" to identify Yahweh.

The Synoptics do not present Mary as an important person and, outside of the birth narratives, this is the only place she appears in Matthew; John portrays her as a believer. No one really understands what Jesus is doing here. These friends of Jesus, and possibly His family, thought He was crazy, but it is true, when we don't understand what someone is doing, sometimes we incorrectly surmise they are insane. It's one of life's great tragedies when a person isn't understood, and accepted, by those closest to them until after they are dead; that was the case with Jesus and it must have hurt deeply.

True family and friendship are based on two factors that are at least as important as blood relationship. First, there are common ideals and second, there are common experiences. If there is no sense of family among church members, the church is missing its primary task. I personally like adding "brother" or "sister" to a fellow-believer's name because we are truly brother and sister in the Lord. The "people of the land," as the Pharisees and Greeks called the common people, should find love, acceptance, support and understanding within the walls of the church.

"Christ's preaching was plain, easy, and familiar, and suited to his hearers. His mother and brethren stood without, desiring to speak with him, when they should have been standing within, desiring to hear him (MH)." Luke 8:19 does suggest they may have tried but could not get in because of the crowd, but it should be noted that there are times when family, and family obligations, must come after the Lord's work. We must be careful, however that we don't use ministry as an excuse to ignore our familial responsibilities. Paul warns, "But if anyone doesn't provide for his own, and especially his own household, he has denied the faith, and is worse than an unbeliever" (1 Tim. 5:8).

You may have noticed that Joseph isn't mentioned, in fact, he hasn't been mentioned since the event in the Temple when Jesus was twelve years old, as recorded in Luke 2:39-52. Many suggest that this indicates that he was dead by this time. While it is probably a good guess, we simply do not know.

Note—if your translation omits verse 47, that is because it isn't found in some of the older texts; some think it was borrowed from Mark 3:32. Either way, with or without the verse, the meaning is not changed.

I have a problem with the depiction of Mary as an active participant in Jesus' ministry since His miracle at Cana in "The Chosen." One reason is this section of Scripture which indicates that not only was she not involved, but that she also may have had some concerns, at this time. There is little question that toward the end of His ministry, she was present, but at an unknown level.

Are Your Ears Working?
Matthew 13:1-9

On that day Jesus went out of the house, and sat by the seaside. [2] Great multitudes gathered to him, so that he entered into a boat, and sat, and all the multitude stood on the beach. [3] He spoke to them many things in parables, saying, "Behold, a farmer went out to sow. [4] As he sowed, some seeds fell by the roadside, and the birds came and devoured them. [5] Others fell on rocky ground, where they didn't have much soil, and immediately they sprang up, because they had no depth of earth. [6] When the sun had risen, they were scorched. Because they had no root, they withered away. [7] Others fell among thorns. The thorns [thistles] grew up and choked them. [8] Others fell on good soil, and yielded fruit: some one hundred times as much, some sixty, and some thirty. [9] He who has ears to hear, let him hear."

Here, Matthew introduces us to Jesus' use of parables. (Actually, Matthew 7:24-27 and 11:16-17 are also classified as parables.) This is an important event, because it is a turning point in His ministry; He leaves the synagogue, the local assembly, and goes to the seashore where the people are.

To those who are honestly searching, the truth becomes clear. We must be careful not to read too much into parables, forcing them to say what they don't mean. Each parable has a central meaning unless otherwise specified by Jesus. (LASB, p. 1568).

Let's explore parables in general before we begin because they are a very old and common form of teaching. The Greek word *parabole* was used forty-five times in the LXX to translate the Hebrew word *mashal*. The literal meaning is "cast alongside" and refers to the use of an illustration to make the meaning clearer and more easily understood. Most of us can't remember Sunday's sermon, but we will probably remember a good story or illustration from it for years!

We use several grammatical forms in language arts today to help make things clearer for our readers or listeners. A simile describes one thing as being "like" another. A metaphor says that one thing is another. An allegory assigns meaning; often abstract meaning, to things or ideas; often with hidden meanings. There are several advantages to the use of parables. Some of them are:

1. They present truth in an understandable form. Abstract concepts are difficult for many of us to grasp; parables give us a word picture which is easier to "see" and understand.

2. They begin where the listener is and takes them where the speaker wants to take them. Most of Jesus' parables were taken from the activities around Him and were intended to teach ordinary, uneducated people, not to be dissected in our study with a pile of books before us. By using concepts people can understand and showing how they relate to the idea being taught, we are better able to learn.

3. They grab the listener's interest and keep it. When a teacher tells stories about people and events of interest to us, we pay closer attention and learn more.

4. They allow us to discover what the truth is for ourselves. They do not tell us what we think; they ask us to draw our own conclusions from the facts presented.

5. They hide the truth from those whose minds are already made up or are too lazy to think for themselves. The open mind learns, the closed mind is offended (DSB, p. 55-56).

A parable usually has one main point and may use any or all of the above figures of speech; so, in seeking to understand parables, we should always ask, "What did this mean to the original hearers," we must be careful to resist two extremes: forcing parables to be allegories and forcing only one meaning on the parable. One other caution which is applicable to all Scripture, not just parables, it is okay to ask, "What does this parable or Scripture say to us today?" But we can't make it say the opposite of what it would have said to the original hearers.

This first set of parables total seven which may be significant since seven is a sacred number. The first four were told to the multitude and the other three were spoken to the disciples privately.

Another thing remarkable in the structure of these parables is, that while the first of the Seven—That of the Sower—is of the nature of an Introduction to the whole, the remaining Six consist of *three pairs*– the Second and Seventh, the Third and Fourth, and the Fifth and Sixth, corresponding to each other; each pair setting forth the same general truths, but with a certain diversity of aspect. All this can hardly be accidental (CCE).

Now to address the passage we want to look at: It was common practice for a farmer to "broadcast" his seed and then plow or rake it into the ground, that practice is still followed for some crops today. Naturally, some of the seed would be wasted, but he was trusting in a harvest that would provide food for his family and seed for the next crop from the seed that took root.

In identifying the various objects that make up the parable, "the path, rocky places, etc.," Jesus is simply acknowledging things they already knew would be part of a farmer's field. Certainly, some seed "sprang up quickly," and "when the sun came up, the plants were scorched…" These pictures, and those that followed, would not be lost on His audience, but they apparently were on the Pharisees. The next section addresses what this parable means.

What is the function of ears? They are for listening, but many of us use them only to hold up our glasses or to stuff hearing aids into and still don't hear what's going on around us. Very often parents spell things around small children so the kids won't know what they are saying, however, the children soon catch on. Maybe we should try harder to hear what we should and try to ignore that which is not our business. "He who has ears to hear, let him hear."

The Purpose of Parables
Matthew 13:10-17

The disciples came, and said to him, "Why do you speak to them in parables?"

[11] He answered them, "To you it is given to know the mysteries of the Kingdom of Heaven, but it is not given to them. [12] For whoever has, to him will be given, and he will have abundance, but whoever doesn't have, from him will be taken away even that which he has. [13] Therefore I speak to them in parables, because seeing they don't see, and hearing, they don't hear, neither do they understand. [14] In them the prophecy of Isaiah is fulfilled, which says,

'By hearing you will hear, and will in no way understand; Seeing you will see, and will in no way perceive: [15] for this people's heart has grown callous, their ears are dull of hearing, they have closed their eyes; or else perhaps they might perceive with their eyes, hear with their ears, understand with their heart, and would turn again; and I would heal them' (Isa. 6:9-10).

[16] "But blessed are your eyes, for they see; and your ears, for they hear. [17] For most certainly I tell you that many prophets and righteous men desired to see the things which you see, and didn't see them; and to hear the things which you hear, and didn't hear them.

Matthew's introduction of the parable of the farmer not only introduces parables in general, but he includes a brief lesson on how to understand them. Please remember parables are not intended to hide meaning, but to reveal it; meaning is there if you don't look too hard for it. "Parables serve the double purpose of *revealing* and *concealing;* presenting 'the mysteries of the kingdom' to those who know and relish them… but to those who are insensible to spiritual things yielding only…some temporary entertainment (CCE)."

The word "mysteries" in verse 11 is a good translation because it does not carry the power of the Greek word *musteria*, which would literally be "mystery" and had special meaning when used in connection with any ancient religion. A convert was trained in understanding the "mysteries" connected with the worship of his god(s), then when a presentation of their "secrets" was made, they would understand, but the uninstructed would only be confused. This was true of the "mystery religions" of the Romans and Greeks that were developing at the same time Jesus was teaching.

In a sense, Christianity is a "mystery religion;" that is to say, it can only be fully understood from the inside. It requires both an encounter with Jesus as Savior and instruction from the Scriptures; without these two experiences, it is not possible to understand God's message to us.

There are two strange statements in verse 12, "whoever has, to him will be given" and "whoever doesn't have, from him will be taken away even that which he has." Is that fair? Fair or not, it is certainly a reality of life. If you do not use the skills and talents you have, what will happen to them? If you use what you have, what happems? If it is true in these areas, why wouldn't it be true in the spiritual realm also?

Verse 13 is a problem for some, Jesus says, "Therefore I speak to them in parables, because seeing they don't see, and hearing, they don't hear, neither do they understand." Some take this statement to mean that Jesus was trying to keep people from understanding. What Jesus is actually saying is that unless He makes it simple, no one will understand and some, whose minds are not open, will never understand because they are looking for something "deeper" than is there on the surface. We must approach Scripture with an open heart and an open mind and, in the case of parables use the old KISS (Keep It Simple Stupid) method.

Jesus did not come to hide God's truth, but to make it clear and He selected teaching methods that would accomplish that end. God is speaking to us all the time, but are we listening? Notice the Isaiah 6 quotation "…they have closed their eyes," it is not God who closed their eyes, they closed them themselves. We need to be very careful that we do not do the same thing. "Jesus brought into reality what the prophets and OT saints desired to see and hear, that is the fulfillment of OT promises (NLTSB, p. 1604)."

Notice also the progression: "perceive with their eyes, hear with their ears, understand with their heart…" Conviction begins with seeing a problem, this causes us to want to hear or learn more about it, then being convicted something needs to be done and ends with our doing something about the problem. The scribes and Pharisees chose to closed their eyes, what will you do?

How to Understand Parables
Matthew 13:18-23

"Hear, then, the parable of the farmer. [19] When anyone hears the word of the Kingdom, and doesn't understand it, the evil one comes, and snatches away that which has been sown in his heart. This is what was sown by the roadside. [20] What was sown on the rocky places, this is he who hears the word, and immediately with joy receives it; [21] yet he has no root in himself, but endures for a while. When oppression or persecution arises because of the word, immediately he stumbles. [22] What was sown among the thorns, this is he who hears the word, but the cares of this age and the deceitfulness of riches choke the word, and he becomes unfruitful. [23] What was sown on the good ground, this is he who hears the word, and understands it, who most certainly bears fruit, and produces, some one hundred times as much, some sixty, and some thirty."

Clearly this parable can be interpreted from two different directions. The first method focuses on the soil and there are four types that Jesus points out and describes.

1. The people who have chosen to close their ears are like "seed sown along the path," there is no opportunity for any growth because it is gobbled up by the birds and small animals.

2. The people who get excited quickly; they go up like a sky rocket. Unfortunately, like a rocket, there is only great light and noise, and then nothing. This is the "seed that fell on rocky places." Because, they lack spiritual depth, they have no staying power, they become offended and just as quickly they are gone. They used to say it isn't how high you jump, but how straight you walk when you land that really matters.

3. The people who put the concerns of life ahead of the things of the spirit represent the "seed that fell among the thorns." They may approach their responsibilities toward Christ with an attitude something like, "Well, I have to make a living, don't I?" "But Jesus said to him, 'No one, having put his hand to the plow, and looking back, is fit for God's Kingdom.'" (Luke 9:62).

4. The people who are receptive are the seeds that "fell on good soil." What was the result? It "produces a crop, yielding a hundred, sixty or thirty times what was sown." The Psalmist reminds us: "He who goes out weeping, carrying seed for sowing, Will assuredly come again with joy, carrying his sheaves." (Ps. 126:6).

The most profound teaching in this method is also the simplest. The meaning is not buried, but is like diamonds lying in the dirt, right there on top waiting to be picked up. But, like the Pharisees, if you want, you can always kick a little dirt over them and say you can't find anything.

However, there is a problem with this first method, it changes the parable into an allegory, so many scholars do not think this interpretation actually came from Jesus; but it must have come from an authoritative source because it has always been held in high regard by the Church. Why not from Jesus?

The second approach, which looks at the "sower," would then be the preferred method of interpretation. Every farmer knows that not all of the seeds he plants will produce fruit. However, he also knows that if he doesn't plant seeds, he can't harvest anything. He must have faith or he will have no crop.

Can it be that that is what is meant by the parable addressed to Jesus' followers, then and now? He knew that ministry, whether by pastors or people, would be difficult. There would be people who would close their ears to the message. There would be people who would get excited, then fall away. There would be people who would be supportive for a while, then drop out. He also knew that some of the seed would grow and blossom and produce fruit. That fruit would provide a harvest sufficient not only to sustain them and others, but to provide the seeds for future crops.

"Though there is mention made of the heart, yet this sowing is referred to as hearing without understanding. For whether the seed is received in the heart or not, yet he that sows, sows to the heart (GN)."

Don't Be too Quick to Judge
Matthew 13:24-30

He set another parable before them, saying, "The Kingdom of Heaven is like a man who sowed good seed in his field, [25] but while people slept, his enemy came and sowed darnel weeds (darnel is a weed grass (probably bearded darnel) that looks very much like wheat until it is mature, when the difference becomes very apparent) also among the wheat, and went away. [26] But when the blade sprang up and produced fruit, then the darnel weeds appeared also. [27] The servants of the householder came and said to him, 'Sir, didn't you sow good seed in your field? Where did these darnel weeds come from?'

[28] *"He said to them, 'An enemy has done this.'*

"The servants asked him, 'Do you want us to go and gather them up?'

29 "But he said, 'No, lest perhaps while you gather up the darnel weeds, you root up the wheat with them. 30 Let both grow together until the harvest, and in the harvest time I will tell the reapers, "First, gather up the darnel weeds, and bind them in bundles to burn them; but gather the wheat into my barn."'"

This passage has always been surrounded by differences of opinion about its interpretation. There are two primary views: one, the minority view, says it is the words of Jesus and should be taken at "face value." Second, many have suggested that Mark 4:26-29 is the source and Matthew has adapted the information to produce this version, so I provide the Mark passage for your consideration.

He said, "The Kingdom of God is as if a man should cast seed on the earth, and should sleep and rise night and day, and the seed should spring up and grow, though he doesn't know how. For the earth bears fruit: first the blade, then the ear, then the full grain in the ear. But when the fruit is ripe, immediately he puts forth the sickle, because the harvest has come."

I have a little trouble accepting the second opinion because the major thrust, the weeds and separation (judgment) at the harvest are completely omitted. Remember, when Jesus says, "The Kingdom of Heaven is like..." He is saying there is something about the Kingdom of Heaven which can be compared to that thing or that experience. He is not saying, "The Kingdom of Heaven is..."

An "enemy" is not usually needed to plant the weeds, because every field has its weed seed awaiting tilling and irrigating, so is there a need to warn us that there is an "enemy" at work? Yes, there is! Satan is alive and well and active both in the world and in the church? We need to always be very aware that while Satan is at work, the Holy Spirit is here to lead us in the work we are called to do.

In Palestine there was a plant called bearded darnel which looks just like the wheat they would have planted and it isn't until the plants produced their "fruit" that they could really tell them apart. The danger in pulling the weeds before that time was simply that you might pull as much wheat as weeds.

The "servants" are the followers of Jesus, the disciples then and the church now, and they seem to be a different group than the "harvesters." Certainly, if this is a picture of the final judgment, that would be correct.

Looking at this section as a parable, verse 30 contains the point Jesus is making, "Let both grow together..." The church must always be aware that some of its membership may be weeds, but it must also be careful to wait until the fruit appears to make the determination; judgment is best left to God.

If we decide to judge others now, we're saying we want a weedless field so we must remove the weeds from our field and we have become Pharisees who "strain out a gnat, and swallow a camel" (Matt. 23:24b). That very thing has happened many times in many denominations as factions have sought to "weed out" those who are not following the Lord like they think they should, usually they are seen as "liberals."

The lesson for us to learn here is that God will do the judging, so leave it to Him. I would suggest that it is appropriate for us to be ruthless with our sin, but willing to allow God to deal with the sin of others.

A Growing Faith
Matthew 13:31-32

He set another parable before them, saying, "The Kingdom of Heaven is like a grain of mustard seed, which a man took, and sowed in his field; ³² which indeed is smaller than all seeds. But when it is grown, it is greater than the herbs, and becomes a tree, so that the birds of the air come and lodge in its branches."

Stagg says, "These parables [the parables of the mustard seed and the leaven] seem to be paired, contrasting the magnitude and might of the Kingdom of Heaven with its seemingly small and unpromising beginnings in Jesus (BBC, p. 157)." In this quote, Stagg gives us the main point of the parable, the beginning was small, but it has grown into a mighty Kingdom.

The mustard plant we know about is different than the mustard plant of Canaan. It was not the smallest seed that grew into a tree, the cypress seed was smaller, but it was a proverb for smallness in Jewish culture. In Luke 17:6 Jesus seized upon its size to demonstrate the power of faith: "...If you had faith like a grain of mustard seed..."

Mustard was grown for its seeds as well as for use as a vegetable. Rabbinic law prohibited its planting in the garden, so it was planted in the field and often grew to ten or more feet tall; birds perching in it to eat its seeds were a common sight.

The Kingdom of Heaven, like the mustard plant, begins small and grows and grows until it is a large and beautiful thing. This parable is great because it contains the promise that the Kingdom will grow into what God intends.

Clearly, the symbolism of the parable echoes Daniel 4:11-12:

The tree grew, and was strong, and its height reached to the sky, and its sight to the end of all the earth. The leaves of it were beautiful, and it had much fruit, and in it was food for all. The animals of the field had shade under it, and the birds of the sky lived in its branches, and all flesh was fed from it.

From an allegorical perspective, there is great symbolism in the things Jesus chose. In Jewish tradition, birds nesting in tree branches were representative of the Gentiles coming to enjoy the blessings of the Kingdom of God.

This is, above all, a parable of hope. How can a baby born in an obscure village, a man condemned to death on a Roman cross, be the Savior of the world? That's exactly how this is a parable of hope, both to His early disciples and to us today.

Can Evil Be Good?
Matthew 13:33-35

He spoke another parable to them. "The Kingdom of Heaven is like yeast, which a woman took, and hid in three measures (literally, three sata. 3 sata is about 39 liters or a bit more than a bushel of meal), until it was all leavened."

³⁴ Jesus spoke all these things in parables to the multitudes; and without a parable, he didn't speak to them, ³⁵ that it might be fulfilled which was spoken through the prophet, saying,

"I will open my mouth in parables;

I will utter things hidden from the foundation of the world" (Ps. 78:2).

Have you noticed the most important aspect of this teaching style? Each of the parables is built around something that was a common sight or event in the lives of the people He taught. When we teach, we should also draw upon things our pupils are already familiar with.

When we see yeast referred to in the NT, it is usually in a negative, evil sense. Here it is used positively. The Holy Spirit can use our teaching to "grow" the Kingdom. "This parable, while it teaches the same general truth as the foregoing one, holds forth, perhaps, rather the *inward* growth of the kingdom, while 'the Mustard Seed' seems to point chiefly to the *outward* (CCE)."

The preaching of the gospel works like leaven in the hearts of those who receive it. The leaven works certainly, so does the word, yet gradually. It works silently, and without being seen…yet strongly; without noise, for so is the way of the Spirit, but without fail. Thus it was in the world (MH).

Three measures (a bushel or 39 liters) would have provided bread for a fairly large family. The yeast used would be a starter, a small piece of dough left from the last batch. The message of the yeast is: the kingdom doesn't come from without, but from within. In the Old Testament, leaven always represented evil, but evil does not triumph over good. Because of this, it must have been very difficult for the Pharisees to accept this parable as valid. However, it is a good example because yeast changes the very nature of the dough. Without it, the dough would be more like a cracker than bread. With it, the dough is transformed and becomes "light" and tasty. Barclay lists five major areas where the "yeast" of Christianity changed the world:

1. The individual man. Look at what Paul says:
    Or don't you know that the unrighteous will not inherit God's Kingdom? Don't be deceived. Neither the sexually immoral, nor idolaters, nor adulterers, nor male prostitutes, nor homosexuals, nor thieves, nor covetous, nor drunkards, nor slanderers, nor extortionists, will inherit God's Kingdom. Such were some of you, but you were washed. But you were sanctified. But you were justified in the name of the Lord Jesus, and in the Spirit of our God. (1 Cor. 6:9-11).

2   The life of women. Women were property of their fathers until married and property of their husbands after marriage, in many non-Christian cultures, that is often still true today. In Christ "There is neither Jew nor Greek, there is neither slave nor free man, there is neither male nor female; for you are all one in Christ Jesus." (Gal. 3:28).

3. The weak and ill. The first institution for the care of the blind was founded by Thalasuis, a Christian monk; the first free "clinic" by Apollonius, a Christian merchant; the first hospital by Fabiola, a Christian woman.

4. The aged who were no longer able to be productive and were therefore a nuisance to be disposed of as quickly as possible.

5. The children. In pagan cultures children were routinely "exposed" and left to die if they were sickly or the wrong sex, a practice continued in some places in our world today and the unborn are often aborted if they are "inconvenient." Child labor laws were the results of concerned Christians. "But when Jesus saw it, he was moved with indignation, and said to them, 'Allow the little children to come to me! Don't forbid them, for God's Kingdom belongs to such as these.'" (Mark 10:14).

The formula Matthew uses: "Jesus spoke all these things to the crowd in parables; he did not say anything to them without using a parable," may indicate that the collection of parables at one time possibly ended here. We should also remember that this verse only applies to this situation, because Jesus used several other forms in His teaching.

"…that it might be fulfilled" is better translated "fulfilling" and is part of Matthew's desire to remind us of the many prophesies in the Old Testament about the Messiah. The quotation, as noted in the text is from Psalm 78:2.

Leave Judgment to God
Matthew 13:36-43

Then Jesus sent the multitudes away, and went into the house. His disciples came to him, saying, "Explain to us the parable of the darnel weeds of the field."

37 He answered them, "He who sows the good seed is the Son of Man, 38 the field is the world; and the good seed, these are the children of the Kingdom; and the darnel weeds are the children of the evil one. 39 The enemy who sowed them is the devil. The harvest is the end of the age, and the reapers are angels. 40 As therefore the darnel weeds are gathered up and burned with fire; so will it be at the end of this age. 41 The Son of Man will send out his angels, and they will gather out of his Kingdom all things that cause stumbling, and those who do iniquity, 42 and will cast them into the furnace of fire. There will be weeping and the gnashing of teeth. 43 Then the righteous will shine like the sun in the Kingdom of their Father. He who has ears to hear, let him hear.

It's interesting to me that neither Mark nor Luke gives an interpretation of the parable and Matthew again interprets it point by point, as if it is an allegory, but it isn't difficult to recognize and appreciate the symbolism.

If it is a parable, as Matthew says, the one main point "shot out" is that Christians and pagans live together in the world until the end of the age. At that time, "The Son of Man will send out his angels, and they will gather out of his Kingdom all things that cause stumbling, and those who do iniquity," (verse 41).

We must be careful that we don't become the Righteous Judge and attempt to do God's work. "It is possible that this parable served to caution the church against rashly expelling questionable members from its fellowship. ... More likely... [the] concern is with the impatience of those who wanted God to act immediately in outward and final judgment... (BBC, p. 159)."

When we assume the role of judge, we are disobedient to God's demands on our life and risk destroying good people along with those we consider bad; we must judge only ourselves. "But to stretch this so far as to justify allowing openly scandalous persons to remain in the communion of the Church, is to wrest the teaching of this parable to other than its proper design, and go in the teeth of apostolic injunctions (see 1 Cor. 5) (CCE)."

The judgment scene here is horrific for the "weeds."

What terrific strength of language—the "casting" or "flinging" is expressive of indignation, abhorrence, contempt…" the furnace of fire" denoting the fierceness of the torment: the "wailing" signifying the anguish this causes; while the 'gnashing of teeth' is a graphic way of expressing the despair in which its remedilessness issues (CCE)! (See Matthew 8:12)

But for the "wheat" it means blessings beyond our expectation.

Barclay points out five lessons this parable should teach:

1. That we must be on our guard, because there is a hostile power at work in the world waiting to destroy the good seed.

2. That it is [sometimes] hard to distinguish between Christians and pagans.

3. That we should not to be too quick to judge others; judgment must be based on a person's entire life, not just one episode.

4. That judgment does come in the end; we must be patient and allow God to judge when he is ready.

5. That only God has the right to judge.

Some scholars believe that the parable, verses 24-30 and its interpretation here weren't the words of either Jesus or Matthew. They believe the words were added toward the close of the first century to address the problem of what to do about heretics who were members and teachers in the congregation. That would make the situation similar to the claim that the book of Ruth was introduced at the time of Ezra and Nehemiah when persecution of those who had married foreigners began.

If what they say is true, it still "sounds like Jesus" who was always hard on sin but easy on sinners. Without substantiation, we should prefer to believe the Bible is the Bible and scholars are subject to error. "Those who will shine like the sun in God's Kingdom stand in contrast to those who receive his judgement (LASB, p. 1570)."

What Would You Give Everything For?
Matthew 13:44-46

"Again, the Kingdom of Heaven is like a treasure hidden in the field, which a man found, and hid. In his joy, he goes and sells all that he has, and buys that field.

[45] *"Again, the Kingdom of Heaven is like a man who is a merchant seeking fine pearls,* [46] *who having found one pearl of great price, he went and sold all that he had, and bought it."*

These two parables teach the same basic lesson, finding the Kingdom of Heaven is a joyous event because it is of infinite worth. Another paradox of Christianity is this: Salvation is free, but it costs you everything.

The banks in the ancient world were not available to ordinary people and the safest place for treasure was to bury it in the ground. In fact, there was a Rabbinic saying that the safest place for money is in the earth.

Palestine was in constant turmoil with more wars fought on its soil than most ancient Near-East countries; people would bury their valuables in the hope that when the trouble was over, they could return and dig them up. The dream of finding a buried treasure is still one of the most popular themes of literature, movies, and television.

The story Jesus used would be familiar to His audience because there were people who spent their lives looking for these treasures. Some think Jesus is encouraging people to do something improper; however, there was a rabbinic law that says what a person finds belongs to him and doesn't need to be reported to anyone. I remember a popular jingle; "finders keepers, losers weepers."

Remember a parable stresses one main point and nothing else really matters so notice that the man found the treasure and he sacrificed everything to get it. However, unlike the merchant, when he claimed the treasure, he had his money back and then some. "And while the one parable represents the Kingdom as 'found without seeking,' the other holds forth the Kingdom as 'sought and found' (CCE).

Jesus again said, "The Kingdom of Heaven is like..." He tells us what it is like, but what is the Kingdom of Heaven? Is it what Jesus prayed in the Model Prayer, "Let your Kingdom come. Let your will be done, as in heaven, so on earth." (Matt. 6:10)? If that is the case, to enter the Kingdom is to do the Will of God.

Pearls held a special place in the hearts of ancient people and they were sought not only for their monetary value, but for their beauty. People enjoyed handling and studying them, so it wasn't unusual for a merchant to go to great lengths to find and purchase exceptional pearls.

The implication of the parable is that there are many pearls, but only "one pearl of great price." There are many things that we can become involved in, good things, helpful things; but to know and do the Will of God is the only "One of great price."

While the treasure seeker got his money back, the merchant was left with only the pearl; however, neither felt they had "sacrificed" to obtain their treasure. Possibly, if we understood the joy of knowing and doing God's Will, we would use the word sacrifice less. As Paul said, "However, I consider those things that were gain to me as a loss for Christ." (Phil. 3:7).

Both the treasure and pearl were found as the results of a search. We don't know how long they searched, but it doesn't appear that they were just "stumbled" over. Whether the search takes a lifetime or only a few minutes, it is worth the effort.

Fishin' or Sortin'?
Matthew 13:47-50

"Again, the Kingdom of Heaven is like a dragnet, that was cast into the sea, and gathered some fish of every kind, [48] which, when it was filled, they drew up on the beach. They sat down, and gathered the good into containers, but the bad they threw away. [49] So will it be in the end of the world. The angels will come and separate the wicked from among the righteous, [50] and will cast them into the furnace of fire. There will be the weeping and the gnashing of teeth."

There were two main ways of fishing in Israel. One used a net designed for casting; the fisherman would stand on the shore or wade out a little way into the water and, watching carefully until a fish swam into his area, he would quickly cast the net and encircle his prey. This method required a sharp eye, quick reflexes, and great patience, but it did allow for selective fishing.

The second method, which is the one Jesus uses here, was a drag-net pulled behind two boats. The net had weights on the bottom and floats on the top, so it stood upright, like a wall in the water. As it was pulled along it caught everything in its path. This method is indiscriminate and the fish were not separated until the net was dragged up on shore.

"There are many in the Church who nevertheless are not of the Church, and therefore at length will be cast out: but the full and perfect cleansing of them is deferred to the last day (GN)." The Kingdom of Heaven draws people with many different motives, attitudes, cultures, and moral convictions. The words "good" and "bad" translate the Greek words *kala* and *sapra* and describe fish that were edible or inedible, based on either taste or Jewish dietary law.

There are two generally held views of the church. One states that the church is an exclusive body, reserved for people who are totally committed to their calling in Christ. It is for people who are "different" from the people of the world. This might have been the view of the Pharisee's who sought to set up a pure "church," but not Jesus. The major problem with this viewpoint is simply this: who will do the judging? Several times in both the Old and New Testaments we are warned that we are not to judge, God is the Righteous Judge, He will do it at the right time.

We have attempted to avoid using the word judge by "setting up standards" or becoming "fruit inspectors." We have said that there are certain people who should not be allowed to prepare or serve communion. Certain people should not teach Sunday school or sing in the choir or pastor churches. This isn't because we judge them, we wouldn't do that, but they don't meet our "standard." By the way, our "standard" has been given to us by God, or so we, and the Pharisees, believe.

The other view about the church is the inclusive view. It holds that the church and its offices and tasks must be open to all people, regardless of race, color, national origin, social status, or social acceptability. I believe that is the lesson of the parable. However, since I do not meet some people's standards, it is natural that I would take that position.

Another thing the parable teaches is this: judgment, separation of the "good" and "bad," will occur but it is left in the hands of the One who is qualified to judge. If we can learn to accept people where they are and allow them to develop into the best people they can be, they will be happier and so will we.

Notice also, "They sat down" to do their work. This was a quiet, deliberate sorting with no chance of making any error. It was done by those who were qualified to do the sorting. Do not fear! The fact that judgment is delayed doesn't mean that it will not take place. So, should we be fishin' or sortin'?

Stop and Think for a Minute
Matthew 13:51-52

Jesus said to them, "Have you understood all these things?"

They answered him, "Yes, Lord."

[52] He said to them, "Therefore every scribe who has been made a disciple in the Kingdom of Heaven is like a man who is a householder, who brings out of his treasure new and old things."

This little interlude is addressed to the Disciples and is an opportunity to stop, catch our breath and reflect on what Jesus has been doing. We talk a lot about the purpose and mission of a Christian, but what is the purpose Jesus has been emphasizing?

Remember, what Jesus said:

Don't think that I came to destroy the law or the prophets. I didn't come to destroy, but to fulfill. For most certainly, I tell you, until heaven and earth pass away, not even one smallest letter or one tiny pen stroke shall in any way pass away from the law, until all things are accomplished. (Matt. 5:17-18). Neither are we to "destroy," or change the Law.

Certainly, Christians have been called to a higher standard than existed under the Law, but that standard is one imposed by God on "us," first person, not on "them," third person. Paul urged us, "For if we discerned ourselves, we wouldn't be judged." (1 Cor. 11:31). Once again, we must be hard on ourselves and easier on others leaving their judgment to God. It isn't our responsibility to develop the standard to impose on other people. Consider the words of Jesus about judging others, "Don't judge, so that you won't be judged. For with whatever judgment you judge, you will be judged; and with whatever measure you measure, it will be measured to you" (Matt. 7:1-2).

While our passage mentions scribes, Jesus implies that we, all of us, are to be teachers. The best teaching we can do is by role-modeling, showing, and living what we believe before our family, friends, and everyone we come in contact with. To underscore this, look at these examples from Paul:

- "Be imitators of me, even as I also am of Christ." (1 Cor. 11:1).
- "Brothers, be imitators together of me, and note those who walk this way, even as you have us for an example." (Phil. 3:17).
- "For you know how you ought to imitate us. For we didn't behave ourselves rebelliously among you…" (2 Thess. 3:7).
- "Let no man despise your youth; but be an example to those who believe, in word, in your way of life, in love, in spirit, in faith, and in purity." (1 Tim. 4:12).
- "…in all things showing yourself an example of good works; in your teaching showing integrity, seriousness, incorruptibility…" (Titus 2:7).

We may not like it, or we may not accept it, but we, each of us are role models.

Paul is not the only one who stresses role modeling. "Take, brothers, for an example of suffering and of patience, the prophets who spoke in the name of the Lord." (James 5:10). Peter gets into the act telling us about the model Jesus provided "For to this you were called, because Christ also suffered for us, leaving you an example, that you should follow his steps…" (1 Pet. 2:21). This doesn't even consider the many calls of Jesus Himself for us to live properly in the world.

Can there be any question? We are to be models of Christianity; not judges of orthodoxy. We can show through the life we live far better than by trying to inflict our standard on them. This allows them to translate the Christian lifestyle into their own understanding. It then becomes "indigenous," or native, to them.

The old tradition of apprentice, journeyman, and master follows the pattern of teaching through modeling. Many years ago, the apprentice actually lived with his master/teacher.

The second important thing a teacher does is answer questions the pupil may have and put into words those things they may not understand. This can best be done by drawing on our own experiences. Good or bad, we had them, we need to use them! This is the "old" and "new" that we can bring out of "our storeroom."

Through faith in Him, Jesus freed us from the consequences of our past, but He didn't undo and remove it. Those events were common to other people, by examining them in the light of our salvation experience, and seeing God's hand at work, we can relate these experiences in a new way. We can help others see that God is at work in their lives even as He was in ours.

The knowledge and talents we had before coming to Christ did not evaporate when we become Christians, but now they are available to be used to glorify God and bring others to Him. Certainly, if our ability was thievery or some other evil, we must put it behind us, however, even that can become a part of our testimony of God's work in our lives.

Often people think they must give up "something" to accept salvation; that is not true. In salvation we get "something," "The thief only comes to steal, kill, and destroy. I came that they may have life, and may have it abundantly." (John 10:10). A changed life may mean that we will want to give up "something," but that will be our decision. Hopefully none of us behaves the way we did when we were first converted; we are growing and will continue to grow if allowed to. We will develop our own standard, but it may be different than that of others, as it should be.

Paul urged us:

Now accept one who is weak in faith, but not for disputes over opinions. One man has faith to eat all things, but he who is weak eats only vegetables. Don't let him who eats despise him who doesn't eat. Don't let him who doesn't eat judge him who eats, for God has accepted him. Who are you who judge another's servant? To his own lord he stands or falls. Yes, he will be made to stand, for God has power to make him stand. … For none of us lives to himself, and none dies to himself (Rom. 14:1-4 and 7).

Familiarity Breeds Contempt…
Matthew 13:53-58

When Jesus had finished these parables, he departed from there. [54] Coming into his own country, he taught them in their synagogue, so that they were astonished, and said, "Where did this man get this wisdom, and these mighty works? [55] Isn't this the carpenter's son? Isn't his mother called Mary, and his brothers, James, Joses, Simon, and Judas (or, Judah)? [56] Aren't all of his sisters with us? Where then did this man get all of these things?" [57] They were offended by him.

But Jesus said to them, "A prophet is not without honor, except in his own country, and in his own house." [58] He didn't do many mighty works there because of their unbelief.

His own country would be Nazareth, where He was raised. To describe Jesus as "the carpenter's son" as Matthew does, would be appropriate, even if Joseph were already dead, as many scholars suppose. However, the Greek word *tekton* can be translated "builder" and means more than a simple carpenter, it means a craftsman. Children were rarely, if ever, identified by their mother because inheritance came through the father's family.

According to custom, any Jewish man could be invited to teach in the synagogue and it was common practice for a visitor to be asked to share and, as today, they would enjoy hearing from "home town" kids who went off and returned. However, we aren't always ready to accept what they have learned; after all,

138

we knew them when they were snotty nosed, little brats. "They imagined that they knew all that there was to know about Him, but they were mistaken (TNTC, p. 141)." In many cultures, a child's heritage determines their lot in life. They raised the question, "How can a mere carpenter's son be anything special?" and they were offended by him.

It's ironic, but the hardest place to teach is often among family and old friends. The attitude of His old neighbors toward Him, the boy and young man who had worked among them, maybe even made something for them, destroyed any opportunity for blessing by His ministry. Were they the only people in Galilee who didn't know about His healing and teaching? I doubt it.

Barclay points out that every Sunday half of the sermon is preached by the congregation. This is true because the congregation sets the atmosphere for the message. That atmosphere can either erect "a barrier through which the preacher's words cannot penetrate" or it can create "such an expectancy that even the poorest sermon becomes a living flame (DSB, p. 92)."

I would add that the congregation runs the pastor's words through the filter of their education, experience, and interaction with him, and the words they receive may not be the words that are spoken. You yourself know that some people cannot hear what certain individuals say.

Again, Jesus cautions us not to judge a person because of who we think he is. Family, background, education, none is the measure of a messenger of God. Only the words he, or she, speaks are appropriate for determining whether God is leading and speaking through them or not.

If the Holy Spirit leads the speaker and we come expecting to hear God's message, even those we might consider "least" will bless and instruct us, more importantly, those who don't know Jesus will have the chance to come face to face with Him.

Matthew says Jesus "…didn't do many mighty works there because of their unbelief." Is faith required for miracles? Study the miracles of Jesus and you will find that most required the exercise of some kind of faith. They were asked if they believed, to reach out a hand, or go and do something. Some faith response was usually required.

Have we become so familiar with the Bible and the work of the church that we can't continue to learn? Have we heard the teachers and preachers so often that we don't need to hear them anymore? Has familiarity with the Gospel bred contempt for it in our hearts and minds?

The End of John the Baptizer?
Matthew 14:1-12

At that time, Herod the tetrarch heard the report concerning Jesus, [2] and said to his servants, "This is John the Baptizer. He is risen from the dead. That is why these powers work in him." [3] For Herod had laid hold of John, and bound him, and put him in prison for the sake of Herodias, his brother Philip's wife. [4] For John said to him, "It is not lawful for you to have her." [5] When he would have put him to death, he feared the multitude, because they counted him as a prophet. [6] But when Herod's birthday came, the daughter of Herodias danced among them and pleased Herod. [7] Whereupon he promised with an oath to give her whatever she should ask. ⁸ She, being prompted by her mother, said, "Give me here on a platter the head of John the Baptizer."

⁹ The king was grieved, but for the sake of his oaths, and of those who sat at the table with him, he commanded it to be given, ¹⁰ and he sent and beheaded John in the prison. ¹¹ His head was brought on a platter, and given to the young lady: and she brought it to her mother. ¹² His disciples came, and took the body, and buried it; and they went and told Jesus.

Herod Antipas was tetrarch of Galilee and Perea and is usually just called Herod in the New Testament; tetrarch means "ruler of a fourth." He was a fairly good king and built many buildings and founded the city of Tiberius, named for the emperor. Herod wanted to kill John much earlier, because he feared that John might lead a revolt against him; you may recall that Herod the Great lived in constant fear of anyone who appeared to have the heart of the people. John was extremely popular and that popularity was the only thing that kept Herod from killing him earlier.

There are two ways to look at why Herod killed John. First, Josephus, the Jewish historian, thinks it was because John was so popular with the people, Herod was suspicious and didn't trust John's motives. Second, the Gospel writers say it was because John told the truth. Telling the truth to anyone with that much power over you can be dangerous.

From John's perspective, Herod had broken two laws of God. He divorced his wife and, even worse, he married his sister-in-law, which, except in the case of a brother dying without an heir, was prohibited under Jewish law.

About Herodias Barclay says, "...she was stained by a triple guilt...a woman of loose morals and of infidelity...a vindictive woman... (DSB, p. 94)." She was a woman who wasn't beneath using her own daughter to gain her revenge. However, she did remain faithful to Herod Antipas. When Caligula banished him to Gaul, and she could have remained in Rome, but she chose to go with him into exile.

The Gospels don't supply the daughter's name; but we learn from the writings of Josephus that she was the daughter of Herod Philip and Herodias, and a granddaughter of Herod the Great, who subsequently married her uncle Philip, the tetrarch of Ituraea and Trachonitis who was the son of Herod the Great and Cleopatra. Historically we know her as Salome and she was probably no more than an early teenager or she would probably have been married already.

A royal princess in an oriental court would have been very sheltered, rarely appearing in public and certainly not dancing at a banquet like this, and definitely not this kind of dancing. This wasn't a presentation of "Swan Lake" and for Herod to allow his stepdaughter to dance in this manner indicates the depravity of his court. For Herod to have been so "pleased," there was probably very little left to the imagination and he was so impressed he made a foolish promise that subsequently cost John the Baptizer his head. (We should note that, while unjust, it was a part of the larger Plan.)

Although royalty had the option of marrying later than common people, girls were often married as soon as they were able to bear children and their marriages were often for political purposes. Marriage within the family, especially among the nobility, was common and continued into the 19ᵗʰ century. England's Queen Victoria was related to most of the ruling families in Europe at the outbreak of World War I.

You can run from a guilty conscience, but you can't hide. Like his father, Herod Antipus was a troubled man. When Jesus appeared on the scene, he apparently thought his old enemy John had returned to haunt him. John and Jesus were cousins and Origen tells us of a tradition that they looked alike. These were very superstitious people, but it is hard to say whether Herod thought John had actually risen from the dead or if Jesus' preaching was like hearing John again. So, based on their beliefs either view could be argued.

Today psychologists might label Herod a "people pleaser," he was more concerned with pleasing his wife and guests than doing what he knew was right. Taking a stand is important, but when you know the stand you are taking is wrong, that's weakness not strength.

In divorcing his first wife, Herod began his own downfall. Aretas, king of Arabia, his father-in-law, was greatly offended by the action and attacked and defeated him. He was rescued and returned to power by turning to Rome for help. When Philip died, Agrippa succeeded him with the title King, which was a problem for Herodias so he reluctantly went to Rome to plead for the same title, but lost everything when Caligula banished him to Gaul (France).

Feeding Five Thousand by Faith
Matthew 14:13-21

Now when Jesus heard this, he withdrew from there in a boat, to a deserted place apart. When the multitudes heard it, they followed him on foot from the cities.

[14] Jesus went out, and he saw a great multitude. He had compassion on them, and healed their sick. [15] When evening had come, his disciples came to him, saying, "This place is deserted, and the hour is already late. Send the multitudes away, that they may go into the villages, and buy themselves food."

[16] But Jesus said to them, "They don't need to go away. You give them something to eat."

[17] They told him, "We only have here five loaves and two fish."

[18] He said, "Bring them here to me." [19] He commanded the multitudes to sit down on the grass; and he took the five loaves and the two fish, and looking up to heaven, he blessed, broke and gave the loaves to the disciples, and the disciples gave to the multitudes. [20] They all ate, and were filled. They took up twelve baskets full of that which remained left over from the broken pieces. [21] Those who ate were about five thousand men, besides women and children.

Barclay reminds us that Galilee was a small country, 50 miles north to south and 25 miles east to west, but according to Josephus, who may have exaggerated some, there were 204 towns and villages with a population of 15,000 or more (DSB, p. 98). No wonder it was so hard to escape the crowds of people.

This is the only miracle of Jesus that appears in all four gospels. The central idea the writers are presenting here is the compassion Jesus had for common people. In the formal temptation by the devil (4:2-4) Jesus wouldn't use His power to help Himself, but over and over we see Him using that same power to help others. Further "…what was being enacted before the people was not a simple feeding, but a dress rehearsal for the Messianic Feast (AB, p. 179)."

How often we get disgusted with people asking for food, money, and taking up our time, but Jesus always seemed to have time for them. I wonder whose mission was more important, His or ours? Barclay warns, "...we must never be too busy for people, and we must never even seem to find them a trouble and a nuisance... We must never deal with people with one eye on the clock... (DSB, p. 99-100)." Is that an "Ouch!" or an "Amen!"?

Jesus broke the bread, but the disciples handed it out. Jesus worked through people then and He still does now; "...the disciple is helpless without his Lord, but...the Lord is helpless without his disciple (DSB, p. 101)."

John 6:9 says, "There is a boy here who has five barley loaves and two fish, but what are these among so many?" So, the source of the food was this boy, not the disciples. Here are some interesting questions: "Do you suppose of all the people there, only one boy had food? Or was he the only one unselfish enough to risk offering what he had?" How often children, and "little people" are more willing to give what they have. "We often feel that our contribution to Jesus is meager, but he can use and multiply what we give him… (LASB, p. 1572)."

Sometimes we discount the healing miracles because there is the psychological to deal with, however when Jesus exercises power over nature, there is no easy way to explain it away and we are forced to look at them in a different light. "Faith can put no limit on God's power (BBC, p. 163)."

"All Jewish meals were sacred, and the words taking, blessed, broke, and gave are normal ones for a host at any Jewish meal (BBC, p. 163)." There can be no question that there was plenty of food because when the meal was over, each disciple still had a full basket.

The text says, "Taking the five loaves and the two fish and looking up to heaven, he gave thanks and broke the loaves. Then he gave them to the disciples, and the disciples gave them to the people." I take that to mean that what Jesus gave the disciples was only a piece of the bread and fish, they in turn broke it and the miracle continued until there was plenty and even some left over. It may be heresy, but it is even possible that those in the crowd participated in the breaking and multiplying.

Most commentators take the approach that Jesus Himself broke the loaves over and over until there was enough, I think that is illogical. For Jesus to have broken enough to feed that many people would have taken hours and He was in the process of developing His disciples and future leaders of the church. I don't see anything in the text that precludes either interpretation.

How large was the crowd, we don't know, but there was a minimum of 5,000 men and an unknown number of women and children, so it could have easily been 10,000-15,000.

There may be no significance to the twelve baskets of leftovers, but it is interesting that there were twelve tribes of Israel, so it could indicate that there was enough to feel all of Israel, not just those who were there that day. God's desire was, and is, to provide for all of His children.

Do You Have Faith to Walk on Water?
Matthew 14:22-33

Immediately Jesus made the disciples get into the boat, and to go ahead of him to the other side, while he sent the multitudes away. [23] After he had sent the multitudes away, he went up into the mountain by himself to pray. When evening had come, he was there alone. [24] But the boat was now in the middle of the *sea, distressed by the waves, for the wind was contrary. ²⁵ In the fourth watch of the night, (the night was equally divided into four watches, so the fourth watch is approximately 3:00 A. M. to sunrise.) Jesus came to them, walking on the sea (see Job 9:8). ²⁶ When the disciples saw him walking on the sea, they were troubled, saying, "It's a ghost!" and they cried out for fear. ²⁷ But immediately Jesus spoke to them, saying, "Cheer up! It is I! (or, I AM!) Don't be afraid."*

²⁸ Peter answered him and said, "Lord, if it is you, command me to come to you on the waters."

²⁹ He said, "Come!"

Peter stepped down from the boat, and walked on the waters to come to Jesus. ³⁰ But when he saw that the wind was strong, he was afraid, and beginning to sink, he cried out, saying, "Lord, save me!"

³¹ Immediately Jesus stretched out his hand, took hold of him, and said to him, "You of little faith, why did you doubt?" ³² When they got up into the boat, the wind ceased. ³³ Those who were in the boat came and worshiped him, saying, "You are truly the Son of God!"

As Barclay says, "The lesson of this passage is abundantly clear but what actually happened is not (DSB, p. 104)." In the prior passage, Jesus fed the multitude and now "Immediately Jesus made the disciples get into the boat and go on ahead of him to the other side..."

John is the only one who tells of the effort of the people to make Jesus their king, "Jesus therefore, perceiving that they were about to come and take him by force, to make him king, withdrew again to the mountain by himself" (John 6:15). When Matthew says that "Jesus made the disciples get into the boat" and precede Him to the other side of the lake, he may be reflecting the same idea.

Because the miraculous feeding happened at the time of the Passover (John 6:4), it would be natural for the crowds to believe Jesus would become their Messiah in a political sense. The annual celebration of deliverance from Egypt always rekindled hope for deliverance from Rome. It may even be that the disciples were encouraging the crowds to press their claims upon Jesus. So Jesus had to force them into the boat, to get them away from the crowds, whom He then dispersed (BBC, p. 164).

Matthew here is describing a group of miracles: Jesus' walking on the water, Peter walking on the water, and the calming of the storm. "Walking on the sea" could be explained as walking on the shore near the sea, because the Greek phrase used in verse 26 (*epi tes thalasses*) could refer to walking by or at the edge of the water, but the evidence is too strong to accept this interpretation. There are too many details in the event to suggest just walking on the shore. We would also have to do something with the boat and with Peter sinking in fear in only a few inches of water. There are just too many problems with that approach.

We don't have to face our difficulties alone. Very early the church recognized that the lesson here is that Christ comes to His followers in the storms of their life, if not to deliver them, at least to go through it with them. "No sooner had a need arisen, than Jesus was there to help and to save (BBC, p. 105)."

Matthew has a collection of stories about Peter that show his weaknesses and recovery from them. "The 'Rock' was not rocklike, yet he was Christ's, as are all who accept his care (BBC, p. 164)." Matthew shows that Christ doesn't fail even those who fail Him (BBC, p. 164). Barclay says, "There is no passage in the New Testament in which Peter's character is more fully revealed than this. It tells us three things about him."

1. Peter often acted on impulse, without thinking about what he was doing. But there are worse things than that, because Peter's was ruled by his heart; his heart was always in the right place and the instinct of his heart was always love.

2. Because he acted on impulse, he often failed and came to grief. Jesus always wanted a man to look at a situation before he acted. He was totally honest with men. A great deal of Christian failure is from acting upon an emotional moment without counting the cost.

3. Peter never really failed, because at the moment of failure he reached for Christ and every time he fell, he rose again and was brought closer to Him. "As has been well said, a saint is not a man who never fails; a saint is a man who gets up and goes on again every time he falls (DSB, pp. 106-7)."

In the letters of St. Francis of Sales:

St. Francis has noticed a custom of the country districts in which he lived. He had often noticed a farm servant going across a farmyard to draw water at the well; he also noticed that, before she lifted the brimming pail, the girl always put a piece of wood into it. One day he went out to the girl and asked her, "Why do you do that?" She looked surprised and answered, as if it were a matter of course, "Why? To keep the water from spilling...to keep it steady!" Writing to a friend later on, the bishop told this story and added: "So when your heart is distressed and agitated, put the Cross into its centre [sic] to keep it steady!

In every time of storm and stress, the presence of Jesus and the love which flows from the Cross brings peace and serenity and calm (DSB, p. 106).

The power of God is available, but not for "magic" tricks or to show off. It is available to allow us to minister to those around us who may be hurting. "Special supports are promised, and are to be expected, but only in spiritual pursuits; nor can we ever come to Jesus, unless we are upheld by his power (MH)."

Time to Minister…Again?
Matthew 14:34-36

When they had crossed over, they came to the land of Gennesaret. [35] When the people of that place recognized him, they sent into all that surrounding region, and brought to him all who were sick; [36] and they begged him that they might just touch the fringe (or, tassel) of his garment. As many as touched it were made whole.

They landed in a fertile plain on the northwest side of the Sea of Galilee. There can be no question of Jesus' fame or popularity, because it didn't take long for word of His arrival to spread and people to begin arriving seeking His help.

At first glance these few lines seem rather unimportant, just a simple transition between major events. However, there is something worth noticing. Barclay points out two things:

1. The beauty of it. As soon as Jesus appears anywhere people begin crowding and asking for His help; which He never refused. Everyone who came to Him, He healed. There is no indication that He preached or taught here; just that He healed.

2. The sadness of it. The sad fact is that there were hundreds, possibly thousands of people who were only interested in Jesus for what they could get from Him. After they were healed, they weren't prepared to follow Him any further.

It has always been true: people want the privilege of Christianity without its responsibilities. It has always been true that many remember God only when they need Him. Ingratitude toward God and Jesus Christ is the worst of all sins and there is no sin we commit more often.

Jesus taught men what God was like by showing them what God is like. He didn't just tell men that God cared; He showed them how much God cares. There isn't much use preaching the love of God without showing it.

Everywhere He went, He was crowded by people demanding His attention. Yet, He was always patient with them in spite of the fact that their primary interests were for their own welfare or gratification. Paul encourages, "But you, brothers, don't be weary in doing what is right. (2 Thess. 3:13)"

When Traditions Hurt You
Matthew 15:1-11

Then Pharisees and scribes came to Jesus from Jerusalem, saying, ² "Why do your disciples disobey the tradition of the elders? For they don't wash their hands when they eat bread."

³ He answered them, "Why do you also disobey the commandment of God because of your tradition? ⁴ For God commanded, 'Honor your father and your mother' (Ex. 20:12; Deut. 5:16) and, 'He who speaks evil of father or mother, let him be put to death' (Ex. 21:17; Lev. 20:9). ⁵ But you say, 'Whoever may tell his father or his mother, "Whatever help you might otherwise have gotten from me is a gift devoted to God," ⁶ he shall not honor his father or mother.' You have made the commandment of God void because of your tradition. ⁷ You hypocrites! Well did Isaiah prophesy of you, saying,

⁸ 'These people draw near to me with their mouth, and honor me with their lips; but their heart is far from me. ⁹ And in vain do they worship me, teaching as doctrine rules made by men'" (Isa. 29:13).

¹⁰ He summoned the multitude, and said to them, "Hear, and understand. ¹¹ That which enters into the mouth doesn't defile the man; but that which proceeds out of the mouth, this defiles the man."

Barclay considers this one of the most important passages in the Gospels because it "represents a head-on clash between Jesus and the leaders of orthodox Jewish religion (DSB, p. 109)." It's certainly one of the most shocking statements Jesus ever made because it not only went against the statements of the scribes and Pharisees, but it wiped out all the food laws of Leviticus. Like their pagan neighbors, the Pharisees had sought to please God by following a long list of rules and rituals, dietary restrictions were only a part of those rules.

"The charge against the disciples is not that of breaking the Law, but of setting aside the *tradition of the elders* (AB, p. 184)." Traditions are important to all of us, but they often carry more weight than law, or common sense would dictate. If we have always done something in a certain way, we are very reluctant to change that way, even if there is a better way of doing it. This seems to be especially true of religious traditions and that's the way it was with the Pharisees. They considered the oral tradition to have the same authority as the written Law, but in practice the oral law carried more influence than Scripture. Possibly Jesus' greatest conflict with the Pharisees was His rejection of this conviction.

For the Jews, washing hands, especially, before a meal was more a matter of religious ritual than a desire to remove germs and dirt. (Germs, as a cause of disease weren't even discovered until the 19th century.) This ceremonial washing was done several times during the day, including any time they had been in the market place where Gentiles might be encountered. It was intended to cleanse any casual contact with any unclean thing that would have defiled them. Here Jesus denied any distinction between clean and unclean objects and/or persons.

These rules were primarily set forth in Leviticus, and most had sensible origins:

1. Handling dead bodies could easily transmit disease.
2. Animals sacred to heathen religions would associate the person with that religion.
3. Some animals carry parasites that can infect humans.
4. The ban on the consumption of blood was associated with the thought that life is related to blood.

Jesus attacked the heart of the problem in His challenge to the practice of declaring property *korban*, which was the practice of dedicating something to God. On the surface, this appears to be a good practice; however, it was typically used to avoid helping someone in need. "In this way an oral tradition could empty God's word of meaning (AB, p. 184)." By invoking it, a Jew could refuse to give money to anyone in need, because they might use it improperly so the person should be sent away empty handed. Do you refuse to give to beggars because "they'll just buy wine with it!"?

It's a great thing to dedicate financial resources to the Lord's work, to other worthwhile charities, and, as of this writing; there can be significant tax benefits in doing so. However, be careful that your obligations are handled properly, including those to your family.

When a parent's wants called for assistance, they pleaded, that they had devoted to the temple all they could spare, even though they did not part with it, and therefore their parents must expect nothing from them (MH).

Jesus always stressed the purpose of the Law against the letter of the Law. He said:

Don't think that I came to destroy the law or the prophets. I didn't come to destroy, but to fulfill. For most certainly, I tell you, until heaven and earth pass away, not even one smallest letter or one tiny pen stroke shall in any way pass away from the law, until all things are accomplished. (Matt. 5:17-18).

That doesn't mean Jesus superseded the Law, because He went on to say:

Whoever, therefore, shall break one of these least commandments, and teach others to do so, shall be called least in the Kingdom of Heaven; but whoever shall do and teach them shall be called great in the Kingdom of Heaven. (Matt. 5:19).

For many people, including the Pharisees, duty to God was, and is, expressed in outward observances. What takes place in the heart or the mind isn't as important as what one does. Yet it is on the inside that the desire to sin is spawned. "Religion can never be founded on any ceremonies or ritual; religion must always be founded on personal relationships between man and God (DSB, p. 117)." Jesus always put people above religion. "Because of a greater commitment to their traditions, the Pharisees rendered God's law nonbinding… (NLTSB, p. 1608)" Sadly, we hold some of our traditions in the same way. "Traditions should help us understand God's laws better, not become laws unto themselves (LASB, p. 1573)"

There is an interesting statement in verse 10, "He summoned the multitude, and said to them…" so apparently the encounter with the Pharisees was somewhat private and now Jesus includes the "multitude," which could well have included Gentiles, to make His statement about what is true defilement.

Jesus chose Isaiah's words to criticize the religious leaders of His day, to repeat to the Pharisees (Isa. 29:13). I'm sure they knew them all too well. "The Pharisees knew a lot about God, but they didn't know God (LASB, p. 1574)."

We need to be very careful about interpreting the Bible. "Additions to God's laws reflect upon his wisdom, as if he had left out something which was needed, and which man could supply; in one way or other they always lead men to disobey God (MH)."

What Is Clean or Unclean?
Matthew 15:12-20

Then the disciples came, and said to him, "Do you know that the Pharisees were offended, when they heard this saying?"

13 But he answered, "Every plant which my heavenly Father didn't plant will be uprooted. 14 Leave them alone. They are blind guides of the blind. If the blind guide the blind, both will fall into a pit."

15 Peter answered him, "Explain the parable to us."

16 So Jesus said, "Do you also still not understand? 17 Don't you understand that whatever goes into the mouth passes into the belly, and then out of the body? 18 But the things which proceed out of the mouth come out of the heart, and they defile the man. 19 For out of the heart come evil thoughts, murders, adulteries, sexual sins, thefts, false testimony, and blasphemies. 20 These are the things which defile the man; but to eat with unwashed hands doesn't defile the man."

When Jesus talks about a "plant which my heavenly Father didn't plant," He may be referring to the Oral Tradition or oral law referred to in the prior section that had become more important than the actual Law. Jesus warns that a plant like that "will be pulled up by the roots." "The shocked reaction of the Pharisees was understandable, since Jesus appeared to be setting aside the legal distinctions between ritually clean and unclean food (AB, p. 185)."

It is much easier to follow a list of rules; to eat only certain things and wash your hands in a certain way, than it is to love the unlovely and spend your time and money helping the needy. Faith that is true faith (at the risk of being redundant) involves a personal relationship with God and our fellow-man in an *agape* attitude. True faith can never be satisfied by dos and don'ts as we have already seen.

It is so true…

…that nothing which enters from without can really defile us; and that only the evil that is in the heart, that is allowed to stir there, to rise up in thought and affection, and to flow forth in voluntary action, really defiles a man! … that the first shape which the evil that is in the heart takes, when it begins actively to stir, is that of "considerations" or "reasonings" on certain suggested actions (CCE).

"We work hard to keep our outward appearance attractive, but what is deep down in our heart (where others can't see) is more important to God (LASB, p. 1574)." Once again Jesus emphasizes that the attitude, why we do what we do, is more important than what we actually do. Man sees only the action, but God sees the heart. Sometimes we get so tired of trying to help the same people out of the same situations, but if that is what it takes, let's do it. "The heart is deceitful above all things, and it is exceedingly corrupt. Who can know it? (Jer. 17:9) "...for there is no sin in word or deed, which was not first in the heart (MH)."

As you lead people down the path toward God, be careful, anyone who claims to be an authority in interpreting God's Word can become a "blind guide," who causes himself and the one(s) he is helping to be hurt. We must speak, but we must be careful when we speak as an authority.

When Self Gets in the Way
Matthew 15:21-28

Jesus went out from there, and withdrew into the region of Tyre and Sidon. [22] Behold, a Canaanite woman came out from those borders, and cried, saying, "Have mercy on me, Lord, you son of David! My daughter is severely possessed by a demon!"

[23] But he answered her not a word.

His disciples came and begged him, saying, "Send her away; for she cries after us."

[24] But he answered, "I wasn't sent to anyone but the lost sheep of the house of Israel."

[25] But she came and worshiped him, saying, "Lord, help me."

[26] But he answered, "It is not appropriate to take the children's bread and throw it to the dogs."

[27] But she said, "Yes, Lord, but even the dogs eat the crumbs which fall from their masters' table."

[28] Then Jesus answered her, "Woman, great is your faith! Be it done to you even as you desire." And her daughter was healed from that hour.

This event is important because it shows Jesus' compassion for all people, even foreigners and former enemies of the Jews. At about that time, Josephus wrote: "Of the Phoenicians, the Tyrians have the most ill-feeling towards us," yet that was the very place Jesus went.

The end of His ministry was approaching and He once more withdrew from the opposition of the Pharisees and teachers of the law with His disciples where He encountered a Canaanite woman who must have heard about His amazing power to heal. The Jews, part of the "covenant," were offended by the conduct of Jesus and His disciples and challenged His authority at every opportunity, but this pagan woman, showed great faith and asked only for His grace and her request was granted. The fact that she called Jesus "Son of David" showed that she had some recognition of Jesus as the Messiah who would heal the people.

Since Jesus' didn't quiet her, His disciples begged Him to stop her persistent cries. They may mean "Send her away without helping her," because they think she is bothering Him or because they are annoyed and embarrassed. But the words could also be translated "Send her away with her request granted."

Jesus' reference that He was sent to "the lost sheep of the house of Israel" may mean that some of the Jews are not "lost" which would make sense, however I am sure that they were not the people the Jewish elders thought they were. Possibly Jesus wanted His disciples and the Canaanite woman to recognize that the Kingdom and its benefits must first be offered to the Jews.

The woman knelt before Jesus and cried, as only the mother of an afflicted child could, "have mercy on me!" But Jesus made certain that she understood the historic distinction between Jew and Gentile. Jesus' short discussion with her follows the well-known attitude of the Pharisees which supposes that the "children" are the people of Israel and the "dogs" are Gentiles.

To call a person a dog was a deadly and a contemptuous insult. The Jew spoke with arrogant insolence about "Gentile dogs," "infidel dogs," and later "Christian dogs." Dogs were ceremonially unclean scavengers that lived in the streets; they were savage and often carried disease. Barclay reminds us of two important elements of oral communication, the tone and body language used and the actual words chosen for that communication.

The tone and the look can make all the difference in our understanding. We can call a person a scoundrel with a smile and a laugh and it shows that we really love that individual. The word Jesus chose for dogs was not the street dogs, but the one for pets.

She didn't argue that Jesus should make an exception for her, or that she had a right to His mercy. She even abandoned the use of "Son of David" and just asked for His help. She was confident that even if she could not sit down as a guest at the table, she wanted to receive a "crumb" of God's mercy. Barclay points out some things about this woman we should notice:

1. She had love. In her heart there was the love for her child which is the reflection of God's love for His children. Love made her approach Jesus.

2. She had faith. (a) It was a faith which grew in contact with Jesus. She came with a kind of superstition…she ended by calling Jesus Lord. (b) It was a faith which worshipped. She began by following; she ended upon her knees; she began with a request; she ended in prayer.

3. She had indomitable persistence. She would not be discouraged. …she was in deadly earnest.

4. She had cheerfulness. She was in the midst of trouble; she was passionately in earnest; and yet she could smile. She had a certain sunny-heartedness about her.

If we are going to achieve our desires, we must be like this Canaanite woman; we cannot allow self to get in the way.

More to Heal and Feed
Matthew 15:29-39

Jesus departed there, and came near to the sea of Galilee; and he went up into the mountain, and sat there. [30] Great multitudes came to him, having with them the lame, blind, mute, maimed, and many others, and they put them down at his feet. He healed them, [31] so that the multitude wondered when they saw the mute speaking, the injured healed, the lame walking, and the blind seeing – and they glorified the God of Israel.

32 Jesus summoned his disciples and said, "I have compassion on the multitude, because they continue with me now three days and have nothing to eat. I don't want to send them away fasting, or they might faint on the way."

33 The disciples said to him, "Where should we get so many loaves in a deserted place as to satisfy so great a multitude?"

34 Jesus said to them, "How many loaves do you have?"

They said, "Seven, and a few small fish."

35 He commanded the multitude to sit down on the ground; 36 and he took the seven loaves and the fish. He gave thanks and broke them, and gave to the disciples, and the disciples to the multitudes. 37 They all ate, and were filled. They took up seven baskets full of the broken pieces that were left over. 38 Those who ate were four thousand men, besides women and children. 39 Then he sent away the multitudes, got into the boat, and came into the borders of Magdala.

Again, Jesus refuses to send away hungry people; I might even suggest people who should have come prepared with a "sack lunch." Is there a lesson in this for us? While the five thousand fed in 14:13-21 were probably Jews, this group is very likely Gentiles, as indicated by the phrase, "And they glorified the God of Israel" in verse 31; still it made no difference to Jesus.

Some suggest the two multitudes are actually the same, but besides the number of people listed, there are several other significant details that are different. In the first feeding, they sit on the grass, indicating it possibly took place in the spring. In the second, they sit on the ground, which could mean the grass has died from the summer sun.

There are a different number of loaves used, five verses seven. The words used to describe the baskets they used for the leftovers are different. The one used in the first feeding is *kophinoi* which was a basket resembling a bottle with a long narrow neck and used by the Jews to carry food. But this basket is a *sphurides* which was a large hamper-like basket and was often large enough to carry a man; it was the kind Gentiles generally used. Finally, in the next section, Jesus refers to them as separate events.

Sometime ago a commentator pointed out that Jesus ended each stage of His ministry by placing a meal before those He taught. The feeding of the five thousand came at the conclusion of His ministry in Galilee, this feeding came after His brief ministry in Gentile territory and His final meal was the Last Supper at the end of His earthly ministry.

What's with the disciples? How long ago was it that Jesus fed the 5,000? "How easily we throw up our hand in despair when faced with difficult situations. Like the disciples, we often forget that if God has cared for us in the past, he will do the same now (LASB, p. 1575)."

Feeding Jews was one thing, but feeding Gentiles was another thing. The Jewish leaders had very little use for Gentiles believing they were intended only for the fires of Hell, but here is Jesus, not only healing and teaching them, but feeding them. Often, we are tacitly just like those leaders, especially when we are dealing with other races, ethnicities, and illegal immigrants.

Each time we have seen Jesus, He was ministering to people by teaching and healing. When it was necessary, He also fed them. His concern has always been for the whole person, not just for the spiritual. We must be very careful that we don't put so much emphasis on the spiritual that we neglect other needs.

Again, we can ask about the leftovers. Why seven baskets? It could be because they thought there were seven nations in the Gentile world and these remnants were sufficient to provide for all of them. Deuteronomy 7:1 lists seven nations occupying the Promised Land that God would drive out before the Israelites, "When the Lord your God brings you into the land you are entering to possess and drives out before you many nations—the Hittites, Girgashites, Amorites, Canaanites, Perizzites, Hivites and Jebusites, seven nations larger and stronger than you" (NIV).

What's A Little Yeast?
Matthew 16:1-12

The Pharisees and Sadducees came, and testing him, asked him to show them a sign from heaven. [2] But he answered them, "When it is evening, you say, 'It will be fair weather, for the sky is red.' [3] In the morning, 'It will be foul weather today, for the sky is red and threatening.' Hypocrites! You know how to discern the appearance of the sky, but you can't discern the signs of the times! [4] An evil and adulterous generation seeks after a sign, and there will be no sign given to it, except the sign of the prophet Jonah."

He left them, and departed. [5] The disciples came to the other side and had forgotten to take bread. [6] Jesus said to them, "Take heed and beware of the yeast of the Pharisees and Sadducees."

[7] They reasoned among themselves, saying, "We brought no bread."

[8] Jesus, perceiving it, said, "Why do you reason among yourselves, you of little faith, 'because you have brought no bread?' [9] Don't you yet perceive, neither remember the five loaves for the five thousand, and how many baskets you took up? [10] Nor the seven loaves for the four thousand, and how many baskets you took up? [11] How is it that you don't perceive that I didn't speak to you concerning bread? But beware of the yeast of the Pharisees and Sadducees."

[12] Then they understood that he didn't tell them to beware of the yeast of bread, but of the teaching of the Pharisees and Sadducees.

There are two sections to this passage. In the first, verses 1-4, the Pharisees look for a sign, also touched upon in Matthew 12:38-39, the second section discusses the problem of "yeast," or "leaven," in some translations.

"This is the only place in the NT where the Sadducees are represented as being outside Judea (AB, p. 192)." The Pharisees and the Sadducees were the religious leaders and teachers of the Jews, but only on five occasions does Matthew put them together in a passage (3:7; 16:1, 6, 11, 12; 22:34). This is undoubtedly because of the great differences between them. But, as mentioned earlier, there is an Arab proverb that say, "The enemy of my enemy is my friend." That was certainly true with these two groups. If politics makes strange bedfellows, so does hate. It would be difficult to find two groups that disagreed more about politics, religion, and the Roman occupation than these two groups.

The fact that they wanted to see a "sign from heaven" isn't so bad; they believed, as do many of us, that if a teacher was a proper teacher sent from God, there should be some way to validate it. The problem is that Jesus had been performing "signs" since His ministry began and they had ignored them. Their problem wasn't with the eyes, but with the heart.

…they desired a sign of their own choosing: they despised those signs which relieved the necessity of the sick and sorrowful, and called for something else which would gratify the curiosity of the proud. It is great hypocrisy, when we slight the signs of God's ordaining, to seek for signs of our own devising (MH).

To call them "An evil and adulterous generation" may seem crude, but it was a common assertion used by Old Testament prophets to describe those who weren't faithful to God. Whatever sign He gave, they would twist and use against Him. We should also remember that evil and adultery don't just happen; they are deliberate choices people make.

Unfortunately, for them, the only "sign" Jesus would give them at this time was His presence. Just as God sent Jonah to Nineveh, He sent Jesus to them. The fact that they could understand what the weather would be like makes it clear that they actually knew Jesus was the Messiah they looked for. We might say, "It was as plain as the nose on their faces." After the three days and three nights in the grave and His resurrection, they would have their "sign" for sure, if they still wanted and would receive it.

Many people, like these Jewish leaders, say they want to see a miracle so that they can believe. But, Jesus knew that miracles never convince the skeptical. Jesus had been healing, raising people from the dead, and feeding thousands, and still people wanted him to prove himself… With all this evidence, those who won't believe are either too proud or too stubborn (LASB, p. 1576).

The problem with the "bread" and "yeast" is actually greater than might appear on the surface. How could the disciples forget about the feeding of the two multitudes? That would be impossible! But, how could Jesus multiply bread if they forgot to bring any?

There had to be a baker there. Couldn't they just go buy some bread? There was a major problem; they were in Gentile territory so the bread would have been baked by Gentiles and thus it would be "unclean." Have they forgotten that Jesus made no distinction between "clean" and "unclean"?

Jesus seizes the opportunity and uses it to teach them something very important: "be on your guard against the yeast of the Pharisees and Sadducees." "Yeast" was used by the Jews as a symbol of the effect an evil influence could have on a person's life. The Pharisees were good people, but they were more interested in appearance than results and the Sadducees placed prosperity above faithfulness to God. We must be on guard! Satan is constantly giving us little things that seem good and certainly harmless, but have the potential to destroy our testimony and even our lives, if we allow them to.

There are cults and sects that use and claim the Bible as their source of "truth." They have a form of godliness and come close to the truth, but they vary slightly, a little "yeast," from it and that takes them far from the truth of the Word of God.

Who Do You Say Jesus Is?
Matthew 16:13-20

Now when Jesus came into the parts of Caesarea Philippi, he asked his disciples, saying, "Who do men say that I, the Son of Man, am?"

[14] They said, "Some say John the Baptizer, some, Elijah, and others, Jeremiah, or one of the prophets."

15 *He said to them, "But who do you say that I am?"*

16 *Simon Peter answered, "You are the Christ, the Son of the living God."*

17 *Jesus answered him, "Blessed are you, Simon Bar Jonah, for flesh and blood has not revealed this to you, but my Father who is in heaven. 18 I also tell you that you are Peter and on this rock I will build my assembly, and the gates of Hades (or Hell) will not prevail against it. 19 I will give to you the keys of the Kingdom of Heaven, and whatever you bind on earth will have been bound in heaven; and whatever you release on earth will have been released in heaven." 20 Then he commanded the disciples that they should tell no one that he was Jesus the Christ.*

This passage has possibly been used and abused by preachers and teachers more than any passage in the Bible. Some see it as installing Peter as the lead pastor, and even the first Pope, and some have gone about binding and releasing people and things willy-nilly. However, you cannot successfully argue from Scripture, history, or tradition that Peter wasn't the leader of the early church, the *ekklēsia* (assembly), and remained such until James the half-brother of Jesus comes on the scene and becomes the leader of the "mother" church at Jerusalem, and Peter, like Paul, becomes an itinerate preacher-teacher and missionary.

The time of His death was rapidly approaching and again Jesus takes His disciples aside to spend some time alone with them. Caesarea Philippi was about twenty-five miles northeast of the Sea of Galilee at the foot of Mount Lebanon, outside the territory of Herod Antipas and was an area that was very "religious."

It was originally called *Panium* (from a cavern in its neighborhood dedicated to the god *Pan*) and *Paneas*. Philip, the tetrarch, the only good son of Herod the Great, in whose dominions *Paneas* lay, having beautified and enlarged it, changed its name to *Caesarea*, in honor of the Roman emperor, and added *Philippi* after his own name, to distinguish it from the other *Caesarea*, on the northeast coast of the Mediterranean Sea (CCE).

There were at least fourteen temples to the ancient gods nearby; it contained the source spring of the Jordan with its great importance to Judaism, and Herod the Great had built a temple where Caesar Augustus was worshiped as a god before he died and was proclaimed a god by the Roman senate, which was the normal way of doing things.

Since time was running out, Jesus wanted to know if anyone recognized who He was, even among the disciples. It was (and is) difficult, dare I suggest impossible, to take an uncommitted position about who Jesus is. As C. S. Lewis said, He is either who He said He is or He is a liar or a lunatic. There is no middle ground, because Jesus placed himself above Moses in the Sermon on the Mount when He gave the "but I tell you…" passages (Matt. 5:21-48). No rabbi or prophet would dare say anything like that, it would be blasphemy. In fact, that was the "charge" He was convicted of by the "council" that allowed His accusers to ask for the death sentence (Matt. 26:65).

The people identified Jesus with some outstanding individuals: "John the Baptizer, Elijah, Jeremiah or one of the prophets." There are many religious groups that recognize Jesus as being a good person, some a prophet, and others a faultless man and a "son of god," as they define a god. However, none but Christianity gives Him the status of being the unique Son and only Savior that Peter does here. Peter's assertion is recorded slightly differently in the three gospels: Matthew has, "You are the Christ, the Son of the living God." Mark simply says, "You are the Christ." And Luke says, "The Christ of God."

His identification with John the Baptizer who was only recently beheaded and was very popular with the people, or Elijah, who didn't die but was take to heaven in whirlwind (2 Kings 2:1 ff) or Jeremiah who was widely expected to be raised from the dead, wasn't much of a stretch for many people because they didn't yet see Jesus as Messiah "material."

How you respond to the question "Who am I?" is up to you, no one else can answer it for you. Your experience must be a firsthand, personal discovery, as the Holy Spirit makes God known to you. "Christianity never consists of 'knowing about' Jesus; it always consists in 'knowing Jesus' (DSB, p. 138)."

The discussion about Peter and the "rock," "keys" and "binding" and "loosing" has been greatly debated by individual Christians and by entire Christian denominations. If we allow it to be, it can be very divisive, so understanding that what Jesus is saying is important!

When we look at Peter's life, we don't see a person who stands firmly, like a rock. Can it be that Jesus gave him the nick name to encourage him to be more "rock-like"? If that is true, it worked. We see in Acts 3:11-4:22 that rocklike strength coming to the front and tradition tells us that when he stood trial before the Roman courts, he never wavered.

Most of us know that Peter is Greek for "rock" and Cephas means "rock" in Aramaic. (According to the *Anchor Bible*, the use of Peter as an actual name did not exist before this time (AB p. 195)). In Greek, there are two words translated rock. The large rock, *petra*, and the small rock or stone, *petros*. The Passage says, "And I tell you that you are *petros*, and on this *petra* I will build my church." So, Peter is the stone, but who, or what, is the large rock Jesus will use to build upon? Jesus Himself is that rock. It is "my church," Jesus' church and He can be the only cornerstone.

Therefore thus says the Lord Yahweh, "Behold, I lay in Zion for a foundation a stone, a tried stone, a precious cornerstone of a sure foundation. He who believes shall not act hastily." (Isa. 28:16b)

Peter does show "flashes" of brilliance and here is one of them, calling Jesus a prophet didn't provide a foundation to build upon, but Peter's assertion did. "There could be a church without Peter, none without Christ (BBC, p. 173)." The large rock was, is, and forever will be Jesus "the Christ, the Son of the living God."

In Greek, there is a distinction between the "gates of Hades" and the "gates of Hell," as some translations have it. Hades is the equivalent of *Sheol* in the Old Testament and was believed to be the place the dead awaited their final judgment. In modern English it might be better rendered "place of the dead" and could also be translated the "power of death." There is no way that the gates of Hades can stand up against the battering ram of the Church of the living God.

It seems strange to me that Peter seems to be the only one of the twelve to speak up at this time. Some suggest that he was only the spokesman for the others; then why weren't the others blessed?

We'll look at the power to bind and loose when we get to chapter 18.

The Cost of Discipleship
Matthew 16:21-28

From that time, Jesus began to show his disciples that he must go to Jerusalem and suffer many things from the elders, chief priests, and scribes, and be killed, and the third day be raised up.

²² Peter took him aside, and began to rebuke him, saying, "Far be it from you, Lord! This will never be done to you."

²³ But he turned, and said to Peter, "Get behind me, Satan! You are a stumbling block to me, for you are not setting your mind on the things of God, but on the things of men." ²⁴ Then Jesus said to his disciples, "If anyone desires to come after me, let him deny himself, and take up his cross, and follow me. ²⁵ For whoever desires to save his life will lose it, and whoever will lose his life for my sake will find it. ²⁶ For what will it profit a man, if he gains the whole world, and forfeits his life? Or what will a man give in exchange for his life? ²⁷ For the Son of Man will come in the glory of his Father with his angels, and then he will render to everyone according to his deeds. ²⁸ Most certainly I tell you, there are some standing here who will in no way taste of death, until they see the Son of Man coming in his Kingdom."

"From that time…" marks a change in direction, from an emphasis on the Kingdom of Heaven to Jesus' coming death and resurrection. His disciples had been with Him a considerable time, around three years, but, because of their preconceived notions about the Messiah, they still hadn't yet come to grips with the nature of the Kingdom. Ultimately, they did, but it wasn't until after the resurrection that the light turned on for them. We need to be careful that our preconceived ideas don't get in the way of people wanting to come to Jesus, but not like we think they should. It is more than just saying the right words!

Jesus recognized that His mission would lead Him to Jerusalem and death, so He spoke plainly as He tried to explain it to the disciples, but it didn't sit well with them, especially Peter, who was probably still expecting a political Messiah. When Peter offered to protect Jesus, Satan was undoubtedly there. Satan had offered a political solution in chapter 4:8-9, now, at his suggestion, Peter was suggesting it. Man's way is to seize the moment, to use force if necessary; God's way is not man's way.

What does Jesus mean when He says, "Get behind me, Satan! You are a stumbling block to me…"? Origen thought what Jesus meant was, "Peter, your place is 'behind' me, not 'in front' of me." Barclay suggests that the command Jesus gives Peter is "Begone 'behind' me!" Peter was to be the follower, not the leader. I'll lead the way; you follow me (DSB, p. 149-150). But, when you look at the rest of the statement, "for you are not setting your mind on the things of God, but on the things of men" I believe it makes the whole thing clear and we really don't need to strain for an answer.

Proverbs 14:12 says, "There is a way which seems right to a man, but in the end, it leads to death." Often, we allow the good to rob us of the best; we go the wrong way because the right way doesn't seem to make sense. Jesus' suffering and death didn't make sense to Peter, but to made perfect sense to God. Peter loved Jesus and he didn't want Him to die, from that side of the cross, it makes perfect sense.

The Gospel is filled with paradoxes, but none is greater than verse 25, "For whoever wants to save his life will lose it, but whoever loses his life for me will find it." For that matter, how can that be true? How can the cross, an implement of death bring life? If we take the dictionary definition of life, it cannot.

However, if we take the other teachings of Jesus that say to keep something you must give it up, then it makes perfect sense. Well then, do we have to die to gain life? Yes and no. The answer is in being dead to self, but alive to Christ.

Since dead people don't worry about anything, we don't worry about anything. Since dead people don't make demands, we don't make demands. If the motivation is self, we must die to that desire. If we don't, we will miss both the Will of God for our lives and we won't be the best self we can be. Being a living dead person is the hardest thing we will ever be called upon to do.

Self-denial for us usually means to give up some luxury. However, in Christian circles, it should mean to dethrone self and place God on the throne of our life. This is the difference between living and just existing. Jesus said, "...take up his cross and follow me," Luke added "daily." This calls for a voluntary action of our own free will and it means to give up personal goals and desires in favor of God's will. It is the natural out-growth of self-denial. We are like children playing "follow the leader" and Jesus is the leader we must follow.

What kind of world was it when Matthew recalled these words of Jesus? It was between 80 and 90 AD and these were difficult days of persecution for the church. Some Christians deserted the faith rather than facing the hardness of these trials.

When Jesus used this picture of his followers taking up their crosses to follow him, the disciples knew what he meant. Crucifixion was a common Roman method of execution and condemned criminals had to carry their cross through the streets to the execution site (LASB, p. 1577).

To follow Jesus meant loss of comfort and the possibility of death.

In verse 26, Jesus raises two interesting questions: "For what will it profit a man, if he gains the whole world, and forfeits his life? Or what will a man give in exchange for his life?" He is pointing out that it may be possible to accomplish our goals for wealth and possessions, but in doing it we may lose far more important things: family, friends, health, even our relationship Him.

What of Jesus' promise, "there are some standing here who will in no way taste of death, until they see the Son of Man coming in his Kingdom."? If He means by that His "second coming," then He didn't keep His promise. I think He means His death and resurrection, the coming of the Holy Spirit. This could also refer to the "Transfiguration" that would soon take place, the coming of the Holy Spirit in power at Pentecost, or even the destruction of Jerusalem in 70 AD. All that happened before many of those died. There aren't two sets of rules, Jesus also won by losing. As my old NT prof might say, "you pay your money and you take your choice..." and Judas didn't live to see it.

A brief study of Kingdom Theology indicates that Christ's Kingdom came with His announcement of it and continues today. It will be culminated when He returns when the current age will cease and His eternal Kingdom will be established.

The Transformation
Matthew 17:1-13

After six days, Jesus took with him Peter, James, and John his brother, and brought them up into a high mountain by themselves. ² He was transfigured before them. His face shone like the sun, and his garments became as white as the light. ³ Behold, Moses and Elijah appeared to them talking with him.

⁴ Peter answered, and said to Jesus, "Lord, it is good for us to be here. If you want, let's make three tents here: one for you, one for Moses, and one for Elijah."

⁵ While he was still speaking, behold, a bright cloud overshadowed them. Behold, a voice came out of the cloud, saying, "This is my beloved Son, in whom I am well pleased. Listen to him."

⁶ When the disciples heard it, they fell on their faces, and were very afraid. ⁷ Jesus came and touched them and said, "Get up, and don't be afraid." ⁸ Lifting up their eyes, they saw no one, except Jesus alone. ⁹ As they were coming down from the mountain, Jesus commanded them, saying, "Don't tell anyone what you saw, until the Son of Man has risen from the dead."

¹⁰ His disciples asked him, saying, "Then why do the scribes say that Elijah must come first?"

¹¹ Jesus answered them, "Elijah indeed comes first, and will restore all things, ¹² but I tell you that Elijah has come already, and they didn't recognize him, but did to him whatever they wanted to. Even so the Son of Man will also suffer by them." ¹³ Then the disciples understood that he spoke to them of John the Baptizer.

The word "transfigured" is the Greek word *metamorphothe*, which is usually translated "transformed" or "changed" because it describes metamorphous, the process that changes a caterpillar into a butterfly. Both Mount Tabor and Mount Hermon have been suggested as the possible site of the event, but Mount Tabor was an armed fortress with a castle, so it seems unlikely.

Because of its proximity to Caesarea Philippi, Mount Hermon seems more logical. It rises to an altitude of 9,400 feet and can be seen from the Dead Sea over one hundred miles away, however, it seems unlikely that the activity took place at the summit; the air would be too thin for sustained activity. Further, it probably took place in the evening or at night because Luke says, "Now Peter and those who were with him were heavy with sleep… (Luke 9:32a)."

Why would Jesus go up on this mountain? We have seen that it was Jesus' practice to go aside to pray, but usually He went alone; this time He took the "inner circle" of disciples with Him. It may be to prepare for the closing days of His ministry on earth.

While they were on the mountain, something strange happened, Jesus' face began to shine "like the sun" and His "…garments became as white as the light." This is reminiscent of Moses experience on Sinai when he received the Law (Ex. 34:29). We can couple that with the "bright cloud" and the voice from the cloud that said, "This is my beloved Son, in whom I am well pleased. Listen to him." The last time we heard the voice of God was at Jesus' baptism (Matt. 3:17b) when the message was: "This is my beloved Son, with whom I am well pleased." In both Greek and English, the first part of the message is the same.

The "bright cloud" recalls the *Shekinah* glory of God in the Old Testament; that is the glory that appeared to Moses on Sinai and materialized to lead the Israelites out of Egypt in the pillar of smoke and cloud. It is the glory that appeared in the Tabernacle and Temple.

It may seem strange that Moses and Elijah appeared and talked to Jesus, but that could be because they symbolize both the Law and the prophets and showed the connection between the Old and New Covenants. They were the cream of Jewish religion; they laid the foundation and now Jesus would finish the building. Luke is the only writer to tell us what was discussed, His impending crucifixion (Luke 9:31).

We have often asked when Jesus truly knew about His mission, His messianic consciousness. It is certainly possible that this was one of the times He learned about what would happen. His "departure," actually His "exodus" was very near. "Exodus" was a word that carried great images for the Jews. It reminded them of Gods deliverance from Egypt and His provision for them in the wilderness. God will also be with Jesus during His exodus.

Again, Jesus didn't want the disciples to talk about what they had seen; and we need to remember that there is a right time for everything. We might also say that they didn't fully understand what was happening now, but they would after the resurrection and ascension. The time to tell about this scene is after the "Son of Man has been raised from the dead." Some translations say "raised," not "risen." "Raised" is probably the better translation and implies someone else, God the Father, does the raising.

The mountain was a spiritual peak for Jesus and a great encouragement to the disciples. Peter was always a man of action and had to do something, why not just stay there? Like Peter, we often want to stay on the mountain, but the ministry is in the valley.

Faith to Move a Mountain
Matthew 17:14-21

*When they came to the multitude, a man came to him, kneeling down to him, and saying, *[15]* "Lord, have mercy on my son, for he is epileptic, and suffers grievously; for he often falls into the fire, and often into the water. *[16]* So I brought him to your disciples, and they could not cure him."*

*[17] Jesus answered, "Faithless and perverse generation! How long will I be with you? How long will I bear with you? Bring him here to me." *[18]* Jesus rebuked him, the demon went out of him, and the boy was cured from that hour.*

[19] Then the disciples came to Jesus privately, and said, "Why weren't we able to cast it out?"

*[20] He said to them, "Because of your unbelief. For most certainly I tell you, if you have faith as a grain of mustard seed, you will tell this mountain, 'Move from here to there,' and it will move; and nothing will be impossible for you. *[21]* But this kind doesn't go out except by prayer and fasting" (NU omits verse 21).*

There are two interesting contrasts between this passage and the prior passage. First, there is the glory of the mountain against the desperation of the valley. Second, there is the power of Jesus against the helplessness of the disciples.

No sooner had Jesus come from the glory of the mountain than He was confronted by a man whose son was seriously ill. He had asked the disciples to heal the boy, but they had failed. Why? They had been given power to drive out demons, "He called to himself his twelve disciples, and gave them authority over unclean spirits, to cast them out, and to heal every disease and every sickness (Matt. 10:1)."

In spite of the failure of the disciples, the father still believed Jesus could help his son. Barclay points out that this is also a modern parable. Often the church is ineffective in its attempt to meet the needs of society, but people still seek Christ. See Dan Kimball's *They Like Jesus but Not the Church*.

We also see in Jesus' ministry the truth of worship; it isn't found in the sanctuary or the prayer closet, but in meeting the needs of people. It is there that people can see and feel the love of God and get a sense of awe in the caring touch of His followers. That doesn't discount the need for the sanctuary or prayer closet; their function is preparation for ministry; they are the "means," but they are not the "end."

The questions, "How long will I be with you? How long will I bear with you?" seem to have been made out of a sense of frustration rather than disgust. Time is running out and still the disciples don't understand. "Jesus' purpose was not to criticize the disciples but to encourage them to greater faith (LASB, p. 1579)."

What does Jesus mean in the statement, "if you have faith as a grain of mustard seed, you will tell this mountain, 'Move from here to there,' and it will move; and nothing will be impossible for you."? What He doesn't mean is an actual mountain. The symbol of a "mountain," as used by the rabbis means a problem that is difficult to solve. There is a clue in verse 21 which Nettle's omits "But this kind doesn't go out except by prayer and fasting." And there is ample Scriptural evidence, and from the life of Jesus, that prayer and fasting are essential in accomplishing the works of the Father.

According to *Nelson's Illustrated Bible Dictionary*, the ancients believed "...epilepsy was caused by the moon; people referred to epileptics as being 'moonstruck,'" which is the English meaning of the Greek word. Some feel that the statement in Psalm 121:6 "The sun will not harm you by day, nor the moon by night" may have that meaning because they believed the sun could cause sunstroke and the moon insanity or "lunacy," which is term still used by some today.

Some have suggested "faith as a grain of mustard seed." means that faith should be nurtured and it will grow into something big and strong and powerful. Although that is true, a case can be made for the idea that just a "speck" of pure faith is sufficient. Many loudly proclaim God's power, but few make use of it. "The extraordinary power of Satan must not discourage our faith, but quicken us to more earnestness in praying to God for the increase of it" (MH)."

Whose Rights Are They Anyway?
Matthew 17:22-27

While they were staying in Galilee, Jesus said to them, "The Son of Man is about to be delivered up into the hands of men, 23 and they will kill him, and the third day he will be raised up."

They were exceedingly sorry. 24 When they had come to Capernaum, those who collected the didrachma coins (a didrachma is a Greek silver coin worth 2 drachmas, about as much as 2 Roman denarii, or about 2 days' wages; it was commonly used to pay the half-shekel temple tax, because 2 drachmas were worth one half shekel of silver; A shekel is about 10 grams or about 0.35 ounces) came to Peter, and said, "Doesn't your teacher pay the didrachma?" 25 He said, "Yes."

When he came into the house, Jesus anticipated him, saying, "What do you think, Simon? From whom do the kings of the earth receive toll or tribute? From their children, or from strangers?"

26 Peter said to him, "From strangers."

Jesus said to him, "Therefore the children are exempt. 27 But, lest we cause them to stumble, go to the sea, cast a hook, and take up the first fish that comes up. When you have opened its mouth, you will find a stater coin (a stater was just exactly enough to cover the half-shekel temple tax for two people). Take that, and give it to them for me and you."

Once again Jesus warned His disciples about His coming death. It is amazing that with all the warnings they were so unprepared for it when it came. It also seems that they focused on His death, not His resurrection; on the loss, not on the hope. Maybe that's natural, no matter how long we might have to prepare for the death of a loved one, we are never ready for it. And the fact that we will be reunited with our Christian family members doesn't stop us from mourning as though we will never see them again.

Only Matthew records the strange story of the fish, which could have been a St. Peter's fish, a "mouth breeder," common to that area, with the money in its mouth. The fact that he had been a tax collector may have been the impetus for Matthew reporting it to us. This is an interesting episode, in that Jesus does what He doesn't have to do and appears to use His power for His own benefit. But it showed that He was willing to give up His rights rather than push them.

It cost a lot of money to run the Temple. There were sacrifices of a year-old lamb in the morning and evening; some were provided, but most had to be raised or purchased. The offerings required wine, flour and oil. There was incense, the priest's robes, repairs, and other costs to be paid. The money to pay for those things had to come from somewhere. It sounds like a church, doesn't it? Well, it was.

During the return from Egypt an "offering," that became a tax on all males over twenty, was established to finance the needs of the Tabernacle. This was in addition to the other offerings and sacrifices that were required (Ex. 30:13-15). The amount was equal to about two day's pay. "The question seems to imply that the payment of this tax was *voluntary,* but *expected;* or what, in modern phrase, would be called a 'voluntary assessment' (CCE)."

Once again, Peter acts, by answering the question, without thinking or consulting Jesus "...putting Jesus and the disciples in an awkward position. Jesus used this situation, however, to emphasize his kingly role (LASB, p. 1579)."

The tax was collected in the synagogue in the spring, but if it wasn't paid at the appropriate time, it had to be paid directly to the Temple in Jerusalem which, is the setting for this encounter. Someone reminded Peter about the tax. Peter didn't know what to do about it, and Jesus seized the opportunity to demonstrate a great truth.

He raised the question "From whom do the kings of the earth receive toll or tribute? From their children, or from strangers?" It is obvious that the family of the king doesn't pay taxes; it is the rest of the population. "Therefore the children are exempt." As the Son, Jesus was free of the tax, so why should He pay it? The key is something we have seen before. Jesus said it was "lest we cause them to stumble..." The word "stumble" is the Greek word we have seen before that was used for the "bait stick" in an animal trap.

160

David, the shepherd boy, asked what is the reward for killing the giant Goliath who was menacing King Saul's army? In 1 Samuel 17:25, "The men of Israel said, 'Have you seen this man who has come up? He has surely come up to defy Israel. The king will give great riches to the man who kills him, and will give him his daughter, and will make his father's house tax-free in Israel.'"

At the time Matthew wrote, the Temple tax didn't just go to the upkeep of the Temple, but also to Rome for the maintenance of heathen temples. However, sometimes there is a greater good than my right to do or not do something. Knowing when to insist upon them and when to forego them is crucial. Paul gives us two clues:

1. "Therefore if food causes my brother to stumble, I will eat no meat forevermore, that I don't cause my brother to stumble" (1 Cor. 8:13).

2. "But if anyone says to you, 'This was offered to idols,' don't eat it for the sake of the one who told you, and for the sake of conscience. For 'the earth is the Lord's, and all its fullness'" (1 Cor. 10:28).

Stagg says: "The human family never moves ahead significantly to more meaningful life except where someone is willing to surrender personal rights for the good of others (BBC, p. 180)."

What about the "fish"? Wouldn't this miracle not only show Jesus using His power for personal gain, but also send the wrong signal to His followers? Yes, it would. Therefore, it probably shouldn't be taken literally. Barclay says there are three reasons we should take the message symbolically:

1. God does not send miracles to enable us to do what we can quite well do for ourselves.

2. This miracle transgresses the great decision of Jesus that He would never use His miraculous power for His own ends.

3. If this miracle is taken literally, there is a sense in which it is even immoral (DSB, pp. 171-2).

We cannot just sit around and wait for God to have the banker deliver the money we need. Peter was a fisherman, Jesus' message to Him could have been, "go to work, you will find enough money from the sale of the fish to pay the tax for both of us."

The True Mark of Greatness
Matthew 18:1-11

In that hour the disciples came to Jesus, saying, "Who then is greatest in the Kingdom of Heaven?"

² Jesus called a little child to himself, and set him in the middle of them, ³ and said, "Most certainly I tell you, unless you turn, and become as little children, you will in no way enter into the Kingdom of Heaven. ⁴ Whoever therefore humbles himself as this little child, the same is the greatest in the Kingdom of Heaven. ⁵ Whoever receives one such little child in my name receives me, ⁶ but whoever causes one of these little ones who believe in me to stumble, it would be better for him that a huge millstone should be hung around his neck, and that he should be sunk in the depths of the sea.

⁷ "Woe to the world because of occasions of stumbling! For it must be that the occasions come, but woe to that person through whom the occasion comes! ⁸ If your hand or your foot causes you to stumble, cut it off, and cast it from you. It is better for you to enter into life maimed or crippled, rather than having two hands or two feet to be cast into the eternal fire. ⁹ If your eye causes you to stumble, pluck it out, and cast it from you. It is better for you to enter into life with one eye, rather than having two eyes to be cast into the Gehenna (or Hell) of fire. [10] See that you don't despise one of these little ones, for I tell you that in heaven their angels always see the face of my Father who is in heaven. [11] For the Son of Man came to save that which was lost.

Barclay feels that chapter 18 "is a most important chapter for Christian Ethics... It singles out seven qualities which should mark the personal relationship of the Christian." They are:

1. humility (vs. 1-4)
2. responsibility (vs. 5-7)
3. self-renunciation (vs. 8-10)
4. individual care (vs. 11-14)
5. discipline (vs. 15-20)
6. fellowship (vs. 19,20)
7. spirit of forgiveness (vs. 23-35), (DSB, pp. 172-4).

From Mark 9:33-34 we learn that Jesus began this discussion: "They came to Capernaum. When he was in the house, he asked the disciples, 'What were you talking about on the way coming?' But they said nothing, because on the road they had been talking among themselves about who was the greatest person."

The question is: "Who then is the greatest in the Kingdom of Heaven?" But Jesus turns to the real problem. The heart of the matter isn't "who is the greatest"? The real problem is "unless you turn, and become as little children." Like most of us, the disciples "jockeyed for position," a position of power, not service. If you don't get in, it doesn't matter how great you are!

The keyword in the passage is the word "turn" which the KJV translates "be converted," which carries the correct idea. Jesus says you're going in the wrong direction; the only thing to do is to be converted and turn around and go the other way.

How does that happen? We must "…turn, and become as little children…" Are we willing to humble ourselves and to give up our "adulthood"? Can we give up our right to self-determination and place ourselves under the guidance of someone else? If we can't, Jesus said, "you will <u>in no way</u> enter into the Kingdom of Heaven" [my underline]. "We are not to be *childish* (like the disciples, arguing over petty issues) but *childlike*, with humble and sincere hearts (LASB, p. 1579)."

Why a child? Are children naturally humble? Not my great-grandkids, they're like their grate-grandpa! Why are the characteristics of a child the characteristics of one who "is the greatest in the Kingdom of Heaven"? Because children are totally dependent on someone else for everything they want and need. Therefore, we must trust God like "little children" not just to be great, but even to enter the Kingdom of Heaven. When we studied our "rights" in Matthew 17:24-27 we saw that we must place God's Will before our own will (like a child?). "So long as a man considers his own self as the most important thing in the world, his back is turned to the Kingdom (DSB, p. 175)."

Jesus goes on to stress the importance of equality in the kingdom, "whoever receives…little child." "Receives" carries the weight of acceptance as an equal. Children are often relegated to inferior status and have inferior space and equipment. How many times have you heard "Children should be seen and not heard"? Why? That certainly wasn't Jesus' attitude.

"…causes…to stumble" again goes back to our study of the bait stick. Jesus said it would be better to die than to mislead a "little one." We often think it is cute to encourage a child to do "naughty" things, until they grow up to be obnoxious or criminals and then it is too late!

Who are the "little ones," actually the word could be better translated "insignificant ones" or even common people would do, that Jesus is talking about? Unquestionably they are actual youngsters. But the use of "child" to describe a disciple or student of a teacher was a common idiom, so they could also be those who are young in Christ, those who might be easily mislead by false teachers.

What about the statement "their angels always see the face of my Father who is in heaven"? It suggests to me that we need to be careful how we treat those we might consider unimportant because there is one with direct access to God watching over their affairs. As Jacob was preparing to die, he summoned his children and blessed them. In Genesis 48:16, he said, "…the angel who has redeemed me from all evil, bless the lads…" In Daniel chapter 10 an angel identified as Michael (a great name) says that he has been fighting for Daniel.

Jesus would be leaving and returning to His Father soon and the disciples would be left to carry on the work of building His church and they must understand how it was to work. When I study church polity, and see how church leaders actually work, I'm not sure if we are getting it right today.

Self-importance, ego, is an ever-present problem for many of us. Paul warned: "A man who thinks that he is an important person when he is not, that man fools himself. Let every man test his own work. Then he will be proud of his own work. He will not be proud because he thinks his own work is better than someone else's work. (Gal. 6:3-4)."

In our study of Matthew 5:27-30, we saw the importance of going to whatever extreme necessary to avoid sin. Here it is restated. Nothing should be allowed that will lead us into sin.

The Joy of Recovery
Matthew 18:12-14

"What do you think? If a man has one hundred sheep, and one of them goes astray, doesn't he leave the ninety-nine, go to the mountains, and seek that which has gone astray? [13] If he finds it, most certainly I tell you, he rejoices over it more than over the ninety-nine which have not gone astray. [14] Even so it is not the will of your Father who is in heaven that one of these little ones should perish.

This is a classic example of Jesus' use of the parable. It is simple; there are only two characters, a sheep that has gone "astray," rather than "one that is lost" as some translations have it, and a searching shepherd. For them, it was a familiar scene, a shepherd seeking a sheep that has wandered away from the flock.

Most of the flocks belonged to the entire village rather than to an individual family, so they were herded by two or three shepherds. If one sheep wandered away, one of the shepherds could easily leave the rest of the flock and search for the lost sheep. The commitment to the herd and the village was absolute and the shepherd would stay out until the sheep was found, either dead or alive.

The pasture in Palestine was along a narrow ridge that runs the length of the country and there were many ravines and gullies a sheep could wander into and be lost, become a meal for a wild animal or die of exposure unless rescued by a shepherd. Sheep are one of the very few animals that need human assistance to thrive.

The picture of the shepherd and the sheep was a common picture used by the Jews to describe their relationship with God in the Old Testament and by Jesus for the relationship between God and man. The helplessness of sheep is legendary and so is the dedication of the shepherd. The picture is a natural one so the interpretation should also be natural:

1. God's love is personal, individual. Is the one sheep more important than the ninety-nine? No! But neither is it less important. To God, it is worth looking for.

2. God's love is patient. No matter how many absurd, foolish things we do, God still loves us. We usually don't waste much time on people who repeatedly blow it, but God isn't like that.

3. God's love is searching. He doesn't wait for the sheep to find its way home; He goes looking for it. We're often willing to take a person back, if they return and apologize and after a period of "probation." Not so with God.

4. God's love is joyous. He wants us to serve only Him, but there isn't any recrimination for past sins.

One more point, this sheep was originally part of the flock and wandered away. (Although it applies, He's not talking about evangelism but conservation!) We don't know why, maybe it was the music, maybe it was the pastor, for whatever reason, it separated itself from the flock, but the shepherd sought and brought it back. "The shepherd's joy is also the joy of the Father; the purpose of pastoral care is so God will not lose any of his sheep (NLTSB, p. 1615)."

How does this apply to us? Do we sometimes get confused about our role? Do we think we're the shepherd instead of a sheep? If we will concentrate on doing our job, and of enjoy our role, it will make a big difference in us and those we serve. Paul says, "But the fruit of the Spirit is love, joy, peace, patience, kindness, goodness, faith, gentleness, and self-control. Against such things there is no law (Gal. 5:22-23)." Did you notice that "fruit" is singular? All of those things rolled together make our "fruit." We don't single out one of them or omit any of them. We need to work on that in ourselves, not in others.

The Model for Church Discipline
Matthew 18:15-20

"If your brother sins against you, go, show him his fault between you and him alone. If he listens to you, you have gained back your brother. [16] But if he doesn't listen, take one or two more with you, that at the mouth of two or three witnesses every word may be established (Deut. 19:15). [17] If he refuses to listen to them, tell it to the assembly. If he refuses to hear the assembly also, let him be to you as a Gentile or a tax collector. [18] Most certainly I tell you, whatever things you bind on earth will have been bound in heaven, and whatever things you release on earth will have been released in heaven. [19] Again, assuredly I tell you, that if two of you will agree on earth concerning anything that they will ask, it will be done for them by my Father who is in heaven. [20] For where two or three are gathered together in my name, there I am in the middle of them."

If a professed Christian is wronged by another, he ought not to complain of it to others, as is often done merely upon report, but to go to the offender privately, state the matter kindly, and show him his conduct. This would generally have all the desired effect with a true Christian, and the parties would be reconciled (MH).

Barclay says, "In many ways this is one of the most difficult passages to interpret in the whole of Matthew's gospel (DSB, p. 187)." The main problem is that these don't sound like and may not be the actual words of Jesus. The word translated "assembly" is usually translated "church" and only appears in the gospels here and in Matthew 16:18a "And I tell you that you are Peter, and on this rock I will build my church… (NIV)" That church didn't actually start until Pentecost.

Another problem with attributing it to Jesus is that Jesus was compassionate toward "Gentile[s] and tax collectors." He never spoke of them in the same way the Jews did.

A third problem is that the passage seems to place a limit on forgiveness which is contrary to the passage that follows: "Then Peter came and said to him, 'Lord, how often shall my brother sin against me, and I forgive him? Until seven times?' Jesus said to him, 'I don't tell you until seven times, but, until seventy times seven.' (Matt. 18:21-22)." Because the passage stresses the importance of reconciliation and restoration of relationships, Matthew is possibly adapting a saying of Jesus to address a problem in the church that we don't know about.

There are three important elements in any act of discipline, they are: the reason for it, the attitude of the person taking the initiative, and the method used. The reason for the encounter is probably the most important element and should be to restore the relationship, not to uncover or remove the one who messed up. That the offended person would take the initiative is a new idea, but often the one wronged is in a better position to recognize and resolve the problem than the one who was offended. We cannot just sit back and wait for the offender to come to us; we must go to them.

We also need to check our attitude. If it is condescending, we may widen the breech instead of closing it. Paul encourages, "Brothers, even if a man is caught in some fault, you who are spiritual must restore such a one in a spirit of gentleness; looking to yourself so that you also aren't tempted (Gal. 6:1)." By taking the initiative, we may find that there isn't a real problem at all, just a misunderstanding. This could save a great deal of embarrassment for everyone concerned.

Jesus outlines a four-step procedure:

1. Attempt to reconcile with only the other party involved present. Meeting face-to-face, not over the telephone and certainly not in a letter, email, or text is the best and quickest way.

2. Attempt to reconcile with the aid of one or two friends. "One witness shall not rise up against a man for any iniquity, or for any sin, in any sin that he sins. At the mouth of two witnesses, or at the mouth of three witnesses, shall a matter be established (Deut. 19:15)." The purpose of the "witnesses" is to help in the reconciliation not to establish the offense.

3. Bring the problem to the church. Secular courts should be avoided whenever possible and the church should serve as a "reconciliation court" to help resolve and restore relationships, but the decision should be made by the parties, "not" the church.

4. Recognize that no fellowship exists and continue to minister to, witness to, and love both the parties with the goal of restoration.

Verse 18 says "Most certainly I tell you, whatever things you bind on earth will have been bound in heaven, and whatever things you release on earth will have been released in heaven" and is one of the most difficult passages found in Scripture. Undoubtedly, it was used to sell "indulgences," or "get out of Hell free cards," during the Dark Ages.

This verse doesn't give the church blanket authorization to go around "binding" and "loosing" people for the sin they commit. However, through the relationships we build, we can build a family that will last into eternity. On the flip side, failure to love people into a lasting relationship could condemn them to an eternity of separation from God in Hell.

Verse 19 has often presented problems for Christians. Jesus says, "…I tell you, that if two of you will agree on earth concerning anything that they will ask, it will be done for them by my Father who is in heaven." Taken literally, as we often do, it can mean a promise of anything; even things that are not good for us or that would hurt someone else. That isn't what the passage means. The fact that each of us has probably agreed with someone about something that didn't come about testifies to that. Then, what does the passage mean? And what are the "rules" to be followed in this kind of prayer?

1. Prayer must not be self-centered. "You ask, and don't receive, because you ask with wrong motives, so that you may spend it for your pleasures (James 4:3)." A prayer which would help me, but hurt others is never acceptable to God. When prayer is for the benefit of others, not self, its motives are correct.

2. Prayer must always be within the will of God. Barclay says most of our prayers are for escape, not victory. The best example is the prayer of Jesus in the garden, "My Father, if it is possible, let this cup pass away from me; nevertheless, not what I desire, but what you desire." (Matt. 26:39b). He wasn't delivered from the Cross, but he was given victory over it.

There is another promise here in verse 20, "For where two or three are gathered together in my name, there I am in the middle of them." The Holy Spirit isn't present just in the large, crowded churches, but He is also in the small Bible study group. Yes, and in the camp or by the fishing stream, if you will seek Him there.

When I was a kid, there was a group, almost a "cult," of those who went around "agreeing" about things they wanted. They got the idea from the King James Version, "…if two of you shall agree on earth as touching anything that they shall ask, it shall be done for them of my Father which is in heaven" (Matthew 18:19). It almost became a mantra for them. As above, that isn't what Jesus meant by it.

The Problem of Forgiveness
Matthew 18:21-35

Then Peter came and said to him, "Lord, how often shall my brother sin against me, and I forgive him? Until seven times?"

²² Jesus said to him, "I don't tell you until seven times, but, until seventy times seven. ²³ Therefore the Kingdom of Heaven is like a certain king, who wanted to reconcile accounts with his servants. ²⁴ When he had begun to reconcile, one was brought to him who owed him ten thousand talents. (about 300 metric tons of silver) ²⁵ *But because he couldn't pay, his lord commanded him to be sold, with his wife, his children, and all that he had, and payment to be made.* ²⁶ *The servant therefore fell down and knelt before him, saying, 'Lord, have patience with me, and I will repay you all!'* ²⁷ *The lord of that servant, being moved with compassion, released him, and forgave him the debt.*

²⁸ *"But that servant went out, and found one of his fellow servants, who owed him one hundred denarii (about one sixtieth of a talent, or about 1.1 pounds of silver), and he grabbed him, and took him by the throat, saying, 'Pay me what you owe!'*

²⁹ *"So his fellow servant fell down at his feet and begged him, saying, 'Have patience with me, and I will repay you!'* ³⁰ *He would not, but went and cast him into prison, until he should pay back that which was due.* ³¹ *So when his fellow servants saw what was done, they were exceedingly sorry, and came and told to their lord all that was done.* ³² *Then his lord called him in, and said to him, 'You wicked servant! I forgave you all that debt, because you begged me.* ³³ *Shouldn't you also have had mercy on your fellow servant, even as I had mercy on you?'* ³⁴ *His lord was angry, and delivered him to the tormentors, until he should pay all that was due to him.* ³⁵ *So my heavenly Father will also do to you, if you don't each forgive your brother from your hearts for his misdeeds."*

Immediately following the discussion about church discipline, we address the problem of forgiveness and the emphasis on reconciliation continues. This may be where Paul picks up the concern:

But all things are of God, who reconciled us to himself through Jesus Christ, and gave to us the ministry of reconciliation; namely, that God was in Christ reconciling the world to himself, not reckoning to them their trespasses, and having committed to us the word of reconciliation. We are therefore ambassadors on behalf of Christ, as though God were entreating by us. We beg you on behalf of Christ, be reconciled to God (2 Cor. 5:18-20).

Barclay says that we owe a "great deal to the fact that Peter had a quick tongue (DSB, p. 193)." It was this impetuousness that provided many of Jesus' best teachings opportunities; this time it is amplification about forgiveness.

The background of Peter's question is probably the rabbinic teaching that you were only required to forgive a person three times. That concept undoubtedly came from the series of condemnations Amos used in his sermons: Amos 1:3a says, "Thus says Yahweh: 'For three transgressions of Damascus, yes, for four, I will not turn away its punishment...'" In 1:6, he says the same about Gaza. And in 1:9, it is Tyre; in 1:11, Edom; in 1:13 Ammon; in 2:1, Moab; in 2:4 Judah; ending in 2:6 with Israel. If God only forgave three times, why should anyone else forgive more?

Surely there must be a limit to the need to forgive. In suggesting seven times, both a sacred and complete number, Peter was offering more than twice the number of times that even God was supposed to have offered to forgive and he may have expected to be complimented for his liberality. Instead, Jesus took the opportunity to again teach the importance of forgiveness, which is important because there is no forgiveness from God unless we have also forgiven. "So speak, and so do, as men who are to be judged by a law of freedom. For judgment is without mercy to him who has shown no mercy. Mercy triumphs over judgment (James 2:12-13)." And Jesus taught, "For if you forgive men their trespasses, your heavenly Father will also forgive you. But if you don't forgive men their trespasses, neither will your Father forgive your trespasses (Matt. 6:14-15)."

Verse 22 has been translated both "seventy-seven times" and "seventy times seven." Which is correct? We don't know. Jesus words could be a reversal of the attitude of Lamech in Genesis 4:23-24 "Lamech said to his wives, 'Adah and Zillah, hear my voice, You wives of Lamech, listen to my speech, For I have slain a man for wounding me, a young man for bruising me. If Cain will be avenged seven times, Truly Lamech seventy-seven times.'" As Stagg says, "To keep count would betray the lack of the real spirit of forgiveness, however few or many times one presumed to forgive another (BBC, p. 185)." It isn't endless revenge, as was often the practice, but endless forgiveness that is taught here.

The parable which Jesus used as an example is a picture which contrasts God's forgiveness of man's sin against Him with a man's sin against another man. The debt owed God is so great it can never be paid; it can only be discharged by forgiveness. The other debt is as ridiculously small as the debt to God is large, several million dollars, against, a few hundred dollars.

Matthew Henry suggests three things we should notice:

1.   The master's wonderful clemency. The debt of sin is so great, that we are not able to pay it.

2.   The servant's unreasonable severity toward his fellow-servant, notwithstanding his lord's clemency toward him.

3.   The master reproved his servant's cruelty. The greatness of sin magnifies the riches of pardoning mercy; and the comfortable sense of pardoning mercy, does much to dispose our hearts to forgive our brethren (MH).

Verse 35 is explicit: "So my heavenly Father will also do to you, if you don't each forgive your brother from your hearts for his misdeeds." Ouch" Is forgiveness an option? Not in the least!

Marriage, Divorce and Celibacy
Matthew 19:1-12

When Jesus had finished these words, he departed from Galilee, and came into the borders of Judea beyond the Jordan. [2] Great multitudes followed him, and he healed them there. [3] Pharisees came to him, testing him, and saying, "Is it lawful for a man to divorce his wife for any reason?"

[4] He answered, "Haven't you read that he who made them from the beginning made them male and female (Gen. 1:27), [5] and said, 'For this cause a man shall leave his father and mother, and shall join to his wife; and the two shall become one flesh' (Gen. 2:24). [6] So that they are no more two, but one flesh. What therefore God has joined together, don't let man tear apart."

[7] They asked him, "Why then did Moses command us to give her a bill of divorce, and divorce her?"

[8] He said to them, "Moses, because of the hardness of your hearts, allowed you to divorce your wives, but from the beginning it has not been so. [9] I tell you that whoever divorces his wife, except for sexual immorality, and marries another, commits adultery; and he who marries her when she is divorced commits adultery."

[10] His disciples said to him, "If this is the case of the man with his wife, it is not expedient to marry."

[11] But he said to them, "Not all men can receive this saying, but those to whom it is given. [12] For there are eunuchs who were born that way from their mother's womb, and there are eunuchs who were made eunuchs by men; and there are eunuchs who made themselves eunuchs for the Kingdom of Heaven's sake. He who is able to receive it, let him receive it."

"When Jesus had finished these words," marks the end of Matthews's fourth discourse of the five he offers. This section, chapters 19-25, with emphasis on judgment will widen the gulf between Jesus and the Jewish rulers and is an interlude before the final discourse.

Plato taught that men were originally double their size; however, they became arrogant so the gods cut them in half. It was only when the two halves found themselves and married that a man and a woman, could be truly complete and truly happy (DSB, pp. 203-4). This is probably where the term "better half" to describe a spouse may come from. And, if you know me, I will probably launch into a lesson in Greek mythology. Each of us is complete in Jesus, but we are also probably more effective working together as a team. "Two are better than one, because they have a good reward for their labor (Ecc. 4:9)."

The Jews had a higher view of marriage than most cultures and considered marriage a "sacred duty." In fact, the Hebrew word, *kiddushin*, used for marriage means sanctified or consecrated and was often used to refer to something dedicated to God.

They took seriously the command of "Be fruitful and multiply. Increase abundantly in the earth, and multiply in it (Gen. 9:7)." For a Jewish man, to fail to marry meant he was killing his posterity. We might remember that Jesus' first miracle took place at a wedding in Cana in Galilee where He and His disciples were guests (John 2:1-11). "Where does this leave homosexual marriage? At best, it is a human invention without biblical precedent (LASB, p. 1582)."

It appears that the Jews were also as preoccupied with divorce and remarriage, as Americans are, because this is the second time Matthew has Jesus addressing the problem with the Pharisees (see Matt. 5:31 ff.). And, each passage has contained the "exception clause," but there is a little different twist here. Mark, which is thought by some to an older book, and therefore, more accurate, doesn't have either the "for any reason?" or "except for sexual immorality" phrases. Further, as I mentioned earlier, for Jesus to have taken "sides" in an ongoing debate would have been unthinkable.

Moses "...tolerated a relaxation of the strictness of the marriage bond – not as approving of it, but to prevent still greater evils (CCE)." The "grounds" for divorce were important and until "no-fault" divorce came along, most divorces in America were for "incompatibility" or "irreconcilable differences" or you may also read that, "for an unwillingness to suppress ego and desire."

The "grounds" for a Jewish divorce are found in Deuteronomy 24:1a, "When a man takes a wife, and marries her, then it shall be, if she finds no favor in his eyes, because he has found some unseemly thing in her..." The Rabbinic Schools of Shammai and Hillel hotly debated the meaning of the passage with Shammai focusing on "unseemly" and Hillel on "no favor."

The root meaning of "unseemly" is "nakedness" or "shamefulness," but in fact, any behavior that would cause the family to be shamed or to "lose face" could be considered "unseemly." Shammai interpreted this to mean only adultery. Divorce had become so common people lost track of who was married to whom. It was for that reason that Moses tried to establish some control over it.

All divorce represents a failure, some kind of selfishness that places "my" desires above God's leadership. But the question often asked is this: "Did Jesus rule out divorce except for adultery?" As always, the answer is harder than the question and it isn't a simple "yes" or "no." To suggest that a person could be abusive and expect a spouse to remain in that situation, as long as there is no adultery involved is ludicrous.

In responding to the question Jesus refocused the attention where it belonged. "In God's image He created him; male and female He created them (Gen. 1:27b)," "Therefore a man will leave his father and his mother, and will join with his wife, and they will be one flesh (Gen. 2:24)." God's ideal was always one husband and one wife for life. That works best when both are subject to each other under God and, unfortunately, many of us Christians still allow our egos to get in the way.

Remember that God wanted His people to marry within the body of believers. The Law said an Israelite was not to marry a Canaanite, lest they be tempted to accept the spouse's gods (Ex. 34:10-17 and Deut. 7:3-4). Paul instructed the church at Corinth, "Do not be unequally yoked together with unbelievers" (2 Cor. 6:14a) and while it isn't addressing marriage specifically, we have properly made that application. It could also address business partnerships and other relationships.

In Ephesians 5, Paul showed how a marriage relationship should function. In using the model of the church, He emphasizes the need for both parties to be Christians. Paul also addressed the problem faced by a believer whose spouse didn't believe. He stated that if the unbelieving partner is willing to live with the Christian, then they should remain married, which could result in his or her salvation (1 Cor. 7:14).

The word Jesus used for "sexual immorality" is usually translated "fornication" and could apply to premarital infidelity as opposed to adultery, which can only happen after marriage. Possibly this is what Jesus had in mind as the only appropriate grounds for divorce. "God designed marriage to be indissoluble. Instead of looking for reasons to leave each other, husbands and wives should concentrate on how to stay together (LASB, p. 1582)" We consider every day an anniversary and try to find something to celebrate. It's hard to fight when you're partying!

There are many who feel that this statement forbids remarriage? Does it? No! Sin is any failure to meet God's standard. There are ample passages from Jesus and Paul and others assuring forgiveness of any sin, except one and divorce and/or remarriage isn't that sin, even if you're a fundamentalist Christian. However, if a person does remarry, there are always problems, including the former spouse and former in-laws. If there are children by the former union, they are seriously impacted and may never get over the divorce of their parents and refuse to accept the new step-parent. Generally, kids aren't as excited about a new "parent" as their parent is about a new partner. A good "rule of thumb" for total acceptance is to double the child's age at the time of the union. Therefore, a baby will generally accept the new "parent" quickly, while a teenager may be out of the house before it happens.

There is only one Scriptural alternative lifestyle to marriage; celibacy. Paul said, "Now concerning the things about which you wrote to me: it is good for a man not to touch a woman. But, because of sexual immoralities, let each man have his own wife, and let each woman have her own husband (1 Cor. 7:1-2)."

Choosing a single-lifestyle is something that shouldn't be done hastily and cannot be done by a Christian to allow them to "play the field." It should be done only because it satisfies a "call" by God to service.

"Clement of Alexander...said 'The true eunuch is not he who cannot, but he who will not indulge in fleshly pleasures' (DSB, p. 207)."

There are few commands in Scripture. Certainly, the Ten Commandments and several orders that came through the prophets and writers of the New Testament, but mostly what we have laid down in Scripture are principles which we must carefully and prayerfully apply to our lives.

Consider the problems of keeping the fourth commandment:

Remember the Sabbath day, to keep it holy. You shall labor six days, and do all your work, but the seventh day is a Sabbath to Yahweh your God. You shall not do any work in it, you, nor your son, nor your daughter, your male servant, nor your female servant, nor your livestock, nor your stranger who is within your gates… (Ex. 20:8-10).

Was there no work done on the Sabbath in Israel? No? Sacrifices were still offered and babies were circumcised. Cows were still milked and animals and families fed. How could the commandment be kept then? It could be kept in spirit and in principle. So, we must try our best to follow the principles God has laid down for us.

What Is the Place of Children in the Church?
Matthew 19:13-15

Then little children were brought to him, that he should lay his hands on them and pray; and the disciples rebuked them. [14] *But Jesus said, "Allow the little children, and don't forbid them to come to me; for the Kingdom of Heaven belongs to ones like these."* [15] *He laid his hands on them, and departed from there.*

These few verses could be attached to the section above because they conclude Jesus' teaching about the family that was begun in verse 1, but I want to treat them separately. I will say, as Tasker reminds us: "…the welfare of children must always be a primary concern of Christians in coming to decisions about divorce (TNTC, p. 184)." Like me, most of us focus on what we want, not what's best for our children.

In verse 14, the KJV says, "Suffer (meaning "allow") little children, and forbid them not…" That is an unfortunate translation. The word used is the same root word used in Acts 8:36 which is translated, "See, here is water; what doth <u>hinder</u> me to be baptized?" (KJV). The thrust is as the WEB has it to "allow…don't forbid." The theme of Acts: "…preaching God's Kingdom, and teaching the things concerning the Lord Jesus Christ with all boldness, without <u>hindrance</u>" (Acts 28:31). This is the same root word.

Here is Jesus, a man probably misunderstood by, but greatly admired by, the crowds. It would be natural for these superstitious mothers to want Jesus to touch their babies, which is literally the word used, with His "magic" [my word] hands, maybe some of the magic would rub off on them.

Equally naturally, the disciples, aware of the pressures on Jesus tried to protect him from the disturbances and the nuisance of these intrusions. It is amazing to me that it may be easier to see the Pope than to see some pastors, priests and bishops. Don't believe me; try to talk directly to famous and not so famous preachers. If you aren't "someone," you'll never get through to them; their staff will "protect" them.

I know they are busy and people can be a nuisance, but people are our "business," even the difficult ones (I'm so glad I don't fit in that category, right Pastor(s)?)

There was no malice on the part of the disciples; it was love and concern for their leader that made them want to protect His valuable time. His time could be shared with some people, teachers, "lawyers," and the like; however, others wouldn't contribute anything of importance and therefore would only waste His time. Boy, did Jesus explode their idea of who is important.

My cousin called my office and asked to speak to me. My phone rang and I picked it up and said hello. She asked, "Mike?" I said "Yes. How are you?" she said, "You don't have your calls screened?" "Nope," I replied, "I learned that dealing with creditors at a company I worked for. I talk to everyone." Of course, I was a small fish in a small pond...

When Jesus said, "...for the Kingdom of Heaven belongs to ones like these," what did He mean? The words "like these" translate the Greek word *toioutos* and is used to denote the character of a person. What is the difference between the character of a child and an adult? A great deal! There are rarely trick questions or hidden agendas, like with the Pharisees. There are rarely requests for special treatment, like the "Sons of Thunder." But there was honest, open love for a teacher who would make time for them.

"Jesus was not sentimental about children, but was fully aware of their frailties. Nevertheless, He undoubtedly believed that...they were more sensitive than adults tend to be to the supernatural world... (TNTC, p. 185)." The denomination I grew up in gave full membership rights to children who accepted Jesus as their Savior and became church members; even allowing them to vote on money matters and calling a pastor. One pastor told me he thought children were less swayed by "material" things than the adults were.

In Mark and Luke, Jesus is more pointed, "Most certainly I tell you, whoever will not receive God's Kingdom like a little child, he will in no way enter into it (Mark 10:15)." "Verily I say unto you, Whosoever shall not receive the kingdom of God as a little child shall in no wise enter therein. (Luke 18:15)." Jesus doesn't want us to be "childish," but childlike! Maybe we should all explore our attitudes and motives a little closer. Is it true that children should really "be seen and not heard," as we used to say? I don't think so!

The Danger of Riches
Matthew 19:16-30

Behold, one came to him and said, "Good teacher, what good thing shall I do, that I may have eternal life?"

[17] He said to him, "Why do you call me good? (MT and TR. NU reads "Why do you ask me about what is good?") No one is good but one, that is, God. But if you want to enter into life, keep the commandments."

[18] He said to him, "Which ones?"

Jesus said, "'You shall not murder.' 'You shall not commit adultery.' 'You shall not steal.' 'You shall not offer false testimony.' [19] 'Honor your father and your mother' (Ex. 20:12-16; Deut. 5:16-20). And, 'You shall love your neighbor as yourself'" (Lev. 19:18)

[20] The young man said to him, "All these things I have observed from my youth. What do I still lack?"

²¹ Jesus said to him, "If you want to be perfect, go, sell what you have, and give to the poor, and you will have treasure in heaven; and come, follow me." ²² But when the young man heard the saying, he went away sad, for he was one who had great possessions. ²³ Jesus said to his disciples, "Most certainly I say to you, a rich man will enter into the Kingdom of Heaven with difficulty. ²⁴ Again I tell you, it is easier for a camel to go through a needle's eye, than for a rich man to enter into God's Kingdom."

²⁵ When the disciples heard it, they were exceedingly astonished, saying, "Who then can be saved?"

²⁶ Looking at them, Jesus said, "With men this is impossible, but with God all things are possible."

²⁷ Then Peter answered, "Behold, we have left everything, and followed you. What then will we have?"

²⁸ Jesus said to them, "Most certainly I tell you that you who have followed me, in the regeneration when the Son of Man will sit on the throne of his glory, you also will sit on twelve thrones, judging the twelve tribes of Israel. ²⁹ Everyone who has left houses, or brothers, or sisters, or father, or mother, or wife, or children, or lands, for my name's sake, will receive one hundred times, and will inherit eternal life. ³⁰ But many will be last who are first; and first who are last.

Is there any logic more illogical than man's logic? The Jews, like us, held two opposite opinions about wealth. Some said riches were a blessing from God upon the righteous, but others claimed wealth was achieved because of wickedness. I guess it depended on whether you are rich or poor which opinion you held. When it came to money, Jesus was concerned about two things, what effect money had on the one who had it and what a person did with their money.

In all three Synoptic Gospels a rich man came to Jesus with a question about salvation. Matthew said, "Good teacher, what good thing shall I do, that I may have eternal life?" The first thing to notice is the words "good thing" which is not in Mark and Luke. Was he asking Jesus "What good deed can I do to buy my way into heaven?" It could be that that's what the Pharisees were trying to do by keeping the minutiae of the Law. At least this rich man was "up front" with his request.

Jesus responded, "But if you want to enter into life, keep the commandments." In the Greek, "keep" carries the impact of "continually keep." When quizzed further, Jesus only listed those commandments related to human relationships, not those related to God. I think that is very interesting. And the man assured Jesus that he had; however, he knew there was still something he should do that he had missed. If that were the case, could he buy that thing?

Jesus' response, "If you want to be perfect…" again uses the Greek word *teleios*, and in this case could be interpreted "true;" true to God. "The man who thinks that the life of the age-to-come can be earned by exact calculation is told to abandon all (AB, p.232)." Maybe the man had kept the Law, at least the letter of the Law, but what about the spirit of the Law? We learn that his attitude was wrong; his riches had taken hold of him and he "went away sad" because he was controlled by his wealth. "Goodness may be reflected in doing, but it belongs to being, i.e., to what one is (BBC, p. 190)."

"For the rich man the difficulty lies to making a choice between caring for his wealth and caring for the things of Christ (AB, p.232-3)." Do you think it strange that Jesus didn't ask everyone else to sell their property? Zacchaeus voluntarily gave away much, but not all, of his riches, but Lazarus apparently didn't give anything away. So, does the command to sell only apply to those to whom riches are a hindrance? Possibly! Probably! "Christ knew that covetousness was the sin which most easily beset this young man…

(MH)." Stagg says that just as a rich man may become a slave to his riches, a poor man may become a slave to his pennies (BBC, p. 192).

The request is for "eternal life." Exactly what would that mean to the man? The Greek word *aionios* means more than just perpetual or timelessness, it is also a quality of life, life like they thought the gods lived.

The statement, "it is easier for a camel to go through a needle's eye, than for a rich man to enter into God's Kingdom" has generated much debate; so much that it often replaces the real thrust of the passage. Some suggest that it means for a camel to enter the city through the small city gate called "the needle's eye," by unloading it and then crawling on its knees; it was a tight fit and difficult to accomplish, but it could be done, but without the cargo.

Some suggest that it means to thread a needle with a ship's hawser, a thick cable called a *kamilos* in Greek, camel is *kamelos*, but there was often little difference in the pronunciation of a long i and a long e.

The third alternative offered is probably the best, that he meant an actual camel and an actual needle. Why? Jesus often used hyperbole, the deliberate exaggeration of figures of speech, to make a point or to teach a truth. And great riches can certainly create a hindrance to all kinds of things.

Good old Peter. He speaks for all of us: "Behold, we have left everything, and followed you. What then will we have?" What's in it for me Lord? Notice what Jesus didn't say, "You jerk, when are you going to learn? This must be the umpteenth stupid question you've asked me!" Instead, He responds in patient love with a promise to the disciples and to those who come after them:

> Most certainly I tell you that you who have followed me, in the regeneration when the Son of Man will sit on the throne of his glory, you also will sit on twelve thrones, judging the twelve tribes of Israel. Everyone who has left houses, or brothers, or sisters, or father, or mother, or wife, or children, or lands, for my name's sake, will receive one hundred times, and will inherit eternal life. But many will be last who are first; and first who are last. (vss. 28b-30.)

We must patiently serve God and allow Him to take care of the details, so keep your attitude right and keep plugging away, because, except for the grace of God, none of us will have eternal life. There are many passages that promise rich rewards to those who are faithful.

How to Be Last
Matthew 20:1-16

"For the Kingdom of Heaven is like a man who was the master of a household, who went out early in the morning to hire laborers for his vineyard. ² When he had agreed with the laborers for a denarius (a denarius is a silver Roman coin worth a common wage for a day of farm labor) a day, he sent them into his vineyard. ³ He went out about the third hour, (time was measured from sunrise to sunset, so the third hour would be about 9:00 AM) and saw others standing idle in the marketplace. ⁴ He said to them, 'You also go into the vineyard, and whatever is right I will give you.' So they went their way. ⁵ Again he went out about the sixth and the ninth hour, (noon and 3:00 PM) and did likewise. ⁶ About the eleventh hour (5:00 PM) he went out, and found others standing idle. He said to them, 'Why do you stand here all day idle?'

⁷ "They said to him, 'Because no one has hired us.'

"He said to them, 'You also go into the vineyard, and you will receive whatever is right.' ⁸ When evening had come, the lord of the vineyard said to his manager, 'Call the laborers and pay them their wages, beginning from the last to the first.'

⁹ "When those who were hired at about the eleventh hour came, they each received a denarius. ¹⁰ When the first came, they supposed that they would receive more; and they likewise each received a denarius. ¹¹ When they received it, they murmured against the master of the household, ¹² saying, 'These last have spent one hour, and you have made them equal to us, who have borne the burden of the day and the scorching heat!'

¹³ "But he answered one of them, 'Friend, I am doing you no wrong. Didn't you agree with me for a denarius? ¹⁴ Take that which is yours, and go your way. It is my desire to give to this last just as much as to you. ¹⁵ Isn't it lawful for me to do what I want to with what I own? Or is your eye evil, because I am good?' ¹⁶ So the last will be first, and the first last. For many are called, but few are chosen."

This is another place where Stephen Langston's chapters and verses in the Bible could be better placed; the first sixteen verses of chapter twenty fit better with the end of chapter nineteen than with the rest of chapter twenty.

"Jesus further clarified the membership rules of the kingdom of Heaven: Entrance is by God's grace alone (LASB, p. 1584)." This parable is significant because it stresses the evenness of God's love for all people and Matthew is the only writer to pick it up. This leads some to suggest that he is again addressing some inequities surfacing in the church, perhaps differences between "classes" of people within the church.

The grape harvest comes at the end of September, just before the fall rains begin. If the grapes aren't gathered before the rain comes, the harvest will be severely reduced, so the owner of the vineyard rushes to get every available worker. The use of vine and vineyard as symbols of Israel was common in the Old Testament.

Notice what happened. The owner "went out early in the morning to hire laborers," which was a common sight. The work day began at dawn and the laborers would gather, much like they gather at the "big box" stores, where the employers knew they would be. For a laborer, failure to get work for even one day could mean a day with little or no food for the entire family.

There was a contract of sorts between those first hired and the owner, "he had agreed with the laborers for a denarius a day" However, he needed more men and about 9 AM he went back, found more unemployed men and told them, "…You also go into the vineyard, and whatever is right I will give you." There still weren't enough men, so at noon, 3 PM and 5 PM he did the same thing. It was common practice and a requirement of the Law that when the day was over, the owner came and paid the workers. Since he paid all of them the same amount, the cry went up: "Owner unfair to laborers! A day's work for a day's pay!" The truth is, only the first workers hired were told their wage, the rest were told "whatever is right I will give you."

As has been well said, 'this parable is in fact the gospel of the penitent thief'. The same paradise awaits both the man who has experienced divine grace in the last hour of his life as him who was first called to be Christ's disciple (TNTC, pp. 190-1).

Our translation has it right! The word often translated "envious" actually means to have an "evil eye," to look at things from a position of mistrust. Bargaining is never a bargain. Has there ever been an agreement where both sides were truly happy? No, because each has had to compromise on something. The important thing about work and pay is the spirit in which each is given. Those who went later went because they were glad they had found work. According to Barclay "A man is not a Christian if his first concern is pay (DSB, p. 226)." Ouch!

The Lord calls people to work in His vineyard, not just for what they can earn, but for the joy of working! "Our relationship with him is to be one of trust and love, with generous giving and receiving (BBC, p. 194)." The "first" went out to work because of what they were going to receive. Was the owner unfair to pay the men who worked only one hour the same thing he paid those who worked twelve hours? That isn't the question.

This parable isn't about collective bargaining and the proper payment of wages! It begins; "For the Kingdom of Heaven is like a man..." what we're talking about is the "Kingdom of Heaven"! The point is that those of us who came along last will be treated the same as those who were there at the beginning. The idea that those who are only humble servants of the Lord, or made "death-bed" confessions, will receive the same reward as those whose name are "up in lights" is difficult to understand. Does that seem fair? No! It is for God to decide, not us, because God is free to reward His servants the way He chooses. You see, "in the kingdom of God all reward is the result of God's grace and not of human merit (TNTC, p. 190)."

Barclay says this parable was "a warning to the disciples." He says: "There are people who think that, because they have been members of a Church for a long time, the Church practically belongs to them and they can dictate its policy. Such people resent what seems to them the intrusion of new blood or the rise of a new generation with different plans and different ways. In the Christian Church seniority does not necessarily mean honour [sic] (DSB, p. 224)."

Still wondering "How to Be Last"? Keep looking out for "number one," that's how! Be more concerned about getting what you "have coming to you" than what you can give others. Maintain an attitude of superiority. You might be able to get to the head of the line here, but you could miss the important line altogether, thereby ensuring that you are indeed last. "The direct object of this parable seems to be, to show that though the Jews were first called into the vineyard, at length the gospel should be preached to the Gentiles, and they should be admitted to equal privileges and advantages with the Jews (MH)."

The Move toward the Cross
Matthew 20:17-19

As Jesus was going up to Jerusalem, he took the twelve disciples aside, and on the way he said to them, [18] "Behold, we are going up to Jerusalem, and the Son of Man will be delivered to the chief priests and scribes, and they will condemn him to death, [19] and will hand him over to the Gentiles to mock, to scourge, and to crucify; and the third day he will be raised up."

With this passage, Jesus deliberately begins to move toward the most difficult part of His mission, His death on the cross. This is the third time He has predicted His death and resurrection. There is a touch of Abraham's attitude and commitment in Jesus' determination.

By faith, Abraham, being tested, offered up Isaac. Yes, he who had gladly received the promises was offering up his one and only son; to whom it was said, "your offspring will be accounted as from Isaac;" concluding that God is able to raise up even from the dead. Figuratively speaking, he also did receive him back from the dead (Heb. 11:17-19).

In spite of the pressure, Jesus' concern was still for the plight of others and not His own distress. We will see many more opportunities when Jesus made the cares of desperate people, and the importance of ministry the priority.

Perhaps the saddest thing anyone, a leader or just an ordinary person, can experience is betrayal. Why? Because betrayal can only come at the hand of a friend! Your enemies are always out to get you and you know it, but when a trusted friend deserts and turns against you, it is the ultimate in betrayal. As a result of this betrayal, Jesus knew He would be turned over "to the chief priests and the scribes." We often say that power corrupts and absolute power corrupts absolutely and these men had absolute power over the religious lives of the Jewish people. In their minds they also had the power to change wrong to right and right to wrong.

About this time, there was a meeting of the Sanhedrin. Caiaphas, the high priest was arguing for the death of Jesus and said, "You know nothing at all, nor do you consider that it is advantageous for us that one man should die for the people, and that the whole nation not perish" (John 11:49b-50). The results of their conference was "…from that day forward they took counsel that they might put him to death" (John 11:53).

Jesus knew they would "condemn Him to death," that He would be turned "over to the Gentiles" who would mock Him, flog Him, and finally crucify Him. How could He endure all this? He knew what was coming; He knew that after three days, He would "be raised up"!

Only Luke adds: "They understood none of these things. This saying was hidden from them, and they didn't understand the things that were said" (Luke 18:34). It's sad that after three years of discipleship they still didn't understand. Yet, many of us have been followers of Jesus for many more years than that and we still don't understand what Jesus is calling us to do.

The Problem of Greatness
Matthew 20:20-28

Then the mother of the sons of Zebedee came to him with her sons, kneeling and asking a certain thing of him. 21 He said to her, "What do you want?"

She said to him, "Command that these, my two sons, may sit, one on your right hand, and one on your left hand, in your Kingdom."

22 But Jesus answered, "You don't know what you are asking. Are you able to drink the cup that I am about to drink, and be baptized with the baptism that I am baptized with?"

They said to him, "We are able."

23 He said to them, "You will indeed drink my cup, and be baptized with the baptism that I am baptized with, but to sit on my right hand and on my left hand is not mine to give; but it is for whom it has been prepared by my Father."

24 When the ten heard it, they were indignant with the two brothers.

25 But Jesus summoned them, and said, "You know that the rulers of the nations lord it over them, and their great ones exercise authority over them. 26 It shall not be so among you, but whoever desires to become great among you shall be (TR reads "let him be" instead of "shall be") your servant. 27 Whoever desires to be first among you shall be your bondservant, 28 even as the Son of Man came not to be served, but to serve, and to give his life as a ransom for many."

There is some indication that James and John may have put their mother up to asking Jesus for the special place of honor, and Jesus responded to them. "You don't know what you are asking. Are you able to drink the cup that I am about to drink…?" Mark says, "James and John...came near to him, saying…" (Mark 10:35). Barclay suggests Matthew was protecting the disciples' reputation. Whoever came, the motive is the same, self-interest.

Barclay feels there may have been a natural reason for the request. He believes that Jesus, James and John were first cousins, that their mothers were sisters identifying her as the Salome mentioned in Mark 15:40 and as the sister of Mary in John 19:25 (DSB, p. 229).

They still saw Jesus as a political leader. Barclay points out the fact that, in spite of the statement from Jesus about His pending death, they still believed He would set up a kingdom and they were loyal and wanted to be in on the "ground floor." In the pagan courts, the place on the right was most prestigious and the one on the left was second. They didn't seem to care who got which, as long as they were both honored in this essentially pagan way.

The "cup," Mark says "baptism," by which Jesus referred is His coming death. The words as used here have no connection with the ordinance we celebrate. Interestingly, those honored in Jesus' greatest hour were two robbers, one on the right and one on the left.

What was the "cup"? James became the first martyr, so it's easy to see his sacrifice, but John seems to have lived a long and productive life, dying in his bed at about one hundred years old. That's it, that's the "cup" and it is different for each of us. One gives his life in martyrdom another gives his life in service.

Thank God the others weren't like James and John! Not so! When they found out what had happened, they became "indignant with the two brothers." The word "indignant" carries a root meaning of "anger." Possibly they were mad they hadn't thought to ask first.

One thing shines clearly through all of this, Jesus didn't get mad and He didn't even seem to get upset. Jesus did what He always did; He loved them and used the moment to teach them what they needed to know. I remember many teachers who struggled to teach me and, like Jesus, when the "aha" moment of understanding came, they were not around to enjoy it.

The disciples hadn't yet learned that honor comes for sacrificial service. To sacrifice means to give up something which you need, not just want, to give yourself, like the "widow's mite." Verse 26 and 27 say, "…whoever wants to become great among you must be your servant, and whoever wants to be first must be your slave." As Tasker correctly states, "those in authority should exercise it, but not in a domineering or oppressive manner (TNTC, p. 195)."

Jesus said He "came not to be served, but to serve, and to give His life as a ransom for many." That means more than giving His life on the cross; He also gave His life in service. Jesus set the standard not by sermon but by example. "The greatest lessons in life are not learned all at once; and the good teacher has patiently to persevere in driving his lesson home (TNTC, p. 194)."

"Ransom" wasn't used by the Jews in a religious sense, it simply meant to rescue. It was and is paid to release someone from something they cannot free themselves from. "Many" is uniquely Jewish and means "all." Jesus died for all men, women, boys and girls.

Carpe Diem!
Matthew 20:29-34

As they went out from Jericho, a great multitude followed him. [30] *Behold, two blind men sitting by the road, when they heard that Jesus was passing by, cried out, "Lord, have mercy on us, you son of David!"* [31] *The multitude rebuked them, telling them that they should be quiet, but they cried out even more, "Lord, have mercy on us, you son of David!"*

[32] *Jesus stood still, and called them, and asked, "What do you want me to do for you?"*

[33] *They told him, "Lord, that our eyes may be opened."*

[34] *Jesus, being moved with compassion, touched their eyes; and immediately their eyes received their sight, and they followed him.*

This event is very much like the one in Matthew 9:27-31:

As Jesus passed by from there, two blind men followed him, calling out and saying, "Have mercy on us, son of David!"

When he had come into the house, the blind men came to him. Jesus said to them, "Do you believe that I am able to do this?"

They told him, "Yes, Lord."

Then he touched their eyes, saying, "According to your faith be it done to you." Their eyes were opened. Jesus strictly commanded them, saying, "See that no one knows about this." But they went out and spread abroad his fame in all that land.

In each of these events there are "two blind men" who cry out for "mercy" and Jesus heals them. In chapter 9, Jesus told them to keep it quiet, but this time there is no admonition to silence; that could be because Jesus was about to enter His final week, so there isn't much point in silence.

Jesus' motivation for healing is "compassion" which doesn't mean pity or sympathy; it is much more; it is something that comes from our inmost being; from the heart. The use of "Lord," doesn't necessarily mean they had accepted Him as Savior because the range of usage in Greek ran from "sir" all the way to "God." However, "Son of David" did carry special overtones because it had Messianic implications, especially at that time in the history of the Jews.

Jesus and the disciples were traveling to Jerusalem for the final confrontation with the Pharisees, as they left Jericho it would be natural that a large crowd would follow them and it was also common for beggars to station themselves along well traveled roads. When the two blind men heard Jesus was coming, they "cried out." This was their opportunity and they seized it! It didn't matter to them that the crowd tried to silence them, they shouted louder; they wouldn't be stopped. They knew their need wouldn't be met unless they seized that moment. They didn't know much about theology or Jesus, but they acted on what they knew and Jesus responded to their need. After they were healed, they followed Him.

The Entrance of the King
Matthew 21:1-11

When they came near to Jerusalem, and came to Bethsphage, (TR & NU read "Bethphage" instead of "Bethsphage") to the Mount of Olives, then Jesus sent two disciples, ² saying to them, "Go into the village that is opposite you, and immediately you will find a donkey tied, and a colt with her. Untie them, and bring them to me. ³ If anyone says anything to you, you shall say, 'The Lord needs them,' and immediately he will send them."

⁴ All this was done, that it might be fulfilled which was spoken through the prophet, saying, ⁵ "Tell the daughter of Zion, behold, your King comes to you, humble, and riding on a donkey, on a colt, the foal of a donkey" (Zech. 9:9).

⁶ The disciples went, and did just as Jesus commanded them, ⁷ and brought the donkey and the colt, and laid their clothes on them; and he sat on them. ⁸ A very great multitude spread their clothes on the road. Others cut branches from the trees, and spread them on the road. ⁹ The multitudes who went in front of him, and those who followed, kept shouting, "Hosanna ("Hosanna" means "save us" or "help us, we pray") to the son of David! Blessed is he who comes in the name of the Lord! Hosanna in the highest!" (Ps. 118:26)

¹⁰ When he had come into Jerusalem, all the city was stirred up, saying, "Who is this?" ¹¹ The multitudes said, "This is the prophet, Jesus, from Nazareth of Galilee."

This is one of the events in Jesus' life that is covered in some form, by all for gospel writers: Mark 11:1-11, Luke 19:28-40, and John 12:12-19.

We begin Jesus' last week on earth with this dramatic event. It was Passover and the city was crowded with about 2.5 million Jews from all over the "world" and who knows how many Gentiles who came to see the spectacle. There can be no mistaking it, this was a Messianic act. The way Jesus entered the city was more like a royal entrance than a triumphal entry. He didn't come riding in on the traditional white horse of a conqueror, but the symbol of a Jewish king, a donkey.

The donkey was one of the first animals tamed by man and is mentioned often in the Bible. A wild donkey was used to describe a headstrong person, but a domesticated donkey was man's obedient servant. These donkeys were about four feet high and usually gray, reddish-brown, or white. Often, they were treated like household pets by the children and decorated with beads and bright ribbons, but the primary purpose was as a work animal to trample seed, turn the millstone and pull the plow.

Donkey caravans transported the freight in ancient times because they could carry great weight for their small size and they required a fraction of the food a horse did. They were safer and more comfortable to ride, so they were ridden by both rich and poor. By riding a donkey when he entered Jerusalem, Jesus signaled His peaceful intentions.

This act was planned by Jesus and predicted in Zechariah 9:9, part of which Matthew quotes, but it refers to the balance of the chapter also. Some suggest Jesus had supernatural knowledge about the donkey; however, the narration seems to indicate that prior arrangements may have been made, the owner was possibly even a follower of Jesus. The fact that this donkey had never been ridden made it especially suited for religious purposes. In acting out His claim, Jesus followed the lead of many prophets in the Old Testament. Jesus was offering Himself to them to be their king and He would begin like Judas Maccabaeus by cleansing the Temple.

In verse 4 we again see Matthew adopting prophesy "…this was done, that it might be fulfilled which was spoken through the prophet…" Be careful that you don't visualize Jesus with a copy of the Septuagint in his hand saying, "Okay, what's next?" Everything that happened in the life of Jesus was common activity. It is also important to remember that there are many more prophesies that refer to acts the Messiah would perform.

The word "Hosanna" is a cry, for help and means "Save [us] now!" "What we have here, therefore, is an ancient liturgical text, a cry to the anointed king for deliverance (AB, p. 252)." As used here, it is not a shout of praise! "Son of David!" and "he who comes" are clearly Messianic and the use of the definite article in "This is the prophet, Jesus, from Nazareth of Galilee" probably carries the same weight; Jesus isn't just "a" prophet, He is "The" Prophet.

Everyone seemed to get caught up in the moment as indicated by the action of the crowd, "…[they] spread their clothes on the road. Others cut branches from the trees, and spread them on the road." It was a common practice in ancient times to greet a very important person this way, much like rolling out the red carpet. Instead of slipping into the city at night for fear of the leaders, he openly arrived and offered himself to the people once again.

Waving palm branches is significant because they were a symbol of Jewish nationalism, much like a flag is to us today. John 12:12-13 says, "On the next day a great multitude had come to the feast. When they heard that Jesus was coming to Jerusalem, they took the branches of the palm trees and went out to meet him, and cried out, 'Hosanna! Blessed is he who comes in the name of the Lord, the King of Israel!'" Has He been willing to meet their expectations of a military conqueror, I have no doubt that all of Israel would have united behind Him to drive out the Romans. Unfortunately for them, that wasn't His calling.

Cleansing the Temple
Matthew 21:12-17

Jesus entered into the temple of God, and drove out all of those who sold and bought in the temple, and overthrew the money changers' tables and the seats of those who sold the doves. [13] He said to them, "It is

written, 'My house shall be called a house of prayer' (Isa. 56:7), but you have made it a den of robbers!"
(Jer. 7:11)

[14] The blind and the lame came to him in the temple, and he healed them. [15] But when the chief priests and the scribes saw the wonderful things that he did, and the children who were crying in the temple and saying, "Hosanna to the son of David!" they were indignant, [16] and said to him, "Do you hear what these are saying?"

Jesus said to them, "Yes. Did you never read, 'Out of the mouth of babes and nursing babies you have perfected praise?'" (Ps. 8:2).

[17] He left them, and went out of the city to Bethany, and camped there.

Jesus was "brave" to enter Jerusalem the way He did, but it was insignificant compared to the act of driving the profiteers from the Temple area, again! The cleansing of the Temple was a prophetic act, not a protest against the practices of the Temple, but the abuses. There are two Greek words translated "temple" and "Temple," notice the capitalization. The former is *hieron*, and applied to the entire thirteen-acre area. The latter is *naos*, the actual building, and could be translated "sanctuary," it contained the Holy Place with the Holy of Holies.

The entire unit included the "Court of the Gentiles," open to everyone; the "Court of Women," entered through the Beautiful Gate, open to all Jews; the "Court of the Israelites," for Jewish men, entered through Nicanor's Gate with a bronze door so large it required twenty men to open or shut, Temple services were conducted there; finally the "Court of the Priests" containing the altar, the seven branched candle stand, the table of showbread and the laver, and the Holy Place with the Holy of Holies.

The scene for Jesus' activities is the "Court of the Gentiles," which was crowded with Jews, arriving for the Passover and Gentiles who had come to see the events. Two great offenses were going on: money changing and animal sales. The problem wasn't that commercial activities were going on so much as the fact that the merchants had turned it into a "den of robbers." They were ripping people off!

If Temple taxes hadn't been paid before the deadline, they had to be paid in Jerusalem at the Temple and in acceptable, Jewish currency. What could be more natural than to make that money available right there at the Temple? The courtesy is worth something. Rationalization is a great thing; I have used it many times to justify doing what I wanted to do.

A trip to the Temple usually required an offering, but there were certain requirements the animals had to meet. They were inspected when brought into the Temple and those that didn't measure up were rejected. Barclay indicates that animals sold inside could cost almost twenty times their price outside. The animals were sold in what he says was the "Bazaars of Annas." Annas just happened to be the name of the High Priest, I suspect, but don't know, if they are the same person.

This exploitation of the simple people by the religious leadership was the first objection Jesus raised. The second objection was that the Temple was to "be called a house of prayer." The only area open to Gentiles was the very place that was jammed with the stalls of bleating animals and money changers clamoring for "customers" and the air of the market place. Does this mean we can't sell things in church, like when we have a guest with books or music to sell? What about gift shops and refreshment stands. Since all areas of our churches are pretty much open to everyone, we aren't taking up the space restricted to nonmembers, so I doubt that the same rules would apply.

Not everyone left when Jesus began to run the merchants out, apparently only those guilty of abuses ran. "The blind and the lame came to him in the temple…" What did Jesus do? He healed them.

The "chief priests and the scribes" also remained and "saw the wonderful things he did." That annoyed them, but when the "children" began "shouting... 'Hosanna to the Son of David,' they became "indignant."

The Death of a Tree
Matthew 21:18-22

Now in the morning, as he returned to the city, he was hungry. ¹⁹ Seeing a fig tree by the road, he came to it, and found nothing on it but leaves. He said to it, "Let there be no fruit from you forever!"

Immediately the fig tree withered away. ²⁰ When the disciples saw it, they marveled, saying, "How did the fig tree immediately wither away?"

²¹ Jesus answered them, "Most certainly I tell you, if you have faith, and don't doubt, you will not only do what was done to the fig tree, but even if you told this mountain, 'Be taken up and cast into the sea,' it would be done. ²² All things, whatever you ask in prayer, believing, you will receive."

There is one significant difference between the Matthew and Mark accounts, the timing of the death of the tree. In Matthew the tree died immediately, in Mark it was dead the next day. This may indicate some development in the story in the time between when Mark and Matthew wrote their Gospels; the "rules" of criticism favor Mark's report.

Figs were important: they were eaten fresh, pressed into cakes, used medicinally and the nation of Israel was compared to a fig tree. The parable in Luke 13:6-9 (see below) undoubtedly applies to the fruitlessness of Israel. Fig trees are unique because they bear two crops each year, one on the old growth and one on new growth. Jesus was hungry. When He saw a fig tree with leaves, He believed there would be figs to eat for breakfast. (Fig buds come on before the leaves, so leaves generally means figs.) But the first crop is generally ripe in June, so it would be unreasonable to expect them in the spring, at Passover.

This situation makes us uncomfortable. What kind of man would condemn a fig tree because it didn't supply His personal needs? It appears the very thing He refused to do in the wilderness, Maybe He meant for us to take this figuratively. Barclay feels the problem may well be that we have confused a parable with an actual incident (DSB, p. 253). Maybe, as the NLTSB suggests, "The cursing of the fig tree is a symbolic gesture depicting God's judgement in Israel for rejecting the Messiah. (p. 1621)."

Luke didn't record this incident in Jesus' life, but he does have a comparable parable in Luke 13:6-9:

He spoke this parable. "A certain man had a fig tree planted in his vineyard, and he came seeking fruit on it, and found none. He said to the vine dresser, 'Behold, these three years I have come looking for fruit on this fig tree, and found none. Cut it down. Why does it waste the soil?' He answered, 'Lord, leave it alone this year also, until I dig around it, and fertilize it. If it bears fruit, fine; but if not, after that, you can cut it down.'"

We have discussed the fact that prophets often used dramatic presentations to drive their point home. That may well be what is happening here. If Jesus approached "Luke's tree," knowing that something was wrong with it because He had had similar experiences with it for the last two years, maybe it had returned to the "wild." I could also wonder if those three years in the parable equate to the approximate three-year ministry of Jesus?

Whatever the problem, it would make a great object lesson. What lesson? Produce or parish! The fig tree provided shade from the heat of the day, but its primary purpose was to provide nourishment. The Jews were to provide God's nourishing "food" to the world, they didn't. Now the church has taken up the task. Any church that doesn't, any Christian that doesn't, is subject to removal. What about your church? What about you?

The death of the tree amazed the disciples and gave Jesus another opportunity to teach. Jesus said with faith "if you told this mountain, 'Be taken up and cast into the sea,' it would be done." Can we simply speak a word and the thing is done? That isn't what Jesus is saying. "Jesus was exhorting the disciples to trust in God and to pray accordingly. He was not offering God's unconditional endorsement of all things they might desire. (NLTSB, p. 1621)"

Faith isn't an easy way to get what we want. Prayer is often answered when it is acted on. When we pray, believe and "put feet to our prayers," we will receive whatever we ask for. When God does His part and we do our part, we will have great results.

What Is Your Authority?
Matthew 21:23-27

When he had come into the temple, the chief priests and the elders of the people came to him as he was teaching, and said, "By what authority do you do these things? Who gave you this authority?"

24 Jesus answered them, "I also will ask you one question, which if you tell me, I likewise will tell you by what authority I do these things. 25 The baptism of John, where was it from? From heaven or from men?"

They reasoned with themselves, saying, "If we say, 'From heaven,' he will ask us, 'Why then did you not believe him?' 26 But if we say, 'From men,' we fear the multitude, for all hold John as a prophet." 27 They answered Jesus, and said, "We don't know."

He also said to them, "Neither will I tell you by what authority I do these things."

There is no question that the "chief priests and the elders of the people" would come and question Jesus' authority. They were the leaders of the people in all matters touching religion and, for the Jews, everything touched on religion, so that was part of their responsibility to the people.

The questions, "By what authority do you do these things?" and "Who gave you this authority?" are separate and distinct questions. Mark records, "John said to him, 'Teacher, we saw someone who doesn't follow us casting out demons in your name; and we forbade him, because he doesn't follow us' (Mark 9:38)." Their power for healing was the "name," but the disciples didn't believe these men had Jesus' "authority," that is, His permission, to use it.

Similarly, it would have been alright with the elders for Jesus to do His work in the "name" of God, but to claim His "authority" to do so would be another matter. They believed that such "authority" could only come from them.

The fact that Jesus didn't challenge their authority to question Him speaks to their right and responsibility, but He did dispute their sincerity, which was underscored by their refusal to rule on John's position. The evidence about John and Jesus was there, but the leaders refused to accept it.

Notice that Jesus refused to argue with them. Their minds were made up, they weren't about to be confused by the facts they could see or by any argument Jesus would give them. "It was not that they could not but that they would not fairly judge John or Jesus (BBC, p. 201)." Following Jesus' example, sometimes it's better not to get into disputes with people and not to argue with them.

The time for direct confrontation hadn't yet come so Jesus refused to give them a direct answer; He still had much to do. Barclay reminds us that it is often harder to bide our time, doing everything at the right time, than to just blurt out the truth and "let the chips fall where they may."

The chief priests tried to put Jesus on the defensive but, as He often did, He took charge. When you can take control, you can direct the conversation the way you want it to go. The question Jesus asked of them had much more serious consequences: "The baptism of John, where did it come from? From heaven or from men?" It was their responsibility to examine prophets and determine their validity. They couldn't answer without compromising and condemning themselves and in not answering they made themselves insignificant. They put themselves squarely between the proverbial rock and a hard place with their response, "We don't know." It was an admission that they would do their duty only when it suited them.

Be careful when you say "The Lord told me..." it can be one of Satan's greatest traps. Consider the effect such "revelations" from God have had on some televangelists and denominations.

Respect for Authority
Matthew 21:28-32

But what do you think? A man had two sons, and he came to the first, and said, 'Son, go work today in my vineyard.' ²⁹ He answered, 'I will not,' but afterward he changed his mind, and went. ³⁰ He came to the second, and said the same thing. He answered, 'I go, sir,' but he didn't go. ³¹ Which of the two did the will of his father?"

They said to him, "The first."

Jesus said to them, "Most certainly I tell you that the tax collectors and the prostitutes are entering into God's Kingdom before you. ³² For John came to you in the way of righteousness, and you didn't believe him, but the tax collectors and the prostitutes believed him. When you saw it, you didn't even repent afterward, that you might believe him.

The Jews intellectually recognized that the Kingdom of God was more than a physical realm, but they didn't want to accept the spiritual aspect of it. They ignored John's preaching and discounted the miracles of Jesus. Stagg says, "…authority is respected by obedience, not by lip service. The chief priests and elders… [only] implied that they had respect for authority (BBC, p. 202)."

There are three versions of this parable in existence. In the first, the first son says "no" but changes his mind and goes, the second agrees but does nothing and the first son is approved by Jesus. The second version reverses the order and the third version follows the order of the first, but approval is given to the son who didn't go work in the vineyard.

The parable shows two groups of people; those who claim to be something but don't follow up in the way they live, they only give lip service. There is also a group that doesn't claim to follow a particular belief, but live its precepts more closely than those who claim it. The parable doesn't show either group to be the acceptable one.

There can be no mistake, the son who said he would obey and did not were the Jewish leaders. The "tax collectors and the prostitutes" were those who initially said "no," but changed their minds and did as the father wanted.

Barclay says:

The key to the correct understanding of this parable is that it is not really praising anyone. [...but] is setting before us a picture of two very imperfect sets of people, of whom one set were none the less better than the other. Neither...was the kind of son to bring full joy to his father (DSB p. 259).

The ideal person is the one whose profession and actions in life are the same.

Perverted Authority
Matthew 21:33-46

"Hear another parable. There was a man who was a master of a household, who planted a vineyard, set a hedge about it, dug a wine press in it, built a tower, leased it out to farmers, and went into another country. [34] When the season for the fruit came near, he sent his servants to the farmers, to receive his fruit. [35] The farmers took his servants, beat one, killed another, and stoned another. [36] Again, he sent other servants more than the first: and they treated them the same way. [37] But afterward he sent to them his son, saying, 'They will respect my son.' [38] But the farmers, when they saw the son, said among themselves, 'This is the heir. Come, let's kill him, and seize his inheritance.' [39] So they took him, and threw him out of the vineyard, and killed him. [40] When therefore the lord of the vineyard comes, what will he do to those farmers?"

[41] They told him, "He will miserably destroy those miserable men, and will lease out the vineyard to other farmers, who will give him the fruit in its season."

[42] Jesus said to them, "Did you never read in the Scriptures, 'The stone which the builders rejected, the same was made the head of the corner. This was from the Lord. It is marvelous in our eyes?' (Ps. 118:22-23).

[43] "Therefore I tell you, God's Kingdom will be taken away from you, and will be given to a nation producing its fruit. [44] He who falls on this stone will be broken to pieces, but on whomever it will fall, it will scatter him as dust."

[45] When the chief priests and the Pharisees heard his parables, they perceived that he spoke about them. [46] When they sought to seize him, they feared the multitudes, because they considered him to be a prophet.

Technically this is not a parable, it is an allegory. What's the difference? A parable generally has only one main point and the devices (details and images) used are not intended to carry specific meaning. An allegory may have only one main point, but there is significance found, or buried, in the details used to create the story.

As we continue to examine the general subject of authority, we come to this allegory patterned after Isaiah 5:1-7

Let me sing for my well beloved a song of my beloved about his vineyard. My beloved had a vineyard on a very fruitful hill. He dug it up, gathered out its stones, planted it with the choicest vine, built a tower in the middle of it, and also cut out a wine press therein. He looked for it to yield grapes, but it yielded wild grapes.

Now, inhabitants of Jerusalem and men of Judah, please judge between me and my vineyard. What could have been done more to my vineyard, that I have not done in it? Why, when I looked for it to yield grapes, did it yield wild grapes? Now I will tell you what I will do to my vineyard. I will take away its hedge, and it will be eaten up. I will break down its wall, and it will be trampled down. I will lay it a wasteland. It won't be pruned nor hoed, but it will grow briers and thorns. I will also command the clouds that they rain no rain on it.

For the vineyard of Yahweh of Armies is the house of Israel, and the men of Judah his pleasant plant: and he looked for justice, but, behold, oppression; for righteousness, but, behold, a cry of distress.

The nation of Israel was often called God's vineyard in the Old Testament and that's the symbolism Jesus used here. This vineyard has been properly prepared with a "wall, winepress" and "watchtower" and is ready to rent out; there were many absentee landlords in Israel, so everyone understood what was happening.

The "farmers" who rented the "vineyard" began plotting almost from the beginning. By rejecting the owner's "servants" and in killing the "son," the "farmers" were actually rejecting the owner's authority over his vineyard and their contract or covenant for occupancy.

Undoubtedly the "servants" represented the prophets, including John the Baptizer, whom God had sent to bring the Jews back to His way; however, they were abused and killed. Stagg says, "God sent his Son into a world which already had killed his prophets. This was love's calculated risk (BBC, p. 203)."

By killing the son, they thought the "owner" would have to agree to their terms, after all the owner had no one left. By rejecting Jesus, the "capstone," the Jews will be rejected. Peter says:

But you are a chosen race, a royal priesthood, a holy nation, a people for God's own possession, that you may proclaim the excellence of him who called you out of darkness into his marvelous light: who in time past were no people, but now are God's people, who had not obtained mercy, but now have obtained mercy (1 Pet. 2:9-10).

Barclay believes this allegory teaches us three things about God: He trusts men, He built the vineyard and entrusted it to men to take care of; He is patient with men, He sent messenger after messenger to them; and in the end, He will judge men.

He says it teaches four things about men: mankind is privileged; God provided everything needed in the vineyard; mankind is free to do whatever he/she wants to do; mankind must answer to God; and mankind's sin is deliberate.

He says it also teaches two things about Jesus: Jesus clearly claims to be the Messiah, chosen by God to redeem His people; and Jesus knew what was ahead for Him and was still willing to accept it (DSB, pp. 263-264).

That "God's Kingdom will be taken away from you…" means, "Either the privilege if being God's chosen nation no longer belonged to the Jews; or the religious leaders had lost the privilege of being leaders of God's people (NLTSB, p. 1622)"

God has given us the "tools" we need to know and share His love with others, but it's up to us to use them. We must be careful when we make up our mind what to do with that love.

The Danger of Presumption
Matthew 22:1-14

Jesus answered and spoke again in parables to them, saying, [2] "The Kingdom of Heaven is like a certain king, who made a marriage feast for his son, [3] and sent out his servants to call those who were invited to the marriage feast, but they would not come. [4] Again he sent out other servants, saying, 'Tell those who are invited, "Behold, I have prepared my dinner. My cattle and my fatlings are killed, and all things are ready. Come to the marriage feast!"' [5] But they made light of it, and went their ways, one to his own farm, another to his merchandise, [6] and the rest grabbed his servants, and treated them shamefully, and killed them. [7] When the king heard that, he was angry, and sent his armies, destroyed those murderers, and burned their city.

[8] "Then he said to his servants, 'The wedding is ready, but those who were invited weren't worthy. [9] Go therefore to the intersections of the highways, and as many as you may find, invite to the marriage feast.' [10] Those servants went out into the highways, and gathered together as many as they found, both bad and good. The wedding was filled with guests. [11] But when the king came in to see the guests, he saw there a man who didn't have on wedding clothing, [12] and he said to him, 'Friend, how did you come in here not wearing wedding clothing?' He was speechless. [13] Then the king said to the servants, 'Bind him hand and foot, take him away, and throw him into the outer darkness; there is where the weeping and grinding of teeth will be.' [14] For many are called, but few chosen."

There is a similar story in Luke 14:16-24:

But he said to him [a man sitting at the table with him], "A certain man made a great supper, and he invited many people. He sent out his servant at supper time to tell those who were invited, 'Come, for everything is ready now.' They all as one began to make excuses.

The first said to him, 'I have bought a field, and I must go and see it. Please have me excused.'

Another said, 'I have bought five yoke of oxen, and I must go try them out. Please have me excused.'

Another said, 'I have married a wife, and therefore I can't come.'

That servant came, and told his lord these things. Then the master of the house, being angry, said to his servant, 'Go out quickly into the streets and lanes of the city, and bring in the poor, maimed, blind, and lame.'

The servant said, 'Lord, it is done as you commanded, and there is still room.'

The lord said to the servant, 'Go out into the highways and hedges, and compel them to come in, that my house may be filled. For I tell you that none of those men who were invited will taste of my supper.'

There are, as you can see, many differences between them. It is "…more probable that Jesus used the same theme…to teach different aspects of truth on what were entirely different occasions (TCNT, p. 206)."

In this parable, Jesus more openly claims that He is the Messiah the Jews had been longing for. If the President of the United States invited you to dinner, would you consider it a social invitation that you could accept or reject? Would you be more concerned that you might not agree with his policies and politics than with the opportunity to attend such a great event? Although some have rejected invitations, most accept them without even thinking about it. Similarly, the invitation from an oriental king wasn't one that could be rejected with impunity. The "king" here of course refers to God the Father.

When the feast was ready, servants were sent to tell the guests to come. Those who were wise were ready.

In this culture, two invitations were expected when banquets were given. The first asked the guests to attend, the second announced that all was ready. In this story the king invited his guests three times, and each time they rejected his invitation (LASB, p. 1588).

Will Heaven be empty? Not if this parable is true because the wedding hall is going to be "filled." But, based on the parable, its occupants may not all be the people we expect.

It is suggested that one of the customs of the day was to provide gifts and appropriate dress for the guests. "The scene depicted is that of the Son judging his own Kingdom. The man…had attempted to enter…without prior repentance' (AB, p. 269)." The fact that the doors are open to everyone doesn't mean the entry standards are changed; entrance to the wedding hall is still on the King's terms. The "king" "noticed a man there who was not wearing wedding clothes." This was a "white tie" affair and the text implies that proper clothes were made available, but he chose not to wear them. Isaiah 61:10 says:

I will greatly rejoice in Yahweh! My soul will be joyful in my God; for he has clothed me with the garments of salvation. He has covered me with the robe of righteousness, as a bridegroom decks himself with a garland, and as a bride adorns herself with her jewels.

There are two applications for this parable; the immediate application and the future application. Following on the heels of the denunciation of the Jewish leaders, the parable drove home the point of their infidelity to their mission. Again, Jesus reminded them that their rejection of the Messiah opened the door widely for people they considered unacceptable, "the people of the land," "both good and bad."

Tasker raises the question in verse 7, "his armies;' evokes the query 'Would Jesus have implied that the Roman legions which destroyed Jerusalem were God's armies?' (TNTC, p. 208)" I ask "Why not?" The same suggestion is made in the Old Testament about armies that invaded and punished Israel. The parable may also allude to the coming destruction of Jerusalem in 70 AD because, sadly, it wasn't long after these words were spoken that their rejection of the invitation led to their destruction at the hand of God's army, in this case the Roman legions.

From a larger perspective, there is also an application for us today. The invitation to the Kingdom is compared to the invitation to a wedding party, not a funeral. If you miss the Kingdom, you miss great joy.

There is also a warning. Those who refused to attend had good things to do; one went "to his field, another to his business." But they were not excused. We must be careful that the good doesn't crowd out the best.

Barclay suggests that verse 7, "The king was enraged. He sent his army and destroyed those murderers and burned their city" wasn't part of the original parable, but was inserted by Matthew in retrospect since he was writing after the destruction of the temple. If they had accepted Jesus and God's way of love, none of that had to happen.

Those first invited were presumptuous; they assumed the "king" would overlook their slight; they were wrong. The guest who came improperly clothed assumed that it didn't matter how he dressed; he too was wrong. We may all be trying to get to the same place, Heaven, but we must do it on God's terms, not on ours.

No person, group, or church can claim exclusivity of being "God's chosen people." The invitation is open to everyone regardless of their heritage, nationality, or any other demographic we can define.

About Citizenship
Matthew 22:15-22

Then the Pharisees went and took counsel how they might entrap him in his talk. [16] They sent their disciples to him, along with the Herodians, saying, "Teacher, we know that you are honest, and teach the way of God in truth, no matter whom you teach, for you aren't partial to anyone. [17] Tell us therefore, what do you think? Is it lawful to pay taxes to Caesar, or not?"

[18] But Jesus perceived their wickedness, and said, "Why do you test me, you hypocrites? [19] Show me the tax money."

They brought to him a denarius.

[20] He asked them, "Whose is this image and inscription?"

[21] They said to him, "Caesar's."

Then he said to them, "Give therefore to Caesar the things that are Caesar's, and to God the things that are God's."

[22] When they heard it, they marveled, and left him, and went away.

We have just seen three direct, pointed attacks by Jesus on the Jewish leadership. Now it's their turn and, with carefully designed questions they attempt to force Jesus to discredit Himself publicly. Be careful when you try to trap someone, your brilliantly laid snare may spring and catch you.

The seriousness of this situation was underscored by the fact that the Pharisees and Herodians, normally in bitter opposition to each other, joined forces to attack Jesus. Remember, "the enemy of my enemy is my friend..." The Pharisees opposed the payment of taxes to the Roman government, but the Herodians, who wished to support the heirs of Herod the Great disagreed. It's sad when anyone becomes a one issue person, but they had. What was their issue? "Get Jesus!"

As an occupied country, the Israelites were required to pay taxes to a pagan government they hated. Here the tax addressed was the poll tax, similar to the Temple tax which amounted to just over a day's wages. This poll tax was particularly odious to the Jews because there were theological implications. To pay taxes to a king was to recognize his right to rule over them and they would consider it a personal affront to God. However, they recognized Caesar because they carried his coins in their purses.

The question, "Is it lawful to pay taxes to Caesar, or not?" was potentially explosive, even treasonous, and they phrased it in such a way that they expected a "Yes" or "No" answer. Randall Terry stated, "He who frames the question wins the debate." That is a good statement, but not always true; as was the case here. Jesus wasn't fooled by their flattery; He "perceived their wickedness…"

The Greek word is actually "give" not "pay," as some translations have it and the intent is to make it more demeaning. Jesus didn't use fancy footwork to avoid the problem, but handled it in a way not anticipated by anyone. Stagg says, "The alternative to 'straddling the fence' is not necessarily to fall off on one side or the other. It may be to demolish the fence (BBC, p. 206)."

The timelessness of Jesus' teaching is bound up in the fact that He laid down principles, not laws, for His followers to live by; application is left up to the individual believer. Christians are citizens of two worlds and have responsibilities to both. "Both God and Caesar have their rights; therefore paying taxes to one is not to rob the other of his due (TNTC, p. 210)."

We get angry with people because they violate the rules we have made up. We have a way to do everything, but often it isn't the same way others do it. Therefore, they must be wrong. Is it more important that the bed is covered neatly by the sheets or must it have "hospital corners" or does it need to be made at all? Remember, "I think..." can be the beginning of a prejudicial statement.

Misunderstandings about the Resurrection
Matthew 22:23-33

On that day Sadducees (those who say that there is no resurrection) came to him. They asked him, [24] saying, "Teacher, Moses said, 'If a man dies, having no children, his brother shall marry his wife, and raise up offspring (or, seed) for his brother.' [25] Now there were with us seven brothers. The first married and died, and having no offspring (or, seed) left his wife to his brother. [26] In the same way, the second also, and the third, to the seventh. [27] After them all, the woman died. [28] In the resurrection therefore, whose wife will she be of the seven? For they all had [were married to] her."

[29] But Jesus answered them, "You are mistaken, not knowing the Scriptures, nor the power of God. [30] For in the resurrection they neither marry, nor are given in marriage, but are like God's angels in heaven. [31] But concerning the resurrection of the dead, haven't you read that which was spoken to you by God, saying, [32] 'I am the God of Abraham, and the God of Isaac, and the God of Jacob?' (Ex. 3:6). God is not the God of the dead, but of the living."

[33] When the multitudes heard it, they were astonished at his teaching.

The Sadducees were few in number and came from the leading families of Israel. The high priest and most of the powerful members of the priesthood were Sadducees, as were many of the wealthy lay people. They enjoyed many privileged positions in society and got along well under Roman rule. Anything that might change the order and authority could affect their status and this could account for their desire to preserve things as they were.

They rejected the oral and written commentary on the Law of Moses called "the tradition of the elders," and this put them in direct conflict with the Pharisees who considered the traditions as important as the Law itself. The Sadducees accepted only the Pentateuch, the first five books of the Bible, as binding.

They didn't believe in a bodily resurrection of the dead, nor the immortality of the soul because they weren't mentioned in the Law of Moses; that meant they didn't believe in a system of rewards or punishments after death. They didn't believe in angels or spirits, and they believed that a man was responsible for his own prosperity or misfortune. They interpreted the law literally and tended to impose strict justice as opposed to mercy toward the offender. Most of the Jews saw their eternity as being invested in their progeny, in keeping their family name alive among the tribes of Israel.

They were neither liberal nor conservative; they simply wanted to maintain the *status quo*. The question they posed was intended to prove the ludicrousness of the doctrine of the resurrection and was one they loved to argue with the Pharisees. We should also notice that they didn't state the law of levirate marriage correctly. The brother wasn't required to have "offspring" for the deceased brother, only a child. After the first child, the rest of the children accrued to the father.

It's interesting how Jesus approached the problem by correcting their misunderstanding of the Scripture and the power of God to do whatever He wills. He showed that the life to come wasn't simply an extension of this life, but was on an entirely new plane. By quoting Exodus 3:6 in verse 32, Jesus showed that the roots of belief in life after death were in fact found in the Pentateuch.

Our understanding of the resurrection is extremely limited, partly because we don't have vocabulary to explain the unexplainable; "streets paved with gold," a "crystal sea," etc. are terms we can use to attempt to understand something of Heaven. Family relationships, will they exist in Heaven? We see the earthly family as one of the highest forms of love, and so it is, on earth. But in the eternal will my wife and I share a "mansion"? I really don't think so. Heaven will be so much more than we can imagine, that I think we limit it with these ideas.

Possibly the statement "but are like God's angels in heaven…" has been used to support the popular belief that people become angels in heaven and float around on clouds and play harps, although I'm not sure where the last part comes from, maybe from the vision in the book of Revelation.

I do believe it is important to recognize that God is not just the God of the living, but He is also God of the dead (Romans 14:8). That's why Jesus used the present tense saying, "I am the God of Abraham, and the God of Isaac, and the God of Jacob?" rather than the past tense, "I was…" As Jesus said to Martha, "I am the resurrection and the life. He who believes in me will still live, even if he dies. Whoever lives and believes in me will never die" (John 11, 25b-26a).

What Is the Greatest Commandment?
Matthew 22:34-40

But the Pharisees, when they heard that he had silenced the Sadducees, gathered themselves together. *35 One of them, a lawyer, asked him a question, testing him.* *36 "Teacher, which is the greatest commandment in the law?"*

37 Jesus said to him, " 'You shall love the Lord your God with all your heart, with all your soul, and with all your mind' (Deut. 6:5) 38 This is the first and great commandment. 39 A second likewise is this, 'You shall love your neighbor as yourself' (Lev. 19:18). 40 The whole law and the prophets depend on these two commandments."

There is a difference of opinions about the purpose of this question; Matthew and Luke say it was to "test" Jesus while Mark makes it appear to be a sincere inquiry. In fact, it would appear that Jesus and this scribe had much in common and may have parted as friends. Whatever the intent, the answer Jesus gave would be the same.

The Pharisees had managed to expand the Ten Commandments into 613 laws, 365 were "you shall not" and 248 were "you shall." They also developed a hierarchy of laws, in which some were considered to be more important and more binding than others.

In one swooping statement, Jesus destroyed the Pharisee's legalistic structure with its 613 laws and unnumbered interpretations of them. However, in removing their system, He imposed a greater system, a system of love…it is much easier to follow do's and don't's because you can look them up and you don't have to think about what you're doing or the results of it. You can say, "I was only obeying orders." That has been tried and it didn't stand up in court!

We know that for the scribes and Pharisees religion consisted of following a set of rules and liturgies. Jesus tried to return them to true religion which begins by loving God. The verse He selected was part of the Shema, "You shall love Yahweh your God with all your heart, with all your soul, and with all your might (Deut. 6:5)." The Greek word translated "soul," is *psuche* and may mean life, mind or self. The "mind" is *diomoai* and is the rational or reasoning part of a human being. So, Jesus is referring to the totality of the person's being. It isn't enough to mentally love God; we must also love Him with our time, our talent, and our treasure.

What begins in God must be reflected in our life among people so, the second greatest commandment, if you will the co-commandment, is "…you shall love your neighbor as yourself" (Lev. 19:18b). If you will allow it, these are two sides of the same coin; in order to do one, you must be doing the other. In each of the gospels, they are placed together. In his first epistle, the Apostle John says:

If a man says, "I love God," and hates his brother, he is a liar; for he who doesn't love his brother whom he has seen, how can he love God whom he has not seen? This commandment we have from him, that he who loves God should also love his brother. (1 John 4:20-21).

Earlier John recorded

In this the children of God are revealed, and the children of the devil. Whoever doesn't do righteousness is not of God, neither is he who doesn't love his brother. For this is the message which you heard from the beginning, that we should love one another…We know that we have passed out of death into life, because we love the brothers. He who doesn't love his brother remains in death. (1 John 3:10-11, 14). There is no middle ground, you either love both God and people or you don't love either. Is this a difficult saying? Yes, it is! What shall we do about it?

David's Lord or David's Son?
Matthew 22:41-46

Now while the Pharisees were gathered together, Jesus asked them a question, [42] saying, "What do you think of the Christ? Whose son is he?"

They said to him, "Of David."

[43] He said to them, "How then does David in the Spirit call him Lord, saying,

[44] 'The Lord [Yahweh] said to my Lord, sit on my right hand, until I make your enemies a footstool for your feet?' (Ps. 110:1).

[45] "If then David calls him Lord, how is he his son?"

[46] No one was able to answer him a word, neither did any man dare ask him any more questions from that day forward.

Before we get to the main problem addressed, notice verse 43, "How then does David in the Spirit call him Lord, saying…" Very often we think the Holy Spirit wasn't present, or at least not operational, in the Old Testament world, except on some special, short-term assignments. That simply is not true. He was active in creation and remained active thereafter. The problem is that they, and we, often don't recognize His activity, and He hadn't yet come in power (Acts 2:1-4).

It may be difficult for us to understand these exchanges between Jesus and His antagonists, but it was a common thing for men to discuss, debate and even argue this type of question. The scribes and Pharisees weren't totally closed minded and enjoyed debate very much, however, like us, they seldom changed their position because they thought they were right.

This particular question may be difficult for us to understand and we may wonder why it's even in the Bible. But, remember the Bible was written for those who first received it. The primary meaning is theirs and we need to try to understand what's happening to see how it applies to us. It was not an attempt to embarrass them; it was an honest attempt to teach them. In an effort to help the Pharisees and Sadducees understand and possibly even accept Him, Jesus asked them a searching question about the "Messiah." "Is the Christ David's son or David's Lord?" Is this an innocent or obscure question? It is neither!

The Jews believed "The Messiah" or "the anointed one" would be empowered by God's spirit to deliver His people and establish His Kingdom. He would be the King of the Jews; a political leader who would defeat all their enemies and bring about a new golden age of peace and prosperity. The title comes from the Old Testament custom of anointing a person with oil to set them aside for a special task, we might call it ordination, and they became a "messiah" in this case. In the Old Testament, "messiah" is used more than 30 times about kings, priests, the patriarchs and even the Persian King Cyrus. It is used in connection with King David who, for them, became the model for the messianic king who would come.

By the time of Daniel, 6th century BC, "Messiah" began to be used as the title of a king who would come in the future, between the "present age" and the "age to come." When the Jews were struggling against their political enemies, he came to be thought of as a political, military ruler. In the New Testament we learn that they thought The Messiah would come soon to perform miracles and to deliver His people; then He would live and rule them forever.

Since David was the great king and conqueror, "The Messiah" was thought of in the same light. The most common title for the coming messiah was "Son of David" and he was expected to restore the honor of Israel and avenge all the indignities forced upon them.

The quotation Jesus chose for His response was a psalm of David, "Yahweh says to my Lord, 'Sit at my right hand, until I make your enemies your footstool for your feet'" (Ps. 110:1) which was one the Pharisees considered to have messianic interpretation. The word "LORD," as many translations have it, (with capital letters) is *Yahweh*, God the Father, the second "Lord" refers to the coming "Messiah."

The problem Jesus poses is this, "How can The Messiah be David's Lord if He is David's son?" Clearly, He cannot be! Jesus, The Messiah, isn't David's son, He is David's Lord. Their understanding didn't go far enough. The Messiah is not the Son of David, He is the Son of God!

The Messiah couldn't be thought of in terms of an earthly kingdom because He was/is King of a Heavenly Kingdom. This was true for them and it is true for us. This is the clearest claim Jesus has made so far about who He really is.

Do as I Say, Not as I Do?
Matthew 23:1-12

Then Jesus spoke to the multitudes and to his disciples, [2] saying, "The scribes and the Pharisees sat on Moses' seat. [3] All things therefore whatever they tell you to observe, observe and do, but don't do their works; for they say, and don't do. [4] For they bind heavy burdens that are grievous to be borne, and lay them on men's shoulders; but they themselves will not lift a finger to help them. [5] But all their works they do to be seen by men. They make their phylacteries (See Deut. 6:8) broad, enlarge the fringes (or tassels) of their garments, [6] and love the place of honor at feasts, the best seats in the synagogues, [7] the salutations in the marketplaces, and to be called 'Rabbi, Rabbi' by men. [8] But don't you be called 'Rabbi,' for one is your teacher, the Christ, and all of you are brothers. [9] Call no man on the earth your father, for one is your Father, he who is in heaven. [10] Neither be called masters, for one is your master, the Christ. [11] But he who is greatest among you will be your servant. [12] Whoever exalts himself will be humbled, and whoever humbles himself will be exalted.

Jesus was condemning, not commending the scribes and the Pharisees. Barclay says the two great commandments can be reduced to two principles "reverence" and "respect." "...reverence for God, for God's name, for God's Day, for the parents God has given us...respect for a man's life, for his possessions, for his personality, for his good name, for oneself (DSB, p. 285)."

"Moses' seat" was a chair in each synagogue that symbolized the origin of the Law and the scribes traced their teachings back to Moses himself. The chair was prominently placed at the front of the synagogue and the teacher spoke from there. In this passage, it is used metaphorically and refers to the fact that they claimed the same authority Moses had. "Bind" as used here is a technical word meaning to forbid.

Like many teachers and preachers, the lives of the Pharisees did not match their message. They required meticulous adherence to their rules and regulations while finding loop holes for themselves. After several attempts to discredit Him, they couldn't find anything! Jesus addressed the multitudes and His disciples "to openly indict the religious leaders for their numerous failures to conform to God's righteous standards (NLTSB, p. 1625)."

They made religion a burden when it was meant to be a blessing. Barclay suggests the test of true religion is this: "Does it make it wings to lift a man up, or a deadweight to drag him down? ... Does it carry him, or has he to carry it? (DSB, p. 285)." "For him that is taught in the word to give respect to him that teaches, is commendable; but for him that teaches, to demand it, to be puffed up with it, is sinful. How much is all this against the spirit of Christianity! (MH)."

These leaders made a great show of their piety by exaggerating their "phylacteries" and "tassels." The "phylacteries" were leather cases, containing Scripture verses, worn on their arms and forehead (Ex. 13:9). The "tassels" were a fringe on the corners of their garments (Deut. 22:12). They were to be reminders of God's commandments, but they had changed; they had become symbols of rank, they were medals of religious piety common to any system that focuses on rules and regulations. They called people's attention to the religiousness of the person wearing them instead of pointing others to the living God. "Experience has shown with what tenacity the traditionalist will defend provisions which have long been irrelevant (AB, p. 278." It has well been said, the seven last words of the church are: "We never did it that way before."

"Rabbi" means "my master" or "my teacher." "Father" was a title used by the Rabbis, because they considered themselves to be the spiritual father of the people and thus more important than even their biological father. Christians should stand on level ground, like brother and sister; each has their own gift, but none is more important than any other in the congregation.

This passage does not rule out titles of respect, they are appropriate. Paul said, "Therefore give everyone what you owe: if you owe taxes, pay taxes; if customs, then customs; if respect, then respect; if honor, then honor (Rom. 13:7)." However, true respect must come from the "respecter," it cannot be demanded by the "respectee." You may demand obedience, but respect must be earned.

I was involved in a Non-profit Management Seminar and they were introducing an exciting "new" theory in management: "Servant Leadership" which they said originated in a YMCA back east. I raised my hand and referred them to this passage. All Christian leadership should be based on this model.

Woe to You...
Matthew 23:13-36

"Woe to you, scribes and Pharisees, hypocrites! For you devour widows' houses, and as a pretense you make long prayers. Therefore you will receive greater condemnation.

[14] *"But woe to you, scribes and Pharisees, hypocrites! Because you shut up the Kingdom of Heaven against men; for you don't enter in yourselves, neither do you allow those who are entering in to enter.*

(Some Greek manuscripts reverse the order of verses 13 and 14, and some omit verse 13, numbering verse 14 as 13. NU omits verse 14.) ¹⁵ *Woe to you, scribes and Pharisees, hypocrites! For you travel around by sea and land to make one proselyte; and when he becomes one, you make him twice as much of a son of Gehenna (or Hell) as yourselves.*

¹⁶ *"Woe to you, you blind guides, who say, 'Whoever swears by the temple, it is nothing; but whoever swears by the gold of the temple, he is obligated.'* ¹⁷ *You blind fools! For which is greater, the gold, or the temple that sanctifies the gold?* ¹⁸ *'Whoever swears by the altar, it is nothing; but whoever swears by the gift that is on it, he is obligated?'* ¹⁹ *You blind fools! For which is greater, the gift, or the altar that sanctifies the gift?* ²⁰ *He therefore who swears by the altar, swears by it, and by everything on it.* ²¹ *He who swears by the temple, swears by it, and by him who was living (NU reads "lives") in it.* ²² *He who swears by heaven, swears by the throne of God, and by him who sits on it.*

²³ *"Woe to you, scribes and Pharisees, hypocrites! For you tithe mint, dill, and cumin, and have left undone the weightier matters of the law: justice, mercy, and faith. But you ought to have done these, and not to have left the other undone.* ²⁴ *You blind guides, who strain out a gnat, and swallow a camel!*

²⁵ *"Woe to you, scribes and Pharisees, hypocrites! For you clean the outside of the cup and of the platter, but within they are full of extortion and unrighteousness (TR reads "self-indulgence" instead of "unrighteousness").* ²⁶ *You blind Pharisees, first clean the inside of the cup and of the platter, that its outside may become clean also.*

²⁷ *"Woe to you, scribes and Pharisees, hypocrites! For you are like whitened tombs, which outwardly appear beautiful, but inwardly are full of dead men's bones, and of all uncleanness.* ²⁸ *Even so you also outwardly appear righteous to men, but inwardly you are full of hypocrisy and iniquity.*

²⁹ *"Woe to you, scribes and Pharisees, hypocrites! For you build the tombs of the prophets, and decorate the tombs of the righteous,* ³⁰ *and say, 'If we had lived in the days of our fathers, we wouldn't have been partakers with them in the blood of the prophets.'* ³¹ *Therefore you testify to yourselves that you are children of those who killed the prophets.* ³² *Fill up, then, the measure of your fathers.* ³³ *You serpents, you offspring of vipers, how will you escape the judgment of Gehenna (or Hell)?* ³⁴ *Therefore behold, I send to you prophets, wise men, and scribes. Some of them you will kill and crucify; and some of them you will scourge in your synagogues, and persecute from city to city;* ³⁵ *that on you may come all the righteous blood shed on the earth, from the blood of righteous Abel to the blood of Zachariah son of Barachiah, whom you killed between the sanctuary and the altar.* ³⁶ *Most certainly I tell you, all these things will come upon this generation.*

Robinson calls this section "the rolling thunder of Christ's wrath;" certainly, it is the most severe denunciation of the Jewish leadership found in the Gospels. The New Testament gives indication that Jesus strongly rejected the teaching and practice of the Pharisees, those who follow a list of do's and don't's. But we still tend to like rules to point to which "prove" our worthiness or acceptability.

Unfortunately, we often hear it "preached" that way… preaching "down" to people almost with glee in our voices. "You're finally going to get yours!" But keeping in mind the context and looking at the very next verse filled with pathos, reread it as a cry of pain for the "lostness" of these elders!

The word "woe" is *ouai* in Greek and it isn't so much an actual word as it is an utterance carrying both sorrow and disgust. Here it comes from the broken heart of God. We might use something like "augh!" This expression was aimed at religious people, not at the prostitutes and tax collectors. it was meant to awaken the religious to their need to repent.

Verse 13 is especially condemning:

Here they are charged with *shutting heaven* against men: in Luke 11:52 they are charged with what was worse, *taking away the key*– "the key of knowledge" –which means, not the key to open knowledge, but knowledge as the only key to open heaven. A right knowledge of God's revealed word is eternal life, as our Lord says (see John 17:3; 5:39); but this they took away from the people, substituting for it their wretched traditions (CCE).

We have already seen that the word "hypocrite" originally meant "one who answers" and came to refer to the dialogue used by actors; so, it came to be the word that meant actor. In Jesus' time it meant pretender, to play a part. Jesus is saying the leaders wore the actor's mask and costume, but their hearts weren't in it.

Israel's entire life focused on their being the Chosen People.

Being a religious leader in Jerusalem was very different from being a pastor in a secular society today. Israel's history, culture, and daily life centered around its relationship with God. The religious leaders were the best known, most powerful, and most respected of the leaders. Jesus made these stinging accusations because the leaders' hunger for more power, money, and status had made them lose sight of God, and their blindness was spreading to the whole nation (LASB, p. 1591).

Excluding verse 14, there are seven statements that begin "Woe." Since seven is a number indicating completion, possibly Jesus is saying the Pharisees are totally condemned. Also, remember, most of these things He condemned are things that we should be doing, they are good things. What are the problems?

1. Their rules kept people away from the Living God. Pagan people were attracted to Judaism, but the leaders made it so difficult that they "shut the Kingdom of Heaven in men's faces."

2. They were evangelistic, mission minded, but exclusive. "The greatest of all heresies is that sinful conviction that any Church has a monopoly of God or of this truth, or that any Church is the only gateway to God's Kingdom (DSB, p. 291)."

3. Keep your word always, not just when God is a "party" to it. Since God hears every word we utter He is a party to every promise.

4. Be careful to follow God in the details while also following the principles behind them; misplaced priorities, majoring on the unimportant things. To "strain out" is to filter, be careful which filter you select.

5. Attention to appearance while ignoring the reason for the appearance. The Greek word used for "greed" is actually robbery; "self-indulgence" would also be a good translation of the Greek. Concern for dotting i's and crossing t's can be overdone.

6. Be real; don't appear to be something you are not. Barclay warns, "There is nothing harder than for a good man not to know that he is good; and once he knows he is good, his goodness is gone, however he may appear to men from the outside (DSB, p. 297)."

7. Truthfulness. The statement, "...you are children of those who killed the prophets..." could mean "like father, like son." Stagg says it means, "Go ahead and complete what your fathers began! (BBC, p. 214)." In the history of mankind, how many wars have been fought in God's name?

8. The martyrs on Jesus' list show His familiarity with the Hebrew Scriptures because they included the first and last men mentioned in those scriptures, from Genesis, the first book, through 2 Chronicles, the last book of their history. Coincidentally they run from A to Z in the English alphabet, but not in the Hebrew or Greek alphabets so don't make something special of this.

Matthew says "...you shut up the Kingdom of Heaven against men..." while Luke suggests "...you took away the key of knowledge" (Luke 11:52a). By our traditions have we also shut the Kingdom to some who would follow Christ? Jesus' judgment isn't against cleanliness, "but against excessive concentration on ritual cleanliness or defilement of eating and drinking vessels (AB, p. 280)."

It is suggested that the stricter Jews would strain anything they drank through a gauze fabric lest they swallow a gnat, the smallest unclean animal, and that is probably the picture here. But they are swallowing whole a camel, the largest unclean animal. How often we do the same thing!

I doubt that any of us have killed any modern-day prophets, or are even related to anyone who has. But I can recall in the 1950's when many of us made disparaging remarks about the "tongues" movement, even insisting that it was of the devil. Have we discouraged and/or hindered someone spreading the Good News of Jesus? Or have we done what we could to encourage and assist them on their way? What do you think? When you stand before God, will you be a helper or a hinderer?

The Agony of Rejection
Matthew 23:37-39

"Jerusalem, Jerusalem, who kills the prophets, and stones those who are sent to her! How often I would have gathered your children together, even as a hen gathers her chicks under her wings, and you would not! [38] *Behold, your house is left to you desolate.* [39] *For I tell you, you will not see me from now on, until you say, 'Blessed is he who comes in the name of the Lord!'"* (Psalm 118:26).

At this point in His ministry the elders have rejected Jesus' mission and message and with the statement "your house is left to you desolate" He indicates that He will not return to the Temple again. "It is possible that Jesus used these words with deliberate reference to the desolation and destruction so vividly portrayed in Jer. xii [Jer. 12] particularly in view of the you would not let me [statement] of vs. 37 (AB, p. 284)." Verses 38 and 39 also find root in Jeremiah.

Jerusalem wasn't just the capital city of the nation; it was the most important city in the world to the Jews, wherever they lived. Thus, there is great pathos in the voice of Jesus as He mourns over what Jerusalem represented and the influenced it had on righteous people all over the world. This is not the voice of the judge; it's the voice of the lover. "Where the mercy of God was greatest, it was there that there was the greatest wickedness and rebellion, and at length the sharpest judgments of God (GN)."

Is there anything sadder than this? The destiny of the Jews had been decided, not by God, but by their leaders. Those who have strong views that God's Will is always going to be done in spite of those who stand in His way need to be careful when they say that. As this passage shows, that simply isn't so. "The Lord is not slow concerning His promise, as some count slowness; but is patient with us, not wishing that any should perish, but that all should come to repentance (2 Pet. 3:9)." One person can set in motion the refusal of God's Will for a family, a church, even a nation. Certainly, there are penalties for those who reject God's Will, but it has still been rejected. Their penalty was severe, "your house is left to you desolate."

Jesus said, "How often I would have gathered your children together, even as a hen gathers her chicks under her wings, and you would not!" Clearly, Jesus' Will and God's Will are the same, that all would be saved. The rulers of the Jews were not willing. Barclay points out four great truths this passage teaches:

1. The patience of God: The Jews had rejected, even killed, every prophet God sent them, yet God continued and even sent His Son to them to woo them back.

The appeal of Jesus: Jesus never tried to force them into the Kingdom, He stood with outstretched, loving arms to welcome them, but they refused.

2. The deliberation of man's sin: In spite of the wonderful things Jesus did for the people, even the nation, they chose to go their own way.

3. The consequences of rejecting Christ: In about forty years, the nation, intended to point everyone to God, was erased from the maps of the world. Today it exists only because of the beneficence of the United States and other western nations.

The symbol of protection used here was a common expression for God's protection of His people. One of the blessings Boaz pronounces on Ruth is: "May Yahweh repay your work, and a full reward be given to you from Yahweh, the God of Israel, under whose wings you have come to take refuge" (Ruth 2:12). Just as a hen will give her life to protect her chicks from danger, Jesus gave His life for us.

What we call "free moral agency" is a double-edged sword. The freedom to choose carries with it the possibility of blessing or ruin. How we choose is more important than we know. "Our Lord declares the miseries the inhabitants of Jerusalem were about to bring upon themselves, but he does not notice the sufferings he was to undergo (MH)."

The *Shekinah* glory that once inhabited Solomon's Temple and now was present in the person of Jesus was about to be withdrawn once again from the presence of the Jews. "Jerusalem and her children had a large share of guilt, and their punishment has been signaled. But ere long, deserved vengeance will fall on every church which is Christian in name only (MH)." I have often said "the trouble with making a decision is that you don't know if it is right or wrong until it is too late." Choose well.

Reading the Signs of the Times
Matthew 24:1-14

Jesus went out from the temple, and was going on his way. His disciples came to him to show him the buildings of the temple. ² But he answered them, "You see all of these things, don't you? Most certainly I tell you, there will not be left here one stone on another, that will not be thrown down."

³As he sat on the Mount of Olives, the disciples came to him privately, saying, "Tell us, when will these things be? What is the sign of your coming, and of the end of the age?"

4 Jesus answered them, "Be careful that no one leads you astray. 5 For many will come in my name, saying, 'I am the Christ,' and will lead many astray. 6 You will hear of wars and rumors of wars. See that you aren't troubled, for all this must happen, but the end is not yet. 7 For nation will rise against nation, and kingdom against kingdom; and there will be famines, plagues, and earthquakes in various places. 8 But all these things are the beginning of birth pains. 9 Then they will deliver you up to oppression, and will kill you. You will be hated by all of the nations for my name's sake. 10 Then many will stumble, and will deliver up one another, and will hate one another. 11 Many false prophets will arise, and will lead many astray. 12 Because iniquity will be multiplied, the love of many will grow cold. 13 But he who endures to the end, the same will be saved. 14 This Good News of the Kingdom will be preached in the whole world for a testimony to all the nations, and then the end will come.

There is no doubt that a very strong sense of nationalism was on the rise in Palestine, primarily through the Zealot party, at this time. The early letters of Paul also express an indication of an early "return" of the Messiah to establish His Kingdom and this section underscores that urgency.

A great deal of the prediction-seeking on the part of NT students has come from a lack of understanding of the forms and imagery of Jewish apocalyptic … It must not be forgotten that crisis of any kind in both political and social circumstances tends to produce a particular kind of thinking, speaking and writing…

In no area has the confusion been more widespread than in the interpretation given to the "coming" of The Man [Messiah] (AB, p. 286-7).

That confusion is greater in that Jesus is probably referring to two "comings;" a coming (or we might say "going") to the Father and a "second" coming to the world.

Which of these "comings" is He addressing in each of the pronouncements in the next two chapters of Matthew which address the fall of Jerusalem, the increased nationalistic activity, the Second Coming, and the end of the age?

The section from 24:1-26:2 is "eschatological in nature and practical in purpose (BBC, p. 215)" and, because it contains both literal and symbolic language, it is both difficult and subject to a great deal of scholarly debate and speculation. According to Webster, eschatology is, "the branch of theology which deals with the final end of man and of the world." It comes from two Greek words, *eschatos* meaning last and *logos* meaning word. "…when will these things be?" and "What is the sign of your coming, and of the end of the age?" aren't easily understood or answered. Do they refer to the destruction of Jerusalem or the *parousia*, that is the Second Coming of Christ?

But Jesus seems anxious that the disciples should not suppose that these two 'judgments' would necessarily follow in immediate chronological sequence… He warns them not to be misled by deceptive utterances of false Messiahs…and not to imagine that events which might seem to be cataclysmic…were infallible signs that the end was near (TNTC, p. 223).

For Christians, it involves the recognition of God's hand at work bringing the world to conclusion and judgment. While this section has some of the elements of apocalyptic writing, it does not use the "full blown" symbolism of either Daniel or Revelation.

As always, Jesus "seized the moment" when His disciples were ready to learn He was ready to teach. "Jesus went out from the temple, and was going on his way. His disciples came to him to show him the buildings of the temple." The beautiful temple, with its gleaming white marble and gold overlay, was one of the wonders of the world ancient. It shined so brightly in the sun that it was hard to look directly at it, however, before all the disciples were dead it would be totally destroyed.

Their response was "...when will these things be? What is the sign of your coming, and of the end of the age?" showed that they were ready to learn. The best time to teach anything is when the student wants to learn.

The introduction is the most important part of any lesson plan because you cannot teach until you have the pupil's attention. In Greek, their question is actually "when will [all] this happen?" That means not only the *eschaton*, the end of the age, and the *parousia*, the coming of the Lord in power, but the destruction of the Temple.

Jesus broke them into their separate parts because the Temple would be destroyed within forty years, but the end and the return of Christ would not come until much later. Depending on your understanding of eschatology (and how God ACTUALLY chooses to do it) the end of the age and the return of Christ may be separate events.

The destruction of the Temple had to be on such a scale as to be unimaginable to the disciples, "there will not be left here one stone on another that will not be thrown down." Speaking about that destruction, Josephus recorded in his history, *Wars of the Jews*:

...wondering probably, how so massive a pile could be overthrown, as seemed implied in our Lord's last words regarding it. Josephus, who gives a minute account of the wonderful structure, speaks of stones forty cubits long [*Wars of the Jews,* 5.5.1] and says the pillars supporting the porches were twenty-five cubits high, all of one stone, and that of the whitest marble [*Wars of the Jews,* 5.5.2]. Six days' battering at the walls, during the siege, made no impression upon them [*Wars of the Jews,* 6.4.1]. Some of the under-building, yet remaining, and other works, are probably as old as the first temple (CCE). [The first Temple was built around 957 BC.]

Precisely, "What is the sign of your coming, and of the end of the age?" First, Jesus' emphasis isn't on a time, but on the fact that we should be prepared. "Be careful that no one leads you astray" He warned, and the so-called New Age movement, which can be traced back to ancient Babylon, is only the most recent attempt to do that.

Jesus warns, "For many will come in my name, saying, 'I am the Christ,' and will lead many astray." A Zealot named Bar Cocheba was acclaimed "Messiah" by Rabbi Akiba during the Jewish-Roman wars (66-70 AD) which led to the destruction of Jerusalem and many have tried to claim the title before and since, including one of my wife's cousins.

"You will hear of wars and rumors of wars...nation will rise against nation, and kingdom against kingdom..." Someone estimated that there have been about 300 religious wars. I'm not sure if that includes the ones going on now or not. Remember, Jesus doesn't want us to get involved in these messianic movements and "holy wars" that would (will) come.

Among natural disasters to come are "famines, plagues, and earthquakes in various places." Matthew reports an earthquake at Jesus' crucifixion (Matt. 27:54) and His resurrection (Matt. 28:2). But these are only the "beginning of birth pains." More is to come…

I don't think Jesus is trying to make a chronological list of things when He says in verse 9 "Then they will deliver you up to oppression, and will kill you." I think it is more along the idea of "Another thing that will happen is…" As always, Jesus makes it clear that being a disciple, a follower, isn't going to be easy. You can expect to be persecuted, hated, and put to death. All of this is because ministry was done "for my name's sake." Unfortunately, "many will stumble, and will deliver up one another, and will hate one another." Serving Christ isn't a trip on the "Love Boat," it is a "tour of duty" on a man-of-war.

As far as we know, John was the only disciple to die a "natural" death and it wasn't because the Romans didn't try to kill him but God had His hand on John to accomplish what needed to be done by this the final disciple.

False prophets will continue to "arise, and will lead many astray." "…iniquity will be multiplied; the love of many will grow cold." Many of these things have already happened and some are happening right now. What remains? I don't know!

Who will be saved? Jesus said, "…he who endures to the end, the same will be saved." Does that mean a Christian can lose their salvation? I believe the Scripture says "No," but many of my friends don't agree. It is certainly something to think about. Stagg says, "The test of salvation is not verbal profession but faithful obedience to God's will (BBC, p. 218)." This admonition is similar to the challenge to the seven churches in Revelation. Here the call is to endure and there it is to conquer, but the idea is the same, we cannot just drift along, we must be involved both as individuals and as churches. We may not we dealing with persecution, but believers in many parts of the world are!

The good news here is that the "Good News of the Kingdom will be preached in the whole world for a testimony to all the nations, and then the end will come." If there is anything remaining to be done, this may be it, but I doubt it. Couldn't Jesus return at any time?

What of the prophecy in verse 2, "…there will not be left here one stone on another that will not be thrown down"? When Jerusalem was destroyed in 70 AD, the Temple was burned and the gold overlay on the walls melted and ran into the cracks in the walls and floor. Roman soldiers literally dismantled the building turning over every stone to retrieve the gold.

Time to Flee
Matthew 24:15-28

"When, therefore, you see the abomination of desolation, (Dan. 9:27; 11:31; 12:11) which was spoken of through Daniel the prophet, standing in the holy place (let the reader understand), [16] then let those who are in Judea flee to the mountains. [17] Let him who is on the housetop not go down to take out the things that are in his house. [18] Let him who is in the field not return back to get his clothes. [19] But woe to those who are with child and to nursing mothers in those days! [20] Pray that your flight will not be in the winter, nor on a Sabbath, [21] for then there will be great oppression, such as has not been from the beginning of the world

until now, no, nor ever will be. ²² Unless those days had been shortened, no flesh would have been saved. But for the sake of the chosen ones, those days will be shortened.

²³ "Then if any man tells you, 'Behold, here is the Christ,' or, 'There,' don't believe it. ²⁴ For there will arise false christs, and false prophets, and they will show great signs and wonders, so as to lead astray, if possible, even the chosen ones.

²⁵ "Behold, I have told you beforehand. ²⁶ If therefore they tell you, 'Behold, he is in the wilderness,' don't go out; 'Behold, he is in the inner rooms,' don't believe it. ²⁷ For as the lightning flashes from the east, and is seen even to the west, so will be the coming of the Son of Man. ²⁸ For wherever the carcass is, there is where the vultures (or eagles) gather together.

There can be little question that this passage refers to the destruction of Jerusalem which occurred in 70 AD, but before it happened there was a long, drawn-out struggle. Defended by religious fanatics, Jerusalem was difficult to conquer, so the Roman General Titus (not the author of the book of Titus) starved them out.

Josephus took part in the siege and tells us that 97 thousand were taken into slavery and 1.1 million died. Those who heeded Jesus advise, "…let those who are in Judea flee to the mountains" escaped the horror.

"The abomination of desolation" which Daniel referred to is generally considered to be the sacrifice of a pig, 167 BC ca., on the altar in the Temple by Antiochus Epiphanes, the king of Syria. During the inter-biblical period; it was the rallying point when Judah Maccabee led the Jews to overthrow their oppressors. In this case, the expected "abomination" could have been the eagles on the Roman standard carried by all Roman Legions that were "planted" by the conquering troops in the Temple area. It is also reported that Caligula attempted to have a statue of himself erected in the Temple in 38 AD. During such a time of turmoil, it would be natural for the Jews to look for a messiah, and many false messiahs and prophets arose to attempt to deliver them.

Faith in nationality has often been fatal because God is rarely (do I dare say never?) on the side of any one nation. Impossible? No, because He has often used heathen nations to bring judgment on His people and on other nations and He loves ALL people.

> Therefore he brought on them the king of the Chaldeans, who killed their young men with the sword in the house of their sanctuary, and had no compassion on young man or virgin, old man or gray-headed: he gave them all into his hand (2 Chr. 36:17).

> Yahweh rejected all the offspring of Israel, afflicted them, and delivered them into the hands of raiders, until he had cast them out of his sight. …until Yahweh removed Israel out of his sight, as he said by all his servants the prophets. So Israel was carried away out of their own land to Assyria to this day. (2 Kings 17:20, 23).

As a result of the warnings in verses 15-22, the final split between the followers of Christ and Judaism occurred as the Roman Legions approached Jerusalem under the command of Titus and the Christians fled to Pella as they had been warned to do.

Jesus warned, in verse 26 "if anyone says, 'he is in the wilderness,'…or, 'he is in the inner rooms,' don't believe it." Even if they work miracles, do not believe it, because Satan can counterfeit almost any miracle he wants to.

What if Jesus comes and we do not know it? The answer to that problem is found in verse 27 "For as the lightning flashes from the east, and is seen even to the west, so will be the coming of the Son of Man." This passage indicates that there will be no secret coming the second time; everyone in the world will know about it.

The Signs of the Lord's Return
Matthew 24:29-31

But immediately after the oppression of those days, the sun will be darkened, the moon will not give its light, the stars will fall from the sky, and the powers of the heavens will be shaken; (Isa. 13:10; 34:4) [30] *and then the sign of the Son of Man will appear in the sky. Then all the tribes of the earth will mourn, and they will see the Son of Man coming on the clouds of the sky with power and great glory.* [31] *He will send out his angels with a great sound of a trumpet, and they will gather together his chosen ones from the four winds, from one end of the sky to the other.*

The statement, "…immediately after the oppression..." (translated "tribulation" in the KJV) refers back to verse 21, "for then there will be great oppression, such as has not been from the beginning of the world until now, no, nor ever will be." There is a lot of symbolism in these verses.

Peter says "But this is what has been spoken through the prophet Joel… The sun will be turned into darkness, and the moon into blood, before the great and glorious day of the Lord comes." (Acts 2:16 and 20). Both passages probably use symbolic language. The idea is that there will be such turmoil that the entire cosmos will be turned upside down and inside out. The first time, Jesus came as a servant, the second time; He will come as the conquering king. The power the Jews wanted Him to display the first time certainly will be displayed the second time.

The much anticipated "Day of the Lord" was generally accepted as being a particular day, or short period of time, at the end of age. It is the day God's Will and Purpose for humankind would be fulfilled. At that time, Jesus will be recognized as King by the whole world. He will cleanse heaven and earth and prepare them for eternity.

"Woe to you who desire the day of Yahweh! Why do you long for the day of Yahweh? It is darkness, and not light. As if a man fled from a lion, and a bear met him; Or he went into the house and leaned his hand on the wall, and a snake bit him. Won't the day of Yahweh be darkness, and not light? Even very dark, and no brightness in it? (Amos 5:18-20)

This is probably the earliest occurrence in the Bible of the phrase, "the day of Yahweh."

Isaiah says it will be a time of judgment, "Wail; for the day of Yahweh is at hand! It will come as destruction from the Almighty (Isa. 13:6)" "Behold, the day of Yahweh comes, cruel, with wrath and fierce anger; to make the land a desolation, and to destroy its sinners out of it (Isa. 13:9)."

Jeremiah adds:

For that day is of the Lord, Yahweh of Armies, a day of vengeance, that he may avenge him of his adversaries: and the sword shall devour and be satiate, and shall drink its fill of their blood; for the Lord, Yahweh of Armies, has a sacrifice in the north country by the river Euphrates (Jer. 46:10).

Isaiah and Joel also call it a time of restoration: "For Yahweh will have compassion on Jacob, and will yet choose Israel, and set them in their own land. The foreigner will join himself with them, and they will unite with the house of Jacob" (Isa. 14:1).

It will happen afterward, that I will pour out my Spirit on all flesh; and your sons and your daughters will prophesy. Your old men will dream dreams. Your young men will see visions. And also on the servants and on the handmaids in those days, I will pour out my Spirit. I will show wonders in the heavens and in the earth: blood, fire, and pillars of smoke. The sun will be turned into darkness, and the moon into blood, before the great and terrible day of Yahweh comes. It will happen that whoever will call on Yahweh's name shall be saved; for in Mount Zion and in Jerusalem there will be those who escape, as Yahweh has said, and among the remnant, those whom Yahweh calls. (Joel 2:28-32).

The New Testament talks about the day of the Lord Jesus Christ, a moment at the end of time when Jesus will return for the believers. "...who will also confirm you until the end, blameless in the day of our Lord Jesus Christ (1 Cor. 1:8)." "... [you, the church] are to deliver such a one to Satan for the destruction of the flesh, that the spirit may be saved in the day of the Lord Jesus (1 Cor. 5:5)." "...as also you acknowledged us in part, that we are your boasting, even as you also are ours, in the day of our Lord Jesus (2 Cor. 1:14)." "...so that you may approve the things that are excellent; that you may be sincere and without offense to the day of Christ... (Phil. 1:10)."

Barclay points out three things we should notice:

1. God has not abandoned the world. It is not abandonment that God contemplates; it is intervention.

2. An increase in evil should not discourage us. It is not the prelude to destruction; it is the prelude to recreation.

3. Both judgment and a new creation are certain (DSB, p. 309).

"The value of these pictures is not in their details...but in the eternal truth which they conserve; and the basic truth in them in that, whatever the world is like, God has not abandoned it (DSB, p. 309)."

LASB says:

Jesus, talking about the end times, telescoped near future and far future events, as did the Old Testament prophets. Many of these persecutions have already occurred, more are yet to come. But God is in control of even the length of persecutions. He will not forget his people. This is all we need to know about the future to motivate us to live rightly now (LASB, p. 1594).

The Lesson of the Fig Tree
Matthew 24:32-44

"Now from the fig tree learn this parable. When its branch has now become tender, and produces its leaves, you know that the summer is near. [33] Even so you also, when you see all these things, know that it is near, even at the doors. [34] Most certainly I tell you, this generation (the word for "generation" (genea) can also be translated as "race") will not pass away, until all these things are accomplished. [35] Heaven and earth will pass away, but my words will not pass away. [36] But no one knows of that day and hour, not even the angels of heaven (NU adds "nor the son"), but my Father only.

37 "As the days of Noah were, so will be the coming of the Son of Man. 38 For as in those days which were before the flood they were eating and drinking, marrying and giving in marriage, until the day that Noah entered into the ship, 39 and they didn't know until the flood came, and took them all away, so will be the coming of the Son of Man. 40 Then two men will be in the field: one will be taken and one will be left; 41 two women grinding at the mill, one will be taken and one will be left. 42 Watch therefore, for you don't know in what hour your Lord comes. 43 But know this, that if the master of the house had known in what watch of the night the thief was coming, he would have watched, and would not have allowed his house to be broken into. 44 Therefore also be ready, for in an hour that you don't expect, the Son of Man will come.

We have said that a parable has one main point and the point here is as simple as the Girl Scout and Boy Scout motto: "Be prepared." Twice we are warned to be ready. In verse 42, Jesus says, "Watch therefore…" and in verse 44, "…be ready…" Jesus is coming. What else needs to be said?

The statement, "this generation will not pass away until all these things are accomplished" has been much debated. Who does it apply to and what does it mean? We don't know for sure, but "this generation" was probably those people alive at that time. We have indications from Paul and the histories of the early church that the first century Christians did expect Jesus' immediate return. If we accept that interpretation, the parable would probably refer to the signs of the increasing tension between the Roman government and the Jews that concluded in the destruction of Jerusalem in 70 AD.

Some scholars prefer to believe the prophecy refers to Jesus' return at the end of the age and some consider it material which supports the "rapture of the church." Some suggest by the fact that Jesus didn't know when the end would come, that He was talking about the end of the age and His return. Undoubtedly, Jesus had limitations while He was on earth, He was confined to a body and could only be in one place at a time, that He didn't know when the end would come should not surprise us. Verse 36 says, "But no one knows of that day and hour, not even the angels of heaven, but my Father only."

Because of the strong statement in verse 36, Barclay says conjecture about the Lord's return "is nothing less than blasphemy, for the man who speculates is seeking to wrest from God secrets which belong to God alone. It is not any man's duty to speculate; it is his duty to prepare himself and watch (DSB, p. 315)." Tasker adds, "It is very strange that in spite of these words so many have wasted their time in the vain attempt to decide for themselves the date when the *parousia* may be expected (TNTC, p. 231)." Yet many well-meaning people spend their lives trying to figure it out rather than trying to reach people so they will not be doomed. As has been pointed out, our job is to be ready when the bridegroom comes!

The day Jesus returns, what kind of day will it be? A day just like any other day! As the days of Noah were, so will be the coming of the Son of Man. For as in those days which were before the flood they were eating and drinking, marrying and giving in marriage, until the day that Noah entered into the ship… (Verse 38).

Verses 40 and 41 say we will be going about our normal duties. There is a sad note repeated in those two verses, and in Luke's record, "one will be taken and the other one will be left." The division, who goes and who stays, is both interesting and unfortunate. It will cut across family lines, occupational lines, national lines and any other line you can think of.

Again, some see in this passage the "rapture" of the church. Certainly, that is possible, but make no mistake about it, in God's own time and in His own way, Jesus will come for His own. "Christ's second coming will be swift and sudden. There will be no opportunity for last-minute repentance or bargaining. The choice we have already made will determine our eternal destiny (LASB, p. 1595)."

The Faithful and Wise Servant
Matthew 24:45-51

"Who then is the faithful and wise servant, whom his lord has set over his household, to give them their food in due season? ⁴⁶ Blessed is that servant whom his lord finds doing so when he comes. ⁴⁷ Most certainly I tell you that he will set him over all that he has. ⁴⁸ But if that evil servant should say in his heart, 'My lord is delaying his coming,' ⁴⁹ and begins to beat his fellow servants, and eat and drink with the drunkards, ⁵⁰ the lord of that servant will come in a day when he doesn't expect it, and in an hour when he doesn't know it, ⁵¹ and will cut him in pieces, and appoint his portion with the hypocrites. There is where the weeping and grinding of teeth will be.

Again, Matthew stresses the fact that believers are to be ready. Verse 46 says: "Blessed is that servant whom his lord finds doing so when he comes." "One is not saved by his works, but he is judged by them (BBC, p. 222)." Whatever God has given you to do, do it the best you can.

The word "servant" is *doulos* which means "bond slave." The followers of Jesus are not employees; they have given themselves to Him and, as Paul says, "For he who was called in the Lord being a bondservant is the Lord's free man. Likewise he who was called being free is Christ's bondservant. (1 Cor. 7:22)."

What is the reward for service, a vacation, no a promotion, a job with more responsibility. That's the way it works on the job and that's the way it works in the Kingdom. Verse 47 tells us, "…he [the lord] will set him over all that he has."

The danger for us is to assume that the "lord" will stay away a long time, and will not come today, if He comes at all; after all, it's been 2,000 years and Jesus hasn't come yet. That kind of presumption can lead to many abuses of privilege. We have already seen that Jesus will come unexpectedly. Verse 50 reminds us, "…the lord of that servant will come in a day when he doesn't expect it, and in an hour when he doesn't know it."

The phrase "cut him to pieces" translates the Greek word *dichotomesei* which literally means to cut in two pieces, but can also be used to express the idea of being cut off or removed and the balance of the passage agrees with that idea.

The Wise and Foolish Virgins
Matthew 25:1-13

"Then the Kingdom of Heaven will be like ten virgins [bride's maids], who took their lamps, and went out to meet the bridegroom. ² Five of them were foolish, and five were wise. ³ Those who were foolish, when they took their lamps, took no oil with them, ⁴ but the wise took oil in their vessels with their lamps. ⁵ Now

while the bridegroom delayed, they all slumbered and slept. ⁶ But at midnight there was a cry, 'Behold! The bridegroom is coming! Come out to meet him!' ⁷ Then all those virgins arose, and trimmed their lamps. ⁸ The foolish said to the wise, 'Give us some of your oil, for our lamps are going out.' ⁹ But the wise answered, saying, 'What if there isn't enough for us and you? You go rather to those who sell, and buy for yourselves.' ¹⁰ While they went away to buy, the bridegroom came, and those who were ready went in with him to the marriage feast, and the door was shut. ¹¹ Afterward the other virgins also came, saying, 'Lord, Lord, open to us.' ¹² But he answered, 'Most certainly I tell you, I don't know you.' ¹³ Watch therefore, for you don't know the day nor the hour in which the Son of Man is coming.

Only Matthew records this parable on watchfulness, which has been subject to allegorical interpretation about Jesus' return at the end of the age and, given its placement with other "end time" parables that is probably His intent. It is impossible not to see the richness of the allegorical symbols and it is easy to jump in and begin dissecting it. In that setting, for example, Jesus is the "bridegroom" and the "virgins" represent the people of the world. When the "bridegroom" delayed His return, some people became complacent, but others remained prepared.

However, I believe it should be interpreted as a parable and, while it addresses Jesus' return, it can also apply to His advent, His first coming. That being the case it would mean the unmentioned bride would then represent Israel and the church.

Certainly "the Kingdom of Heaven" isn't "like ten virgins..." but it can be "compared" (KJV) to their experience in this parable. What was their experience? Some were prepared and accepted; some were not prepared and were rejected. "There is a time for preparation and a time when it is too late to prepare (BBC, p. 223);" this is the main point of the parable.

The events described still take place in parts of the Near East today and can be loosely compared to our custom of driving the bride and groom around town in decorated cars with horns honking. The big difference is that we go away for the honeymoon while they held open house for a week in their new home.

To travel at night involved a certain amount of risk and failure to carry extra oil would be like going out with weak batteries in the flashlight and no spares. What will you do when the light fails? Those who were unprepared didn't just miss the processional, they missed the whole party!

The Jews had the Scripture, but more importantly they had the actual writers of the Scripture. Because of this, they should have been prepared for the coming of the Messiah. The danger, and the admonition, isn't against sleeping, both groups slept. The danger is in being unprepared for the bridegroom. Since they were not prepared to receive him, the Jews were replaced by the Gentiles.

> You will say then, 'Branches were broken off, that I might be grafted in.' True; by their unbelief they were broken off, and you stand by your faith. Don't be conceited, but fear; for if God didn't spare the natural branches, neither will he spare you (Rom. 11:19-21).

In verse 12, "I don't know you," uses the perfect tense of the verb which could suggest "I have not known you." It's sad but anyone who has the opportunity for blessings can refuse to accept them.

Reward for Faithful Stewardship
Matthew 25:14-30

"For it is like a man, going into another country, who called his own servants, and entrusted his goods to them. [15] *To one he gave five talents, (a talent is about 30 kilograms or 66 pounds (usually used to weigh silver unless otherwise specified)) to another two, to another one; to each according to his own ability. Then he went on his journey.* [16] *Immediately he who received the five talents went and traded with them, and made another five talents.* [17] *In the same way, he also who got the two gained another two.* [18] *But he who received the one talent went away and dug in the earth, and hid his lord's money.*

[19] *"Now after a long time the lord of those servants came, and reconciled accounts with them.* [20] *He who received the five talents came and brought another five talents, saying, 'Lord, you delivered to me five talents. Behold, I have gained another five talents besides them.'*

[21] *"His lord said to him, 'Well done, good and faithful servant. You have been faithful over a few things, I will set you over many things. Enter into the joy of your lord.'*

[22] *"He also who got the two talents came and said, 'Lord, you delivered to me two talents. Behold, I have gained another two talents besides them.'*

[23] *"His lord said to him, 'Well done, good and faithful servant. You have been faithful over a few things, I will set you over many things. Enter into the joy of your lord.'*

[24] *"He also who had received the one talent came and said, 'Lord, I knew you that you are a hard man, reaping where you did not sow, and gathering where you did not scatter.* [25] *I was afraid, and went away and hid your talent in the earth. Behold, you have what is yours.'*

[26] *"But his lord answered him, 'You wicked and slothful servant. You knew that I reap where I didn't sow, and gather where I didn't scatter.* [27] *You ought therefore to have deposited my money with the bankers, and at my coming I should have received back my own with interest.* [28] *Take away therefore the talent from him, and give it to him who has the ten talents.* [29] *For to everyone who has will be given, and he will have abundance, but from him who doesn't have, even that which he has will be taken away.* [30] *Throw out the unprofitable servant into the outer darkness, where there will be weeping and gnashing of teeth.'*

This parable stresses the importance of dealing with the context of a Scripture passage. When we recognize that this is a part of Jesus' teaching directed to the Pharisees, the original application of this passage is different from our usual application. The original application probably made the unfaithful steward a representative of the scribes and Pharisees.

Their expressed goal was "to build a fence around the Law," to protect it. Unfortunately for them, Jesus had come to free people from those restrictive interpretations. He called for exploring new vistas of God's love and they weren't ready to make the investment.

Originally the word "talent" was a certain weight, so its value would depend on the material weighed. Naturally, gold would be worth more than silver or copper. The talent was the heaviest unit of weight in the Hebrew system and was equal to about 3000 shekels and varied from about 66-138 pounds, depending on which of four systems was used. Later usage applied it to money; instead of referring to a talent of gold people would just refer to a talent.

Ignoring the context, the point is simple, those who use what God gives them will be given more and those who try to keep what they have will lose it. This is a valid interpretation and is probably the best application for today.

In this teaching we can see four things that are important:

1. God gives people different "talents." What we have has come from God. We have different gifts, interests, and abilities, because each of us is unique.

2. The reward for a job well done is greater responsibility, not relaxation.

3. The greatest and saddest tragedy is not failing but in failing to try, sitting on the sidelines instead of getting in the game. The measure of greatness in found in attempting great things.

4. The way to keep something is to use it.

Sadly, many people make excuse for their failures. Like the Pharisees, in attempting to justify himself, the unfaithful servant attacked the character of his master. Many people claim that their lack of success is because of someone else, not their own failure. The Jews had been given much, but they had hidden it in the ground. We must be careful lest we do the same thing. Largely as a result of this parable, "talent" came to refer to abilities also. My dad wouldn't keep a job. It wasn't that he couldn't, it was that everyone he worked for was dishonorable. I've had quite a number of employers and all but a very few were fine people. My dad just needed an excuse to quit and move us to another town.

What about Jesus' return? What should our attitude be?

Jesus is coming back - we know this is true. Does this mean we must quit our jobs in order to serve God? No, it means we are to use our time, talents, and treasures diligently in order to serve God completely in whatever we do. For a few people, this may mean changing professions. For most of us, it means doing our daily work out of love for God (LASB, p. 1596).

It is worthwhile to note that the master gave each servant a different amount "to each according to his own ability." God never expects more from us than we are able to do. We are not all judged by the same standard, but by a standard specifically designed for us and our SHAPE, if I may borrow from Rick Warren's *Purpose Driven Life* illustration again.

The Basis for Judgment
Matthew 25:31-46

"But when the Son of Man comes in his glory, and all the holy angels with him, then he will sit on the throne of his glory. [32] Before him all the nations will be gathered, and he will separate them one from another, as a shepherd separates the sheep from the goats. [33] He will set the sheep on his right hand, but the goats on the left. [34] Then the King will tell those on his right hand, 'Come, blessed of my Father, inherit the Kingdom prepared for you from the foundation of the world; [35] for I was hungry, and you gave me food to eat. I was thirsty, and you gave me drink. I was a stranger, and you took me in. [36] I was naked, and you clothed me. I was sick, and you visited me. I was in prison, and you came to me.'

[37] "Then the righteous will answer him, saying, 'Lord, when did we see you hungry, and feed you; or thirsty, and give you a drink? [38] When did we see you as a stranger, and take you in; or naked, and clothe you? [39] When did we see you sick, or in prison, and come to you?'

[40] "The King will answer them, 'Most certainly I tell you, because you did it to one of the least of these my brothers, (the word for "brothers" here may be also correctly translated "brothers and sisters" or "siblings") you did it to me.' [41] Then he will say also to those on the left hand, 'Depart from me, you cursed, into the eternal fire which is prepared for the devil and his angels; [42] for I was hungry, and you didn't give me food to eat; I was thirsty, and you gave me no drink; [43] I was a stranger, and you didn't take me in; naked, and you didn't clothe me; sick, and in prison, and you didn't visit me.'

[44] "Then they will also answer, saying, 'Lord, when did we see you hungry, or thirsty, or a stranger, or naked, or sick, or in prison, and didn't help you?'

[45] "Then he will answer them, saying, 'Most certainly I tell you, because you didn't do it to one of the least of these, you didn't do it to me.' [46] These will go away into eternal punishment, but the righteous into eternal life."

While this is a parable, it is also far more than a parable, it is a prophesy of the coming and final judgment. Stagg calls it "the standard or principle of judgment, which is one's true relationship to Christ as reflected in his ministry to the least of his people, especially in their situations of need (BBC, p. 226)," and it is a favorite passage of mine.

Except at his trial before Pilate, this is the only place Jesus refers to himself as King. The picture comes from Ezekiel, "As for you, O my flock, thus says the Lord Yahweh: 'Behold, I judge between sheep and sheep, the rams and the male goats'" (Eze. 34:17). It was common practice to pasture sheep and goats together and separate them at night.

"All the nations" are involved in this event and they are all judged by the same criterion, not their belief or profession of faith in Jesus, but by their actions. The "sheep" and "goats" were easy for a Jewish shepherd to identify, they looked very different. While the "righteous" and "cursed" are not as easy to spot, but the "King" has no difficulty in separating them.

"In a sense, Jesus does not so much judge as declare judgments already made by the Father (BBC, p. 227)." It's important to recall that the standard of judgment is the same for all people and it's a standard that everyone can meet; its ministry in the simple things: a meal, some clothes, caring for the sick, etc. "If we really wish to delight a parent's heart...help his child (DSB, p. 326)."

The deeds described here, often called "deeds of mercy," were acts of compassion shown to the helpless... These good deeds are not attempts to merit God's favor; rather, they arise from a love for Christ that results in compassion toward others... (NLTSB, p. 1631)

The surprising thing to me is that neither group seems to be surprised or alarmed about those included with them. It isn't until after judgment is pronounced that they are surprised and even then, their focus is not on being with the wrong crowd, but in justifying their inaction.

The ministry provided by the "righteous" was to respond, in a spontaneous manner, to the needs of hurting people. They did not think of themselves as doing something for the Lord, they were just helping people in need. "Place a mouse before a cat and one sees what a cat is; place a person in need before a true child of God and one sees what a child of God is (BBC, p. 227)."

Much like the unfaithful steward in the prior passage, the "goats" try to place the blame for their failure not on themselves but on God, "when did we see you...and didn't help you?" In other words, Jesus, if You had told us it was You, we'd have done something, but we're not going to help people who are lazy, or won't help themselves, that sends the wrong message.

What about the "the least of these my brothers"? Who are they? There has been a great deal of discussion and debate...

Some have said they are the Jews; others say they are all Christians; still others say they are suffering people everywhere. Such a debate is much like the lawyer's earlier question to Jesus, "Who is my neighbor?" (Luke 10:29). The point of the parable is not the *who*, but the *what* - the importance of serving where service is needed (LASB, p. 1597).

This is a statement about the judgment, "eternal fire," "eternal punishment," and "eternal life" all use the same Greek word *aionios* for "eternal," therefore the length of time is the same for all. If Heaven lasts forever, then Hell must also last forever and if Hell doesn't last forever, then Heaven can't last forever. You can't have it the way you want it. I should also point out that *aionios* can also refer to a quality of life, a life far superior to anything we can understand in this age.

Again, we see the condemnation is on the negative, as it was with the previous parable.

...it is not so much positive wrong-doing that evokes the severest censure, as the utter failure to do good. The sins of omission are seen to be even more damning than the sins of commission...those on the left hand are severely punished for failing to notice the many opportunities for showing kindness which had been given them (TNTC, p. 239).

It is my personal conviction that the sins of omission are deliberate decisions to do nothing; they are not simply oversights involving things we didn't see. We make a decision "not to get involved"!

In eternity, there is a new dimension to time. It is no longer reckoned by the ticking of a clock or the vibrating of a quartz crystal. There is a timelessness about it. I'm sorry but I believe the words to "Amazing Grace" are wrong... "When we've been there 10,000 years..." Eternity is one great, long day. Revelation 22:5a says, "There will be no night, and they need no lamp light; for the Lord God will illuminate them. They will reign forever and ever."

It is suggested that this is also a picture of the judgment of the Church; I would suggest it could be a judgment of church membership. Far too many of us place our faith in the fact that we have "joined the church," a common expression in the Southern Baptist churches I have been part of. As important as formal identification with a local church is, it isn't the end all for salvation.

The Plot Thickens
Matthew 26:1-5

When Jesus had finished all these words, he said to his disciples, [2] "You know that after two days the Passover is coming, and the Son of Man will be delivered up to be crucified."

³ Then the chief priests, the scribes, and the elders of the people were gathered together in the court of the high priest, who was called Caiaphas. ⁴ They took counsel together that they might take Jesus by deceit, and kill him. ⁵ But they said, "Not during the feast, lest a riot occur among the people."

Each year in remembrance of the Exodus, a Pascal lamb was killed at the Temple and was eaten between sundown and midnight. Passover, which began on the fourteenth day of Nisan, was the time all Jews who could do so were expected to go to Jerusalem for its celebration and to worship in the Temple.

"Matthew makes it clear. Mark and Luke do not, that Jesus knew that it would be at the coming Passover, due to begin in two days' time, that he would be handed over to the Roman authorities for crucifixion (TNTC, P. 241)." Peter states, "…being delivered up by the determined counsel and foreknowledge of God, you have taken by the hand of lawless men, crucified and killed (Acts 2:23)" making it clear that all these things where with the knowledge and consent of the Father.

While Jesus didn't seek His own death, He did accept and anticipate its inevitability. Here again He was aware of what is about to happen and warned His followers about it.

As I have said, scholars have often debated when Jesus knew His mission and that He would die by crucifixion, which wasn't the Jewish method of execution, that was stoning, His "Messianic consciousness." Whenever it was, He certainly knew it all at this time, for He says, "the Son of Man will be delivered up to be crucified."

The leaders of the Jews: "…took counsel together that they might take Jesus by deceit, and kill him." They didn't need to meet and decide what to do about Him; they had already made up their minds about that; they met to decide how they were going to accomplish it.

Caiaphas, the High Priest, was appointed by the Roman governor. The office was intended to be a life-time job and was hereditary from a descendant of Aaron, but it had become almost a revolving door situation. Barclay tells us that between 37 BC and 67 AD there were at least twenty-eight who held the office, an average of less than three years each. By that standard, Caiaphas lasted a long time, from 18-36 AD, so he must have been very willing to cooperate with the Roman governor (DSB, p. 327).

With almost three million people in the city and the high religious and national feelings that would be in the atmosphere, it could have been volatile. In fact, the desire to maintain his office was probably the motivation for not arresting Jesus during the Passover. They had seen how the people responded to Jesus and if they caused a riot, Caiaphas would have been gone very quickly.

The die was cast. There will be no turning back by either Jesus or the Jewish leadership.

Impractical Theology
Matthew 26:6-13

Now when Jesus was in Bethany, in the house of Simon the leper, ⁷ a woman came to him having an alabaster jar of very expensive ointment, and she poured it on his head as he sat at the table. ⁸ But when his disciples saw this, they were indignant, saying, "Why this waste? ⁹ For this ointment might have been sold for much, and given to the poor."

¹⁰ However, knowing this, Jesus said to them, "Why do you trouble the woman? Because she has done a good work for me. ¹¹ For you always have the poor with you; but you don't always have me. ¹² For in pouring this ointment on my body, she did it to prepare me for burial. [13] Most certainly I tell you, wherever this Good News is preached in the whole world, what this woman has done will also be spoken of as a memorial of her."

The record of this event is almost the same in both Matthew and Mark and is so similar in John that we take it to be the same event. Neither Matthew nor Mark identified the woman, but John says she was Mary, the sister of Lazarus and Martha (John 12:3).

A couple of problems we should notice are the timing of the event and the event itself. John says,

Then six days before the Passover, Jesus came to Bethany, where Lazarus was, who had been dead, whom he raised from the dead. So they made him a supper there. Martha served, but Lazarus was one of those who sat at the table with him (John 12:1-2).

And he said Mary "poured it on Jesus' feet" not his head.

Mark said the value of the perfume was "a year's wages" which the disciples considered a "waste." Jesus emphasized that not all Christian service must be "practical" or directed "to the poor." And sometimes it is a good thing to be extravagant. Barclay points out four things:

1. The event shows "love's extravagance," she took her most precious possession and poured it out on Jesus. Love doesn't calculate the cost; it gives until there is nothing left to give. The concern is not that I have given too much, but too little. [Have you ever gone over-board on a gift for a loved one?]

2. It shows that there are times when common sense is forgotten. Only extravagance can show what we want to show. "A gift is never really a gift when we can easily afford it..." [Have you ever done something "stupid" to show your love?]

3. It shows "that certain things must be done when the opportunity arises or they can never be done at all." [It's that old *carpe diem* thing.]

4. It shows "the fragrance of a lovely deed lasts forever...this shines like an oasis of light in a darkening world (DSB, pp. 329-330)."

It's not always easy to decide how much to give, whether in time, talent, or treasure, so it is important to allow God to set the limits.

Where was Jesus when this event occurred? He was "in the house of Simon the Leper..." Why not go to Lazarus' home, it was also in Bethany and there would be no cause for offence? We, as Jesus admonished His followers, should go where we're invited and remain there and minister to those we meet there. Was that a place a "good" Jew would have been? What about a "good" Christian? Should we be in bars, in AIDS wards, in the "red light district"? If there is ministry needed, one of us should be there to provide it!

John 12:4 tells us it is Judas, the treasurer, the betrayer, who raised the objection. Did he only want to get his hands on the money for his own purposes? John 12:6 answers our question? "Now he said this, not because he cared for the poor, but because he was a thief, and having the money box, used to steal what was put into it." "It is not the lack, but the love of money, that is the root of all evil (MH)."

Nard, for that is what this ointment was, was popular with those who could afford it and if this identification of Mary the sister of Lazarus is correct, she could afford it. "The only use of this was to refresh and exhilarate—a grateful compliment in the East, amid the closeness of a heated atmosphere, with many guests at a feast. Such was the form in which Mary's love to Christ, at so much cost to herself, poured itself out (CCE)." Dan Brown might have done better to have identified Mary the sister of Lazarus as Jesus' supposed wife in the *Da Vinci Code*.

The statement, "For you always have the poor with you," doesn't negate our responsibility toward helping poor people and it evokes Deuteronomy 15:11, "For the poor will never cease out of the land." which goes on to say: "Therefore I command you to surely open your hand to your brother, to your needy, and to your poor, in your land." "Rather, by saying this, Jesus highlighted the special sacrifice Mary made for him (LASB, p. 1598)."

Betrayed by a Friend
Matthew 26:14-16

Then one of the twelve, who was called Judas Iscariot, went to the chief priests, [15] and said, "What are you willing to give me, that I should deliver him to you?" They weighed out for him thirty pieces of silver. [16] From that time he sought opportunity to betray him.

There are several passages from Zachariah that bear on these events, but "If all that we can find here is a 'proof text,' we fail to understand the use of the OT in the time of Jesus, and certainly its use in the gospel (AB, p. 317)."

We don't know exactly why Judas offered to betray Jesus, but it has been the subject of a great deal of speculation. Possibly the most popular idea today is that Judas knew Jesus' power and this was an attempt to force Him into a situation where He would have to use that power to save His own life. After all, there is no greater instinct than self-preservation, is there? …not always!

We believe Judas was a Zealot and he may have reasoned that this "push" was needed to begin the revolt around which all the Zealots would rally to throw off the Roman rulers. With Jesus' power, He could easily defeat the Romans. He could be the Messiah they expected, and looked for, the deliverer God had promised. But He would not have been who God wanted Him to be. Sometimes we get tired of waiting for God to act, so we try to "force His hand." We're often like the impatient, hungry buzzard who told his buzzard friend, "Patience my posterior, I'm gonna go kill something!" (At least that's the way I'm allowed to tell the story.)

This event closely followed the extravagant act of Mary anointing Jesus with the costly perfume and Judas' objection and desire to sell it. As we said above, John 12:6 points out Judas' averseness, so another popular idea is that he did it for the money. If it is the desire for money, the price he received from the chief priests wasn't very much, so it was a poor deal.

The price, "thirty silver coins" was the price of a slave; Exodus 21:32 says, "If the bull gores a male servant or a female servant, thirty shekels of silver shall be given to their master, and the ox shall be stoned."

Judas' role was not to tell the "chief priests" where Jesus was, all they had to do was follow the crowds that followed Jesus around to know that; Judas' task was to tell them when Jesus would be alone so He could be taken without fear of the people rescuing Him. Betrayal, and that is what Judas was doing, is a sad thing. Your enemies are always out to get you, but betrayal can only come from a person you trust. Whatever his motives, Judas betrayed his friend, Jesus.

Not to excuse Judas' action, but someone was going to do it. Jesus said, "You know that after two days the Passover is coming, and the Son of Man will be delivered up to be crucified" (Matt. 26:2). Someone, somewhere, in two days would do it because Jesus came to die to atone for our sin, and it was time for it to happen. It can rightly be said that we are as guilty as Judas was because Jesus died for us.

The Final Passover?
Matthew 26:17-25

Now on the first day of unleavened bread, the disciples came to Jesus, saying to him, "Where do you want us to prepare for you to eat the Passover?"

18 He said, "Go into the city to a certain person, and tell him, 'The Teacher says, "My time is at hand. I will keep the Passover at your house with my disciples."'"

19 The disciples did as Jesus commanded them, and they prepared the Passover. 20 Now when evening had come, he was reclining at the table with the twelve disciples. 21 As they were eating, he said, "Most certainly I tell you that one of you will betray me."

22 They were exceedingly sorrowful, and each began to ask him, "It isn't me, is it, Lord?"

23 He answered, "He who dipped his hand with me in the dish, the same will betray me. 24 The Son of Man goes, even as it is written of him, but woe to that man through whom the Son of Man is betrayed! It would be better for that man if he had not been born."

25 Judas, who betrayed him, answered, "It isn't me, is it, Rabbi?"

He said to him, "You said it."

"It is clear that all three Synoptic Gospels regard the last Supper as the Passover meal…[unfortunately] narratives, which are regarded as evidence…are self-contradictory in this matter… (TNTC, p. 244)." In that regard, timing has been a problem with Jesus' last week: what happened when, was there a day "off" when He did nothing that was reported, what is this "supper" and how is it related to Passover and when did Jesus actually die on the cross. For some of us it is important that He be "slain" at the same time as the Passover lambs were being slaughtered by the priests for the people's Passover meals.

Some conservatives believe, as I do, that Jesus was not crucified on Friday, but on Thursday. Why? The conflict comes from passages in John that the crucifixion occurred while the Pascal lambs were being killed. "Now **before** [my emphasis] the feast of the Passover, Jesus, knowing that his time had come that he would depart from this world to the Father…" (John 13:1a). "They led Jesus therefore from Caiaphas into the Praetorium. It was early, and they themselves didn't enter into the Praetorium, that they might not be defiled, but might eat the Passover" (John 18:28) "Now it was the Preparation Day of the Passover, at about the sixth hour [6 AM by the Roman "clock"]. He [Pilate] said to the Jews, 'Behold, your King!'" (John 19:14) "Purge out the old yeast, that you may be a new lump, even as you are unleavened. For indeed Christ, our Passover, has been sacrificed in our place" (1 Cor. 5:7).

Would that invalidate the Synoptic account of the celebration? It could be that the meal took place early because Jesus knew what was happening, but there is no mention of the various Pascal dishes, lamb, bitter herbs, etc., being served. It isn't really important when it happened; the important thing is that it did happen.

It would appear that there were two calendars in use at that time. Under an old, solar calendar, Passover was observed on a fixed day but under the lunar calendar it fluctuated based on the lunar cycle. The second calendar used by some sectarians, and probably the early church, would allow Jesus to observe the actual Passover with His disciples away from the pressure of the Elders and still have been sacrificed as the Pascal lambs were also being slain.

Passover was special. From a theological perspective it was not the most important feast of the Jews, that would have been *Yom Kipper*, but in the hearts of the people it was. It was the goal of every Jew to be in Jerusalem for Passover every time he could and at least once in his lifetime. "Next year in Jerusalem" is still a phrase many use to close the meal [Seder] today.

According to the rules that had developed, the Passover meal was to be eaten within the city of Jerusalem. Because of this, all the residents were required to open their homes to accommodate Jews from all over the world that had come for the occasion.

Verse 18 leaves little doubt that Jesus made preparation for this last meal with the disciples, "He said, 'Go into the city to a certain person, and tell him, "The Teacher says, 'My time is at hand. I will keep the Passover at your house with my disciples.'"'"

An interesting aspect of this passage is that none of the disciples suspect any of the others of being the betrayer, but it appears that each suspected he might be. Certainly, none of them suspected Judas and Jesus did not expose Judas either, although Matthew makes it clear that Jesus knew he was the one.

An interesting thing about Judas both here and when he kisses Jesus in the garden is that Judas is the first to speak. This was a definite no-no, especially in Judaism. A disciple, a pupil, would NEVER speak before the teacher spoke to them. Couldn't Judas have been recognized from the fact that he dipped his hand into the bowl? No, because most of the other disciples had done the same thing. That's the way they ate, "family style."

Institution of the Lord's Supper
Matthew 26:26-29

As they were eating, Jesus took bread, gave thanks for (TR reads "blessed" instead of "gave thanks for") it, and broke it. He gave to the disciples, and said, "Take, eat; this is my body." [27] *He took the cup, gave thanks, and gave to them, saying, "All of you drink it,* [28] *for this is my blood of the new covenant, which is poured out for many for the remission of sins.* [29] *But I tell you that I will not drink of this fruit of the vine from now on, until that day when I drink it anew with you in my Father's Kingdom."*

Some suggest Jesus did not actually eat the meal. Why not? He was as hungry as any of the rest of them. I am not sure why they raise the question and I mention it only because you should to be aware of it. Undoubtedly, Jesus was the host, because He was their leader.

The "new" supper instituted that night was clearly intended to be a memorial of Jesus' sacrifice, He said, "Do this in memory of me" (Luke 22:19b). Each of the Jewish feasts were memorials, that is they had a historical connection with their past, so when we participate in Communion, we need to make the connection with this first Lord's Supper also.

The Passover commemorated their deliverance from slavery in Egypt. Their safety was guaranteed by the blood of a lamb sprinkled on the door post and lentil and the symbolism Jesus used made Him the Pascal lamb sacrificed and sprinkled for us. "This ordinance of the Lord's supper is to us the Passover supper, by which we commemorate a much greater deliverance than that of Israel out of Egypt (MH)."

He used the word "covenant," a word they were very familiar with; God made a covenant with Abraham and renewed it often with the leaders and/or the people. A covenant implies an agreement in which two or more parties will work together, each doing something for the other.

Notice, the bread represents Jesus' body and the cup represents His "blood...poured out for many for the remission of sins." The symbol of "bread" goes beyond just His physical body; it also represents His spiritual body, which is the Church, that is the entire Church universal. The blood, while it symbolizes forgiveness also represents life; "But flesh with its life, that is, its blood, you shall not eat" (Gen. 9:4).

Was Judas there for the Lord's Supper? Matthew and Mark don't make it clear when Judas left. Luke indicates that he didn't leave until after the Supper, he says:

He took bread, and when he had given thanks, he broke, and gave it to them, saying, "This is my body which is given for you. Do this in memory of me." Likewise, he took the cup after supper, saying, "This cup is the new covenant in my blood, which is poured out for you. But behold, the hand of him who betrays me is with me on the table. The Son of Man indeed goes, as it has been determined, but woe to that man through whom he is betrayed! (Like 22:19-22).

John does not tell us when Judas left and doesn't mention the Supper.

I think it would be illogical for him to leave before or during the Seder, if it was in fact the Passover meal, but it is a theological problem for us because it places an apostate at the Communion table and many conservatives don't want Judas to be there. If he was there, he was just the first such person to partake "in a way unworthy" (1 Cor. 11:27b) but he undoubtedly wasn't the last.

It's sad that Christendom has divided over what the Supper means and who should participate, or be excluded, when the church gathers for the memorial, a symbol of unity has become a divisive issue.

False Bravery
Matthew 26:30-35

When they had sung a hymn, they went out to the Mount of Olives.

[31] Then Jesus said to them, "All of you will be made to stumble because of me tonight, for it is written, 'I will strike the shepherd, and the sheep of the flock will be scattered' (Zech. 13:7). [32] But after I am raised up, I will go before you into Galilee."

[33] But Peter answered him, "Even if all will be made to stumble because of you, I will never be made to stumble."

[34] Jesus said to him, "Most certainly I tell you that tonight, before the rooster crows, you will deny me three times."

[35] Peter said to him, "Even if I must die with you, I will not deny you." All of the disciples also said likewise.

The hymn they sang could have been:

Give thanks to Yahweh, for he is good; for his loving kindness endures forever.

Give thanks to the God of gods; for his loving kindness endures forever.

Give thanks to the Lord of lords; for his loving kindness endures forever:

To him who alone does great wonders; for his loving kindness endures forever: (Ps. 136:1-4)

It goes on to tell of God's mighty acts of creation, deliverance from Egypt, and continuing provision for His people, and was the last of several psalms usually sung during the Passover meal.

The Mount of Olives is on a north-south ridge east of Jerusalem and is a prominent feature of Jerusalem's profile. It is a gentle, rounded hill, covered with olive trees, rising to a height of 2,676 feet and overlooks the Temple. It was from the summit of one of those hills that the disciples watched Jesus ascend into heaven (Acts 1:11-12).

The Mount of Olives is mentioned by the prophet Zechariah regarding the return of the Messiah:

His feet will stand in that day on the Mount of Olives, which is before Jerusalem on the east; and the Mount of Olives will be split in two, from east to west, making a very great valley. Half of the mountain will move toward the north, and half of it toward the south (Zech. 14:4).

This supports the belief that when Jesus returns to earth, He will alight on the Mount of Olives, at the same place from which He ascended into heaven. Its proximity to Jerusalem's walls made it a strategic danger. Titus had his headquarters on the northern portion of the ridge during his siege of Jerusalem in 70 AD.

As always, Jesus was more concerned about others than Himself and He tries to prepare them for the days to come.

Jesus said, "I will go before you into Galilee," which could mean He would go on and they would follow later, or that He would be with them and lead them to Galilee. Whatever it meant, they would all return to the region where their ministry together began to regroup and plan how the disciples would continue the mission.

Jesus warned that the disciples would "stumble," which is a good translation because it is the same root word used to identify a person who is offended by or ashamed of someone or some action. Certainly, it was prophetic, because they did run, but like the prodigal, they returned and were welcomed back.

There can be no doubt that Peter was a brave man, but we, like he, must be careful when we boast about what we will do. A person who is brave in one context may be a coward in another and one who is a coward in one context may be very brave in another.

Improper self-confidence, like that of Peter, is the first step to a fall. There is a proneness in all of us to be over-confident. But those fall soonest and foulest, who are the most confident in themselves. Those are least safe, who think themselves most secure. Satan is active to lead such astray; they are most off their guard: God leaves them to themselves, to humble them (MH).

Jesus knew how Peter would respond, but He also knew Peter's heart. Peter wanted desperately to do the right thing, but like many of us, he wasn't prepared at this time. Later, when he had grown stronger, he would be able to stand firm and he did. "While Peter's denial receives the most attention, *all the other disciples* denied or avoided association with Christ as well (NLTSB, p. 1634)."

The Burden of Sacrifice
Matthew 26:36-46

Then Jesus came with them to a place called Gethsemane, and said to his disciples, "Sit here, while I go there and pray." [37] He took with him Peter and the two sons of Zebedee, and began to be sorrowful and severely troubled. [38] Then he said to them, "My soul is exceedingly sorrowful, even to death. Stay here, and watch with me."

[39] He went forward a little, fell on his face, and prayed, saying, "My Father, if it is possible, let this cup pass away from me; nevertheless, not what I desire, but what you desire."

[40] He came to the disciples, and found them sleeping, and said to Peter, "What, couldn't you watch with me for one hour? [41] Watch and pray, that you don't enter into temptation. The spirit indeed is willing, but the flesh is weak."

[42] Again, a second time he went away, and prayed, saying, "My Father, if this cup can't pass away from me unless I drink it, your desire be done." [43] He came again and found them sleeping, for their eyes were heavy. [44] He left them again, went away, and prayed a third time, saying the same words. [45] Then he came to his disciples, and said to them, "Sleep on now, and take your rest. Behold, the hour is at hand, and the Son of Man is betrayed into the hands of sinners. [46] Arise, let's be going. Behold, he who betrays me is at hand."

Jerusalem was a fairly small area on the top of a hill. Every available piece of land was used for buildings so there was no room for gardens so they were built outside the city by wealthy men. Gethsemane was probably such a garden on the Mount of Olives where Jesus may have gone often with His disciples to pray, rest or just to talk with them. From its name we believe the garden was located in an olive grove containing an olive press.

All four gospel writers give special attention to Jesus' final visit to Gethsemane, which was undoubtedly a time of final instruction to the disciples and a time of soul-searching prayer for Jesus. All the disciples went to the garden, but only Peter, James and John went with Jesus to the final location to "watch" and "pray." Jesus asked the three to "watch" while He prayed. We aren't sure if He meant to be on guard for those who were coming to arrest Him or if it had some other meaning.

Nothing shows the humanity of Jesus more this this time in the garden. If He were only God, He wouldn't fear death, because God can't die. If He were only human, He might not have prayed for the Father's Will to be done. But since He was/is the God/man, completely divine and completely human, He could go through with it because He knew what was on the other side. Not once, but three times, His prayer was for God to relieve Him of His coming death. His prayer was not an attempt to disobey God's Will nor to change God's plan; His prayer clearly showed His willingness to obey the Father. "My Father, if this cup can't pass away from me unless I drink it, your desire be done" (verse 42). It also teaches us that we can pray that we might not have to endure difficult, even dangerous, situations and circumstances but should be willing to proceed.

Jesus' desire that the Father's "will be done" would echo what He taught the disciples to pray in the Model Prayer, "Let your will be done, as in heaven, so on earth" (Matt. 6:10b). Talk is cheap. Jesus could not only "talk the talk," He would "walk the walk."

Could Jesus have avoided the cross? As His prayer says, yes, He could have. It was His choice whether to go on with God's plan or quit. If this isn't true then there was no real temptation and this was only a pious lie. Because Jesus faced and overcame such strong temptation, we can identify with Him as a very human, personal Lord and Savior. "For in that he himself has suffered being tempted, he is able to help those who are tempted (Heb. 2:18)."

Few of us have learned to sacrifice; we give out of our left-over money and things we no longer want or need, not out of our poverty.

C. S. Lewis didn't talk about percentage giving. He said the only safe rule is to give more than we can spare. Our charities should pinch and hamper us. If we live at the same level of affluence as other people who have our level of income, we are probably giving away too little. Obstacles include greed for luxurious living, greed for money itself, fear of financial insecurity, and showy pride" (Kathryn Ann Lindskoog, *Hymns for the Family of God* Paragon Associates, Inc. Nashville, Tennessee, 1976, p. 514).

Can we truly sacrifice without feeling the burden of it? Can there be sacrifice without some kind of pain? I think not. But prayer prepares us for any coming difficulty. Barclay says, "Jesus rose from his knees to go to the battle of life. That is what prayer is for. In prayer a man kneels before God that he may stand erect before men (DSB, p. 350)."

We must remember that often the biblical messengers have shown us how weak the biblical leaders were. You wouldn't have fallen asleep at such an important time, would you? Yet, in spite of their weakness, they grew into the larger-than-life people we so admire today.

Paul verified this:

…but God chose the foolish things of the world that he might put to shame those who are wise. God chose the weak things of the world, that he might put to shame the things that are strong; (1 Cor. 1:27). He has said to me, "My grace is sufficient for you, for my power is made perfect in weakness." Most gladly therefore I will rather glory in my weaknesses, that the power of Christ may rest on me. Therefore I take pleasure in weaknesses, in injuries, in necessities, in persecutions, in distresses, for Christ's sake. For when I am weak, then am I strong (2 Cor. 12:9-10).

We could address the question: "Should a person pray for or about something more than once." Verse 44 says, "He left them again, went away, and prayed a third time, saying the same words" I am one of those people who says, "I prayed about it, now I'll leave it to God. However, if Jesus prayed about the same thing three times, I guess it's appropriate for us to pray about something more than once. Possibly it depends on how much we want to see the thing accomplished.

Betrayal and Arrest
Matthew 26:47-56

*While he was still speaking, behold, Judas, one of the twelve, came, and with him a great multitude with swords and clubs, from the chief priests and elders of the people. * [48] *Now he who betrayed him gave them a* *sign, saying, "Whoever I kiss, he is the one. Seize him." ⁴⁹ Immediately he came to Jesus, and said, "Hail, Rabbi!" and kissed him.*

⁵⁰ Jesus said to him, "Friend, why are you here?" Then they came and laid hands on Jesus, and took him. ⁵¹ Behold, one of those who were with Jesus stretched out his hand, and drew his sword, and struck the servant of the high priest, and struck off his ear. ⁵² Then Jesus said to him, "Put your sword back into its place, for all those who take the sword will die by the sword. ⁵³ Or do you think that I couldn't ask my Father, and he would even now send me more than twelve legions of angels? ⁵⁴ How then would the Scriptures be fulfilled that it must be so?"

⁵⁵ In that hour Jesus said to the multitudes, "Have you come out as against a robber with swords and clubs to seize me? I sat daily in the temple teaching, and you didn't arrest me. ⁵⁶ But all this has happened, that the Scriptures of the prophets might be fulfilled."

Judas knew where to find Jesus "Now Judas, who betrayed him, also knew the place, for Jesus often met there with his disciples" (John 18:2). He also knew that Jesus would be alone with His disciples, so it would be a "safe" place for the arrest.

The Pharisees made the fatal mistake of thinking if they eliminated the leader, the movement would die on its own. They weren't concerned about a bunch of uneducated nobodies continuing the work after their leader was dead. The communists made the same mistake with Christians behind the old Iron Curtain.

Judas' greeting, a kiss, was a common greeting for a teacher, but the word used here is one that indicates a gushy show of affection; it is the word used for a lover's kiss meaning "to kiss repeatedly and fervently."

Was the "kiss" to identify Jesus? No. Who came to arrest him? The Temple police! They had to know who Jesus was. They had undoubtedly seen him in the Temple and probably even spied on Him for the High Priest, however they didn't know where to find Him alone, and in the darkness, there were no street lights, they didn't want Him to slip away in the confusion.

Barclay suggests that Judas kissed Jesus, as His teacher, and meant it, then stood back to watch, expecting Jesus would act. Maybe He thought Jesus would step into a phone booth and change into His Super Messiah costume and smite the bad guys, so to speak. Maybe that's why we don't see Judas again until he has decided that his plan has failed and he prepares to commit suicide, as would be in keeping with the Oriental custom of killing oneself to "save face" in the midst of a defeat.

At that moment, Peter was ready to take on the whole mob, even if he had to do it alone. When he drew his sword and cut off the High Priest's servant's ear (John 18:10), that wasn't what he was attempting to do, undoubtedly the servant ducked. How often we have used the wrong approach, sometimes even using an evil method, to try to accomplish something good, but it can't be done. The ends don't ever justify the means.

There are two important things to remember about Jesus' death, it was His choice and it was God's plan. Jesus' weapon was not a sword, but a cross. He didn't have to return to Jerusalem, He didn't have to "take on" the establishment and He could have slipped out in the darkness. He chose not to do those things. "Jesus died, not because men killed him, but because he chose to die (DSB, p. 351)."

How prophetic, "all those who take the sword will die by the sword." In less than forty years, Jerusalem was utterly destroyed and the Jews were scattered again, but the Church has continued to move forward.

Kangaroo Kourt
Matthew 26:57-68

Then all the disciples left him, and fled. ⁵⁷ *Those who had taken Jesus led him away to Caiaphas the high priest, where the scribes and the elders were gathered together.* ⁵⁸ *But Peter followed him from a distance, to the court of the high priest, and entered in and sat with the officers, to see the end.* ⁵⁹ *Now the chief priests, the elders, and the whole council sought false testimony against Jesus, that they might put him to death;* ⁶⁰ *and they found none. Even though many false witnesses came forward, they found none. But at last two false witnesses came forward,* ⁶¹ *and said, "This man said, 'I am able to destroy the temple of God, and to build it in three days.'"*

⁶² *The high priest stood up, and said to him, "Have you no answer? What is this that these testify against you?"* ⁶³ *But Jesus held his peace. The high priest answered him, "I adjure you by the living God, that you tell us whether you are the Christ, the Son of God."*

⁶⁴ *Jesus said to him, "You have said it. Nevertheless, I tell you, after this you will see the Son of Man sitting at the right hand of Power, and coming on the clouds of the sky."*

⁶⁵ *Then the high priest tore his clothing, saying, "He has spoken blasphemy! Why do we need any more witnesses? Behold, now you have heard his blasphemy.* ⁶⁶ *What do you think?"*

They answered, "He is worthy of death!" ⁶⁷ *Then they spit in his face and beat him with their fists, and some slapped him,* ⁶⁸ *saying, "Prophesy to us, you Christ! Who hit you?"*

This is the first of the three events we call "trials" and could probably be best described as a preliminary hearing. "It would seem clear from Matthew's narrative that the Sanhedrin were already in session while Jesus was being arrested (TNTC, p. 253)." Verse 59 says, "…the chief priests, the elders, and the whole council sought false testimony against Jesus, that they might put him to death…" "The verb tense suggests an extended, perhaps desperate, attempt to find any testimony that could lead to a formal accusation… (NLTSB, p. 1635)." We might say, "Let's hang him, then give him a fair trial." Their decision had been made and they weren't going to allow technicalities to get in the way.

They needed a "crime" and enough evidence and testimony to bring Jesus before Pilate, because they didn't have authority to put Him to death themselves. Later, in Acts 6-7, they would kill Stephen without bringing him before Pilate although it is not clear whether Stephen was officially convicted and executed by the Sanhedrin or it was a "lynch" mob without any pretense of a "trial." When my mind is made up, don't confuse me with facts.

Often the question is asked, "Was this a legal meeting?" It wasn't, and doesn't matter unless we have some agenda. If it makes you feel better, it was probably an illegal meeting because everything was supposed to be done in the light of day; breaking the law, when it suits us is not uncommon; some of us do it every time we get on the freeway. Are we going to overturn the decision, say Jesus was convicted before a Kangaroo Kourt, and therefore His sacrifice was invalid? I hope not.

Jesus didn't try to defend Himself, why should He, they weren't open to the truth and, with the number of times He had "turned the tables" on them, He could certainly have "gotten off" leaving us without a Savior. Sometimes it's better to keep quiet than to argue.

Since Jesus claimed to be the "Son of God," this was something that could be taken to Pilate, because they saw the Messiah as a political leader. Strange, they longed for a Messiah who would deliver them from the Romans, but they weren't going to follow Jesus even if He came riding on a white horse.

The Sanhedrin, a council or assembly, was the ruling body and Supreme Court of justice for the Jews during the New Testament period. It was presided over by the high priest and, for the Jews it had authority over all religious, civil, and criminal matters. It was composed of 71 elders and included: Joseph of Arimathea, Gamaliel, Nicodemus, Ananias and the high priests Annas and Caiaphas among its membership. Some have suggested Paul was a member before his conversion, but we don't know for sure.

The Sanhedrin probably grew out of a council of advisors to the high priest when the Jews were ruled by the Persian and Greek empires and started as a group of priests and prominent lay people. As the influence of the scribes grew, they acquired positions also. So, the Sanhedrin came to include Sadducees, the chief priests and elders, Pharisees and scribes. Paul often used their theological differences to his advantage.

After 6 AD, the Sanhedrin's authority was limited to Judea. However, Jews everywhere respected the Sanhedrin and accepted its decisions. In Judea the Romans allowed them to make most of the governing decisions and even allowed them to have their own police force.

Unlike our court system where cases can be appealed; the Jews couldn't appeal the verdict of a lower court to them for review and reversal. They only handled special, important matters and issues the lower courts could not resolve. The Romans reserved the right to interfere or overturn what the Sanhedrin did, as they did with Paul "When a great argument arose, the commanding officer, fearing that Paul would be torn in pieces by them, commanded the soldiers to go down and take him by force from among them, and bring him into the barracks" (Acts 23:10). In practice, it probably didn't happen often.

The sentence of death for blasphemy was an appropriate verdict: "He who blasphemes Yahweh's name, he shall surely be put to death. All the congregation shall certainly stone him. The foreigner as well as the native-born, when he blasphemes the Name, shall be put to death" (Lev. 24:16). However, Jesus wasn't lying. The act of tearing one's clothes was common, especially when hearing blasphemy, but it was forbidden of the high priest: "He who is the high priest among his brothers, upon whose head the anointing oil is poured, and that is consecrated to put on the garments, shall not let the hair of his head hang loose, or tear his clothes" (Lev. 21:10).

Their behavior, "Then they spit in his face and beat him with their fists, and some slapped him, saying, 'Prophesy to us, you Christ! Who hit you?'" was inappropriate but common behavior.

The command, "You shall not give false testimony against your neighbor" (Ex. 20:16) goes beyond simply not lying; it also means if you know the truth, you must tell it. However, that didn't stop them from using false witnesses in an attempt to "convict" Jesus. None of that happened in Jesus' trial.

When Jesus says "I tell you, after this you will see the Son of Man sitting at the right hand of Power, and coming on the clouds of the sky," He says three things. First, He will return, second, He has the honored position to the right of the Father, and finally that He holds the position of power.

The fact that the Gospel writers don't agree on every aspect of the trial, and for that matter, the last days of Jesus, has caused some to be concerned. However, that may be the "best" part…

If there were solid agreement, item by item and step by step, throughout the whole narrative, then there would be grounds for the gravest suspicion. What emerges…is an effort to piece together conflicting and puzzling traditions often preserved in all probability by men who had not close contact with the processes of either Jewish or Roman law, but who clung tenaciously to what they knew or had heard (AB, p. 334).

As you probably know, nothing is more suspicious to a policeman than witnesses who tell exactly the same thing. Because of their different perceptions, eye witnesses can be a real problem to prosecutors.

Three Times? Three Times!
Matthew 26:69-75

Now Peter was sitting outside in the court, and a maid came to him, saying, "You were also with Jesus, the Galilean!"

[70] But he denied it before them all, saying, "I don't know what you are talking about."

[71] When he had gone out onto the porch, someone else saw him, and said to those who were there, "This man also was with Jesus of Nazareth."

[72] Again he denied it with an oath, "I don't know the man."

[73] After a little while those who stood by came and said to Peter, "Surely you are also one of them, for your speech makes you known."

[74] Then he began to curse and to swear, "I don't know the man!"

Immediately the rooster crowed. [75] Peter remembered the word which Jesus had said to him, "Before the rooster crows, you will deny me three times." He went out and wept bitterly.

Again, I ask, was Peter a brave man? Again, I say, "Yes he was!" It took real courage to walk into the courtyard of the high priest, where the first denial occurred; it also took real love for Jesus. Peter didn't have one friend in that group; maybe that's why his courage failed him.

All four Gospels report Peter's denial and this is another example of the church's honesty about the frailty of its leaders. No effort was made to excuse Peter's weakness and no excuses are offered now or in any known writing or tradition.

This is not the kind of story we like told about ourselves, however Mark covered it fully and we believe his material comes directly from Peter himself. Why report this dark hour of one of the heroes of the faith? Because God forgives and uses people who fail; we should not glorify our failure, but we should not forget that God forgives us if we ask Him.

Three times Peter denied Jesus. He started simply:
1. "…he denied it before them all"
2. "…he denied it again, with an oath"
3. "…he began to curse and swear"

The first little "fib" grows into a "little white lie," and before you know it you have a "tiger by the tail."

Certainly, the crowing of the "rooster" was a terrible reminder of his own weakness, but isn't it better to have tried and failed than never to have tried at all? We should remember that failing once doesn't doom us to a life of failure. Plain old Peter became St. Peter and he will be honored as long at the world stands. However, Judas' failure was turned into even greater failure and his name lives on also, but in infamy.

Jesus Before Pilate
Matthew 27:1-2

Now when morning had come, all the chief priests and the elders of the people took counsel against Jesus to put him to death: ² and they bound him, and led him away, and delivered him up to Pontius Pilate, the governor.

Pontius Pilate was the fifth Roman prefect, not perfect nor governor, in Judea. He governed from 26-36 and gave the official order that sentenced Jesus to death. According to Webster, a prefect is: "any of various high officials or magistrates of differing functions and ranks in ancient Rome." He was not the "governor," as some have it and he reported to the governor of Syria (see below).

For Pilate, life and death hung on his mood at the moment. According to Josephus, not much was known about Pilate before 26 AD when Tiberius appointed him to be procurator of Judea. The information available indicates he was probably an Italian born Roman citizen and his family was probably wealthy enough to be part of the middle class. Most likely he held a military post before his appointment to Judea.

According to Matthew 27:19; he was married and his wife, Claudia Procula, lived with him at his headquarters in Caesarea. His territory included Judea, Samaria, and south to the Dead Sea and Gaza. He had total authority over non-Roman citizens in his area (Luke 2:2).

Pilate was never popular with the Jews because he was insensitive to their religious attitudes and he was resolute in enforcing his policies. However, when the Jews reacted with strong displeasure, he often backed down. He riled the Jews when he took money from the Temple treasury to build an aqueduct that would supply water to Jerusalem; the Jews reacted violently and Pilate's soldiers killed many in their rebellion. Nevertheless, Pilate remained in his office for ten years, indicating that Tiberius considered Pilate to be a good administrator.

We don't know what happened to Pilate, but Josephus suggests there was a problem with the Samaritans, who complained to Vitellius, governor of Syria, his superior, who removed him from office and sent him to stand trial before the emperor to account for his conduct. Since Tiberius died before Pilate arrived, he may not have ever been tried.

Eusebius the bishop of Caesarea Palestrina about 314 says he was exiled to Vienne in Gaul where he committed suicide. Another legend says he committed suicide and his body was thrown into the Tiber, but the Tiber was so agitated that the body was removed, transported to Gaul and thrown into the Rhone River.

I spite of several stonings, the Jews could not legally execute anyone without the approval of the Roman authorities so they brought Jesus to Pilate. Pilate's response was, "Take him yourselves, and judge him according to your law." Therefore the Jews said to him, "It is not lawful for us to put anyone to death..." (John 18:31). Their purpose was to lend an air of legality to this episode, because they weren't terribly concerned about executing others, and the Romans didn't interfere unless the victim were a Roman citizen or it suited them. I don't think that Pilate would have even raised an eyebrow if they had stoned Him, but they didn't want to rile Jesus' supporters among the people. The Romans wouldn't care about His "blasphemy," so they needed another charge that would be sufficient for Pilate to take action, "rebellion" was that charge.

Judas Iscariot's Death
Matthew 27:3-10

Then Judas, who betrayed him, when he saw that Jesus was condemned, felt remorse, and brought back the thirty pieces of silver to the chief priests and elders, ⁴ saying, "I have sinned in that I betrayed innocent blood."

But they said, "What is that to us? You see to it."

⁵ He threw down the pieces of silver in the sanctuary, and departed. He went away and hanged himself. ⁶ The chief priests took the pieces of silver, and said, "It's not lawful to put them into the treasury, since it is the price of blood." ⁷ They took counsel, and bought the potter's field with them, to bury strangers in. ⁸ Therefore that field was called "The Field of Blood" to this day. ⁹ Then that which was spoken through Jeremiah (some manuscripts omit "Jeremiah") the prophet was fulfilled, saying, "They took the thirty pieces of silver, the price of him upon whom a price had been set, whom some of the children of Israel priced, ¹⁰ and they gave them for the potter's field, as the Lord commanded me." (Zech. 11:12-13; Jer. 19:1-13; 32:6-9)

Judas Iscariot, the very name carries the suggestion of treachery and betrayal, and has become a slur in the English language. Ironically the name Judas means "praise of the Lord" and was a popular name among the Jews. The term Iscariot distinguishes this Judas from the other disciple named Judas and probably refers to his hometown, Kerioth, in southern Judah, so then Judas was a Judean, and the only disciple not from Galilee.

We don't know much about his life, but we assume Jesus saw something in him or He would not have called him to be a disciple. His name is on three lists of disciples (Matt. 10:2-4; Mark 3:16-19; Luke 6:14-16), but always appears last. He must have been important, because he was the treasurer of the small band of disciples (John 12:6; 13:29).

During the week before Passover, he went to the chief priests and offered to betray Jesus for a reward (Matt. 26:14-16; Mark 14:10-11). As we have seen, he carried out the betrayal in the Garden of Gethsemane, by identifying Jesus, for the Temple guards with a kiss.

Realizing what he had done, Judas attempted to return the money to the priests, but they refused to take it, actually, they couldn't accept it because it was "blood money" and they did have some principles. While Judas admitted that he sinned, he didn't "repent" as the KJV has, but "felt remorse," a better translation of the Greek. It is important to recognize that there is a difference between realizing that we have sinned, and even feeling sorry for it, and repenting of it. We must go the extra step and ask for forgiveness from both God and the person sinned against.

The condemnation, even though not unexpected, might well fill him with horror. But perhaps this unhappy man expected, that, while he got the bribe, the Lord would miraculously escape, as He had once and again done before, out of His enemies' power: and if so, his remorse would come upon him with all the greater keenness (CCE).

The attitude of the Jewish leadership was even worse than that of Judas': "What is that to us? You see to it." Those charged with insuring "justice" were only interested in having things their way. "Not only had they rejected the Messiah, they had rejected their role as priests… Their hatred for Jesus had caused them to lose all sense of right and wrong (LASB, p. 1604)."

Matthew says Judas threw the money down and went out, and hanged himself and the priests bought a potter's field with the money. Acts suggests Judas bought the field and killed himself there. "Now this man obtained a field with the reward for his wickedness, and falling headlong, his body burst open, and all his intestines gushed out (Acts 1:18)." "In this instance, unclean money was used to buy an unclean place for unclean people [gentiles who died in Jerusalem to be buried in] NLTSB, p. 1637)" The field is believed to be located where the Kidron, Tyropoeon, and Hinnom valleys come together.

Undoubtedly Matthew was following the time-honored tradition of quoting from memory and not remembering where the quote was found, I am a member of that "club" also. He attributes Zechariah's quote to Jeremiah:

> I said to them, "If you think it best, give me my wages; and if not, keep them." So they weighed for my wages thirty pieces of silver. Yahweh said to me, "Throw it to the potter, the handsome price that I was valued at by them!" I took the thirty pieces of silver, and threw them to the potter, in Yahweh's house. (Zech. 11:12-13).

Before we are too critical of the priests, don't we sometimes also pick and choose what, when and how we are willing to obey the commands of Christ?

The True King of the Jews
Matthew 27:11-26

Now Jesus stood before the governor: and the governor asked him, saying, "Are you the King of the Jews?" Jesus said to him, "So you say."

[12] When he was accused by the chief priests and elders, he answered nothing. [13] Then Pilate said to him, "Don't you hear how many things they testify against you?"

[14] He gave him no answer, not even one word, so that the governor marveled greatly. [15] Now at the feast the governor was accustomed to release to the multitude one prisoner, whom they desired. [16] They had then a notable prisoner, called Barabbas. [17] When therefore they were gathered together, Pilate said to them, "Whom do you want me to release to you? Barabbas, or Jesus, who is called Christ?" [18] For he knew that because of envy they had delivered him up.

[19] While he was sitting on the judgment seat, his wife sent to him, saying, "Have nothing to do with that righteous man, for I have suffered many things today in a dream because of him." [20] Now the chief priests and the elders persuaded the multitudes to ask for Barabbas, and destroy Jesus. [21] But the governor answered them, "Which of the two do you want me to release to you?" They said, "Barabbas!"

[22] Pilate said to them, "What then shall I do to Jesus, who is called Christ?"

They all said to him, "Let him be crucified!"

23 But the governor said, "Why? What evil has he done?"

But they cried out exceedingly, saying, "Let him be crucified!"

24 So when Pilate saw that nothing was being gained, but rather that a disturbance was starting, he took water, and washed his hands before the multitude, saying, "I am innocent of the blood of this righteous person. You see to it."

25 All the people answered, "May his blood be on us, and on our children!"

26 Then he released to them Barabbas, but Jesus he flogged and delivered to be crucified.

Pilate seemed convinced Jesus wasn't guilty of anything that deserved death (Luke 23:4), and wanted to release Him, but he didn't want to annoy the Jews and risk damaging his career. So, when they insisted on Jesus' crucifixion, Pilate agreed.

The elders knew that they didn't have a capital case except in one area; Jesus' claim to be the Messiah, "the King of the Jews." This was something Pilate couldn't ignore because they could raise that issue with Caesar. The question, "Are you the King of the Jews?" is in response to the charge they brought Pilate, but at no time have we seen Jesus making such a claim. His response, "So you say," could have also been translated as a question, "Do you say so?" In fact, in light of the interchange, it seems to be a more likely response.

He remained silent possibly because to speak wouldn't have helped His cause and He didn't want to change the outcome; this is precisely why He came to earth. The Jews had made up their minds and Pilate was too weak to stand up to them even after being warned by his wife (verse 19). There is irony in the fact that the only one willing to do anything on Jesus' behalf was an out and out pagan like Pilate.

Pilate is a good example of a person who rises to the top over the bodies of those below him. He recognized Jesus' innocence and had authority to acquit Him, but gave in to the demands of the crowd rather than risk a setback in his career. However, in this case I must say, "Thank you Pilate!"

An interesting point, there is ample evidence that Barabbas' name was Jesus Barabbas, so the crowd was actually asked, "Which Jesus will you have me release?" Barabbas simply means son of Abbas. Verse 22 seems to suggest that also, "What then shall I do to Jesus, who is called Christ?" Barabbas was a "rebel," according to John 18:40 and Matthew calls him a "notable [notorious] prisoner," (verse 16), who was selected by the mob to be released instead of Jesus. Pilate offered to release either Christ or Barabbas and the mob demanded that he release Barabbas and crucify Christ; there is no further mention of Barabbas in the New Testament after he was released.

It seems unlikely that the people would all respond, "May his blood be on us, and on our children!" It was probably a few leaders who got the crowd into it. When Matthew was written down, there was a great deal of stress between the Jews and the early church and unfortunately this verse has been used by some to justify anti-Semitism. To suggest that the Jews alone were responsible for Jesus' sacrifice is to suggest they are the only ones who need salvation through His sacrifice.

Flogging was a normal part of the crucifixion process and the other two victims presumably were flogged also. The scourge was a whip used for punishment. In the Old Testament, the word is used to identify punishment, by man (1 Kings 12:11) or God (Isa. 10:26). The Mosaic Law allowed a wicked person to be whipped with forty blows (Deut. 25:2-3) but thirty-nine was the normal maximum to avoid going over the limit.

In the New Testament, it was common to scourge a prisoner, to "loosen the tongue," before questioning him "...the commanding officer commanded him to be brought into the barracks, ordering him to be examined by scourging, that he might know for what crime they shouted against him like that (Acts 22:24)." This whip had a handle with one or more leather cords or thongs attached to it. Often the cords were knotted or weighted with pieces of metal or bone, to make it "more effective."

Referring to the scourging of Jesus, in his prophecy about the coming Messiah, the prophet Isaiah said, "But he was pierced for our transgressions. He was crushed for our iniquities. The punishment that brought our peace was on him; and by his wounds we are healed (Isa. 53:5)."

There is no middle ground with Jesus. In choosing not to choose or deny Him, you have decided to deny Him. "Washing your hands of a tough situation doesn't cancel your guilt. It merely gives you a false sense of peace (LASB, p. 1605)."

The Fool King
Matthew 27:27-31

Then the governor's soldiers took Jesus into the Praetorium, and gathered the whole garrison together against him. [28] They stripped him, and put a scarlet robe on him. [29] They braided a crown of thorns and put it on his head, and a reed in his right hand; and they kneeled down before him, and mocked him, saying, "Hail, King of the Jews!" [30] They spat on him, and took the reed and struck him on the head. [31] When they had mocked him, they took the robe off of him, and put his clothes on him, and led him away to crucify him.

Originally the Praetorium referred to the headquarters of the Praetorian Guard which was a special company of Roman soldiers who were bodyguards for the emperor and stayed in the city of Rome. By New Testament times, they were sent to the provinces to guard Roman officials as well. They were an elite corps whose salaries and privileges were much better than other Roman soldiers. The Praetorian Guard was disbanded in the third century because it had become so powerful, even threatening the authority of the emperor. The full complement was about six hundred men, so it is unlikely that the entire detachment was in Jerusalem, it was probably only a small company there to protect Pilate.

The scourging, in which the condemned man was beaten nearly to death was completed, but the soldiers weren't finished yet. Normally the victim was taken immediately to be crucified, but they wanted to play a little game. They heard that He was a "king," so they decide to play "king" with Him.

The purple robe, the crown of thorns, and the staff, all were symbols of mockery. The soldiers took thorn bushes and made a crown for their "fool king" and forced it on His head, Matthew, Mark and John, all report it. To the Greeks and Romans, crowns were a symbol of honor and authority but Jesus' "crown" was probably only intended to make Him look foolish. "The soldiers ridiculed the idea that one like Jesus could be any kind of king. Their criterion of power was altogether different (BBC, p. 243)."

Injury was added to insult. After the scourging, Jesus' back would have been cut up severely. When the robe was placed on His back, the fluid would begin attaching to it. When it was removed, probably unceremoniously, the pain would be excruciating and the wounds would begin to bleed again. This was not a small price Jesus paid for our salvation.

However, the attitude of the soldiers was different than that of Caiaphas and his followers. The soldiers responded to orders and saw a chance to have a little fun. They acted out of ignorance while the Jews and Pilate knew what they were doing.

What the soldiers thought made Jesus look foolish, because its symbols were opposites: thorns for gold, a reed for a scepter, a worn-out robe for a flashy, regal robe; were appropriate for Him. Most of His ministry was a contrast of opposites.

The Crucifixion
Matthew 27:32-44

As they came out, they found a man of Cyrene, Simon by name, and they compelled him to go with them, that he might carry his cross. [33] When they came to a place called "Golgotha", that is to say, "The place of a skull," [34] they gave him sour wine (or, vinegar) to drink mixed with gall. When he had tasted it, he would not drink. [35] When they had crucified him, they divided his clothing among them, casting lots, (TR adds "that it might be fulfilled which was spoken by the prophet: 'They divided my garments among them, and for my clothing they cast lots;'" [see Psalm 22:18 and John 19:24]) [36] and they sat and watched him there. [37] They set up over his head the accusation against him written, "THIS IS JESUS, THE KING OF THE JEWS."

[38] Then there were two robbers crucified with him, one on his right hand and one on the left. [39] Those who passed by blasphemed him, wagging their heads, [40] and saying, "You who destroy the temple, and build it in three days, save yourself! If you are the Son of God, come down from the cross!"

[41] Likewise the chief priests also mocking, with the scribes, the Pharisees, (TR omits "the Pharisees") and the elders, said, [42] "He saved others, but he can't save himself. If he is the King of Israel, let him come down from the cross now, and we will believe in him. [43] He trusts in God. Let God deliver him now, if he wants him; for he said, 'I am the Son of God.'" [44] The robbers also who were crucified with him cast on him the same reproach.

As the soldiers led the exhausted Jesus away, He must have been struggling under the weight of the cross beam so the commander pressed "a man from Cyrene, named Simon...to carry the cross" for Him. Barclay says, "That which to Simon had seemed his day of shame became his day of glory (DSB, p. 366)." Mark tells us he was the "father of Alexander and Rufus" (Mark 15:21), which suggests that Simon, and his family, may have become followers of Jesus. Paul says, "Greet Rufus, the chosen in the Lord, and his mother and mine" (Rom. 16:13). We don't know for sure but it could be the same one Mark refers to.

According to the author of the book of Hebrews, Golgotha was a hill outside the city walls "Therefore Jesus also, that he might sanctify the people through his own blood, suffered outside of the gate (Heb. 13:12)."

Crucifixion was a common method of torture and execution used by the Romans, but it was reserved for slaves and criminals, no Roman citizen could be crucified. It was used by many nations of the ancient world, including Assyria, Media, and Persia. Alexander the Great crucified 2,000 inhabitants of Tyre when he captured the city.

Nails or leather thongs were used to secure the victim to a crossbeam attached to a vertical stake. Blocks or pins were sometimes attached to the stake to give the victim support as he hung from the crossbeam. Sometimes the feet were nailed to the vertical stake.

As the victim hung there, the blood couldn't circulate to the vital organs and gradually exhaustion and exposure brought on death, but usually it took several days. If the victim had been badly beaten, he usually didn't live very long. To hasten death, executioners sometimes broke the victim's legs so they couldn't support their body to keep the blood circulating so death came more quickly, as was the case of the other two crucified with Jesus. Usually, bodies were left to rot or to be eaten by scavengers. The charge against the victim was often attached to the cross as a warning to others.

It was also common for the bodies to be publicly displayed by hanging them from stakes on the stockade wall to discourage civil disobedience or to mock defeated military foes (Gen. 40:19; 1 Sam. 31:8-13). There is no biblical evidence that the Jews used crucifixion for execution because the Law ordered death by stoning (Leviticus 20:2; Deut. 22:24), but it did allow public display of the criminal's body "on a tree" (Deut. 21:22), with limitations, "If a man has committed a sin worthy of death, and he is put to death, and you hang him on a tree; his body shall not remain all night on the tree, but you shall surely bury him the same day; for he who is hanged is accursed of God; that you don't defile your land which Yahweh your God gives you for an inheritance." (Deut. 21:22-23) and there is no evidence that the tree was a cross.

Following his conversion to Christianity, Constantine discontinued the practice because the cross was a sacred symbol of Jesus' love for us, God's power to save us, and our commitment to Christian discipleship.

Why did Jesus refuse the "sour wine to drink mixed with gall"? In spite of the numerous sermons covering the subject, we really don't have the foggiest idea and speculation would be ludicrous, so why do it? The clothes became property of the executioners so "they divided his clothing among them, casting lots." We are also told, "and they sat and watched him" not to keep Him from escaping, but to ensure that His friends didn't rescue him.

Is there significance in the fact that "two robbers [were] crucified with Him"? No and yes. No, because multiple executions were common. Yes, because Jesus' attitude and forgiveness were the same all the time, whether He was having a "good day" or a "bad day" Jesus cared about other people.

While He as on the cross, Jesus was attacked by three groups:

1. The two thieves, subsequently one of them repented.
2. People passing by, Golgotha was on the road into Jerusalem and those traveling into the city thought He must be a very bad person, or He wouldn't have been crucified.
3. Jewish officials who offered to believe if He would come down from the cross.

In the days of public execution this would have been a common occurrence.

We have trouble understanding the attitude of these people at Jesus' execution, but history shows that people were the same into the 19th century and probably are today. Verse 39 says, "Those who passed by blasphemed him, wagging their heads…" a common thing for people to do. After all, the person being executed can't hurt you now, so it's your turn to show your "courage."

There was great irony in the mockery of the elders of Israel, "He saved others, but he can't save himself…" How very true. Jesus could not "save himself" if He was going to save "others," but their assertion "He trusts in God" was right on target. There can be no question of His trust in God because just about everyone else has deserted Him. He could have saved Himself, but He chose not to do it!

The End?
Matthew 27:45-56

Now from the sixth hour (noon) there was darkness over all the land until the ninth hour (3:00 PM). ⁴⁶ About the ninth hour Jesus cried with a loud voice, saying, "Eli, Eli, lima (TR reads "lama" instead of "lima") sabachthani?" That is, "My God, my God, why have you forsaken me?" (Ps. 22:1)

⁴⁷ Some of them who stood there, when they heard it, said, "This man is calling Elijah."

⁴⁸ Immediately one of them ran, and took a sponge, and filled it with vinegar, and put it on a reed, and gave him a drink. ⁴⁹ The rest said, "Let him be. Let's see whether Elijah comes to save him."

⁵⁰ Jesus cried again with a loud voice, and yielded up his spirit. ⁵¹ Behold, the veil of the temple was torn in two from the top to the bottom. The earth quaked and the rocks were split. ⁵² The tombs were opened, and many bodies of the saints who had fallen asleep were raised; ⁵³ and coming out of the tombs after his resurrection, they entered into the holy city and appeared to many. ⁵⁴ Now the centurion, and those who were with him watching Jesus, when they saw the earthquake, and the things that were done, feared exceedingly, saying, "Truly this was the Son of God."

⁵⁵ Many women were there watching from afar, who had followed Jesus from Galilee, serving him. ⁵⁶ Among them were Mary Magdalene, Mary the mother of James and Joses, and the mother of the sons of Zebedee.

We, from the Middle Ages on, have focused on the physical suffering of Jesus on the cross, that wasn't true in the first century:

…the early Christian proclamation [was] of the cross as a 'trophy' and sign of victory. The harm done by such concentration is still with us. The cry of triumph…is unhappily still misunderstood by some as an utterance of patient resignation (AB, p. 353).

The Synoptic Gospel writers use the Jewish "clock" for telling time while John uses the Roman method. The "sixth hour" was noon and the "ninth hour" was 3:00 PM so the darkness, during the brightest part of the day, lasted three hours and was far too long for an eclipse.

Some have suggested the sky was black because God "turned His back" on His Son while He bore the sins of the world. Stagg reminds us, "God was never nearer than at Golgotha as Jesus gave himself in full obedience to the Father's will (BBC, p. 246)." I suggest the same is true of us; sometimes we have to struggle through things; I think it's called "testing" but God doesn't abandon us! Paul says, "…namely, that God was in Christ reconciling the world to himself" (2 Cor. 5:19a).

We have identified seven "sayings" of Jesus from the cross. Matthew and Mark have one Luke and John each have three more. The cry, "'Eli, Eli, lima sabachthani?' That is, 'My God, my God, why have you forsaken me?'" has some confusion. The origin is undoubtedly Psalm 22:1. Barclay says this is "the most staggering sentence in the gospel record. (DSB, p. 368)." He suggests Jesus was possibly reciting Psalm 22 which, "though it begins in complete dejection, ends in soaring triumph (DSB, p. 368)."

The first problem is that it is in Aramaic, not in Hebrew. Aramaic began to emerge about 2000 BC and eventually replaced many languages spoken in the Ancient near East and was the common language at the time of Jesus. The New Testament was written in Greek, but the language Jesus and the disciples spoke was probably Aramaic. Christians outside Palestine probably did not speak Aramaic, so Jesus' quotes in Aramaic had to be translated into Greek for them.

Another problem is the confusion "Some of them who stood there, when they heard it, said, 'This man is calling Elijah.'" Because Elijah did not die, but was translated, taken up in a chariot, "the common belief was [he came to] the that aid of the distressed (AB, p. 350)." Did they simply misunderstand? That is possible. Did they intentionally misunderstand? Why not? They twisted everything else Jesus said, why not this also?

Matthew tells us, "Jesus cried again with a loud voice, and yielded up his spirit." John tells us what He said, "When Jesus therefore had received the vinegar, he said, 'It is finished.' He bowed his head, and gave up his spirit" (John 19:30). Jesus did not die of exhaustion like the others did; He gave up His life for us. "It is finished" is the translation of the Greek word *tetelestai* which is the shout of triumph given by the winner of a great event. "So, then, Jesus died a victor with a shout of triumph on his lips (DSB, p. 370)."

When the soldiers proclaim, "Truly this was the Son of God." They were making a great statement, but probably not the one we'd like them to make. The definite article "the" is not in the best Greek texts and they came from a polytheistic society; Zeus was the "father" of their gods, they could well be saying, "This man was another son of Zeus."

A heavy "veil" in the Temple separated the Holy Place from the Holy of Holies; the Most Holy Place and wasn't a veil as we think of veils. Josephus tells us it was four inches thick and that horses tied to each side couldn't tear it apart. Only the high priest was allowed to go behind that curtain and that was only one day each year, *Yom Kipper*, the Day of Atonement (Lev. 16:2). However, when Jesus died on the cross, Matthew tells us "…the veil of the temple was torn in two from the top to the bottom." It was as though the finger of God cut through it like a knife. "Josephus records the appearance about AD 30 of a star resembling as sword and a spontaneous opening of the gates of the Temple (Josephus, *War* 6.5.3-4) (NLTSB. P. 1639)."

Is there symbolism is the tearing of the curtain? Certainly, there is, but more importantly, there is fact! With Jesus' sacrifice, we enter a totally new era of relationship with God. We are no longer on the outside trying to look in, which would have been impossible. No longer is a High Priest necessary to go into the Holy Place, where we are not allowed to go, to offer a sacrifice for us. We can now go boldly, but humbly before our God and Father ourselves.

One of the strange events, "The tombs were opened, and many bodies of the saints who had fallen asleep were raised…" is often skipped over, but this act proves "that death was overcome: and the resurrection of the dead followed the resurrection of Christ (GN)." Who were these "holy people"? Possibly some were followers of Jesus who had died, but I'm sure that not all of them were disciples. Most assuredly, some of these were people who followed the Mosaic Law, in other words, they were Old Testament "believers."

Because of these unusual events, "Jesus' death, therefore, could not go unnoticed. Everyone knew something significant had happened (LASB, p. 1607)."

The writers tell us, "Many women were there watching from afar…" We should not read anything into the fact that they were there or that they were "watching from afar…" because women would not normally crowd around the scene of an execution, men would do that. The important thing is that they were there.

They had followed Jesus for many years and they were still following. "Among them were Mary Magdalene, Mary the mother of James and Joses [that is the mother of Jesus], and the mother of the sons of Zebedee…" and suggests to me that there were others also. Acts 1:21-22 infers the disciples and other followers were also there, somewhere. What Jesus had to do now, He had to do alone, but He had not been totally deserted.

The Burial of the Savior
Matthew 27:57-61

When evening had come, a rich man from Arimathaea, named Joseph, who himself was also Jesus' disciple came. [58] This man went to Pilate, and asked for Jesus' body. Then Pilate commanded the body to be given up. [59] Joseph took the body, and wrapped it in a clean linen cloth, [60] and laid it in his own new tomb, which he had cut out in the rock, and he rolled a great stone to the door of the tomb, and departed. [61] Mary Magdalene was there, and the other Mary, sitting opposite the tomb.

Jewish, early Christian custom, and common sense required burial the same day as death, and the Mosaic Law required an executed criminal be buried the same day (that wasn't the custom of other nations where a body could be displayed for months as a warning as we have already seen).

Because of their ceremonial uncleanness, tombs were usually some distance from where people lived. In special cases, like David and other kings, tombs were built inside the city walls or in a garden near their home. Tombs were usually either natural hillside caves or, like Joseph's tomb, they were carved out of the hillside. If the cave wasn't large enough for the number of bodies expected, it was enlarged by excavation.

In small families, places for the bodies were cut out of the side or the floor of the cave. To the right of the entrance to the "Garden Tomb" is space for two bodies laid side-by-side with a niche for bones at the head and between the two spaces. Because there is room for two bodies, we think it was a family tomb for the parents and children. Once the body had decomposed, the bones would be stacked in the tomb, or placed in an ossuary and it was ready for the next family member that died.

Under Roman law, the relatives of a criminal could claim the body for burial, but if there was no one to claim it, the body was left on the cross for scavengers to eat or until it rotted. Since none of Jesus' relatives was in a position to claim His body, Joseph of Arimathaea was allowed to do so.

All four gospels report that Joseph went to Pilate and was given permission to remove and bury Jesus; however, it takes all four writers to get a good picture of him. Matthew says he was "a rich man from Arimathaea, named Joseph, who himself was also Jesus' disciple…" Mark says "Joseph of Arimathaea, a prominent council member who also himself was looking for God's Kingdom… (Mark 15:43)"; Luke adds "Behold, a man named Joseph, who was a member of the council, a good and righteous man (he had not consented to their counsel and deed), from Arimathaea, a city of the Jews, who was also waiting for God's Kingdom (Luke 23:50-51);" John has "…Joseph of Arimathaea, being a disciple of Jesus, but secretly for fear of the Jews… (John 19:38b)."

While Joseph was from Arimathea, the fact that he had prepared a tomb in Jerusalem indicated his move was "lock, stock, and barrel" to Jerusalem. Since he was a prominent, wealthy member of the Council, this would give him easy access to Pilate.

Rabbinic law prevented the reuse of the tomb of an executed criminal and it is suggested that Jesus' burial was meant to be temporary, only until after the Passover when His body would be properly prepared and He would be reburied; we know Jesus rose from the dead, but most of His followers did not expect it. As with most of Jesus' life and ministry, there is nothing unusual going on here.

Many legends have sprung up about Joseph. One of the most famous is that Philip sent Joseph from Gaul to England to preach the Gospel; they say he took the chalice used in the Lord's Supper with him that, contrary to the "evidence" of *The Da Vinci Code*, that chalice became the Holy Grail and great quest of the King Arthur legends.

Matthew Henry reminds us that in life Jesus had no home and in death He had no tomb. He trusted the Father to provide what He needed and the Father was faithful. We need to do the same!

John tells us that Nicodemus "…who at first came to Jesus by night, also came…" accompanied him (John 19:39) and they prepared the body as best they could in the time available before sundown. The writers also tell us that the women at the crucifixion followed and kept watch.

Securing the Tomb
Matthew 27:62-66

Now on the next day, which was the day after the Preparation Day, the chief priests and the Pharisees were gathered together to Pilate, [63] saying, "Sir, we remember what that deceiver said while he was still alive: 'After three days I will rise again.' [64] Command therefore that the tomb be made secure until the third day, lest perhaps his disciples come at night and steal him away, and tell the people, 'He is risen from the dead;' and the last deception will be worse than the first."

[65] Pilate said to them, "You have a guard. Go, make it as secure as you can." [66] So they went with the guard and made the tomb secure, sealing the stone.

The "Preparation Day" had become a euphemism for Friday, the day to prepare for the Sabbath. Why doesn't Matthew call it Friday then? Possibly because the "Preparation Day" referred to was to prepare for the Passover and actually occurred on Thursday. That would make both Thursday and Friday "Preparation Days" and holy days, Sabbath days if you like. Again, the importance is not in the day of the week Jesus died, but the fact that He died!

If we use the accepted Christian calendar as our authority, then the day following the "Preparation Day" would have been the Jewish Sabbath. Either we have the calendar wrong or this is a great violation of their Law. To enter Pilate's Hall was inappropriate for them, but to do it on a Sabbath would have been the ultimate hypocrisy.

The Jews wanted the tomb sealed to prevent any fraud on the part of the disciples. Interesting, isn't it? The Jews were concerned about a resurrection. Apparently, they were paying closer attention to what Jesus said than His disciples were. This seemed to be a good move for them and it proved to be good for us also because it provided objective, Roman soldiers as witnesses to the events of Sunday morning.

The Jews believed that if they could keep Jesus in the tomb for three days, it would provide evidence to the world that He was in fact dead. They believed the spirit hovered near the body for three days before it departed; you could say they believed no one was officially dead until after three days had passed, another reason for three days and three nights. I believe they wanted to open the tomb and show (ta-da!) the body of the imposter.

Both Jews and Christians believed the tomb was empty; they only disagreed about how it became empty. The Jews claimed that the body had been stolen by the disciples while the Christians claimed Jesus had been raised from the dead by the power of God.

Many people attempt to shut Jesus out of their lives by sealing him in some tomb or other, but there is no tomb that can contain a resurrected Savior.

The Resurrection
Matthew 28:1-10

Now after the Sabbath, as it began to dawn on the first day of the week, Mary Magdalene and the other Mary came to see the tomb. [2] Behold, there was a great earthquake, for an angel of the Lord descended from the sky, and came and rolled away the stone from the door, and sat on it. [3] His appearance was like lightning, and his clothing white as snow. [4] For fear of him, the guards shook, and became like dead men. [5] The angel answered the women, "Don't be afraid, for I know that you seek Jesus, who has been crucified. [6] He is not here, for he has risen, just like he said. Come, see the place where the Lord was lying. [7] Go quickly and tell his disciples, 'He has risen from the dead, and behold, he goes before you into Galilee; there you will see him.' Behold, I have told you."

[8] They departed quickly from the tomb with fear and great joy, and ran to bring his disciples word. [9] As they went to tell his disciples, behold, Jesus met them, saying, "Rejoice!"

They came and took hold of his feet, and worshiped him.

[10] Then Jesus said to them, "Don't be afraid. Go tell my brothers (the word for "brothers" here may be also correctly translated "brothers and sisters" or "siblings") that they should go into Galilee, and there they will see me."

At the heart of the Gospel message is the resurrection of Jesus; without a resurrection, there is no message. As mentioned in the last section, both Jews and Christians agreed Jesus' tomb was empty. The question was "Why?" or "How!"

Christ rose the third day after his death; that was the time he had often spoken of. On the first day of the first week God commanded the light to shine out of darkness. On this day did He who is the Light of the world, shine out of the darkness of the grave…(MH).

How poetic! How correct! And we have celebrated "Easter" morning every Sunday since.

A "spiritual resurrection" would mean nothing to either The Jews or the Disciples. It's important to recognize that initially His followers believed His body had been stolen also. To both, Jews and Christians, resurrection meant a bodily resurrection.

Some of the women who had been at the cross were the first to see the risen Lord. Right after dawn on the Sabbath, as soon as it was safe to go out, they went to the tomb. You can't believe the followers of Jesus were irreligious or insensitive to Jewish laws or these women wouldn't have waited until after the Sabbath.

The text seems to indicate the earthquake occurred after the women arrived, if that is correct, it wasn't for the purpose of letting Jesus out or they would have seen Him leave. The quake was only to show that the tomb was already empty.

The "appearance" of the angel, "like lightning" with clothing as "white as snow" so terrified the guards they apparently passed out. It isn't uncommon; men have often been unable to stand up to the things women deal with as a part of being a mother. The angel's message was direct, "Don't be afraid, for I know that you seek Jesus, who has been crucified." Don't forget that the first thing Jesus wants to do for all of us is to drive out our fears, then he challenged them to enter the empty tomb and finally to go tell the disciples. You cannot tell the good news until you are confident it is true.

It was only after they had seen the empty tomb that Jesus came to them and confirmed the fact that He was indeed alive. His greeting, "Rejoice!" is indicative of the occasion. Recognition that Jesus lives is more than a greeting, it is cause for rejoicing. But, don't stop there, "Don't be afraid. Go tell my brothers…" and probably means His disciples. People must hear the good news before they can accept it. The satisfied customer will win more converts to any "product" than a salesman. That's true of the "product" of salvation also.

The Big Lie
Matthew 28:11-15

Now while they were going, behold, some of the guards came into the city, and told the chief priests all the things that had happened. ^{12} When they were assembled with the elders, and had taken counsel, they gave a large amount of silver to the soldiers, ^{13} saying, "Say that his disciples came by night, and stole him away while we slept. ^{14} If this comes to the governor's ears, we will persuade him and make you free of worry." ^{15} So they took the money and did as they were told. This saying was spread abroad among the Jews, and continues until today.

The women went to report their discovery and encounters and so did the guards. Why would the guards go to the chief priests? Remember, there were Temple guards, employed by the Council to maintain order in the Temple area, but these guards weren't Temple guards. How do we know they weren't? The Jews wouldn't need to ask permission to post their own guards nor would they need to protect them, however if the "governor" found out Jesus body was missing, Roman guards would be subject to death for allowing its removal.

"The chief priests and the elders used the deception which they expected the disciples to use (AB, p. 359)." It's time for Plan B, so the Counsel met and devised a plan. What did they do? They paid the guards to lie. Plan B is often a desperate attempt to win a "battle." "This saying was spread abroad among the Jews, and continues until today." This indicates that at the writing, probably after the fall of Jerusalem in 70 AD, the story was still being told.

In some cultures, paying bribes is a way of doing business, but in ancient Israel, it was expressly against the law (see Exodus 20:16 and 23:8). They say "every man has his price." We don't know how much the guards were paid, but these were men who didn't make much money, so anything would be welcomed by them. However, since tomb robbery was common in the ancient world, they probably should have just stuck with that story by itself.

But this falsehood disproved itself. Had the soldiers been all asleep, they could not have known what passed. If any had been awake, they would have roused the others and prevented the removal; and certainly, if they had been asleep, they never would have dared to confess it; while the Jewish rulers would have been the first to call for their punishment (MH).

The Jews had done everything they could to discredit Jesus while He was alive: they illegally tried Him; they lied to Pilate about Him; they couldn't keep Him in the grave so they lied about His resurrection. However, truth is always stronger than lies. The story that should have been stopped in its tracks in the first century has more believers today than at any time in the church's history.

About the resurrection, Chuck Colson, one of the Nixon Watergate "plumbers" said:

I know the resurrection is a fact, and Watergate proved it to me. How? Because 12 men testified they had seen Jesus raised from the dead, then they proclaimed that truth for 40 years, never once denying it. Every one was beaten, tortured, stoned and put in prison. They would not have endured that if it weren't true. Watergate embroiled 12 of the most powerful men in the world—and they couldn't keep a lie for three weeks. You're telling me 12 apostles could keep a lie for 40 years? Absolutely impossible.

The Great Commission
Matthew 28:16-20

But the eleven disciples went into Galilee, to the mountain where Jesus had sent them. [17] When they saw him, they bowed down to him, but some doubted. [18] Jesus came to them and spoke to them, saying, "All authority has been given to me in heaven and on earth. [19] Go, (TR and NU add "therefore") and make disciples of all nations, baptizing them in the name of the Father and of the Son and of the Holy Spirit, [20] teaching them to observe all things that I commanded you. Behold, I am with you always, even to the end of the age." Amen.

How ironic that Jesus chose Galilee for His final brief discourse and the commissioning of the disciples. Yes, He was from Galilee and most of the twelve were Galileans. Yes, He often "retreated" to Galilee to escape the pressure of dealing with the Elders. However, Jerusalem was the religious center of the Jewish universe.

Possibly more sermons have been preached from this passage than any other passage in the Bible. Why not, it's the greatest challenges to the church on record?

The other Gospel writers record many of Jesus' appearances to various groups of people, but Matthew doesn't and we don't know why. He jumps right into this appearance in Galilee. Notice there are only eleven disciples left in the group, Judas didn't return to them and a successor hadn't yet been selected.

We often say, "Seeing is believing," but Matthew reported, "When they saw him, they bowed down to him, but some doubted." John tells us, "Jesus said to her, 'Didn't I tell you that if you believed, you would see God's glory?' (John 11:40)." We have it backwards, when we believe, then we will see.

Is the Bible reliable? Is it an honest account of what happened? Verses like verse 17 help us know that it is. If Matthew hadn't reported that "some doubted" there might be room for us to wonder about his honesty, but the open honesty of the failing of the great people of the Bible serve to prove its factuality. "Doubt is perhaps not the opposite of faith, but only faith's misgiving. ... The opposite of faith is not doubt, but cynicism (IB, p. 621)."

Notice the baptismal formula, "in the name of the Father and of the Son and of the Holy Spirit." It isn't names; it is "name," singular. This is the earliest recorded Trinitarian formula stated in Scripture. The phrase, "to the end of the age" is more accurately "to the completion of history."

Jesus did three things:

1. He demonstrated His power in many miracles and in His own resurrection. "All authority...has been given to me."
2. He told them to spread the Good News (see below). "…go and make disciples of all nations."
3. He stated that He is with us all the time, present tense, not just future tense. "I am with you always."

Jesus also requires three things of us "as we are going…" is a better translation of the Greek than "go."

1. "make disciples of all nations,"
2. "baptizing them in the name of the Father and of the Son and of the Holy Spirit,"
3. "teaching them to observe all things that I have commanded you."

This appearance shouldn't be confused with what we call the Ascension, recorded in Acts 1:12; this is in Galilee and the Ascension took place from the Mount of Olives near Jerusalem.

The Gospel began with a statement that Jesus was of the royal line of David, and recorded that while still an infant He was acknowledged "King of the Jews" by astrologers from the East. Now after being crucified as "King of the Jews" He has been raised from the dead; and in His glorified state as the risen Christ He claims unreservedly to possess complete authority in heaven and earth. On this note the Gospel ends (TNTC, pp. 273-4).

I can't think of a better way to conclude this brief study! I pray you have been edified and challenged! And now we wait…

While you wait, consider this: Am I a follower of Jesus or am I trusting my good works to get me through the "pearly gates"? Becoming a follower means being a believer and it's as easy as A B C
A…admit that I'm a sinner and need a Savior. I may not be a murderer or a thief, but I've wronged people and in so doing have wronged God. "for all have sinned, and fall short of the glory of God (Romans 3:23)."
B…believe that Jesus died for your sins. "Because Christ also suffered for sins once, the righteous for the unrighteous, that he might bring you to God, being put to death in the flesh, but made alive in the Spirit (1 Peter 3:18)."

C…confess your belief in Him. "that if you will confess with your mouth that Jesus is Lord, and believe in your heart that God raised him from the dead, you will be saved." (Romans 10:9)

You can do that with a simple prayer like this:

"Lord, I know that I'm a sinner, please forgive me and I believe that Jesus died for my sins. I accept Him as my Savior. Amen.

If you have done that, welcome to the family! If you don't feel any different, that's okay, in time you will. Becoming a follower of Jesus, a Christian, is not so much an emotional thing as it is a statement of fact.

If I can help you, you can reach me at mdshepherd0413@gmail.com. Drop me a note and let me know how I can help. God bless!

Made in the USA
Coppell, TX
05 January 2025

43563226R00140